STUDIES IN EVANGELICAL HISTORY AND THOUGHT

British Evangelical Identities Past and Present

Volume 1

Aspects of the History and Sociology of Evangelicalism in Britain and Ireland

STUDIES IN EVANGELICAL HISTORY AND THOUGHT

British Evangelical Identities Past and Present

Volume 1

Aspects of the History and Sociology of Evangelicalism in Britain and Ireland

Edited by
Mark Smith

WIPF & STOCK · Eugene, Oregon

Wipf and Stock Publishers
199 W 8th Ave, Suite 3
Eugene, OR 97401

British Evangelical Identities Past and Present, Volume 1
Aspects of the History and Sociology of Evangelicalism in Britain and Ireland
By Smith, Mark

ISBN 13: 978-1-60608-603-2
Publication date 4/21/2009
Previously published by Paternoster, 2008

This Edition reprinted by Wipf and Stock Publishers by arrangement with Paternoster

Series Preface

The Evangelical movement has been marked by its union of four emphases: on the Bible, on the cross of Christ, on conversion as the entry to the Christian life and on the responsibility of the believer to be active. The present series is designed to publish scholarly studies of any aspect of this movement in Britain or overseas. Its volumes include social analysis as well as exploration of Evangelical ideas. The books in the series consider aspects of the movement shaped by the Evangelical Revival of the eighteenth century, when the impetus to mission began to turn the popular Protestantism of the British Isles and North America into a global phenomenon. The series aims to reap some of the rich harvest of academic research about those who, over the centuries, have believed that they had a gospel to tell to the nations.

Series Editors

For Sarah

Contents

Contributors

Dr Rod Ambler has recently retired from the Department of History at Hull University. His edition of *Lincolnshire Parish Correspondence of John Kaye, Bishop of Lincoln, 1827-53* was published in 2006, and *Churches, Chapels and the Parish Communities of Lincolnshire, 1660-1900,* volume IX in the History of Lincolnshire series, in 2000

Dr Andrew Atherstone is Tutor in History and Doctrine, and Latimer research fellow, at Wycliffe Hall, Oxford. His publications include *The Martyrs of Mary Tudor* (second edition, 2007), *Oxford's Protestant Spy: The Controversial Career of Charles Golightly* (2007), *Oxford* (forthcoming 2008) and, as editor, *The Heart of Faith* (forthcoming 2008).

Dr Kristin Aune is Senior Lecturer in Sociology at the University of Derby, having also taught at the University of Westminster and Ridley Hall, Cambridge. She is the author of *Single Women: Challenge to the Church?* (Paternoster, 2002) and several articles and book chapters on gender and contemporary Christianity. She is co-editor (with Andrew Walker) of *On Revival: A Critical Examination* (Paternoster, 2003) and (with Sonya Sharma and Giselle Vincett) *Women and Religion in the West: Challenging Secularization* (Ashgate, 2008).

Professor David W. Bebbington is Professor of History at the University of Stirling. His publications include *Evangelicalism in Modern Britain: A History from the 1730s to the 1980s* (1989); *The Dominance of Evangelicalism: The Age of Spurgeon and Moody* (2005); and *Victorian Nonconformity* (2nd edn, 2008).

Revd Dr David Goodhew is Director of Ministerial Practice at Cranmer Hall, St John's College, Durham. His published work includes a history of a South African township and research on modern British and South African church history including histories of the Christian Union movement and the Student Christian movement.

Professor John Harvey is an art historian and practitioner. He has written several books, including *Photography and Spirit* (2007), *The Appearance of Evil* (2003), and *Image of the Invisible* (1999). He is Professor of Art at the School of Art, Aberystwyth University, where he teaches Fine Art and Art History'.

Dr Andrew R. Holmes is a Lecturer in Modern Irish History at Queen's University Belfast. He has published widely in the history of Irish Protestantism and is author of *The Shaping of Ulster Presbyterian Belief and Practice 1770-1840* (Oxford, 2006).

Dr David Ceri Jones is a Lecturer in the Department of History and Welsh History at Aberystwyth University. He is the author of *'A Glorious Work in the World': Welsh Methodism and the International Evangelical Revival, 1735-1750* (2004), and is currently writing a history of Calvinistic Methodism during the long eighteenth century.

Dr Ian Jones is Director of St Peter's Saltley Trust and is an Honourary Research Fellow at the University of Manchester. He is author of *The Local Church and Generational Change: Mainstream Christianity in Birmingham 1945-2000* (forthcoming), *Women and Ordination in the Church of England: Ten Years On* (2004) and has co-authored (with Peter Webster) several articles on the history of church music.

Dr Rachel Jordan is the Associate Mission and Evangelism Adviser for the Archbishops' Council of the Church of England. Her recent PhD focussed on Nonconformist women's public ministry in Britain from 1900-1959. Rachel was previously an evangelism adviser at the Church Pastoral Aid Society and has wide experience in mission and evangelism.

Dr David Killingray is Professor Emeritus of History at Goldsmiths College, University of London. He has written widely on aspects of African, Caribbean, Imperial, and English local history, as well as on the Black diaspora. Recent books include *An historical atlas of* Kent (2004, with Terence Lawson), The *United Kingdom Overseas Territories: past, present and future* (2005, with David Taylor), and, *Black voices: the shaping of our Christian experience* (2007, with Joel Edwards). He has just completed a book on African soldiers in the Second World War.

Dr Ian Randall supervises research at Spurgeon's College, London, and the International Baptist Theological Seminary, Prague. He has published many articles and several books, including *The English Baptists of the Twentieth Century* (2005), *A School of the Prophets* (2005), *What a Friend we have in Jesus* (2005) and *Spiritual Revolution: The Story of OM* (2008). He is a Fellow of the Royal Historical Society

Dr Mark Smith is University Lecturer in Local and Social History at the University of Oxford. He is the author of *Religion in Industrial Society: Oldham and Saddleworth 1740-1865* (1994) *Doing the Duty of the Parish: Surveys of the Church in Hampshire 1810* (2004) and editor with Stephen Taylor of *Evangelicalism in the Church of England c.1790-c.1900* (2004)

Dr Brian Talbot is the Minister of Broughty Ferry Baptist Church, Dundee. His published work includes: *Search for a Common Identity The Origins of the Baptist Union of Scotland 1800-1870* (2003); *Standing on the Rock The History of Stirling Baptist Church 1805-2005* (2005); 'Fields are White unto Harvest', in Randall and Cross (eds), *Baptists and Mission* (2007)

Dr Peter Webster is Editorial Controller of British History Online (Institute of Historical Research). His published work to date has addressed the place of music and the visual arts in the twentieth-century churches. Forthcoming work includes a book-length study of Michael Ramsey, Archbishop of Canterbury.

Dr Martin Wellings is a Methodist minister, and is President of the World Methodist Historical Society. In addition to articles on evangelical and Methodist history, his published work includes *Evangelicals Embattled. Responses of Evangelicals in the Church of England to Ritualism, Darwinism and Theological Liberalism 1890-1930* (2003).

Dr Eryn White is Senior Lecturer in the Department of History and Welsh History, specializing in the history of Wales in the eighteenth century. Her published work includes *The Welsh Bible* (2007) and she is co-author of the *Calendar of Trevecka Letters* (2004).

Introduction

British Evangelical Identities: Locating the Discussion

A Movement in Search of Definitions

Evangelicalism is probably the most over-defined religious movement in the world. To a large extent this is a straightforward consequence of its diversity – few Protestant denominations are untouched by its influence and the organisations locating themselves within the evangelical fold are legion. A necessary outcome of the diversity of the organisational expressions of Evangelicalism is a multiplicity of explanations of what that evangelicalism means – commonly expressed in credal statements like bases of faith, and covenants. Such material contains much that is common to the mainstream of orthodox Christianity, especially in its Western forms,[1] and much scholarly ingenuity could be expended in distilling the evangelical essence from the shared Christian deposit.[2]

In identifying an evangelical organisation, church or movement with a particular doctrinal position such formulations are at one level simply a description of the beliefs the members of the group share in common, though they typically also intend to demarcate evangelical from non-evangelical belief. They may, therefore, be prescriptive as well as descriptive. They erect a doctrinal fence line around evangelicalism and prescribe the nature of the theological convictions that are essential to membership of the group. The two basic convictions underlying this phenomenon – that true doctrine can be held and that its holding is not

---

[1] A clear example of this can be found in, J. Stott, *Evangelical Truth A personal plea for unity* (Leicester: IVP, 1999), passim. Stott's starting point is that evangelical belief is neither a recent innovation nor a deviation from Christian orthodoxy and he develops his exposition along traditional Trinitarian lines.

[2] See, for example, A. McGrath, *Evangelicalism and the Future of Christianity* (London: Hodder & Stoughton, 1993); R. Turnbull, *Anglican and Evangelical?* (London: Continuum, 2007).

an unimportant matter – are a significant feature of the movement. A clear example would be the succession of bases of faith published by the Inter-Varsity Fellowship (later the Universities and Colleges Christian Fellowship) which were intended at the outset to demarcate its conservative evangelicalism from the broader forms of Protestantism to be found in the Student Christian Movement and elsewhere. David Goodhew's account in this volume of the 1950 summit meeting between representatives of the SCM and the IVF shows the ramifications of this phenomenon in practice. The SCM delegation placed a strong emphasis on unity, with fellowship preceding doctrinal agreement. The IVF delegates, on the other hand, saw fellowship as a product of union around agreed doctrinal truths expressed in propositional form. Moreover, their understanding of salvation history as the story of the preservation of a faithful remnant made the 'scandal of division' less of an issue for them than for their interlocutors.

So crucial has the issue of doctrine been for conservative evangelicals that Dr Martyn Lloyd-Jones (himself a leading member of the IVF delegation in 1950), for example, addressing the conference of the International Federation of Evangelical Students over two decades later, in 1971, could assert, 'the necessity of opposition to doctrinal indifferentism' and 'the constant necessity for definition':

> We are not simply defining the Christian in general, but we are defining the evangelical Christian, and we do that, of course, because we believe that ultimately the evangelical faith is the only true expression *in doctrine* of the Christian faith itself.[3]

Though not universal this sense of the 'necessity for definition', understood primarily in doctrinal terms, is sufficiently pervasive to be regarded in itself as a mark of evangelicalism.[4]

A second approach to the definition of evangelicalism, though with a less luxuriant ecology than the doctrinal description/prescription, also flourishes in contemporary discourse – the academic description/analysis. Occasionally, especially when located in the field of philosophical theology or intellectual history, these analyses manifest a similar structure to the doctrinal definitions proposed by evangelical

---

[3] Addresses published in D. M. Lloyd-Jones, *What is an Evangelical?* (Edinburgh: Banner of Truth, 1992), 17. Italics added.

[4] Not all evangelicals manifest this trait but it is certainly widespread and more conservative evangelicals often manifest frustration with imprecision in this area on the part of their brethren. See, for example, R. Burrows, *Dare to contend! A call to Anglican evangelicals* (Newcastle upon Tyne: Jude Pubications, 1990), especially 25-32, O. Barclay, *Evangelicalism in Britain 1935-1995 a personal sketch* (Leicester: IVP, 1997), 9-12.

groups themselves. A good recent example of this kind of writing would be Harriet Harris' discussion of the relationship between evangelicalism and Fundamentalism, which argues for a congruence between the two movements on the basis of a shared biblical foundationalism.[5] More commonly, however, such analyses emerge from the work of religious and social historians and sociologists and so tend to emphasise the social and organisational forms and practices that characterise evangelicalism in addition to its doctrinal distinctives. There is a growing tendency here, mischievously or otherwise, to use the terminology of Euclidean geometry to characterise the definition on offer.[6] Thus we have the Ward 'hexagon' – six themes tying together the thought world of early evangelicalism – mostly intellectual in character but also including a devotion to 'small group religion'.[7] Arriving only a little later came the Larsen 'pentagon' – four mainly doctrinal features plus a characteristic participation in evangelical networks.[8] Both Larsen and Ward, of course, are making conscious reference to the major player among the Euclidean structures – the 'Bebbington quadrilateral'. David Bebbington's definition of evangelicalism as perennially manifesting four characteristics ('Biblicism', 'Crucicentrism', 'Conversionism' and 'Activism') clearly represents the hybridising approach to defining evangelicalism and indeed even the doctrinal characteristics are primarily explored in terms of their impact on the culture, practice and spirituality of the movement than as intellectual commitments alone.[9] First appearing in 1989, the quadrilateral rapidly became remarkably widespread in both academic and more popular discussions of

---

[5] H. Harris, *Fundamentalism and Evangelicals* (Oxford: Clarendon Press, 1998).

[6] It may be only a matter of time before commentators take to referring to the Lausanne pendedecagon.

[7] W. R. Ward, *Early Evangelicalism A Global Intellectual History* (Cambridge, Cambridge University Press, 2006), 4.

[8] T. Larsen, 'Defining and Locating Evangelicalism', in, Larsen and D. J. Treier (eds.), *The Cambridge Companion to Evangelical Theology* (Cambridge, Cambridge University Press, 2007), 1.

[9] D. W. Bebbington, *Evangelicalism in Modern Britain A History From The 1730s To The 1980s* (London: Unwin Hyman, 1989), 1-16. Though the book uses the word 'quadrilateral' only once. There has also been some resort to less rigid metaphors. Graham Kings, for example, has recently used the image of different forms of watercourse to characterise the identity of three varieties of Anglican evangelicalism in, G. Kings, 'Canal, River and Rapids: Contemporary Evangelicalism in the Church of England', *Anvil*, 20 no 3 (2003), 167-184. He has, however, since reverted to a more geometrical metaphor in the form of the Mercedes logo. G. Kings, 'Exploring a new way of understanding evangelical unity Mercedes-Benz and evangelicals in the Church of England?' *Church of England Newspaper*, (22 June, 2007), 9.

Anglophone evangelicalism in Britain and overseas, especially in America,[10] and, as Tim Larsen has pointed out, its reception is itself a phenomenon worthy of investigation.[11] Derek Tidball, writing in 1994 – only five years after the publication of the book – pronounced that the quadrilateral, 'has quickly established itself as near to a consensus as we might ever expect to reach.'[12]

This was, perhaps inevitably, given the movement's restless drive for definition and re-definition, an optimistic pronouncement and Bebbington's quadrilateral has come under increasing challenge in the last few years. Perhaps the best example of such a challenge from a British source can be found in Garry Williams' Tyndale Lecture of 2002.[13] There Williams launched an attack on Bebbington's identification of the origins of evangelicalism with the Enlightenment and made an alternative case for continuity with the Puritans and Reformers. Perhaps the most interesting part of the article is the closing paragraph, which spells out what Williams sees (in an act of stepping 'outside the realm of history') as the consequences of deciding to locate evangelical origins in the sixteenth and seventeenth centuries rather than the eighteenth – consequences that turn out to be confessional in nature.

> If we think that Evangelicalism began in the 1730s then Wesley and Edwards become its most important fathers. This means that Evangelicalism was from its origin equally divided between Reformed and Arminian theology; neither could claim to be the mainstream doctrinal position. In this sense it is easy to see how Bebbington's analysis serves to give a strong foothold to Arminianism within the Evangelical movement by making foundational one of its most noted proponents. If, however, we reconsider the origins of Evangelicalism and find that it is a Reformational and Puritan phenomenon, then the picture looks very different.... Evangelicalism then becomes aboriginally Reformed on the doctrine of election rather than divided. The position taken by John Wesley on election becomes a deviation along with that of Philip Melanchthon and his Lutheran followers, and Jacobus Arminius and the Remonstrants. With such an historical perspective, Reformed theology

---

[10] It forms the basis, for example, of the general preface for the series in which the present volume appears.

[11] Larsen, 'Defining and Locating Evangelicalism', 1-2, and Larsen, 'The Reception Given *Evangelicalism in Modern Britain* since publication', in M. Haykin and K. J. Stewart (eds.), *Continuities in Evangelical History: Interactions with David Bebbington* (Downers Grove, IL.: IVP) forthcoming.

[12] D. J. Tidball, *Who Are The Evangelicals?* (London: Marshall Pickering, 1994), 14. Though Tidball, anticipating Larsen, also wanted to draw attention to the networking propensity of evangelicals.

[13] G. J. Williams, 'Was Evangelicalism Created by the Enlightenment', *Tyndale Bulletin*, 53.2 (2002), 283-312.

> becomes the authentic Evangelical mainstream of three centuries, and the historical case for the foundational status of Arminianism is undermined.[14]

This argument is of interest in a number of respects not least in its implicit reliance on tradition in a style often associated with Catholic polemics of the sixteenth and seventeenth centuries. However, it is also authentically evangelical in at least two respects. First is its commitment to discerning the essence of true evangelicalism; the angels of remnant theology clearly hover over its willingness to write off a large majority of twenty-first century evangelicals as deviants from the mainstream. Here, of course, the argument is reversible – are modern evangelicals deviants from the Puritan mainstream or are the Puritans better understood as atypical evangelicals – with a generally narrower theology especially on the scope of the atonement?[15] Indeed in noting the rise of Arminian style theologies within the movement, Williams may have helpfully pointed to another way in which evangelicalism has been shaped by its Enlightenment context. Second is its evident commitment to 'the constant necessity for definition' – with a sharp eye to the possibilities for turning the academic descriptive/analytical mode to prescriptive uses.

Indeed, for some conservative evangelicals at least, the diversity of evangelicalism and the anxiety about definition which is its reflex leads to discomfort with the descriptive mode itself, especially in its more sociological varieties, and an assumption that valid definitions must be normative in both form and intention. Writing in 1993, for example, the Anglican conservative evangelical Melvin Tinker condemned a volume of essays written by staff and other associates of Wycliffe Hall[16] precisely because

---

[14] Ibid., 312.

[15] The argument from aboriginality is of course much more difficult to make when evangelicalism is considered not only as continuous with seventeenth century Anglophone Reformed Christianity but also with German-speaking Lutheran Pietism. See, for example, W. R. Ward, *The Protestant evangelical awakening* (Cambridge: Cambridge University Press, 1992).

[16] R. T. France and A. E. McGrath, *Evangelical Anglicans Their Role and Influence in the Church Today* (London: SPCK, 1993).

> Instead of testing matters doctrinally, it is done phenomenologically – it is a book descriptive of what some professing evangelicals believe rather than prescriptive of what they should believe.[17]

Definition and Identity

Despite possible qualifications to Bebbington's account, it remains the most serviceable definition of evangelicalism for the period covered by the essays in this volume and will be found in dialogue with some and underlying much of what follows. Nevertheless this volume is *not* concerned with the definition of evangelicalism in either mode but rather with the related but different issue of evangelical identity. That is, it is concerned with evangelicalism in practice, evangelicalism as experienced, evangelicalism as felt and expressed rather than as dissected or distilled. It therefore necessarily presents a contextual rather than essentialist account of the movement. In so doing, it draws attention to an issue that the enterprise of definition frequently seeks to erase or overcome – that evangelicalism in practice is never met with in its pure form. Evangelical identity is not the identity of evangelicalism the abstract form but the identity of Evangelicals – the people and the communities they establish – and is therefore always encountered as a hybrid with other sources of identity. In the United Kingdom one may meet Presbyterian evangelicals and Baptist evangelicals, male evangelicals and female evangelicals, English evangelicals and Northern Irish evangelicals, black evangelicals and white evangelicals, reformed evangelicals and charismatic evangelicals, but never mere evangelicals.[18] Even in their most inclusive multi-national multi-denominational organisations and gatherings the multiple sources of evangelical identity can be seen on display. They are both undeniably evangelical, but there is a world of difference between 'New Wine' and 'New Horizon'.[19] Evangelicalism may be indigenised within, corrupted

---

[17] M Tinker, 'Bending Over backwards', *Evangelicals Now*, (Sept. 1993), 17 For similar views, see M. Thompson ' Saving the heart of Evangelicalism', in M. Tinker (ed.), *The Anglican Evangelical Crisis* (Fearn: Christian Focus, 1995), 28-9.

[18] Even this statement barely scratches the surface of the multiple sources of identity shared by different groups of evangelicals and the subgroups to be found within them.

[19] New Wine is a charismatic evangelical network its name reflecting its emphasis on new life in the Spirit. Its first summer conference, in 1989, attracted some 2,400 people and it has since generated a series of new initiatives including a youth oriented network called Soul Survivor (www.new-wine.org). Its website contains a statement of 'values'. New Horizon also began a large summer conference in 1989 on the campus of the University of Ulster at

by, in tension with, or transforming the contexts in which it is encountered (and perhaps all four simultaneously) but those contexts and the multiple refractions of evangelicalism they produce are an inescapable part of the phenomenon. In the face of this heterogeneity, the plural form 'evangelical identities' is used intentionally to describe the subject of this volume.

Evangelical identities are in one sense the identities felt and expressed by those who regard *themselves* to be evangelical and therefore sometimes persist in groups which have ceased to be regarded as evangelical more widely. To this extent evangelical identity may contest definition. Such identities, however, are perhaps inevitably unstable – subject to change with prevailing notions of the nature of evangelicalism. Suggestive of such a situation is a comparison of the accounts of Methodism to be found in the English Church Censuses of 1989 and 2005. In 1989, some 34% of Methodist churchgoers described themselves as evangelicals – expressing an evangelical identity predominantly in the liberal evangelical mode described in the essay by Martin Wellings in this volume. By 2005, that proportion had dropped to 18% – mostly evangelicals describing themselves as mainstream or charismatic. There was a corresponding rise in the proportion of Methodists expressing their identity as 'liberal', 'broad' or 'low church'.[20] To some extent these changes in ascription may represent genuine changes in the spirituality and theology of the Methodist church. It is probable, however, that the main cause of the change was the exposure of an inherited identity (an assumption that to be Methodist was naturally to be evangelical in some sense) to a new climate in which evangelicalism was increasingly defined in public discourse in a conservative (or conservative and charismatic) sense and in which conservative evangelicalism was linked in the public mind to controversial positions on human sexuality and even, by association, to the more aggressive stances of the Bush administration in the USA.[21] In these circumstances, the assertion of an evangelical identity ceased to be serviceable to more liberally inclined Methodists who sought more accurate and attractive labels for their position.

More stable expressions of evangelical identity are perhaps closely

---

Coleraine. It traces its spiritual roots back to the Billy Graham revivals of the 1950s and represents a more conservative and sometimes Reformed stream of evangelicalism with a clear basis of faith, like that of UCCF, set out on its website. (www.newhorizon.org.uk).

[20] P. Brierley (ed.), *UK Christian Handbook Religious Trends 6* (London: Christian Research, 2007), 5.15.

[21] It is notable that there was a particularly rapid decline in the proportion of Methodist evangelical self-ascription between 1998 and 2005.

linked to a degree of mutual recognition – especially as exercised within inter-denominational networks and para-church organisations. Those based in universities, for example, have given to generations of undergraduates an opportunity to experience and learn to adopt a conscious evangelical identity – especially in its conservative mode. Shared cultural forms and practices, like hymn-singing and individual bible study, have been important too. In some cases evangelicals have affirmed a common identity by the use of a shared language. In the nineteenth century this was a sufficiently prominent feature of the movement to be parodied by novelists like Charles Dickens, Anthony Trollope and Wilkie Collins. Witness, for example, Drusilla Clack from Collins *The Moonstone*, with her 'precious publications' and 'awakening letters', her 'guilty mazes of Dissipation' and, of course, her 'career of manifest usefulness' in support, inter alia, of the 'British Ladies'-Servants'-Sunday-Sweetheart-Supervision Society'.[22] The echoes of an older evangelical private language survived into the late twentieth century where it could be parodied rather more affectionately in the characters Victoria and Stenneth Flushpool, created by Adrian Plass, with their constant references to 'the natural'.[23] Such languages are, however, constantly re-invented and characteristic usages (like 'resources', meaning merchandise, for example) remain a feature of a common if not universal culture among evangelicals. Mutual recognition may be experienced in warm fellowship at evangelical ecumenical events but it may also rest on a generous and delicate balance between knowledge and ignorance about the actual theology and spirituality of groups accepted within the evangelical fold.

Contexts and Identities

Clearly, evangelicalism has from the outset been subject to constant interplay between the wider movement and local context, between theological conviction and the personalities of leading figures, between ecclesiastical tradition and popular practice (both individual and communal). Together these have shaped evangelical cultures and thus the way in which evangelical identity has been experienced and expressed in different times, places and communities. The intimate and dialectical relationship between evangelicalism and its hosts is a central theme of several of the essays and especially of David Bebbington's essay on evangelicalism and cultural diffusion. He shows that, as with the rest of British society, it has generally been the more highly educated, socially exalted and younger evangelicals who have been the

[22] Wilkie Collins, *The Moonstone* (London, 1868), Second Period, ch 4.
[23] A. Plass, *The Sacred Diary of Adrian Plass Aged 373/4* (London: Fount, 1987).

first to take on cultural innovations, like premillennial eschatology in the early nineteenth century or charismatic worship styles in the late twentieth. However, the means by which such ideas were spread have often been quite particular to the movement, such as the key influence of the pulpit and of mass evangelical gatherings like the Keswick conventions. Moreover, the consequences of these innovations were shaped by the broader national, linguistic and theological contexts in which evangelicals were located. Gaelic-speaking Calvinist Presbyterians, for example, were relatively insulated from innovation as compared to metropolitan English Congregationalists of a similar social standing. Hence, evangelical responses to cultural innovation were, as with those contexts themselves, necessarily diverse and sometimes contradictory in character.

Refractions and Expressions

The remaining essays in the volume address different aspects of the heterogeneous refractions and expressions of evangelical identity in a range of ecclesiastical, social and cultural contexts – denominations, nations, ethnicity and gender, arts and material culture and spirituality. Cumulatively they reveal the complexity and the dynamism of evangelical diversity.

Denominations

The extent to which an evangelical identity can be refracted through the distinctive lens of a particular denominational tradition is particularly apparent in Martin Wellings' discussion of Evangelicalism within twentieth century Methodism. At one level this was a denomination committed, both by its foundational documents and by its traditions, to evangelical Christianity. At the same time, however, Wellings shows how its particular orientation – especially its connexional structure, its relative lack of confessional controls and its emphasis on experience – left Methodism especially open to the influence of modern thought at the end of the nineteenth and early twentieth centuries. The results of higher criticism and ethical concerns about traditional doctrines like penal substitution and eternal punishment had a particularly significant impact on Methodism. Consequently its evangelicalism, in the early and mid-twentieth centuries, was characteristically liberal in form especially at the level of the paid ministry, though a more conservative evangelicalism did persist at the grass roots in some circuits and among some ministerial networks. After the 1960s, however, the rise of more radical streams of liberal theology and the resurgence of conservative forms of evangelicalism nourished from both within and without

Methodism, turned the denomination into a more pluralist one. Now an evangelical identity (increasingly construed in conservative or conservative and charismatic terms) is one option among several and the characterisation of Methodism as a distinctively evangelical denomination is no longer viable.

Similar themes are explored in Brian Talbot's discussion of three prominent nineteenth century Baptists – Jonathan Watson, Francis Johnston and James Paterson – and their links with projects of Baptist union in Scotland. For Watson, the most important priority in his ministry was the discernment and promotion of 'vital Christianity' and this led him into a characteristically evangelical mode of cooperation with other evangelicals from a variety of denominational backgrounds. While sharing such views in the earlier part of his career, Francis Johnston gradually moved to a position that placed a premium on theological agreement over against either denominational loyalty or pan-evangelical co-operation – a particularly divisive position given that his own theological views at the time stood outside the Baptist mainstream. James Paterson, on the other hand, though himself a committed Calvinist, represented a biblicist position that was sceptical of the value of creeds and confessions of faith as more than guidelines for the faithful. Given these differences of view, the presence of both Calvinist and Arminian traditions and the influence of powerful personalities, the path to unity and cooperation even for churches claiming to be both Baptist and evangelical was a rocky one. It was eventually achieved more by mutual recognition of a shared spirituality and identity than an attempt to define its basis in doctrinal terms.

Tensions between evangelical and denominational identities have perhaps been most acute for those evangelicals who are members of theologically-mixed established churches organised (at least in theory) on a territorial parochial basis rather than as gathered congregations. This is particularly clearly exemplified in Rod Ambler's discussion of the dynamics surrounding the building of Holy Trinity, Louth in 1834. There we see a group of awowedly Anglican evangelicals engaged in the apparently unimpeachable project of extending the influence of the established church by the construction of a new church building in an expanding market town under the auspices of an Act of Parliament. At the same time, however, the very prominence of Holy Trinity's evangelical supporters and their link to a wider agenda of reform could not but be seen as a criticism of the existing ministry of the establishment in Louth and their scheme was thus suspected as a party project. Such suspicions were further exacerbated by a distinctively evangelical mode of operations involving the mobilisation of the laity – both male and female – to support the initiative. To what extent, under such circumstances, was it possible to assert evangelical priorities within the denomination without thereby creating or consolidating a church party? Ambler's case study thus exemplifies what might be regarded as a perennial problem for evangelicals within bodies like the Church of England and the Church of Scotland.

National Traditions

The interactions between Evangelical identities and particular national contexts are explored in the essays by Eryn White, David Ceri Jones and Andrew Holmes. Jones and White analyse different aspects of the early years of the Welsh revival and demonstrate the extent to which evangelicalism can become so indigenised as to become a part of the national culture. They also show the capacity of an evangelical identity, transmitted and reinforced by participation in evangelical networks, to transcend and reinterpret the national context. At one level, the revival stood heir to a Welsh Protestantism that had, since the sixteenth century, sought to legitimate itself on the basis of a constructed history of a pure Welsh Christianity stretching back to Joseph of Arimathea, though until recently oppressed by a papal tyranny introduced by the Saxons. It also had continuities with the seventeenth-century Welsh Puritans as part of the slow progress of a long reformation in Wales. At another level, the revival stood apart from this history, critical of the existing state of unawakened Welsh Protestantism and seeking its legitimation directly from the early years of the church described in the pages of the New Testament.

There was a powerful sense among the early Methodists themselves that they did indeed represent something new. Methodism was an amorphous movement whose identity was based as much on a sense of shared experience and common practices, like informal fellowship meetings, as on theology. However, particularly characteristic was the novel *perspective* of the early evangelicals, deeply anchored to be sure in the local context but just as firmly rooted in a wider revival. First through the friendship between Howel Harris and George Whitefield the Welsh Methodists became linked to the contemporary English revival in general and (as it began to divide along theological lines) its Calvinist wing in particular. Then it became further linked to the wider transatlantic and continental European revivals. Crucially, this perspective was not restricted to its leading figures but available to all via preaching and networks of correspondence and was constantly recycled in the burgeoning evangelical press. Even rank and file Methodists could thus think globally (by the standards of the day) and thereby find themselves empowered to act locally. This participation in an international community of the saints was of the essence to early evangelicals – placing their local experience of success or persecution in the context of a wider movement of grace – a new work of God. It is in this context that we should also locate the disputatiousness and divisiveness of the movement, for with God's plan of salvation for the world in their generation at stake, what could be more important than to get it right? However, in the nineteenth century when Welshness was ever more assaulted and asserted and when the Calvinistic Methodist mainstream of the revival, having parted company with the established church, had to make its way in the world of Nonconformity, so it began to promote its own association with that Welshness. The internationalism that had been a keynote of the early revival thus began to give way to an amalgam of evangelical with national identity.

Writing on the particular experience of Northern Irish evangelicals, Andrew Holmes points out the national tendency to construct evangelical identity in historical terms either as a story of providential deliverance with a strong anti-Catholic dynamic and particular reference to the seventeenth century or as a more pietistic story of revivals and missions with particular reference to events in the nineteenth century. Ulster evangelicalism is also characterised by an enduring relationship, forged in the late nineteenth and early twentieth centuries, between evangelical identity and the local expression of British national identity. Though more widespread in the past, this fusion is now rare in Britain and thus, as Holmes notes, places, 'the region out of step with the predominant expressions of evangelicalism in the rest of the United Kingdom.' He goes on to suggest, however, that a more rigorous and creative application of evangelical principles to the historiographical task might both help to rescue Northern Irish evangelicals from the trammels of an identity over-determined by partial or partisan constructions of their own history and also open up new ways of understanding the identity of the movement as a whole. In particular, he suggests, it might be better to seek a more sophisticated understanding of evangelicalism by examining the way ordinary believers have sought to work out their theological principles in practice and in the context of local cultural particularities rather than by engaging with the construction of definitions.

Race and Gender

The relationship of evangelical identity with the experience of race and gender is explored in the essays by David Killingray, Kristin Aune and Rachel Jordan. In respect of race, this phenomenon is most clearly visible in the case of minority communities like the black evangelicals in Britain discussed by Killingray. We should note, however, that it is undoubtedly no less pervasive, though rather less studied, in the case of majority ethnic communities too. Killingray provides a wealth of examples of black evangelicals finding both liberty and a new voice in their faith but his account is also richly suggestive of ways in which black evangelicals used that voice to challenge the tradition itself and especially the depth of its commitment to the priesthood of all believers and to justice in wider society. In a twenty-first century when black evangelicals are exercising an ever greater influence on the character of the movement in Britain as a whole, the context provided by this essay is particularly important in drawing our attention to the fact that this influence is neither unprecedented nor extrinsic to the British evangelical tradition.

Rachel Jordan's discussion of the relationship between matrimony and ministry for female preachers in the first half of the twentieth century raises with particular force the question of the nature of the interaction of evangelical identities with prevailing cultural norms. Here we see four slightly different combinations. The Salvation Army had formally enshrined the public ministry of women in its culture and organisational forms, yet prevailing assumptions about traditional gender roles made it extremely difficult for female officers to be both married and active as ministers. The Methodist and Baptist deaconess orders both expected their members to be single and required them to resign on marriage in a direct correspondence to the marriage bar that operated in other contemporary professions like teaching. The Pentecostal churches, on the other hand, justified female preaching on the basis of an extraordinary call which over-rode the social conventions prevailing within society at large. It was therefore possible for Pentecostal women, both single and married, to enjoy a greater freedom as evangelists and pastors. Even in the Elim church, however, a process of bureaucratisation and consolidation led to a gradual exclusion of women from its ordained ministry in the second generation. Evangelicalism clearly retained a capacity to challenge or even transcend powerfully articulated social norms for the role of women and also to provide a language and a sense of empowerment for women in the exercise of public ministry. Nevertheless, the exercise of that capacity was the exception rather that the rule as evangelical identity remained closely linked to social respectability.

Kristin Aune's essay on constructions of masculinity in the New Frontiers churches draws attention to the extent to which discourses of evangelical identity may themselves shape and be shaped by particular understandings of gender. Moreover, she argues, while leaders in the church may perceive themselves to be responding to a call to establish biblical models of manhood and womanhood and in particular fatherhood and motherhood – their understandings of those models may nevertheless be profoundly shaped by cultural traditions and a contemporary sense of crisis. Even so, as Aune points out there is evidence of negotiation here in which evangelical models are rarely simply the same as 'secular' ones and in any case the latter cannot be entirely separated from the history of the Christian discourse in which they were traditionally expressed. The relationship is thus dialectical and complex and probably uneven in its impact on individual evangelicals.

Cultural Expressions

The relationship of evangelicalism with cultural forms is explored two essays by Peter Webster and Ian Jones and by John Harvey respectively. In their discussion of the relationship between evangelicalism and the adoption of new musical idioms in the Church of England in the twentieth century Webster and Jones raise the issue of the ways in which identity is externally ascribed as well as internally experienced and expressed and draw attention to the importance of activity and 'style' in provoking such external attribution. Although experimentation with new musical forms in church was not limited to nor even particularly characteristic of Anglican evangelicalism in the 1950s and 60s, the adoption of a particular 'soft rock' pop style promoted by the growth of the charismatic movement had by the 1980s become intrinsically identified with evangelicalism in the popular imagination. Indeed it is arguable that given the late twentieth-century fragmentation of the Victorian patterns of liturgy and music in Sunday worship, the adoption of a particular musical style (though moderated by generational preferences) is increasingly constitutive of the identity of most groups within the Church of England and possibly in British Christianity more widely. Nevertheless, in practice, given the suspicions of 'pop' harboured by some more conservative evangelicals, the evangelical forms of Christianity may be both more diverse and more articulate about their diversity than most of the others.

John Harvey provides a critical examination, the expression and representation of evangelicalism through popular material culture – t-shirts, wall plaques, bumper stickers, posters, pencils and other artefacts. Much of this material, as he shows, makes intentional use of low cultural forms to express universal Christian sentiments in a way that seeks to provoke questions from non-Christians, as well as to teach and to promote the remembering or recycling of evangelical ideas and sentiments within the movement. If, as Harvey notes, much of this evangelical kitsch is unsuccessful or even incompetent, especially in the disjunction of word and image associated with some of the material, it is also one manifestation of a perennial evangelical desire to engage (either by appropriation, negotiation or confrontation) with popular culture. This may have been in general more restrained and certainly much less thorough-going in Britain than in North America, whence much of the material is imported, but it is even rarer in much of the rest of British Christianity. Harvey's account goes a fair way towards confirming Richard Holloway's oft-quoted remark that, 'one of the most courageous things about evangelicals is their ability to embrace bad taste for the sake of the gospel.'[24] It might be comforting, nevertheless, at least from the aesthetic point of view, to be presented a little more often with evidence that this is not just a consequence of an inability to tell the difference.

Expressions in Spirituality

Important though the expression of evangelical identity in cultural forms has been, its expression in the spirituality represented in those forms has typically lain even closer to the heart of the movement. Something of the warmth of this spirituality can be glimpsed in Andrew Atherstone's examination of the sermons of Francis Chavasse. Chavasse, one of the most significant Anglican evangelicals of his time and the successor to J. C. Ryle as bishop of Liverpool, was notable for his pastoral preaching. His sermons centred not so much on the explication or defence of his firmly held evangelical doctrine but on using simple language to point his hearers to the person of Christ as a saviour and as a friend. The priority he placed on this also influenced the way he dealt with controversy – being concerned not so much to win the argument as to win for Christ the person from whom he differed. In the late nineteenth century – a period when evangelical identity is often represented as defined in negative terms – against other Christian traditions or the threats of Biblical criticism and Darwinian science, the case of Chavasse shows that it also continued to be expressed in a positive and even optimistic mode. Moreover, at a time when evangelicalism was increasingly seen as under threat, spirituality provided an anchor point for its identity – a confidence that Christ would have the last word. Ian Randall's discussion of evangelical spirituality from the 1880s to the first world war draws attention not only to its warmth but also to its diversity. Beginning with David Gillett's assertion that Evangelical spirituality has tended to value spontaneity over form, inward spirituality over the sacraments, individual salvation over the church and the practice of piety over social involvement, Randall demonstrates that while these characteristics have been present they have never dominated the movement as a whole. Many Anglican evangelicals, for example, continued to place a high

---

[24] R. Holloway, 'Evangelicalism: An Outsiders Perspective', in France and McGrath (eds.), *Evangelical Anglicans*, 182.

value on both liturgy and sacramental worship during this period. The leading Baptist C. H. Spurgeon certainly profoundly distrusted set forms for prayer but was equally profoundly devoted to frequent celebration of Communion with a robust understanding of the real presence in a traditional Calvinist form. Evangelical spirituality was far from a homogenous phenomenon but acted to link evangelicals together at least as much as it divided them. It also retained a capacity to provide a bridge between evangelicals and other Christians of non-evangelical traditions including the exponents of the more Catholic forms of Anglicanism. The ecumenical potential of evangelical spirituality and its notion of an invisible church is further explored in the discussion of Henry Venn's *Life of Francis Xavier.* There in the enlightenment Claphamite evangelical mode of Joseph Milner (persisting as a strand in British evangelicalism even in the harder-edged world of the *Record*)[25] the godliness of a post-reformation Jesuit apostle was allowed to compensate for his theological failings. Even firmly-defined evangelicalism then can retain a capacity for catholic sympathy – a recognition of the possibility that the Holy Spirit might be active in other Christian traditions however inadequate their doctrine.

In his afterword, Derek Tidball points to the remarkable capacity of evangelicalism to provoke criticism both from within and without – a phenomenon which is perhaps inextricably connected with its current position as the most vibrant expression of British Christianity. He locates this vibrancy in a set of three key evangelical theological commitments: to belief in a living, acting and communicating God, to a transforming Gospel of grace and to the authority of the Bible. He also relates it to three sociological strengths: its character as a popular movement (engaging with ordinary people and mobilising the energy of the laity), its flexibility and adaptability in responding to social and cultural change and, at the same time, the strength of its conviction about its core message. Evangelicalism thus combines, in all its remarkable diversity, a considerable level of engagement with contemporary culture with a substantial degree of distance from it. This combination, suggests Tidball, is one of the keys to the current success of evangelicalism and many of the key elements he identifies are explored (in their past and present forms) in the essays presented here. However, given the dizzying diversity of evangelicalism in Britain, which is indeed one of the most prominent features of the contemporary religious landscape, no single set of studies can hope to do more than illustrate a few aspects of the movement. In the current volume, important variations in the experience and expression of

---

[25] For the hardening of evangelical positions in the later 1820s and the role of the *Record* see, for example, Bebbington, *Evangelicalism*, 75-94.

evangelical identity between generations, social classes, theological traditions and English regions have been left relatively unexamined. There is, therefore, clearly plenty of room for further exploration of a movement which, at the start of the twenty-first century shows little sign of flagging in its enterprise, its heterogeneity or its continuing concern with the definition of its own identity.

CHAPTER 1

Evangelicalism and Cultural Diffusion

David Bebbington

The relationship between gospel and culture has been much studied by missiologists in recent years. Andrew Walls of the University of Edinburgh and other experts on the history of world missions have shown that Christianity, especially in its Evangelical form, has proved remarkably adaptable to a wide range of diverse societies, taking up aspects of their ways of life and merging them with the distinctive features of the faith. The gospel, like the Bible, is eminently translatable.[1] That does not mean that theology is merely a function of culture, for it has proved an immensely creative force in its own right in the world of ideas. But the research of missiologists has brought to light something of the closeness of the integration of religion with its human setting, the potential for changes in the relationship over time and the resulting complexity of the interaction between gospel and culture. The same insights can be applied to Britain much more fully than they have been. Evangelical ideas have been part of the surrounding intellectual ambience, have been modified under its influence and have acted and reacted on British society in many and various ways. The object of this paper is to examine one aspect of the way in which Evangelicalism and its host culture in Britain have been related, the process of diffusion. Its subject is therefore the pattern whereby attitudes and opinions have flowed within the movement. Because the processes have taken place over time, they fall within the province of the historian, but because the purpose here is to generalise rather than to particularise they could equally be regarded as the concern of the sociologist, the anthropologist or even, in some respects, the geographer. So the scope of the coverage is broad: how ideas have typically been transmitted within the Evangelical movement over the last two and a half centuries or so.

The subject of culture initially calls for definition. The word, as Raymond Williams showed in his *Culture and Society,* has altered its

---

[1] Andrew Walls, *The Missionary Movement in Christian History* (Edinburgh: T & T Clark, 1996); *The Cross-Cultural Process in Christian History* (Edinburgh: T & T Clark, 2002).

meaning significantly over time and remains rather elusive.[2] Three contemporary usages may be distinguished. First there is the notion of high culture, the expression of civilisation in literature, art and music. The novels of Jane Austen, the canvases of Poussin or the fugues of Bach are quintessential forms of high culture. The word 'culture' is most commonly used in this way in Britain. When we speak of a cultured person, we mean somebody who appreciates Mozart or enjoys reading Homer. Secondly, there is the concept of popular culture, whether revealing itself in peasant customs of the past or in contemporary soap operas. This usage has traditionally been more common in the United States, where the *Journal of Cultural Studies,* published from Bowling Green University, Tennessee, concentrates on topics such as the worldview of Hollywood and the techniques of advertising. But the notion has also become firmly embedded in academic life in Britain, generating its own discipline of 'Cultural Studies'. The third way in which the term is employed is much broader than either of the other two, concentrating not on civilisation, whether high or low, but on the whole web of attitudes prevailing in a society. This is the manner in which the word has normally been used in anthropology, which has even extended it beyond the sphere of ideas to 'material culture', that is the sum of social artefacts. The third meaning of the concept was once confined to specific academic circles in Britain, but more recently it has become familiar in such phrases as the 'enterprise culture' and it is now in widespread use. In its broadest sense, the word can apply to virtually any feature of a society: a society's culture is how it is.

The usage here is an amalgam of all three of these ways of applying the word 'culture'. Evangelicalism has contained expressions of each of them. In the field of worship, for example, organ playing is a technique that can display the characteristics of high culture; flower arrangement in church can sometimes form a part of popular culture; and the raising of hands by charismatic worshippers falls within culture in its broadest definition. The usage that blends all three has advantages because of its all-encompassing quality. It recognises the importance of ideas, and so allows the theology that has been central to Evangelicalism to assume a prominent place in the analysis. Equally, because it embraces material culture, it gives weight to such matters as the architectural style of buildings or the physical shape of tracts. The word 'culture' is therefore being deployed in this paper in a comprehensive sense.

The theme of diffusion also deserves comment. The concept signifies the ways in which ideas or practices have spread over time. It has two chief dimensions, which, though related, must be distinguished. One is

---

[2] Raymond Williams, *Culture and Society, 1780-1950* (London: Chatto & Windus, 1959).

the social. What is upheld by one social group at a particular point can be transmitted to another group either suddenly or gradually, so that an obscure notion can become general. The different groups can be explored to discover which was first to maintain a point of view, which received it from the first and how rapid the process was. Equally, however, diffusion may be a spatial development. The study of how attitudes have passed from one area to another has yielded significant findings. In particular, geographers have examined not just patterns of distribution at a single juncture but also the taking up of innovations first in one place and then in another. It will be valuable to look at both the social and the spatial dimensions of diffusion.

There are various aspects of the relationship between Evangelicalism and diffusion that could be explored. One is the spread of Evangelical religion itself. This is a major theme in Mark Noll's *The Rise of Evangelicalism*. Taking the Evangelical Revival in the United Kingdom and Great Awakening in America jointly as his subject, he shows much of how and why the movement spread during the eighteenth century.[3] A classic account of the same process, though in a fictional microstudy, is George Eliot's 'Janet's Repentance'. In the early nineteenth century an Evangelical clergyman brings the gospel to the town of Milby, meeting a wall of hostility but eventually surmounting it by his diligence.[4] Although there is great scope for study of the introduction of the Evangelical movement into fresh places, that is not the theme of this paper.

Another issue that could be scrutinised is how secular influences were transmitted through Evangelicalism. This topic has become familiar to historians as a dimension of the social control thesis that reached the peak of its popularity in the 1970s. The ruling classes, it was argued by historians sympathetic to a Marxian position, used religion as one of the devices for keeping down the proletariat, especially in the age of industrialisation. A full-blooded instance of this viewpoint can be found in Allan MacLaren's study of Aberdeen in the 1840s, which contends that the Evangelical faith that gave rise to the Free Church of Scotland was primarily a vehicle for disciplining the lower orders.[5] A powerful counterblast was issued in the study of nineteenth-century Sunday schools by Thomas Laqueur, who showed that these alleged agencies of social control did not merely peddle ideas of deference but

---

[3] M. A. Noll, *The Rise of Evangelicalism: The Age of Edwards, Whitefield and the Wesleys* (Leicester: InterVarsity Press, 2004).

[4] George Eliot, 'Janet's Repentance', *Scenes of Clerical Life* (Edinburgh: William Blackwood and Sons, 1858).

[5] A. A. MacLaren, *Religion and Social Class: The Disruption Years in Aberdeen* (London: Routledge & Kegan Paul, 1974).

were authentic expressions of working-class culture. Laqueur's project entailed careful analysis, as far as possible, of the teaching actually transmitted in these largely Evangelical bodies.[6] The results of this kind of study can be illuminating, especially in resisting misrepresentations of Evangelical religion; but again that is not the topic here.

Instead the subject for discussion in this paper is the diffusion of ideas and practices within Evangelicalism. It is about the transmission of what had been indigenised within the movement. How did innovations pass from group to group and area to area? Premillennial teaching about prophecy, for example, became newly popular within the period: what were the processes involved in its dissemination? Again, whereas the gown had traditionally been worn by Anglican clergymen when preaching, Evangelicals influenced by the legacy of the Oxford Movement began to adopt the surplice in the pulpit during the later years of the nineteenth century: who did so and where was it done? The schemes of diffusion within the Evangelical movement are worthy of study in their own right.

It might be thought that the task of identifying any significant pattern would be impossible. When people embraced premillennialism, they did so freely, as a matter of conviction, so that the distribution of those who had adopted it by any given point, it might be expected, would be random. To suggest any group trends might be interpreted as an unjustified assumption of social determinism, a slight on personal responsibility. Free, individual decisions, however, do commonly reveal significant consistencies. The sociological pioneer Emile Durkheim found that even Paris suicides, which might be expected to be among the ultimate expressions of individual autonomy, fell into discernible patterns.[7] That was because those who did away with themselves were subject to the same social pressures as other people and accordingly responded, though in more dramatic fashion than others. Likewise Evangelicals, though enjoying the degree of liberty normally assigned to human beings, were also moulded by the influences that are the common lot of humanity. As members of their communities, as readers and in a host of other ways they were affected by a variety of social factors. To generalise about responses is not to deny responsibility for choices.

What, then, has been the pattern of cultural diffusion among Evangelicals? Initially, we can focus on the social rather than the spatial trends, the way in which different groups adopted beliefs and manners

---

[6] T. W. Laqueur, *Religion and Respectability: Sunday Schools and Working-Class Culture, 1780-1850* (New Haven, CT: Yale University Press, 1976).

[7] Emile Durkheim, *Suicide: A Study in Sociology*, trans. J. A. Spaulding and George Simpson, ed. George Simpson (London: Routledge & Kegan Paul, 1952).

rather than the places where they did so. The predominant overall schema, we may say at the outset, was for novelties to spread from above to below, from an elite to the masses. The great Evangelical MP and champion of the slaves William Wilberforce wrote in 1797 of 'the general diffusion of the sentiments of the higher orders'.[8] Ideas, he was claiming, would trickle down from the top of society to its lower reaches. His view might be discounted as the natural opinion of one of the well-to-do of the time, naturally expecting that the higher orders would automatically be imitated by the rank and file of a deferential population. Again, Wilberforce's conviction might be thought to reflect the presumption of the Enlightenment that the more refined could spread the light of knowledge to the lower orders who had previously been benighted in darkness. It is true that the next age, when Romantic ideas were in currency, stressed the countervailing capacity of the ordinary people, the folk, to retain the admirable qualities of former generations and to transmit them upwards to their superiors. So it should not be assumed that Wilberforce was correct in declaring that the flow of influence was chiefly downwards. Yet on investigation that is exactly what does turn out to be the case with Evangelicals. Normally ideas and practices spread downwards from groups with greater advantages to a wider constituency.

More particularly, three characteristics normally marked those who were affected earlier rather than later by innovations in the Evangelical world. In the first place, they were highly educated. Those with more experience of learning tended to read more extensively and so to be more exposed to fresh ideas. In particular university graduates, who for most of the period could claim to enjoy a form of elite status, were more likely to experiment with new notions. Hence charismatic renewal, far from being the mindless extravagance that was sometimes depicted in the press, initially attracted a disproportionate number of graduates. The church led by Bryn Jones at Bradford, the fulcrum of the largest network of restorationist congregations in the 1980s, for example, included many elders boasting degrees and four holders of doctorates when they were less common than they have since become.[9] Innovations in the Evangelical world normally struck the more educated before the less qualified.

A second variable normally affecting who was likely to embrace novelty was class. In a secular context, a study of Derby in the 1950s

---

[8] William Wilberforce, *A Practical View of the Prevailing Religious System of Professed Christians in the Higher and Middle Classes in this Country Contrasted with Real Christianity*, 4th edn (London: T. Cadell jun. and W. Davies, 1797), 10.

[9] Andrew Walker, *Restoring the Kingdom* (London: Hodder and Stoughton, 1985), 188.

showed that the middle classes usually accepted new ideas more readily than the working classes.[10] The phenomenon was explained as primarily the result of the greater amount of reading done by the middle classes. Just as more education was associated with innovation, so was a higher position on the class scale, and that was because the two were closely related. In the days before free university places, those who could afford a better education were those with higher incomes. A similar pattern has been evident in Evangelicalism. Denominations with a higher social profile have been notably more receptive to new ideas. During the later years of the nineteenth century, Congregationalists were significantly more inclined to liberalise their theology than their near denominational neighbours the Baptists.[11] Their respectability made many of the Congregationalists want, as it were, to smooth off the rough edges of their faith, to domesticate their religion. They showed a greater willingness to accept newer notions of, for example, the universal Fatherhood of God. At the same time, however, Evangelical Anglicans, whose social standing was on average even higher, also embraced novelty in the shape of Keswick holiness teaching, which tended to stiffen theological conservatism.[12] It was not necessarily liberal views that attracted people of superior status; rather it was novelty. So sections of the Evangelical movement with a higher-class position were disproportionately drawn to fresh convictions.

The third most striking factor affecting willingness to take up something new was age. Teenagers and young adults were usually more malleable than their elders. Hence there was normally a generational difference between Evangelicals upholding traditional ways and those wanting to move on. The most innovative body associated with the Evangelical movement in the earlier twentieth century, for example, was the Oxford Group, a network of young people led by the American evangelist Frank Buchman. They would arrive enthusiastically in an area urging the inhabitants to change their lives by an act of surrender, shunning inherited theological terminology in favour of language that offered the fewest barriers to the gospel.[13] They were often Oxford students, as the title of the body suggests, and so they were frequently privileged in terms of academic attainments and social standing as well. As in many other cases, such as the ready

[10] Theodore Cauter and J. S. Downham, *The Communication of Ideas: A Study of Contemporary Influences on Urban Life* (London: Chatto & Windus, 1954).

[11] Mark Hopkins, *Nonconformity's Romantic Generation: Evangelical and Liberal Theologies in Victorian England* (Milton Keynes: Paternoster, 2004).

[12] D. W. Bebbington, *Evangelicalism in Modern Britain: A History from the 1730s to the 1980s* (London: Routledge, 1993), chap. 5.

[13] Bebbington, *Evangelicalism*, chap. 7.

reception of Romantic notions in the 1830s by the early Brethren or the appeal of radical charismatic renewal in the 1980s, the three factors of learning, class and age intertwined.[14] Those who were eager to adopt new ways within the Evangelical movement were primarily the educated, the well-to-do and the young.

What were the mechanisms of diffusion? The most obvious agency among Protestants was the pulpit. Ministers provided teaching for their flocks, usually (until recently) twice each Sunday and often during the week as well. Hence the instruction that the ministers themselves had received was crucial. For many, the colleges where they trained were the chief sources of their distinctive ideas. Fundamentalists in the interwar years spoke darkly of the wells of learning being poisoned by Modernism, in some cases founding new institutions such as the Bible Churchmen's College in Bristol and the School of Evangelism at Barry in South Wales to replace the older tainted bodies.[15] Although by that time most of the theological colleges were in university cities so that it was impossible to isolate candidates for the ministry from wider influences, the colleges did transmit a particular style. Thus at Zion Baptist Church, Cambridge, in the 1950s, a deacon claimed to be able to identify the college background of any visiting preacher within five minutes of the opening of the sermon. Men from Spurgeon's College, for example, were noted for their breezy anecdotes.[16] Ideas flowed from those responsible for training through the ministers to the pews.

A second agency of diffusion was the mass gathering. These were by no means a novelty of the late twentieth century. Dissenting bodies held district association meetings from the later eighteenth century, acting as media for the dissemination of the latest views of doctrine and practice. The Northamptonshire Baptist Association, for instance, was where many of its ministers first heard of the theology of Jonathan Edwards and its sanction for the proclamation of the gospel uninhibited by worries over whether their hearers had been predestined to salvation. The result was a series of discussions that culminated in the foundation

---

[14] D. W. Bebbington, 'The Place of the Brethren Movement in International Evangelicalism', in Neil Dickson (ed.), *The History of the Global Brethren Movement* (forthcoming). Walker, *Restoring the Kingdom*, 188.

[15] W. S. Hooton and J. S. Wright, *The First Twenty-Five Years of the Bible Churchmen's Missionary Society (1922-47)* (London: Bible Churchmen's Missionary Society, 1947), chap. 4. Noel Gibbard, *Taught to Serve: The History of Barry and Bryntirion Colleges* (Bridgend, Glamorgan: Evangelical Press of Wales, 1996).

[16] George Hayden was the deacon. I am grateful to his son, Dr Roger Hayden, for the point.

of the Baptist Missionary Society in 1792.[17] Likewise the annual meetings of Evangelical Anglicans at Islington from 1827 to 1982 attracted around a thousand attenders by the start of the twentieth century to listen to addresses by leading clergy on questions of contemporary policy. The Islington meetings functioned as the magisterium of the movement, usually trying to steady the rank and file in their existing opinions but sometimes urging new courses of action. In 1908, for example, it discussed 'The Church and Social Problems', recommending in a year when the rise of the Labour Party was in the public eye that the clergy should take up questions of politics, municipal life, housing, the treatment of children, the sweated trades and temperance. The theme of social issues was not to be repeated at Islington until 1968. Already, however, sixty years previously, the gathering had given Evangelical clergy the green light for involvement in combating the ills of Edwardian England.[18] Mass meetings could be powerful agents of innovation.

Literature, thirdly, was an extraordinarily important means by which fresh ideas spread. Evangelicals were masters of the art of using publications to disseminate their convictions, founding the prolific Religious Tract Society in 1799 and the mighty British and Foreign Bible Society five years later. Although Bibles were published without note or comment, the tracts engaged with many topics, including even science. Around the middle of the nineteenth century the Religious Tract Society published a monthly series of sixpenny booklets arguing that all spheres of life were providentially ordered and so illustrated the analogies between the scientific and the spiritual worlds. Even a New Zealand caterpillar infected with fungus was deployed to illustrate Christian teaching.[19] Although the chief effect was to reinforce existing beliefs, the exploration of fresh intellectual areas by readers was undoubtedly the result. Denominational periodicals, which contained very diverse material, exercised an even more widespread effect. In the early nineteenth century the *Evangelical Magazine* and the *Methodist Magazine* both sold about twenty thousand copies a month.[20] Such periodicals could be the means of disseminating novelties, as when John Campbell recommended the Gothic style for chapel building in the *Congregational*

---

[17] D. W. Bebbington, 'Remembered around the World: The International Scope of Edwards's Legacy', in D. W. Kling and D. A. Sweeney (eds), *Jonathan Edwards at Home and Abroad: Historical Memories, Cultural Movements, Global Horizons* (Columbia, SC: University of South Carolina Press, 2003), 183-4, 186.

[18] *Record*, 17 January 1908, 57-68.

[19] Aileen Fyfe, *Science and Salvation: Evangelical Popular Science Publishing in Victorian Britain* (Chicago: University of Chicago Press, 2004), 116.

[20] Fyfe, *Science and Salvation*, 49.

Year Book.[21] And separate titles were pervasive. George Warner, a Primitive Methodist minister, was said to have published during his lifetime between 30,000 and 40,000 books and pamphlets commending his brand of teaching about entire sanctification.[22] Although its relative influence declined with the rise of the other media during the twentieth century, Christian literature continued to play a large part in stimulating Evangelicals to take up new causes.

It is also true, in the fourth place, that organisations have been major agencies of diffusion. The Methodist device of the class meeting, a weekly gathering of about a dozen people for fellowship and uplift, was extremely influential in encouraging members to go on to meet fresh spiritual challenges. Small-scale prayer meetings and fellowship groups have been characteristic of the Evangelical movement over the centuries, providing a forum for the dissemination of practices new as well as old. Thus it was in cottage meetings, away from the formalities of chapel services, that female leadership of worship advanced amongst Methodists in the early nineteenth century.[23] A plethora of youth organisations has marked Evangelical history, but the chief among them has undoubtedly been the Sunday school. Over 75 per cent of children in Britain aged 5 to 14 were enrolled in a Sunday school during the Edwardian years.[24] These bodies may have declined during the subsequent century, but Sunday school still retained a major hold on the children of the unchurched population right down until the arrival, around 1960, of the television in the working-class sitting room and of the car in the street outside. Here were institutions that conveyed Evangelical ideas, with their enduring substance and their passing variations, to a very high proportion of the population.

Individuals, fifthly, must not be forgotten. Major figures could exercise an exceptional influence through their personal role, reinforced in print. Edward Irving, the flamboyant minister of the Church of Scotland in London during the 1820s, for example, made an enormous impact on contemporary Evangelicals. Cultivating a friendship with the poet S. T. Coleridge, Irving imbibed many of his distinctive notions together with his whole Romantic style of thinking. The Scottish

---

[21] John Blackburn, 'Remarks on Ecclesiastical Architecture as applied to Nonconformist Chapels', in the *Congregational Year Book* (London: Jackson and Walford, 1847), 161.

[22] J[ohn] Stephenson, *The Man of Faith and Fire: Or, the Life and Work of the Rev. G. Warner* (London: Robert Bryant, 1902), 276.

[23] Deborah Valenze, *Prophetic Sons and Daughters: Female Preaching and Popular Religion in Industrial England* (Princeton, NJ: Princeton University Press, 1985), 41-9.

[24] C. G. Brown, *The Death of Christian Britain* (London: Routledge, 2001), 168.

minister applied the new approach to traditional doctrine and came up with a whole string of fresh readings: the principle of living by faith as a missionary, the expectation of an imminent and personal second advent, the possibility of speaking in tongues and much else were implanted in the Evangelical world by his agency.[25] Other individuals have been hardly less significant. During the twentieth century the influence of Martyn Lloyd-Jones, especially on his native Wales, was immense, leading to the setting up of the Evangelical Movement of Wales to consolidate the forces of the movement in the principality.[26] Equally the pervasive influence of John Stott within and beyond the Anglican world can hardly be underestimated. It was Stott, for example, who did most to persuade conservative Evangelicals to return to a policy of social engagement from which they had previously withdrawn.[27] So individuals could play a decisive part in changes of direction.

By such means as these, therefore, ideas and practices spread through the Evangelical community. The general social pattern of diffusion, as we have seen, was from more elite groups downwards to the rank and file. The predominant flow is clear, reflecting the processes that sociologists have discovered in other fields. Yet, as might be expected, the particular circumstances of Evangelicalism have made the reality of the process far more complex. A sequence of qualifications needs to be made to the overall principle.

Firstly, the nature of the elite within Evangelicalism deserves attention. Secular societies usually contain more than one type of elite, and so it has been in the Evangelical movement. There have been two types of leader, the intellectual and the social. The intellectual group largely consisted of theologians, but also included thinkers in other fields such as Hannah More, the late eighteenth-century friend of Samuel Johnson who wrote novels, improving literature and government propaganda in the wake of the French Revolution.[28] The individuals in this group might be socially superior, as were many of Hannah More's circle such as William Wilberforce, but that was by no means always the case. Writers who exerted considerable sway over the Evangelical world could be people of lowly social standing. One such

---

[25] Bebbington, *Evangelicalism*, chap. 3.

[26] Noel Gibbard, *The First Fifty Years: The History of the Evangelical Movement of Wales, 1948 -1998* (Bridgend, Glamorgan: Evangelical Press of Wales, 2002).

[27] D. W. Bebbington, 'The Decline and Resurgence of Evangelical Social Reform' in John Wolffe (ed.), *Evangelical Faith and Public Zeal: Evangelicals and Society in Britain, 1780-1980* (London: SPCK, 1995), 185, 192.

[28] Anne Stott, *Hannah More: The First Victorian* (Oxford: Oxford University Press, 2003).

was T. B. Smithies, the Methodist editor of innumerable journals in the high Victorian years. From 1851 onwards he was responsible for *The Band of Hope Review, The British Workman, The Children's Friend, The Infant's Magazine, The Friendly Visitor, The Family Friend, The Weekly Welcome, The Band of Mercy Magazine* and the Earlham series of tracts. Smithies, who selected the ideas that met the eyes of millions, was originally a humble insurance clerk.[29] Opinion-formers need not be figures of fame or fortune.

Yet many were individuals of high social standing. Evangelicalism in its heyday was well staffed by the aristocracy and gentry. Nearly every Victorian subscription list boasted a number of peers at its head. Landowners could exert themselves to ensure the spread of new ideas, especially among their own tenants and in the vicinity of their own estates. Thus in 1853 William Macdonald Macdonald, a laird in the parish of Craig on the east coast of Scotland who belonged to the small but stoutly Evangelical English Episcopal denomination, ensured that good literature circulated in the fishing village of Ferryden by opening a reading room at his own expense. Because the reading room was also a coffee room, Macdonald helped to identify Evangelical religion with the temperance movement, a link that became deep-seated in the community.[30] In the twentieth century J. Arthur Rank, enjoying the income from his flour milling empire, could direct resources to causes of which he approved in Methodism. Believing that films could do good as well as harm, he donated projectors to the churches and took up film-making himself, a decision that led him to the create the British cinema industry and eventually to receive a peerage.[31] So the social elite of the country at large could be a powerful factor in the spread of new practices. The Evangelical groupings from which novelties proceeded were primarily intellectual circles, but in the second place included people of high social station.

Nor was the popular culture that evolved within Evangelicalism a unitary phenomenon. In reality – and this is the second qualification of the generalisation – the attitudes of Evangelicals in the pews were remarkably diverse. It is true that the evidence would suggest that there was little significant division between the sexes in terms of the grasp and observance of Evangelical faith. Female spirituality among Evangelical Nonconformists around the middle of the nineteenth

---

[29] G. S. Rowe, *T. B. Smithies (Editor of "The British Workman"): A Memoir* (London: Partridge, 1884), 52-5.

[30] Andrew Douglas, *History of the Village of Ferryden*, 2nd edn (Montrose: The Author, 1857), 55.

[31] D. J. Jeremy, *Capitalists and Christians: Business Leaders and the Churches in Britain, 1900-1960* (Oxford: Oxford University Press, 1990), 350-1.

century was virtually indistinguishable from that of their menfolk.[32] Yet there were other lines of demarcation that were sharper. Even within the British Isles, Evangelicals were diverse in nationality. Wales, unlike England, was dominated for much of the period by Nonconformity and Scotland had its own overwhelmingly Presbyterian tone. Evangelical currents flowing powerfully among Anglicans were likely to make less impact elsewhere in Britain. Language differences could reinforce barriers to the reception of new ideas. Thus it was believed that the first book to teach premillenialism in the Welsh language was not published until 1919, nearly a century after its equivalent in English.[33] Similarly in the Scottish Highlands the Gaelic language functioned as a preservative of orthodox Calvinism.[34] Theology itself, furthermore, erected obstacles to the spread of novelties. Calvinism in particular could be resistant to fresh ways of thinking, so that, for instance, the Strict and Particular Baptists arose in the early nineteenth century through refusing to accept the doctrinal innovations of the age.[35] Consequently the believers in the pew were often protected from change by national, linguistic and theological defences. The rank and file remained notably diverse, for by no means all the novel ideas and practices eventually filtered down to everybody.

A third point to be made is that dissemination was not always intentional. Sometimes it was indeed deliberate, with a section of opinion eager to spread some 'new teaching'. That was true, for example, among Welsh Independents in the early nineteenth century, who posited a middle way between traditional Calvinism and the Arminianism of the Wesleyan Methodists. Taking up what they called the 'New System' from the writings of the theologian Edward Williams, they successfully commended their convictions as well calculated to bring about church growth.[36] In other instances, however, the process of diffusion was unconscious. Because deference was such a potent force in British society, there was much aping of higher social groups by lower ones. Hence in the later nineteenth century, one of the chief factors moulding the style of Nonconformist worship in prosperous urban congregations was the imitation of the decency and order of the Church of England, which was perceived as altogether more

---

[32] Linda Wilson, *Constrained by Zeal: Female Spirituality amongst Nonconformists, 1825-1875* (Carlisle: Paternoster, 2000).

[33] *Christian*, 6 March 1919, 19.

[34] D. E. Meek, *The Scottish Highlands: The Churches and Gaelic Culture* (Geneva: WCC Publications, 1996), 41.

[35] Kenneth Dix, *Strict and Particular: English Strict and Particular Baptists in the Nineteenth Century* (Didcot, Oxfordshire: Baptist Historical Society, 2001).

[36] Bebbington, 'Remembered', 184-5.

respectable. By 1869 one Congregational chapel had a communion table emblazoned with the sacred monogram 'IHS', two reading desks, a gowned minister, repetition of the Lord's Prayer and the *Te Deum*, and even two 'crimson velvet bags' for the offering.[37] The innovations had not been urged on them by the Anglicans; they were simply copied. The process of change could be a matter of the assimilation of attractive options that were in the air.

The general thesis about the flow of influence also needs qualification, fourthly, in respect of its direction. It may normally have been a question of ideas and practices percolating down the social scale, but in some cases the reverse was true. What was at one point confined to the popular level could subsequently be taken up and recommended by leaders of opinion. Thus the distinctive Methodist belief in entire sanctification was in the early nineteenth century a plebeian preoccupation, but from the 1870s it was taken up and propagated by a group of prominent ministers and laymen.[38] The leaders could even find themselves displaced by the led. This was pre-eminently true in the Welsh Revival of 1904-05, when an obscure candidate for the Calvinistic Methodist ministry, Evan Roberts, became a national hero in the principality. Ministers of great experience deferred to Roberts as he spoke at informal services where dozens were converted. He was, said a contemporary, 'like a particle of radium in our midst'.[39] It was certainly possible, especially at times of great stirring, for people of powerful influence to emerge from the grass-roots of the movement.

A fifth consideration is that, if the downward cultural flow could sometimes be reversed, it could also be modified by the direction becoming predominantly, as it were, horizontal rather than vertical, that is at the same social level. Thus the temperance movement, a great enthusiasm of Nonconformist Evangelicals by the opening of the twentieth century, began as a non-religious movement. It was originally, around the 1830s, a cause beloved by secular-minded artisans wanting to improve themselves, and was frowned on by most Evangelicals as another gospel that threatened the true one. But temperance was steadily adopted by Christians of similar social groups, especially by Primitive Methodists, and eventually total abstinence became *de rigueur* for chapel membership.[40] This profound change of

---

[37] *Freeman*, 16 April 1869, 302.

[38] D. W. Bebbington, 'Holiness in Nineteenth-Century British Methodism', in W. M. Jacob and Nigel Yates (eds), *Crown and Mitre: Religion and Society in Northern Europe since the Reformation* (Woodbridge, Suffolk: Boydell, 1993).

[39] Eifion Evans, *The Welsh Revival of 1904* (London: Evangelical Press, 1969), 72.

[40] Brian Harrison, *Drink and the Victorians: The Temperance Question in England, 1815-1872* (London: Faber and Faber, 1971).

manners was primarily due to rubbing shoulders with equals. Again, various influences swept into the British Isles from across the Atlantic. Individual communion cups were first adopted instead of a single chalice as a health precaution in 1894 in the United States. Four years later they were introduced at Thorne Congregational Church near Doncaster and from there spread rapidly throughout the chapel world.[41] The sacred solos of Ira D. Sankey, the singing assistant of the evangelist D. L. Moody, form a more celebrated example of the reception of American innovations.[42] Thus novelty could be assimilated from abroad. There was therefore a transverse pattern of influence operating on British Evangelicalism, both from outside Evangelicalism and from outside Britain.

Each of these qualifications acts as a caveat against seeing too much uniformity in the process of assimilating fresh influences. The social pattern of the dissemination of innovations within Evangelicalism was therefore predominantly from the elite to the masses, but there are many exceptions to the rule. So long as similar reservations are kept in mind, it is also possible, however, to outline the general geographical dimensions of the process. This is the way in which ideas and practices have spread over space. Although it is closely connected with the analysis in terms of social groups, the topic deserves some consideration in its own right.

Geographers who have studied the take-up of innovations have decided that a possible explanation is what they call contagion. On this understanding a preference for some novelty is spread, like a disease, as the result of personal contact. In a classic account of the diffusion of car ownership in Sweden after the First World War, Torsten Hägerstrand showed that at successive dates the fashion for buying vehicles moved from west to east, from the side of the country facing Denmark to the side facing Finland. The possession of motor cars advanced as fresh Swedes admired the gleaming new vehicles owned by their neighbours.[43] Evangelical processes of diffusion seem to have followed a comparable pattern. Some areas have usually been early to adopt change, and other areas have normally lagged behind. The place where fresh ideas have normally been most highly favoured is London, which, as the capital and the largest city, has been the most likely place for novelties to be broached. From there, they have extended to the south-east of England and then steadily advanced outwards. The resulting

---

[41] *Christian World*, 22 November 1894, 871; 9 August 1900, 12; 16 August 1900, 9.

[42] John Kent, *Holding the Fort: Studies in Victorian Revivalism* (London: Epworth, 1978), chap. 6.

[43] Torsten Hägerstrand, *Innovation Diffusion as a Spatial Process*, trans. Allan Pred (Chicago: University of Chicago Press, [1967]).

pattern approximates to that of centre and periphery, a familiar one in historical geography. The spread of charismatic renewal in the earliest period, down to 1963, reflects something of this schema. By that date the new movement had a significant presence in London, the home counties and the south-west, had slightly touched the midlands and Yorkshire but was virtually unknown in the north-east, the north-west and Wales.[44] Renewal had put down roots near the centre, was beginning to affect the inner periphery but had not yet influenced the outer periphery. Contagion would appear to have been at work.

Other geographers, however, have pointed to another spatial process affecting the adoption of novelty. This is the principle of hierarchy, according to which the popularity of innovations is directly related to the size of urban areas. On this interpretation, fresh ways and attitudes would spread from London to the big cities first rather than to immediately adjacent areas, then to rather smaller places and eventually, much later, to rural nooks and crannies. Again, there is some evidence for this pattern appearing in Evangelicalism. To take the same instance as before, renewal was already known in Scottish cities by 1963 when it had not yet reached the northernmost parts of England.[45] Larger places, that is to say, were affected before some of the intermediate territory. Networks of friends, families and former college contacts were at work, linking similar people in different places. Consequently there was a tendency for an urban/rural split to emerge, with cities taking up novelties before the surrounding countryside. This, of course, had been the pattern in the late Roman Empire, when cities were evangelised before their hinterlands, so that the word for countryfolk, *pagani*, became the label for unbelievers, 'pagans'. Equally, however, it was true of the employment of denominational hymn books among Cambridgeshire Baptists in the early 1970s. The city churches sang from the 1962 edition, the larger village chapels by and large used the 1933 edition and the smaller chapels retained the 1900 edition.[46] The larger the place, the more popular were innovations.

A persuasive case has been made out by the geographer Brian Robson for the reality of spatial diffusion normally being a combination of the two processes that have just been outlined. He shows, for example, that the early take-up of telephones in the late nineteenth century was chiefly round London, the result of contagion, and also in large cities, a symptom of hierarchy.[47] An equivalent pattern is evident

---

[44] Peter Hocken, *Streams of Renewal: The Origins and Early Development of the Charismatic Movement in Great Britain* (Exeter: Paternoster, 1986), 112.

[45] Hocken, *Streams of Renewal*, 112.

[46] Personal observation.

[47] B. T. Robson, *Urban Growth: An Approach* (London: Methuen, 1973).

at the same time in the foundation of local Councils of the Evangelical Free Churches, a movement that grew largely spontaneously during the 1890s to co-ordinate the work of the chapels. Most of the earliest Free Church Councils were established in big cities, but then smaller councils were set up in adjacent villages as well as in smaller towns further away. The last parts of the country to be covered by the councils were rural counties without major centres of population such as Dorset and Westmorland.[48] Evangelical phenomena therefore broadly fit the geographers' models for the spread of innovations over space.

For a full picture of the process of diffusion amongst Evangelicals, the spatial dimension must be added to the social. Normally, we may conclude, ideas and practices have first been adopted by an intellectual elite, and to a lesser extent a social elite, specially in London. From there they have spread to the educated, the well-to-do and the young, particularly in the cities. In the twentieth century, as urban segregation by status grew, there are signs that the more prosperous suburbs may have been more liable to change than the city centres, for it was there that the most responsive social groups were chiefly to be found. The role of Holy Trinity, Brompton, during the 1990s, as the epicentre of the Alpha programme of evangelism, however, has shown that churches in favoured parts of inner cities can still have a remarkable capacity for innovation. By contrast, rural areas such as Radnorshire, with congregations that are by and large less well educated, less prosperous and less youthful, have not been notable for path-breaking change. In 2003 the highpoint of the anniversary services of one Baptist chapel in the county was a (very capable) rendition of Sankey solos.[49] The process of diffusion has been neither uniform nor automatic, but it has tended to follow particular lines.

At least two applications arise from this exploration of an aspect of the relationship of gospel and culture. One might be useful for the church in its missionary endeavour. If Evangelicalism has followed such a pattern, there are implications for how the gospel should be presented in particular areas. In a sense the principle is already known and observed. Gospel pop concerts are not normally held in Stornoway. But those concerned with the strategy of mission might be well advised to look for new techniques in what has been done recently and successfully in places slightly larger than their own with a similar social profile. Minehead, for instance, might look to Torquay or Leicester to Birmingham. We may be confident that the process of innovation will persist and continue to have an impact on the effectiveness of

---

[48] D. W. Bebbington, *The Nonconformist Conscience: Chapel and Politics, 1870-1914* (London: Allen & Unwin, 1982), 68.

[49] Sarn Baptist Church from personal observation.

evangelism.

The second application might be more useful for scholarship. Evangelicalism has been a major force in British society, achieving nothing short of cultural dominance in the mid-nineteenth century. Since then it has shrunk to a much smaller element, by 1998 constituting only 2.8 per cent of the English population.[50] Nevertheless it is a far from negligible grouping. What academic study of the movement, in its present as well as its past dimensions, needs to take into account is its huge internal variety. When considered at all, Evangelicalism is often treated as monochrome and unchanging. What study of the process of cultural diffusion illustrates is that, since it has been in constant flux, it has proved a remarkably heterogeneous phenomenon. Lifestyle, organisation, worship and even theology have regularly been moulded and remoulded. Emphases have varied over time and space. Some sense of how Evangelicalism has altered is essential if the place of the churches in modern Britain is to be appreciated. It is also essential to the understanding of modern British culture.

---

[50] Peter Brierley (ed.), *UK Christian Handbook Religious Trends No. 2* (London: Harper Collins, 1999), 12.3.

CHAPTER 2

Understanding Schism: The 1950 Peace Summit between the Student Christian Movement and the Inter-Varsity Fellowship

David Goodhew

On a late winter's afternoon in 1950 two delegations met in total secrecy at a smart London club. A neutral chairman was there to keep order and a stenographer was present, so that both sides could provide a certain record of what was said, should this later be necessary. This might have been a scene from the Cold War. In fact, it was a meeting between the leaders of the Student Christian Movement of Britain and Ireland (SCM) and the Inter-Varsity Fellowship (IVF – subsequently re-named the Universities and Colleges Christian Fellowship, UCCF). One embodied a 'broad' theology, ready to adapt to what it saw as the needs of the times, the other held firm to what it saw as orthodox Christianity. Amongst the participants were Martin Lloyd Jones, a leading Congregationalist preacher and a young postgraduate from Oxford called David Jenkins, later to achieve fame as the bishop of Durham.

The summit of SCM and IVF, Lloyd Jones and Jenkins, embodies one of the most serious splits within modern British Christianity, a split which finds many echoes worldwide.[1] Their encounter in 1950 had been preceded by several half-hearted attempts at reconciliation and was the only serious attempt by the SCM and IVF to resolve their differences. Although it failed, it is crucial to making sense of the division between 'liberal' and 'conservative' versions of Christianity. Modern Evangelicalism is, to a large extent, defined by the terms of this debate. So that meeting on a late winter's afternoon, in a secluded London club, is for evangelicalism of both historical relevance and contemporary importance.[2]

---

[1] A. Hastings, *A History of English Christianity, 1920-85* (London: Collins, 1986), 90.

[2] An example of this process is the liberal/evangelical dialogue by David Edwards, (once head of SCM), and John Stott, (a pillar of IVF), *Essentials: a liberal-evangelical dialogue* (London: Hodder and Stoughton, 1988).

SCM was the most significant Christian organisation operating amongst students in Britain in the first half of the century. In 1910 its Cambridge branch – the Cambridge Inter-Collegiate Christian Union (CICCU) - split from SCM and in 1928 a rival national body, the IVF, was formed. These earlier divisions centred around IVF's stress on a conservative Evangelical view of scripture (whereas SCM was much more open to 'higher criticism') and the penal substitutionary doctrine of the atonement of Christ, which IVF regarded as sacrosanct and which SCM regarded as one theory amongst many.[3] IVF grew gradually and by the 1960s had overtaken the SCM which went into steep decline in the late 1960s.[4]

In 1950 SCM and IVF were evenly matched, with SCM still the dominant force. To the meeting on 1 March 1950 between SCM and IVF each side brought substantial delegations. As well as the two general secretaries Alan Booth (a Methodist who later became Director of Christian Aid) and Douglas Johnson (a layman who belonged to a variety of churches but who was primarily a Presbyterian, heavily influenced by the Brethren and who was General Secretary of IVF from 1928 to 1964) there were several staff members (Oliver Barclay and Phyllis Bennett for IVF; Stephen Burnet, Davis McCaughey, Joan Wright and John Gibbs for SCM), several students (Frank Rhodes, John Sertin and Peter Haile for IVF; James Blackies, David Jenkins and Derek Jefferson for SCM). IVF also brought John Aiken (chair of its Graduate Fellowship) and, most significantly, Martin Lloyd-Jones, its vice-president. IVF's delegation had a slight bias towards Cambridge; SCM's delegation was more clerical than IVF's. In denominational terms, both sides contained a mix of Anglicans and free churchpeople.

Booth began the summit by stressing that, for SCM, the key issue was ecclesiology. Christianity was manifest in community, so true

---

[3] See: D. Goodhew, 'The Rise of the Cambridge Inter-Collegiate Christian Union, 1910-71', *Journal of Ecclesiastical History*, 54, 1, (Winter 2003), 64-65.

[4] The most helpful material includes: Tissington Tatlow, *The Story of the SCM of Great Britain and Ireland* (London: SCM, 1933); *A Survey of Christianity in the Universities* (London, SCM, 1962); Douglas Johnson, *Contending for the Faith* (Leicester: IVP, 1979); Geraint Fielder, *Lord for the Years* (Leicester: IVP, 1988); John Pollock, *A Cambridge Movement* (London: John Murray, 1953); Oliver Barclay, *Whatever Happened to the Jesus Lane Lot?* (Leicester: IVP, 1977); Steve Bruce, 'The SCM and the IVF: a Sociological Study of two Student Movements' (D.Phil., Stirling, 1980); R. Boyd, *The Witness of the SCM* (London: SPCK, 2007); D. Goodhew, 'The Strange Death of the SCM', in C. Binfield (ed.) *Christian Youth Movements: their History and Significance* (forthcoming); Martin Wellings, 'Aspects of Late Nineteenth Century Anglican Evangelicalism: the Response to Ritualism, Darwinism and Theological Liberalism' (D. Phil. thesis, Oxford, 1989), 447-60 ; Goodhew, 'Rise of CICCU'.

discipleship necessitated a common fellowship. Booth used evidence from the Bible and Evangelical tradition to underpin this view and spoke of SCM's need to repent of past divisiveness, noting how separation detracted from witness. The fellowship was open to any with 'faith in Christ', defined in terminology akin to conservative Evangelism.[5] This was challenged by Barclay, who pointed to SCM's openness to Unitarianism:

> *Barclay*: '...you were not previously committed as a Movement to the deity of Christ.'
> *McCaughey*: 'I think the people who formulated it [the SCM basis] thought they were committed as a Movement, but they thought at another point that they were also making it possible for those who came in with difficulties on that point to come in and learn more inside. But it may be that we now, looking back, think that their way of stating it is not our way. That is the history of Christian thought and the life of the Church anyway. There is no need to be frightened about finding ourselves doing that.'[6]

IVF speakers then quizzed SCM's representatives as to how they viewed their predecessors. Booth stressed that SCM was 'constantly reforming itself according to the Holy Scripture', obtaining 'a growing understanding'. McCaughey stressed that 'the Church's life and thought is in one sense always changing, yet at the same time is always being sustained from the same source.' Lloyd-Jones offered a very different view of the value of change:

> I would say that the history of the Church is characterised by the doctrine of the remnant, which has virtually been the same right through. As you say, there may have been great changes in the life of the Church in general, but I maintain that there has been a Remnant which has been virtually in the same position, so that I cannot accept this contention that these changes are of necessity characteristic of the life of the Church. I would not admit that. I should say there should be no change.[7]

This exchange encapsulates the movements' differing views of the past. SCM saw its history in evolutionary terms, changing to fit each new generation. Change was not without limits, but the limits were broad. IVF saw its history as a continual return to the 'old paths', trodden by the faithful remnant.

Lloyd-Jones then pressed Booth as to what the essence of the gospel

---

[5] Westhill College, Birmingham Orchard Learning Centre, SCM Papers, C263 Verbatim report of discussions between delegations of SCM and IVF, 1 March 1950, (hereafter: 'Discussions...1 Mar 1950'), 5-10.
[6] Discussions...1 Mar 1950, 14-15.
[7] Discussions...1 Mar 1950, 16-17.

was. Booth recognised that, under Barth's influence, SCM's gospel had become less dominated by ethics and social thinking and had grown more overtly theological. For Lloyd-Jones the question of shifting convictions was crucial, fearing that a movement which had been more liberal might therefore be promoting 'the sentimental notion of unity' when he wanted 'a theological notion of unity', 'you are in danger of putting the idea and principle of unity before truth and we prefer to put truth first.'[8] Booth and others sought to get away from SCM's past, yet for IVF its present had to be judged in the light of the past or, at least, the past had to be dealt with before the present could be taken seriously.

Booth sought to move the discussion on to the nature of theological statements. For him, SCM could not have a permanent standpoint which would be unchanged in twenty years.

> you can never have that because it is always a human effort your statement is never a perfect reflection, even if only by reason of the fact that words tend to change their particular meaning a little. We are mortal, our words are mortal and partial. Therefore, I could not give a statement that we absolutely stand on, saying 'these words are the words of God.' They would in fact be the words of the SCM and therefore you could not be sure that the Lord as King even of that would not call us to put it differently or to say something different.[9]

IVF speakers stressed the unchanging nature of the gospel: 'Teaching first, doctrine first; there is no fellowship apart from it.'[10] A further problem for Booth was the danger of declaring only a partial gospel: 'if you ever declare a bit of the Christian faith without declaring the whole of it, you have in fact produced something which is a bit of a monster.'[11] But whereas theology was shifting, for Booth the requirement for fellowship was absolute: 'we are bound as Christians to seek to recognize each other in Christ.'[12] McCaughey maintained that 'there is in the New Testament no theology for a divided Church' so the current situation was 'a really frightfully sinful position.' As in previous exchanges SCM speakers saw unity as crucial.

By contrast Lloyd-Jones saw division as 'inevitable': 'It always has been and I cannot see but that it always will be. You have had it throughout the history of the Church'. Puritans and Methodists provided examples of necessary separation for the sake of the gospel:

---

[8] Discussions...1 Mar 1950, 23.
[9] Discussions...1 Mar 1950, 28-29.
[10] Discussions...1 Mar 1950, 41.
[11] Discussions...1 Mar 1950, 56.
[12] Discussions...1 Mar 1950, 30.

'the position we are in is the one that you have had happening before.'[13] Consequently, for him, many who attended church were not fully Christians.[14] For Booth this was far too cut and dried: 'At any point any way in which I describe it [the gospel] to another person means that I (not being the Pope and not laying the claims of the Pope upon myself) know that I have not got it perfectly.' Lloyd Jones called this 'vague sentimentalising' which made any discipline impossible.

McCaughey stressed Christianity was not propositions but an 'event' or 'relationship'. So healing the divisions between SCM and IVF was not about statements but 'much more at the point at which we can worship together and discover those things which we can say together to God in prayer and worship because then we will be in this new relationship which is prior to the propositional statement.'[15] Lloyd-Jones strongly rebutted this view: heresy was always present, even in New Testament times, and had to be dealt with. 'You must state the truth in propositions; the human mind, must have it in that form, not that we say it ends at that.'[16] Following up this statement Barclay tried to pin down SCM's view of the atonement. Booth said he could only give a personal response, for 'who are the SCM to declare what is the true doctrine of the atonement ?' From this Barclay deduced that 'the SCM is not committed to any single doctrine.'[17] Barclay was heavily involved in the running of the IVF and his suspicions came from his perception of local SCM groups whose leadership, he believed, would periodically contain those who were Unitarian or agnostic.[18] Booth countered that such stress on propositions gave a false sense of security, failing to safeguard 'the inwardness of the faith, whereas there is no way, apart from the fellowship of the Holy Spirit, of guarding that inwardness.' Barclay stated that statements were not the only safeguard, but were a necessary part of any safeguard.[19] Barclay accepted that there were faults in the IVF doctrinal statement, but it formed an essential bottom-line.[20] The following exchange exposes both the frank nature of the discussions and the points at issue:

> *Barclay*: What is the Word of God ?
> *McCaughey*: Jesus Christ is the Word of God in the simplest possible terms, saving Dr Lloyd-Jones' presence.

---

[13] Discussions...1 Mar 1950, 33-35.
[14] Discussions...1 Mar 1950, 38-39.
[15] Discussions...1 Mar 1950, 44-46.
[16] Discussions...1 Mar 1950, 46.
[17] Discussions...1 Mar 1950, 46-8.
[18] Discussions...1 Mar 1950, 49-50.
[19] Discussions...1 Mar 1950, 50-1.
[20] Discussions...1 Mar 1950, 53-4.

> *Lloyd-Jones*: How does He judge ?
> *McCaughey*: He judges in the Life of His Church by the power of His Holy Spirit.
> *Lloyd-Jones*: How do we know that it is done ?
> *McCaughey*: Our awareness of Jesus Christ is always by Faith.
> *Lloyd-Jones*: Our awareness ? So it comes to awareness. You tell me he is judging. I want to know how do we become aware of the fact that He has judged ?
> *McCaughey*: That is how I understood your question.
> *Lloyd-Jones*: I do not think you have answered it. You keep saying we are judged by the Word of Jesus Christ. How do we know ?
> *Booth*: You do not know.
> *Chairman*: We are getting into rather deep water....'[21]

Soon after, there was a break for tea.

Next, Booth tried to break the logjam by suggesting that, 'to such a large extent we do believe the same things, at any rate the group in this room' so he suggested that they should meet for joint bible study. This produced the response that it would put fellowship before doctrine. Indeed, Booth's suggestion embodied IVF's unease: they were not bothered whether or not the individuals in the delegation were 'sound', it was the structure they mistrusted.[22]

IVF leaders quizzed SCM delegates on the authority behind their work. McCaughey replied that it was justification by faith.

> ...you say: where is our final authority ? The great corrective principle in all Christian thinking is the doctrine of justification by faith, that you are not justified by right thinking or by correct formulations any more than you are justified in God's presence by proper moral living.

Micklem, the chair, suggested that, since IVF used the bible with non-Christians, they could do so with SCM. Lloyd-Jones was not convinced: 'No, I say you preach to the unconverted. They are not in a position to discuss and I think we have made a great mistake often in discussing with such people instead of proclaiming to them.'[23]

As the discussions entered their final stage, they grew more disjointed and acrimonious. Barclay saw the critical issue as being that mere churchgoing was not enough: personal faith was the key. For Booth what IVF could gain from SCM was a sense that personal faith meant corporate identity.[24] Moreover, for Booth, those outside of

---

[21] Discussions...1 Mar 1950, 51-2.
[22] Discussions...1 Mar 1950, 59, 61.
[23] Discussions...1 Mar 1950, 65.
[24] Discussions...1 Mar 1950, 68, 71.

orthodox Christianity might have much to teach those inside.[25] Sertin, the current president of CICCU, asserted that SCM should simply adopt IVF's doctrinal stance. Barclay felt that 'As a Movement you do not stand for anything particular.'[26] Jenkins took strong exception to this view

> Really this is just an elementary matter of logic. It is quite fantastic. You must really go back and study logical syntax. You cannot postulate things in that 'either/or' fashion.[27]

Afterwards Johnson commented to Booth,

> Your friend from Oxford - David Jenkins - was a picture! He could scarcely contain himself at the enormities propounded by our folk. He was saying 'No, No' and almost breaking his chair with exasperation.[28]

The meeting ended with a prayer. Despite the lack of agreement correspondence continued between the two bodies. Booth and Johnson agreed that defensiveness had, to some extent, warped the discussion on both sides.[29] Booth commented that IVF was akin to Roman Catholicism in its view of infallibility, except that the latter was possessed not by the Pope but by the IVF. Booth continued to see many of the disagreements as 'unreal' and felt the root issue was the nature of theological presuppositions.[30]

Booth had previously desired some kind of peace but he now prepared for war, saying the failure of the talks meant SCM would now be vocal in explaining why it disagreed with IVF.[31] He saw the IVF as mostly to blame: they had 'no theological training at all', and IVF 'exercises the authority of a Church without justification'; 'they believe more in theological definition than in Christian faith'.[32] Two months later Booth called the meeting of 1 March a 'disaster', produced by IVF's 'theological incompetence' rooted in 'a rationalistic and scientific way of thinking'. He was now planning a document for SCM branches advising them on how to deal with IVF,

---

[25] Discussions...1 Mar 1950, 71-72.

[26] Discussions...1 Mar 1950, 74, 76.

[27] Discussions...1 Mar 1950, 76.

[28] SCM C263 D. Johnson to A. Booth, 8 Mar 1950.

[29] SCM C263, D. Johnson to A. Booth, 8 Mar 1950; A. Booth to D. Johnson, 11 Mar 1950.

[30] SCM C263, A. Booth to D. Johnson, 6 Mar 1950.

[31] SCM C263, A. Booth to D. Johnson and A. Booth to N. Micklem, both 6 Mar 1950.

[32] SCM C263, A. Booth to J. Gibbs, 14 Mar 1950.

> Such a document evidently must be written in a truly humble and penitent mood, but must also endeavour to clarify our reasons for believing the IVF to be schismatic and heretical.[33]

The summit's failure had less significance for the IVF; they had not, after all, desired it in the first place. They retained their view that, although there were good people within SCM's ranks, it was doctrinally unsound and that no cooperation was possible.[34] Johnson retained the view that each body had a different job and could compliment each other, similar to the way that Methodism's emphases had in previous centuries balanced those of Anglicanism.[35]

Thirty years after the student David Jenkins clashed with IVF in London, he clashed with the same theological position as the Bishop of Durham, when his views on the resurrection of Christ were called into question.[36] The current split over sexuality within Anglicanism (mirrored in many other churches) comes from the same root and contemporary Evangelicalism often defines itself in terms of a split between liberal and conservative forms of Christianity. Yet, whilst the divide between liberal and conservative Christians is widely recognised as one of the most significant in twentieth century Christianity, little is known of the nature of that divide or of the institutional factors which help to sustain it. An understanding of what divided SCM and IVF and what kept them apart is thus crucial to making sense of Christianity in twentieth century Britain and beyond.

Four major factors and a number of smaller matters underlay the division. Firstly, to be ecumenically inclined was not to be proof from the possibility of schism. In 1910 SCM was energetically promoting unity and, partly for this reason, chose to part company from its conservative Cambridge branch because it was an obstacle to the unity it sought.[37] Then and in subsequent years, IVF had no qualms about separation and, by its remnant theology, almost approved of it. Notwithstanding its central role in ecumenism, SCM remained keener to include those on the fringes of faith than conservative evangelicalism. Even when it was making strenuous efforts to achieve an understanding with IVF, it was also looking at how it might define itself against the latter. Booth's denunciation of IVF as 'schismatic and heretical' shows that, for SCM, the ecumenical omelette might have to be made whilst

---

[33] SCM C263, A. Booth to D. Webster, 16 May 1950.

[34] Fielder, Lord for the Years, 145-6, 186, 204, 237, 243.

[35] UCCF papers, held at UCCF Headquarters, Leicester, Box 113, D. Johnson to A. Booth, 13 November 1950.

[36] T. Harrison, *The Durham Phenomenon* (London: Darton, Longman and Todd, 1985); Hastings, *English Christianity*, 653, 655.

[37] Goodhew, 'Rise of CICCU', 64-65.

cracking a few ecclesiastical eggs.

Above all the divide was a division over the nature of truth. IVF held tenaciously to a view of Christianity in which propositional statements, allied to a conservative view of the Bible were axiomatic. This did not mean that they passed over other aspects of the Christian message, such as emotion or fellowship, but they were immovable on the importance of the propositions they held. By contrast, SCM's theology was far more fluid: at the start of the century it was fairly conservative; between the wars it gave far greater place to ethical and social concerns and often relaxed its views on traditional theological matters; from the late 1930s it was influenced by Barth and grew theologically more conservative. Within these shifts there were continuities. One was a tendency to see truth in a pietistic fashion; of crucial importance was the believer's faith. Christian truth was an event or a relationship, before it was a doctrine. From this sprang an almost mystical faith in the power of personal contact to overcome ideological barriers. Successive SCM general secretaries tried this approach and thereby unwittingly alienated IVF, who took their stress on the value of meetings over doctrinal statements as proof of a doctrinal nebulousness which they were determined to avoid.

A third division was over how each side viewed change. SCM had an essentially evolutionary view of religion. Change was often, though not always, good and it therefore amended its 'Aim and Basis' four times in the years between 1910 and 1950.[38] For IVF the 'old paths' were the best. Truth was a largely unchanging deposit to be passed on amidst the fads and fashions of the age.

Fourthly, the two groups divided over their view of division itself. IVF saw controversy as sometimes necessary and even good, for it clarified the true gospel from the spirit of the age. By contrast, SCM's primary concern was often 'the scandal of division', hence their far greater desire for a rapprochement. This in turn meant that IVF stressed the importance of conversion and was wary of mere 'nominalism' in religion. Conversely, SCM made strenuous efforts to include those on the margins of Christian orthodoxy or who were not Christians at all. IVF's remnant theology helped it weather lean times. SCM's stress on inclusivity came partly from its belief that the true church was a broad body.

For SCM there was also an intellectual gulf between the IVF's 'theological incompetence' and what it saw as its own more 'mature' position. Certainly there were far fewer theological heavyweights on the

---

[38] Tatlow, *Story of the SCM*, 470-486, 613-32 and 810-19; J. David McCaughey, *Christian Obedience in the University: Studies in the Life of the SCM of Great Britain and Ireland* (London: SCM, 1958), 167-73.

IVF side. But the intellectual divide can be seen in other terms. There was a more empiricist side to IVF: key figures such as Johnson, Barclay and Lloyd-Jones held doctorates in science. Conversely, SCM was far more clericalised than IVF, many of whose key figures where lay people. Church tradition played a part. Both movements contained a spread of churches amongst their members, with a predominance of Anglicanism. But, whereas the SCM drew strands from across the theological spectrum, IVF stood firmly within conservative Evangelicalism. In particular, Congregationalist and Brethren emphases had a key role in making them highly suspicious of 'monarchical priesthood'. Personal factors were also significant. Douglas Johnson, was general secretary of the IVF from its foundation in 1928 to 1964. His firm convictions – backed by no little scholarship – were crucial to IVF's position. Although little known outside IVF circles, he was one of the most influential Christians in twentieth century Britain.

An examination of the division between IVF and SCM has a number of lessons for later generations. The twentieth century tends to be seen in terms of ecumenical progress, but the trajectories of SCM and IVF show that it has also seen the rise of new divisions, no less virulent than older ones. Ecumenical bodies tend to focus on reconciliation between mainstream denominations and often ignore more conservative churches. In so doing they may be fighting the easy battles and ignoring the most serious divisions. The division between SCM and IVF is being replicated in splits across a variety of denominations.

Examination of the histories of SCM and IVF is also a reminder of just how significant student Christianity has been for the history of British Christianity. Large sections of the leadership of British (and especially English) Christianity have been conditioned by the experience of the division between SCM and IVF and have replicated the schism across the country. As higher education expanded in Britain during the twentieth century, the establishment and continuation of the divide between IVF and SCM also increased in significance. With the formation of IFES in 1947, the divide became mirrored in international student Christianity. The importance of the schism between the two bodies makes the secret summit between SCM and IVF in 1950 one of the most important moments in the history of British Evangelicalism.

The summit of 1950 was the most serious and the final effort by either SCM and IVF to reach an understanding over a division which had already lasted forty years. After its failure they continued to plough separate furrows, making occasional justifications for their respective positions. Had a rapprochement (even a mild rapprochement) proved possible in 1950 the subsequent trajectory of the two bodies would have been very different. By remaining aloof IVF reinforced its identity which persists, broadly unchanged, to this day. It is not possible to say whether the failure of the 1950 talks led to SCM's later decline in the 1960s and 1970s, but, at the very least, the failure of the talks left SCM more exposed when that decline began.[39] The schism between IVF and SCM was to prove of crucial importance to the history of twentieth century Evangelicalism and the history of the twentieth century church.

---

[39] For an outline of the trajectory of SCM and IVF in the decades after 1950, see: Bruce, 'The SCM and the IVF' and Fielder, *Lord for the Years*.

CHAPTER 3

Evangelicalism in Twentieth-Century Methodism

Martin Wellings

Charting the relationship between British Methodism and evangelicalism in the twentieth century involves dealing with two entities which, like John Wesley himself, seldom kept still for long. Some of the complexities of comparing these evolving phenomena may be illustrated by four soundings taken across the century, beginning with the pivotal year of Methodist Union, 1932, when the three main branches of Methodism (Wesleyan, Primitive and United Methodist) came together to form the present Methodist Church. Embedded in the founding Deed of Union was (and is) a doctrinal clause which made much of the denomination's commitment to 'the evangelical faith'. According to the Deed, Methodism was raised up 'to spread scriptural holiness through the land by the proclamation of the evangelical faith' and the Connexion proudly affirmed its continuing loyalty to its historic doctrines.[1]

Thirty five years later, as Methodists were considering whether to take union a stage further by uniting with the Church of England, a high-profile evangelical Methodist, the Revd and Hon. Roland Lamb, resigned from the Methodist ministry, alleging that the Connexion had abandoned its evangelical principles. In an address to a gathering of evangelicals, Lamb, chair of the Methodist Revival Fellowship, claimed that the Methodist Conference had 'denied its own basic Evangelical standards' by assenting to the union scheme proposed by the Anglican-Methodist Conversations.[2]

So far the picture emerging seems to be one of decline into doctrinal laxity, a familiar model in evangelical polemic. Two other soundings,

---

[1] *The Constitutional Practice and Discipline of the Methodist Church* (2 vols; Peterborough: MPH, 2003), II, 213.

[2] Roland Lamb, 'Revival and Reformation' in *The Challenge of the Reformation for Today* (London: Evangelical Press, 1968), 52. Compare Robert J. Kitching, 'The conservative-evangelical influence in Methodism 1900-1976' (MA dissertation, Birmingham, 1976), 17. I am very grateful to the Revd Bob Kitching for a copy of his dissertation and for the loan of Roland Lamb's pamphlet.

however, qualify this impression. First, the phrasing of the 1932 Deed of Union drew on a Wesleyan Conference report of 1919, drafted to obstruct the attempts of ultra-conservatives to use the Connexion's doctrinal standards as a weapon against advocates of moderate biblical criticism. Debate about evangelical identity, or about Methodism's claim to be an evangelical denomination, was in full swing in the first decades of the twentieth century.[3] Second, despite the resignation of Roland Lamb and several other evangelical leaders, the last quarter of the century witnessed the development of a flourishing conservative evangelical group within the Connexion, one which produced in Donald English the only person since Methodist Union to be elected twice to serve as President of the Conference.[4] The claim of the 1932 Deed that Methodism 'has held from the beginning and still holds' the doctrines of the evangelical faith may seem rather sanguine, but equally the rumours of the death of Methodist evangelicalism seem more than somewhat exaggerated. This paper will attempt a more nuanced account and suggest that the chequered history of evangelicals in Methodism in the twentieth century reflects the broader pattern of evangelical history in the same period.

Few would challenge the place of the Wesleys' Methodism at the heart of the eighteenth century evangelical revival. Although Methodists have needed to learn that the revival cannot be collapsed into the career of John Wesley and that the evangelical movement did not begin at about 8.45 p.m. on 24 May 1738 in Aldersgate Street, the Wesleys' branch of the revival was hugely significant.[5] Throughout much of the nineteenth century Methodism continued to occupy a place at the centre of the evangelical world. Many Methodists were involved in the formation of the Evangelical Alliance in 1846 and Methodists were active in many other non-denominational evangelical societies.[6] At the end of the century, the earl of Harrowby, president of the British

---

[3] *Minutes of (Wesleyan) Conference 1919* (London: Wesleyan Conference Office), 264-5. I have discussed the background to this report in '"Throttled by a dead hand?" The 'Wesleyan Standard' in nineteenth and twentieth century British Methodism', *Methodist History* (Madison, NJ), 37.3 (April, 1999).

[4] On the evangelical groups, see below. Donald English served as President of Conference in 1978 and 1990; his biography has been written by Brian Hoare and Ian Randall: *More than a Methodist* (Carlisle: Paternoster, 2003).

[5] See Mark A. Noll, *The Rise of Evangelicalism* (Leicester: IVP, 2004) for a comprehensive history.

[6] I have discussed Methodist involvement in the EA in 'Evangelicals in Methodism: mainstream, marginal or misunderstood?', *Epworth Review* (Peterborough), 30.4 (October 2003), 39-40. On the evangelical societies in general, see Roger H. Martin, *Evangelicals United. Ecumenical Stirrings in Pre-Victorian Britain, 1795-1830* (Metuchen and London: Scarecrow Press, 1983).

and Foreign Bible Society, suggested that it was time a Methodist was appointed as General Secretary of this flagship of evangelical agencies. Thus in 1899 the Wesleyan John Holland Ritson was appointed. Ritson's brother-in-law, the Wesleyan businessman Williamson Lamplough, was already a member of the BFBS General Committee, and he continued to serve the Society in various offices until his death in 1925. The history of the BFBS records that the brothers-in-law did not always agree: on one occasion they were overheard arguing in Ritson's room and their exchange concluded with this trenchant declaration from the General Secretary: 'No, Williamson: I've quite made up my mind; we will *not* pray about it!'[7]

If Methodism held and cherished an established place in the evangelical world in the late nineteenth century, several distinctive features of Methodist evangelicalism need to be noted. First, Methodist evangelicalism was Arminian rather than Calvinist in its theology. Both Wesleyan and Primitive Methodist doctrinal standards comprised John Wesley's robustly Arminian *Sermons* and his *Notes on the New Testament*.[8] Equally if not more influential in shaping Methodist identity and consciousness was hymnody, and the hymnals of all the strands of divided Methodism were decidedly Arminian. It would be dangerous to claim that their Arminianism made Methodists more open to theological innovation than their Calvinist counterparts, but their firm allegiance to one side of the fault-line which ran through the evangelical movement did separate Methodists from fellow evangelicals in the Reformed tradition and perhaps contributed to a mood of insularity and theological self-sufficiency.[9]

Second, Methodist evangelicalism was activist and experiential rather than intellectual. Methodism had its scholars, but most ministers had far less formal education than their Anglican and Nonconformist counterparts, while the majority of Sunday services in Methodist

---

[7] James Moulton Roe, *A History of the British and Foreign Bible Society 1905-1954* (London: BFBS, 1965), 32-3, 233. On the Lamplough family, see also John A. Vickers, *A Dictionary of Methodism in Britain and Ireland* (Peterborough: Epworth Press, 2000), 197, and on Ritson, *ibid.*, 297 and *Minutes of Conference 1954*, 118-19. The obituary does not quite capture the forcefulness of Ritson's personality.

[8] *Minutes of (Wesleyan) Conference 1919*, 264, define the Wesleyan 'standards' as Wesley's Sermons (specifying the first 44) and Notes. The wording of the Primitive Methodist Deed Poll may be found in A. Lewis Humphries, 'Creed Revision', *Holborn Review* (London), 8.2 (April 1917), 244. The 'doctrines of the Connexion' appear in *The General Minutes of the Primitive Methodist Connexion consolidated by order of the seventy third Conference* (London: James B. Knapp, 1892), 1.

[9] John Scott Lidgett described Methodist theology as 'almost entirely self-enclosed': *My Guided Life* (London: Methuen, 1936), 144-5.

chapels were conducted by local (lay) preachers with no formal training at all.[10] Methodists, moreover, tended not to take a great interest in the discipline of systematic theology. Mark Noll's analysis of eighteenth century evangelicals distinguishes between those concerned with the articulation of right doctrine and those who concentrated on the message of conversion and sanctification.[11] Methodists fell into the second category, inheriting John Wesley's impatience with those who quarrelled over 'opinions', and emphasising Christian experience, evangelism and the quest for holiness. It might be asked how well grounded was Methodism's commitment to traditional evangelicalism: did it rest more on personal experience, habit and evangelistic effectiveness than informed intellectual conviction?[12]

Third, Methodist evangelicalism was connexional rather than congregational in its polity and ethos. Methodists made much of their character as a Connexion. They spoke of 'the Body', of 'our doctrines' and 'our discipline'. They were knit together by publications and institutions, and by the practice of ministerial itinerancy. In constitutional terms, although the balance of power between the centre and the localities varied from church to church – from Wesleyan centralisation to the greater autonomy of Primitive Methodist districts and Free Methodist circuits – the Connexions at national level remained responsible for the selection, training and deployment of ministers, and they held chapel property on a model trust which made secession difficult. Local 'societies' were not independent congregations, but branches of a circuit, served by itinerant and local preachers whose deployment on the preaching plan was determined by the superintendent minister. Moreover, the sense of belonging was important, even for the Free Methodists whose acronym 'UMFC' was sometimes rendered 'usually missing from circuit'.[13] The ethos, rhetoric and structures of Methodism promoted unity, discouraged party

---

[10] The creation of a Theological Institution for Wesleyan ministers in the 1830s was highly controversial, and Primitive Methodist ministers received only a year's training until the 1890s; compulsory training for local preachers did not begin until Methodist Union in the 1930s.

[11] Noll, *Rise of Evangelicalism*, 111.

[12] This is not to suggest that Methodists were incapable of writing systematics: see the works of Richard Watson and William Burt Pope in the nineteenth century and the exposition of Wesley's theology by Randy L Maddox in *Responsible Grace* (Nashville, TN: Abingdon Press, 1994).

[13] Oliver A. Beckerlegge, *A Methodist Life* (Loughborough: Teamprint, 2000), 132. Beckerlegge's *The United Methodist Free Churches* (London: Epworth Press, 1957), 67-73 discusses the balance between connexionalism and local independence in the UMFC.

groupings and made congregational separatism very difficult.[14]

These particular features of Methodist evangelicalism had significant consequences for the movement's response to the broader theologies emerging towards the end of the nineteenth century. Methodist doctrinal standards placed no credal barriers in the way of biblical criticism. Methodism's concern for evangelism and its focus on the experience of salvation and sanctification made it susceptible to 'reverent criticism' and to the argument that the new theology was an effective evangelistic tool. The rhetoric of unity and the structures of a connexional Church rendered isolationism very difficult, even for determined conservatives. Arguably Methodism lacked the intellectual resources, the theological mindset and the separatist polity necessary to sustain a long-term resistance to new theological currents.

In December 1889 Charles Haddon Spurgeon published a polemic against 'down-grade' theology in *The Sword and the Trowel*, lamenting that 'the Gospel of the Lord Jesus Christ is now assailed all along the line. Scarcely a denomination is free from the enemies of the truth....' Reflecting on Spurgeon's lament a month later, the Wesleyan *Preacher's Magazine* commented rather smugly that no cause for complaint had been found with Methodism: the various Methodist Connexions had been given a clean bill of health.[15] This satisfaction was premature. Between 1890 and 1920 Methodism, in common with other denominations, faced the onslaught of 'modern thought'. New critical scholarship challenged traditional assumptions about the Bible. Darwinian biology posed sharp questions not only about the relationship between Genesis and geology but also about the biblical scheme of creation, fall and redemption. A growing chorus of voices questioned the cross-centred theology of traditional evangelicalism, repudiated substitutionary theories of the atonement and rejected the doctrine of eternal punishment. Evangelical ethics also came under scrutiny as the churches struggled to respond to a growing and now predominantly urban population and to the craze for sports and leisure among the young. The limits of orthodox belief and the boundaries of acceptable behaviour were tested in all the churches, and Methodism

[14] The theology of connexionalism is discussed by Brian Beck in 'Some reflections on connexionalism', *Epworth Review* 18.2 (May 1991) and 18.3 (September 1991); the importance of the circuit as a distinguishing feature of village Methodism is noted by Barrie Trinder in *Proceedings of the Wesley Historical Society* [hereafter *PWHS*] (Birmingham) 54.5 (May 2004), 187.

[15] *The Sword and the Trowel* (London), December 1889, 633; *The Preacher's Magazine* (London), January 1890, 45.

was no exception.[16]

In some denominations these issues provoked prolonged and bitter doctrinal and institutional conflict.[17] In the Methodist Connexions, however, few controversies broke out. W. T. Davison's cautious endorsement of higher criticism in a paper read to a meeting of London Wesleyan ministers in March 1891 appalled Spurgeon, but was well received by the audience and accepted by traditionalists as well as progressives.[18] A year later, the young critical scholar A. S. Peake's appointment to a tutorship at the Primitive Methodists' college in Manchester was approved without demur – and the Conference confirmed the appointment annually for thirty-seven years *nemo contradicente*.[19] A more flamboyant modernist than Peake, John Day Thompson, faced criticism in 1896, but the attempt to censure him ended in humiliating failure for the conservatives.[20] The Wesleyans meanwhile rebuked J. A. Beet for his views on eternal punishment in 1902, but accepted the appointment of George Jackson to a chair at Didsbury College eleven years later.[21] Unlike Peake and Beet, Jackson was not an original theologian, and, unlike Thompson, he was not a swashbuckling polemicist. He was a well-read mediator of the 'assured results' of higher criticism, making accessible to a wider public theories which had apparently been regularly taught in Wesleyan colleges since the 1890s. The fact that the conservative campaign against him mustered a mere handful of votes in the Conference, and that it generated ridicule and irritation rather than sympathy for the traditionalists, suggested that a watershed had been passed in British Methodism.[22]

Two questions arise from this brief survey. First, why was the

---

[16] An overview of these issues may be found in chapter 6 of D. W. Bebbington's *Evangelicalism in Modern Britain. A History from the 1730s to the 1980s* (London: Unwin Hyman, 1989).

[17] For the tensions in the Church of England, see my *Evangelicals Embattled* (Carlisle: Paternoster, 2003).

[18] *Methodist Times* (London), 19 March 1891, 289-91; *Sword and Trowel*, May 1891, 249.

[19] John T. Wilkinson, *Arthur Samuel Peake* (London: Epworth Press, 1971), 50-54.

[20] Stuart Mews, 'Against the simple gospel: John Day Thompson and the new evangelism in Primitive Methodism', in Stuart Mews (ed.), *Modern Religious Rebels* (London: Epworth Press, 1993).

[21] David Carter, 'Joseph Agar Beet and the eschatological crisis', *PWHS* 51.6 (October 1998); D. W. Bebbington, 'The persecution of George Jackson: a British fundamentalist controversy', in *Studies in Church History* 21 (Oxford: Blackwell, 1984).

[22] On the aftermath of the Jackson controversy, see my 'The Wesley Bible Union', *PWHS* 53.5 (May 2002).

acceptance of 'modern thought' so swift and so painless? Some of the answers have been outlined already in terms of the position and ethos of late-Victorian Methodism. The new scholarship quickly won the intellectual arguments with the rising generation of college tutors and ministerial students and there was no effective conservative response, let alone a conservative 'school' to argue the contrary case. New views were commended in cautious terms by scholars and publicists whose known orthodoxy and personal evangelical experience were trusted by the denominational leadership, ministers and influential laity. Traditionalists, moreover, were often out of touch and tactically inept, prone to ill-judged and ill-tempered interventions which alienated the moderate middle ground whose support was essential if the Conference was to be rallied against change.

The second question concerns the extent of the change which took place between 1890 and 1920. Was the watershed really the triumph of modernists over fundamentalism, of liberals over evangelicals? Jackson's opponents in the ultra-conservative Wesley Bible Union certainly thought so, and some more recent commentators have concurred with their verdict.[23] Even setting aside the polemical labels, this judgment does not do justice to the enduring presence of evangelical emphases and assumptions within the Methodist Connexions. It is more accurate to propose that in the first part of the twentieth century Methodist evangelicalism was not silenced, but instead transposed into a broadly liberal evangelical key. One test is to take the criteria of the 'Bebbington quadrilateral'[24] - Bible, cross, conversion and action – and to apply it to Methodism in this period. Most Methodists remained committed to the authority and inspiration of Scripture, but not to the dogmas of infallibility and inerrancy. In A. S. Peake, the Primitive Methodists produced a biblical scholar of international renown who was both a confident advocate of higher criticism and also an earnest preacher of a Christ-centred gospel.[25] Some Methodists were certainly drawn to theological systems centred on the incarnation or on the fatherhood of God, but many continued to

---

[23] This is the general tenor of Iain H. Murray, *Wesley and Men Who Followed* (Edinburgh: Banner of Truth, 2003), chapter 11, and of J. J. W. Edmondson's 1990 Durham MA thesis, 'The doctrines of hell and judgment and the need for personal conversion as an index to the development of liberal theology within the theological colleges of the Methodist Church in England from 1907 to 1932'.

[24] Bebbington, *Evangelicalism*, pp. 2-17.

[25] M. Wellings, 'Peake, Arthur Samuel' in Timothy Larsen (ed.), *Biographical Dictionary of Evangelicals* (Leicester: IVP, 2003), pp. 512-14; Ian Sellers, 'A. S. Peake reconsidered', *Epworth Review* 24.4 (October, 1997).

emphasise the cross, albeit without endorsing penal substitution.[26] Most ministers and local preachers urged and preached for conversion, while softening or omitting references to eternal punishment.[27] Moreover Methodists certainly kept busy, combining fervent evangelism with social action, while recasting evangelical activism in a theological framework that had less to say about eschatology, was frankly embarrassed by Adventist millenarianism and made much more of a this-worldly kingdom of God.[28] This is classical liberal evangelicalism, a phenomenon which was developing in the Church of England and in the Free Churches in the years immediately before the First World War, was stimulated by the experience of Forces' chaplains during the War, and flourished in the inter-war period and beyond. One influential manifestation in Methodism was the Fellowship of the Kingdom, an organisation for ministers founded in 1919.[29] Appealing to those who found traditional evangelical ways spiritually stale and intellectually unsatisfying, FK caught a mood and won wide support in the inter-war years, attracting a broad cross-section of the younger ministers.[30]

Not all were won over by the new forms of evangelicalism which spread in the early part of the twentieth century. As noted above, there was a small but vocal backlash at Connexional level against higher criticism and 'modernist' theology which gave Methodism its own minor fundamentalist controversies. More significant was the survival of what might be termed a 'constructive conservative' position, occupying ground between the emerging liberal evangelical consensus and the militant fundamentalists. Foremost among the constructive conservatives in this period were Dinsdale Young and Samuel Chadwick. Young (1861-1938) was minister at Westminster Central Hall from 1914 until his death. An obituary tribute in the *Methodist Recorder* commented that 'by nature, by choice and by ever-deepening

---

26 See, for example, W. Russell Maltby, *Christ and his Cross* (London: Epworth Press, 1935).

27 See, for example, Colin A. Roberts' recollections of Luke Wiseman in R. G. Burnett et al, *Frederick Luke Wiseman. A Commemorative Record* (London: Epworth Press, 1954), 72-3, and Kenneth Hulbert, *Passion for Souls. The Story of Charles H. Hulbert, Methodist Missioner* (London: Epworth Press, 1959), chapter 6.

28 The 1919 Minutes, for example, advertise a series of pamphlets on 'Watchwords of Methodism'. The first is J. Scott Lidgett's *The Kingdom of God,* the third Maldwyn Hughes' *The Meaning of the Atonement.*

29 On Anglican developments, see my *Evangelicals Embattled.* On FK, see Ian M. Randall, *Evangelical Experiences. A study in the spirituality of English evangelicalism 1918-1939* (Carlisle: Paternoster, 1999), chapter 5.

30 For instance, Newton Flew and the celebrated trio of W. E. Sangster, Donald Soper and Leslie Weatherhead. FK also attracted 'definite evangelicals' like Oliver Beckerlegge: *Methodist Life,* 198.

conviction, he belonged to the older evangelical school. He gloried in the Cross, he fed on the Holy Scriptures as the veritable Word of God and he found inspiration, strength and buoyancy for his prodigious labours in joyful anticipation of the coming of his Lord.' Scott Lidgett, clearly no admirer of Young's theology, remarked that 'the unsettlement of the age did not touch him. In so far as he conceived that current teachings were incompatible with the Gospel as he believed and preached it, he either passed them by or dismissed them with a hearty, yet genial, anathema ....'[31] The final point is telling: Young's anathemas were always good-natured. Looking back from the vantage point of the early 1960s, E.W. Tattersall, the *Recorder*'s veteran photographer, recalled Young's sense of humour at the expense of a modernist minister.[32] Although he appeared on the platform of the Advent Testimony Movement and the Bible Testimony Fellowship and lent support from its early days to the Wesley Bible Union, Young's geniality and his secure position within the Connexion marked him off from the disappointed and often dyspeptic fundamentalists of the WBU.[33]

The same might be said of Samuel Chadwick (1860-1932). Theologically conservative, deeply influenced by Wesleyan holiness teaching and committed to evangelism, Chadwick might have become a leader of militant fundamentalism, using his position as Principal of Cliff College, his presidency of the Southport Holiness Convention and the editorship of *Joyful News* to promote the conservative cause. In fact, although Chadwick stood for and commended a conservative Wesleyan evangelicalism, he also evinced spiritual breadth and openness to new ideas, maintained personal friendships with those of different persuasions and revealed an absence of rancour which dismayed and exasperated the militants.[34]

In their different ways Young and Chadwick demonstrated that there was a continuing place within Methodism for those who were not persuaded by liberal evangelicalism. In the next generation the 'constructive conservative' tradition was maintained by leaders like

---

31 *Methodist Recorder*, 27 January 1938, 3, 4.

32 *Methodist Recorder*, 20 July 1961, 11.

33 *Bible Testimony Fellowship Addresses 1923-26, 1928-32* (London: Marshall Bros./Marshall, Morgan and Scott, n.d.,); Harold Murray, *Dinsdale Young. The Preacher. An Intimate Sketch of Dr Dinsdale T. Young* (London: Marshall, Morgan and Scott, n.d.), 73, 79-83, 86. Murray quotes Young in defence of the term 'fundamentalist', but also urging fundamentalists to be loyal, not bitter. Compare the characterisation of fundamentalists in D. W. Bebbington, 'Martyrs for the truth: fundamentalists in Britain', in *SCH* 30 (Oxford: Blackwell, 1993).

34 See my biographical sketch in the *Oxford Dictionary of National Biography*. For an attack on Chadwick by the WBU, see *Journal of the Wesley Bible Union* (Gloucester: F. J. Brooke), Nov. 1915, 245-8.

Colin Roberts (1886-1975), W. E. Sangster (1900-60) and Leslie Davison (1906-72).[35] All three were fervent evangelists and all served as General Secretaries of the Home Mission Department, covering most of the period from 1939 to 1972. Roberts was the initiator of the wartime 'Christian Commando Campaigns' and a key supporter of Bill Gowland's pioneering work in industrial mission in the 1950s. Sangster, Dinsdale Young's successor at Westminster Central Hall, took part in the Filey Convention and supported Billy Graham. Davison was an early advocate of the charismatic movement in Methodism.[36] Although it is impossible to draw clear lines of 'party' demarcation – Sangster remained active in FK as well as the EA and met regularly with Leslie Weatherhead – options other than pure liberal evangelicalism remained open for Methodists.[37]

If this was true among the ministers, it was much more the case at the grass roots of the church. A great deal more work needs to be done on local history to tease out stories of enduring conservatism in societies and circuits,[38] but there is certainly evidence of what has been termed 'folk fundamentalism' in mid-twentieth century Methodism.[39] This denotes a section of the church which ignored or avoided the debates of the early twentieth century, which refused to accept change or remained unaware of new ideas until forcibly confronted by them. When this confrontation happened, resistance could be fierce, as one young minister discovered to his cost when he preached in a rural

[35] See *Minutes of Conference 1976*, 86-7 (Roberts) and *1972*, 179 (Davison); Paul Sangster, *Dr Sangster* (London: Epworth Press, 1962). Paul Sangster insists that without a knowledge of evangelical beliefs 'the life of W. E. Sangster is incomprehensible': *ibid.*, 32. I am grateful to Professor David Bebbington for underlining the importance of W. E. Sangster in this period.

[36] Colin A. Roberts (ed.), *These Christian Commando Campaigns. An Interpretation* (London: Epworth Press, 1945); David Gowland and Stuart Roebuck, *Never Call Retreat. A Biography of Bill Gowland* (London: Chester House Publications, 1990), 54-5, 121. Sangster supported Gowland's vision of the Luton Industrial College (*ibid.*, 150-1); Gowland's account of his evangelistic work in Manchester, *Militant and Triumphant* (London: Epworth Press, 1954), carried forewords by Roberts and Sangster; Sangster, *Dr Sangster*, 181, 223; *Minutes of Conference 1972*, 179; Kitching, 'Conservative-evangelical influence', 23.

[37] The friendship between Sangster and Weatherhead runs through their respective biographies, and each wrote a profile of the other when designated President of Conference: John Travell, *Doctor of Souls. Leslie D. Weatherhead 1893-1976* (Cambridge: Lutterworth Press, 1999), 212; Sangster, *Doctor Sangster*, 122, 204, 304.

[38] In *No Longer Poor Old Droxford* (n.p., 2001), Bob Kitching tells the story of the Droxford (now Meon Valley) Circuit, renowned as a bastion of conservatism.

[39] The phrase is from Stephen B. Dawes, 'In honesty of preaching: 3. "Mind the Gap"', *Expository Times* (Edinburgh), 111.9 (June 2000), 294.

Northamptonshire chapel in the mid-1930s and made it clear that his theology had little room for the 'shed blood'. On leaving the pulpit after the service he was seized by the lapels, given a good shake and told, 'Don't come here with that rubbish again.'[40] Preachers who found congregations responding warmly to a traditional message and approach and expressing appreciation for 'old-fashioned Methodist preaching' were touching the same phenomenon.[41] Persistent conservatism may also be detected in the anxiety expressed at the introduction of the Sunday School syllabus *Partners in Learning* in the 1960s on the grounds that the new material was insufficiently Bible-based.[42]

Some Methodists maintained a traditionalist world-view because they had never consciously encountered anything else. As noted above, FK was a ministerial movement, and there was no real equivalent for lay people. Connexional publications and training courses for local preachers had a limited audience.[43] The institutions which really drew the crowds – the Whitsuntide anniversary and the Derwent Convention at Cliff College, and the Southport Holiness Convention – stood for and articulated an older theology. Methodists, moreover, participated in non-denominational networks which sustained conservative evangelical expressions of Christianity, including local conventions and Bible weeks, the Evangelical Unions in the universities and colleges and the Youth for Christ movement which reached Britain towards the end of the Second World War.

Apart from contact through the well-established networks of Cliff and Southport, conservative evangelical Methodists in the middle decades of the century were nervous about banding together. The malign shadow of the WBU fell across attempts to set up a new evangelical organisation.[44] Two groups which were established in this period took care to emphasise a constructive rather than a polemical purpose. One was the Methodist Group Fellowship, a body with a broadly evangelistic aim, set up in the 1940s by the Revd J. Ernest Bolam

[40] Interview with Mr Eric Lawrence, Wappenham. The minister in question was H.D. Pointon.

[41] Bill Parkinson, *Life lived to the Full*, (Lancaster: Scotforth Books, 2004), 96.

[42] John Munsey Turner, *Modern Methodism in England 1932-1998* (Peterborough: Epworth Press, 1998), 72.

[43] The Connexional Book Steward reported ruefully in 1961 that Methodists were no longer a reading people: interview with Frank Cumbers, *Methodist Recorder*, 30 November 1961, 1.

[44] John H. J. Barker, 'Fifty years a conservative evangelical', *CEIM Newsletter*, Summer 1973, 8-12.

(1885-1979).[45] The other was the Methodist Revival Fellowship, founded in 1952, with a specific commitment to pray for revival. There was some continuity of personnel between MRF and the WBU: the first secretary of the MRF, the Revd J.H.J. Barker, served on the committee of the British Bible Union, successor to the WBU, but the Fellowship's aims were devotional and constructive, not militant.[46]

If the period from 1890 to 1930 saw the development of a dominant liberal evangelical strand in British Methodism in response to 'modern thought', the social, spiritual and intellectual revolution of the 1960s and 1970s destroyed the liberal evangelical hegemony and witnessed the rise of a new conservative evangelical movement as one element within a frankly pluralist church. In these years liberal evangelicalism came under pressure from at least three directions.

First, rapid social change drastically altered the context of all Christian thinking and activity. The assumptions and methods of the inter-war generation, which had been sustainable through the 1950s, no longer seemed acceptable or effective. Faced with plummeting membership, collapsing Sunday schools, a dramatic drop in candidates for the ministry and a fundamental questioning of the nature of mission and vocation, the church started to look for new answers. Liberal evangelicalism suddenly seemed very tired.[47]

Second, partly in response to the changes in society and partly in response to new currents of thought, radical theologians began to challenge accepted orthodoxies with renewed vigour. In the public eye this trend was represented by John Robinson, *Honest to God* and 'South Bank' religion; in Methodism, John Vincent's pungent books and articles dismissed much traditional Methodist theology and practice as wedded to an age which had gone for ever.[48] Creative, abrasive,

---

45 Beckerlegge, *Methodist Life,* 115. Bolam's obituary in *Minutes of Conference 1979,* 61, is more than usually uninformative.

46 Peter Barker, 'Look to the rock from which you were cut', *Headline,* Spring 2002, 5-6; Kitching, 'Conservative-evangelical influence', chapters 3 and 4. MRF was careful to seek Conference permission for the use of 'Methodist' in its title.

47 For a general survey of the period, see Adrian Hastings, *A History of English Christianity 1920-1990* (London: SCM, 1991), part vi, and for the wider cultural background, Arthur Marwick, *The Sixties* (Oxford: OUP, 1998). There is an incisive description of the impact of the 1960s on church life in David Bebbington, 'Evangelism and spirituality in twentieth century Protestant nonconformity', in Alan P. F. Sell and Anthony R. Cross (eds), *Protestant Nonconformity in the Twentieth Century* (Carlisle: Paternoster, 2003).

48 Three articles in the *Methodist Recorder* for 1961 (7 September, 11; 14 September, 9; 21 September, 11) stirred up considerable controversy; *Christ and Methodism* (London: Epworth Press, 1965), subtitled 'Towards a new Christianity for a new age', developed the themes in greater detail.

iconoclastic, the Alliance of Radical Methodists, formed in 1970, twisted the tail of the Connexional establishment.[49] The older generation of tutors in the colleges were unwilling to address the new theology, or incapable of doing so, and when a group of younger academics published *Doing Theology*, a new textbook for local preachers, in 1972, there was a furious response from the traditionalists.[50]

Third, conservative evangelicalism experienced a significant revival. Across the British churches in general conservative morale was boosted by the Billy Graham crusades in the 1950s and underpinned by thirty years of increasingly effective IVF work in the university Christian Unions. Charismatic renewal, another mutation of evangelicalism and tending to be conservative theologically, began to affect traditional churches and to create new ones. Methodists were drawn in to the crusades and to similar evangelistic enterprises.[51] A new generation of evangelical leaders, including Howard Belben and Donald English, emerged from the student work of the IVF.[52] Charismatic renewal touched Methodism. Conservative evangelicalism grew in numbers and in confidence.

Whereas Methodism responded to the developments at the turn of the twentieth century by shifting its centre of gravity in a more liberal direction, the changes of the 1960s and 1970s were too diverse, too extreme and too incompatible to allow the Connexion to follow a similar strategy again. The shape of the emerging new consensus was not a single theological position or liturgical style, but a growing endorsement of pluralism and an acceptance of difference.[53] This

---

[49] George Thompson Brake, *Policy and Politics in British Methodism 1932-1982* (London: Edsall, 1984), 369-70; conversation with the Revd John Newbury, national secretary of ARM in the early 1970s. There is no entry for ARM in the *Dictionary of Methodism.*

[50] Brake, *Policy and Politics*, 367-69; John Stacey, 'Local preachers and theological change (ii)', in Geoffrey Milburn and Margaret Batty (eds), *Workaday Preachers* (Peterborough: MPH, 1995), 279-89.

[51] Leslie Weatherhead commended the 1954 Graham Crusade: Travell, *Doctor of Souls,* 205; Methodists were involved in the 1961 North of England Crusade: *Methodist Recorder*, 3 August 1961, 4; York Methodists were active in the Eric Hutchings crusade in the city in summer 1961: *Methodist Recorder*, 1 June 1961, 3.

[52] Bebbington, *Evangelicalism*, p. 260 (Belben); Hoare and Randall, *More than a Methodist*, 19-37 (English).

[53] Epitomised in Rupert Davies' address to the Conference of 1970, 'Theological reconciler', Kitching, 'Conservative-evangelical influence', 20. Compare the endorsement of pluralism twenty five years later in N. Collinson, 'Where do our doctrinal boundaries lie?', *Epworth Review* 22.1 (January 1995), 6-8. The latter, an address to the 1994 Conference, takes as its starting point the question: 'Given our differences, how do we stay together?'

presented Methodist evangelicalism with both a problem and an opportunity.

The problem was whether continuing participation in a 'mixed' and self-consciously pluralist denomination constituted a failure to witness to evangelical truth and maintain personal integrity. Of course this was not a new challenge. The members of the WBU struggled with the possibility of secession in the 1920s, and twentieth century Methodism lost a steady trickle of evangelical ministers and members who, at different times and for various reasons, decided that they were no longer able to practise their faith conscientiously within the Connexion. The Anglican-Methodist Conversations of the 1960s were a defining issue for some; unsettlement over 'the state of Methodism, its liberalism and lack of evangelical zeal' led four ministers and more than a hundred members in several Lancashire circuits to secede to the Free Methodists in the early 1970s; debates on acceptable expressions of human sexuality in the 1990s and on the Anglican-Methodist Covenant in 2002-3 troubled many. The MRF and its successors regularly addressed the question of 'staying in' or 'going out', and Roland Lamb was not the only leader who chose to resign from Methodism.[54]

The response of most evangelical leaders, however, was to urge the opportunity presented by the new pluralism. If the Connexion was broad enough to embrace the Alliance of Radical Methodists and the Methodist Sacramental Fellowship, surely there must be room for a definite conservative evangelical grouping as well? The nervousness of the 1930s and the tentative organisations of the 1940s and 1950s gave way to the more confident establishment of Conservative Evangelicals in Methodism in 1971, partly in response to an invitation from the President of the Conference, the Revd Rupert Davies.[55] CEIM merged with MRF in 1987 to form Headway, 'a movement of Methodists committed to prayer for revival and witness to the evangelical faith'.[56] By the end of the century Headway was well represented in the Conference and on a range of Connexional bodies, and had set itself the aim of increasing paid-up membership to five thousand.[57] The evangelical voice was heard in the councils of the Connexion, albeit as one partner in a broader conversation.

Two concluding questions may be addressed: how Methodist is

---

[54] Kitching, 'Conservative-evangelical influence', chapter 4; Parkinson, *Life lived to the Full*, 93-4

[55] Kitching, 'Conservative-evangelical influence', chapters 4 and 5.

[56] 'Conservative Evangelicals in Methodism', in Vickers, *Dictionary of Methodism*, p. 77; Headway advertisement in handbook for the 2004 Methodist Conference.

[57] *Headline*, Winter 2001/2, 16-17. Membership figures do not appear to be published.

modern Methodist evangelicalism? And how evangelical is modern Methodism?

Was the revival of conservative evangelicalism in Methodism in the last quarter of the twentieth century essentially native growth from the Connexion's own roots or a wild shoot imported from the wider evangelical world and grafted onto the old stock? Was it a recovery of an older identity or the creation of a new one? There are no simple answers to this. External influences clearly played an important part, among them the charismatic movement and the impact of new worship songs and styles, IVF/UCCF and other pan-evangelical networks and events like Spring Harvest. Evangelicalism has always transcended denominational boundaries and nourished itself through a broad range of networks and contacts. Methodist evangelicals, however, have continued to engage with their own heritage: with the theology of the Wesleys' Methodism, with the emphasis on holiness and with the structures and ethos of a connexional church.

And how evangelical is modern Methodism? Contemporary pluralism makes it very difficult to judge the denomination against a yardstick like the quadrilateral of Bible, cross, conversion and action. The most that can be said is that there is a strong body of opinion within Methodism which remains committed to the authority of Scripture, to a cross-centred gospel, to evangelism and to working out faith in daily life and in social justice, and that this position is recognised and respected within the denomination.[58] An evangelical identity, then, is one, but not the only option, for twenty-first century Methodists.

---

[58] See, for example, the description of approaches to Scripture held within Methodism in the Faith and Order committee report 'A lamp to my feet and a light to my path' (1998), published in *Statements and Reports of the Methodist Church on Faith and Order* (2 vols; Peterborough: MPH, 2000), II, part 2, 644-68 and the place of evangelism in 'Our Calling', adopted by the Conference of 2000.

CHAPTER 4

Competing Voices: Three Contrasting Approaches to the Development of a Distinctive Evangelical Identity amongst Baptists in Nineteenth-Century Scotland

Brian R. Talbot

In the first decade of the nineteenth century in Scotland there were three distinct Baptist streams, the older Scotch Baptists with a clear connexional identity who held to the plurality of elders, together with the 'English' Baptists, who viewed themselves as holding to the same traditions as the English Particular Baptists and the Haldaneite Baptists, those former Scottish Independents who had adopted Baptist principles around the same time as Robert and James Haldane. This latter group were mixed in their ecclesiology with some inclined to Scotch Baptist practices and other members adopting the pastor-deacons leadership pattern of the 'English' Baptists. In the late 1840s there also emerged a short-lived militant Arminian Baptist Union, led by Francis Johnston, which lasted only a few years.[1] It was out of these four movements that Scottish Baptists united in the second half of the nineteenth century. In this chapter the different interpretations of Baptist identity of three of the most prominent and representative Baptists in this period, Francis Johnston, James Paterson and Jonathan Watson will be discussed. Watson, although an 'English' Baptist, held views broadly similar to the leading Haldaneite Baptists. Paterson was a consistent and conservative Particular Baptist throughout his ministry, but Johnston, by contrast, though brought up in Calvinistic Baptist circles, had adopted advanced Arminian views that had emerged out of the teaching of the American evangelist Charles Finney. In his later years, though, his hard-line position mellowed and the adoption of more mainstream views led to his acceptance once again into wider Scottish Baptist ranks. Despite their

[1] Details of these Baptist bodies can be found in B. R. Talbot, *Search for a Common Identity: The Origins of the Baptist Union of Scotland 1800-1870* (Carlisle: Paternoster, 2003).

differences in the years preceding the formation of the Baptist Union of Scotland in 1869, all three men came to a common understanding of Baptist identity in this national body, and were honoured with the Presidency of the Union, Jonathan Watson, the first President in 1869-1870, Francis Johnston the fourth President in 1872-1873 and James Paterson the eighth President in 1876-77.[2]

Jonathan Watson (1795-1878), held the unique position of being the only Scottish Baptist minister who had sought to associate himself with each of the attempts to unite this network of churches, prior to the successful union of 1869. Watson, although raised within Scotch Baptist circles and even serving as a co-pastor of the Dundee Scotch Baptist Church between 1813 and 1815,[3] held to a more open view of the Christian Church and its various denominations. In his views Watson can be identified with a pan-Evangelical movement that in the approximate period 1790 to 1830 had led to significant co-operation between Christians of various traditions in the United Kingdom. Although denominationalism became much more prominent later in the nineteenth century this Baptist minister remained true to the convictions that he had formed early in his life. In an address given to his own congregation in Edinburgh in 1867 in which he reflected on what he had learned during fifty years of pastoral ministry. He noted that:

> We are apt to imagine that all that is true and good lies within our own denomination, a mistake common, I believe, to all denominations; but so much of vital godliness as has come under my observation among all Christian sects, convinces me that 'God is no respecter of persons', and that it is a grievous mistake for believers to confine their affections within any circle short of 'the whole family in heaven and earth'.[4]

At Watson's funeral, Andrew Thompson, minister of Broughton Place United Presbyterian Church in Edinburgh, declared that 'Mr Watson's theology was that of the old school of which your own Haldanes were such eminent representatives'.[5] This Baptist minister held fast to the same theological principles throughout his ministry, but saw no conflict between working for closer ties between Scottish Baptists, at the same time as building bridges with fellow Evangelical Christians in the other

---

[2] 'Past Presidents: Their years of office and the subjects of their addresses', *Scottish Baptist Yearbook* (Glasgow: Baptist Union of Scotland, 2003), 70.
[3] S[amuel] N[ewnam], 'Watson, Jonathan', *Baptist Handbook* (London: Yates and Alexander, 1879), 326.
[4] J. Watson, *Observations suggested by a Pastorate of Upwards of Fifty Years* (Edinburgh: Jonathan Watson, 1867), 2.
[5] 'Watson, Jonathan', *Baptist Handbook*, 327.

Protestant denominations.

The most influential and formative years of Watson's ministry took place at Cupar in Fife. It is instructive to note the two ministers present at the constitution of the Cupar Baptist Church and the induction of Jonathan Watson as its pastor in November 1816.[6] The first was William Innes, pastor of the Elder Street Baptist Church, Edinburgh. Innes's congregation was an open-membership cause, accepting new members by profession of faith rather than the standard approach following believer's baptism, a status unique amongst Baptist churches in the capital city.[7] The second person was Robert Aikenhead, Watson's brother-in-law, the minister of Cowan Street Independent Church, Kirkcaldy. In 1835 Aikenhead's congregation agreed to exercise 'mutual forbearance' with their minister after he had become convinced of the Baptist understanding of this ordinance. It was probably no surprise that Cupar Baptist Church was founded as an open membership congregation, of whom three out of the original twenty-three members were paedobaptists, including the pastor's wife.[8] The constitution of Watson's church was in line with the extraordinary degree of co-operation in ministry between the Baptists and Independents in Fife in the early nineteenth century. In 1825, 'The Fife Home Missionary Association or Itinerating Society' was established to co-ordinate evangelistic activities in the district. All seven of the Independent and probably seven out of the eight Baptist congregations, including Cupar Baptist Church, were participants in this venture.[9] Watson's willingness to seek an inclusive basis of fellowship in his own congregation had prepared him for his role in future years of seeking a similar basis of union amongst the various groups of Scottish Baptists.

It is appropriate next to consider the role the Cupar Baptist minister played in the various attempts to strengthen ties between Scottish Baptists in the nineteenth century. Jonathan Watson had been present at the 1827 meetings called to unite Baptist churches in Scotland. The opening meeting of the group proposing union in April 1827 took place in Elder Street Baptist Church, Edinburgh. Three 'English' Baptist ministers Alexander McLeod of Glasgow, John Gilmour of Aberdeen and Jonathan Watson, took responsibility for leading the main session.

---

6 *A Brief History of Cupar Baptist Church* (Cupar: Cupar Baptist Church, 1936), 8.

7 A. B. Thomson, 'Some Baptist Pioneers in Scotland during the Eighteenth Century and the early years of the Nineteenth', *Scottish Baptist Yearbook* (Glasgow: Baptist Union of Scotland, 1902), 20.

8 *History of Cupar Baptist Church*, 8-9.

9 McNaughton, 'The Congregational Church in Kirkcaldy and other Congregational Churches in Fife from their beginning to 1850' (Th.D thesis, The American Congregational Centre, Ventura, California, 1989), 347.

Watson was invited to preside and to deliver the main address, implying that he had played a significant role in the proceedings of the movement for unity amongst Scottish Baptists.[10] The formal launch of the Baptist Union of Scotland took place at the same venue in June 1827 at which Watson and Robert Murdoch, one of the Cupar deacons who had been a part of the church since its inception in 1816, were present.[11] Watson was one of only six, out of fifteen, Baptists from outside the capital city of Scotland who were invited to serve on the committee of the new body.[12] Watson's zeal for union was clearly evident in his practical support for this venture in the late 1820s.

The 1835 to 1842 Scottish Baptist Association (SBA), a successor body to the 1837 Baptist Union, also attracted the support of the Cupar minister. Minutes of the 1835 annual meetings state that Watson and James Paterson of Glasgow had been appointed preachers for the following year's Association meetings. Watson's support for the SBA was assured though he did not adopt as high a profile as in the late 1820s.[13] In the same way Cupar Baptist Church and its minister were associated with the newly constituted Baptist Union of Scotland that was launched in 1843.[14] This new Baptist Union took over from the SBA and had more ambitious plans and objectives. In its earliest years this union grew in size and effectiveness. The turning point in its fortunes came in 1845 when a proposal to unite the largest Baptist body in Scotland, the Baptist Home Missionary Society, with the Baptist Union was rejected. The man who had attempted to bring the two sides together was Jonathan Watson. This decision was an opportunity lost and as the vision of the Baptist Union continued to narrow, its decline became inevitable.[15] There was, though, a determination to overcome obstacles to union on the part of many leading Baptists in Scotland and as a result of much careful planning between 1856 and 1869 the Baptist Union of Scotland was finally established in 1869.[16] It was fitting that the first President of that union was Jonathan Watson, a man who had

[10] *Circular from Committee of Proposed Baptist Union*, May 4 1827, Waugh Papers, Scottish Baptist History Archive, Glasgow, 2.

[11] *To the Baptist Churches in Scotland*, June 13 1827, Waugh Papers, p. 1.

[12] *To the Baptist Churches in Scotland*, June 13 1827, 1.

[13] Minutes of the Scottish Baptist Association, July 1835, a copy held in the Scottish Baptist History Archive, 2.

[14] Talbot, *Search for a Common Identity* Appendix 5.1, 361-362. Details of this new Baptist Union will be given in reference to Francis Johnston its secretary later in this chapter.

[15] The details of this merger proposal and the changes within that Baptist Union are found in Talbot, *Search for a Common Identity*, 233-240, 247-262.

[16] Talbot, *Search for a Common Identity*, 277-317, explores the various steps of progress that led to the start of the 1869 Baptist Union of Scotland.

sought as enthusiastically as anyone to unite the different groups of Baptists in Scotland.[17] He was in favour of retaining the old Reformed confessions of faith, though he was willing to accept that the majority of his colleagues preferred the modest declaration that the Baptist Union 'shall consist of Churches and Individuals holding Evangelical doctrines', as a basis for membership.[18] Although in some of the details of his understanding of Baptist identity this Baptist patriarch may have differed from many of his younger colleagues, yet the broad principle of an inclusive body to unite Scottish Baptists stemmed from the vision he had promoted as early as 1827 in the first Baptist Union of Scotland.

Francis Johnston (1810-1880) was a charismatic figure with a big vision of what could be achieved by Scottish Baptists in the furtherance of their cause. He was brought up in a Baptist family that had associations with the Rose Street Baptist Church, Edinburgh, where his father James was a trustee.[19] His fiery and passionate nature, though, both attracted and alienated other Baptists as he advocated the issues he deemed to be of the highest priority. The comments of his friends in reflecting on his life and ministry enable us to gain an insight into Johnston's mind . Alexander Wylie, his successor at Marshall Street Baptist Church, Edinburgh, discreetly declared that 'Whatever position he took on any subject it was sure to be pretty decided... Perhaps under no circumstances could one endowed with Mr Johnston's temperament have had a smooth and easy career.'[20] William Landels, noted that: '[Johnston's] excessive zeal sometimes led him to forget –so engrossed was he in his work- that those who differed from him might not like to have their own beliefs assailed…'[21] These insights into the personality of this gifted minister go some way to explaining why he failed to achieve the level of success in ministry that might otherwise have been expected.

The input of Francis Johnston into wider Baptist affairs in Scotland began in 1842 when he returned to his native land to take up the pastorate of Cupar Baptist Church as the successor to Jonathan Watson. He was immediately active in the affairs of the SBA to the extent that he was appointed secretary of the association and invited to prepare the

---

[17] D. B. Murray, *The First Hundred Years The Baptist Union of Scotland* (Glasgow: Baptist Union of Scotland, 1969), 44, with reference to Watson, noted that Scottish Baptists referred to him as 'the Father of the Union as long as he lived.'

[18] *First Report of the Baptist Union of Scotland* (Edinburgh: John Lindsay, 1869), 4, 8-11.

[19] Charlotte Chapel documents, dated from 1824, listing the trustees up to 1848. MSS in the possession of Charlotte Baptist Chapel, Edinburgh.

[20] Wylie, 'Francis Johnston', 46-47.

[21] W. Landels, 'Denominational Reminiscences By an Old Baptist', III, *Scottish Baptist Magazine*, 12.10 (October 1886), 268.

circular letter for the following year. In addition, he persuaded his colleagues to re-name this body as the Baptist Union of Scotland (BUS).[22] The inspirational leadership of Johnston soon drew more churches into the work of the Baptist Union. At the start of this union in 1843 there had been fifteen affiliated causes, but by 1850 at its height this number had risen to thirty-eight churches, but in an era of significant church growth, this figure only represented 38% of Scottish Baptist congregations.[23] The period 1842 to 1845 was one in which Johnston appeared to model an inclusive vision of Baptist identity in Scotland and to which a growing proportion of his colleagues could identify. It was, however, a vision that gained increasing modifications throughout the 1840s.

The first cloud on the horizon was Johnston's resignation from the Cupar pastorate in November 1845 because the majority of the congregation were unwilling to change the 'open membership' policy of the church.[24] Francis Johnston then moved with his family and five ministerial students to Edinburgh with a view to planting a new cause, which in time became the Marshall Street congregation. The second important issue was a decision taken by Johnston to reject the merger proposal by the Baptist Home Missionary Society (BHMS) for union with the BUS. If this proposal had been accepted then all the Baptist bodies in Scotland would have been united under one organisation. Prior to the August 1845 annual meeting of the BUS, Jonathan Watson, on behalf of the BHMS, wrote a letter to the union leadership, 'pressing the homologating of the Union and that Society'.[25] This request had fulfilled the plea for unity that Johnston had made in 1843. The majority of union members were enthusiastic and wished the matter approved 'without delay', though they agreed to remit the matter to the October BUS Executive Committee meeting.[26] Johnston thought differently and by December that year had persuaded his colleagues to veto the proposal on the grounds that the BUS and the BHMS would achieve

---

[22] *An Inquiry into the Means of Advancing the Baptist Denomination in Scotland The Circular Letter of the Baptist Union of Scotland* (Cupar: G. S Tullis, 1843), 6-12. Johnston's vision is discussed in more detail in Talbot, *Search for a Common Identity*, 233-240.

[23] Appendix 4.2 The Proportion of Churches affiliated to The Scottish Baptist Association or The Baptist Union of Scotland, 1827-1879; Appendix 4.3 The Scottish Baptist Association, 1835-1842; and Appendix 5.1 The Baptist Union of Scotland, 1843-1856, in Talbot, *Search for a Common Identity*, 357-362.

[24] Hannen, 'Francis Johnston', 5.

[25] Baptist Union of Scotland Minutes of Annual Meetings, Wednesday August 6, 1845. The MS is in the possession of Bristo Baptist Church, Edinburgh.

[26] The Baptist Union of Scotland Executive Committee Minutes, October 1845. The MS is in the possession of Bristo Baptist Church, Edinburgh.

their goals more effectively by remaining as separate bodies, yet a formal reply was not sent to the BHMS until after the 1846 BUS annual meeting.[27] This decision had alienated the majority of the leading Baptist ministers in Scotland,[28] but instead of conciliation Johnston felt that confrontation would be the best way to move forward his agenda. At this stage in his ministry Johnston had already begun to question the benefits of trying to work with fellow Baptists whose theology and vision were not closely identified with his own aspirations.

The next divisive step was the publication in 1848 of Johnston's magnum opus *The Work of God and the Work of Man in Conversion*. This book was produced at a time of theological ferment in Scotland and must be seen in its context. Johnston was greatly influenced by James Morison, the Evangelical Union leader, whose rationalistic understanding of faith and denial of the primacy of the supernatural influence of the Holy Spirit in conversion stood in sharp contrast to traditional reformed orthodoxy.[29] It is clear that Johnston's book was written for popular consumption rather than as an academic treatise, but referring to Calvinistic doctrine, for example, as that 'in which Satan and his angels and agents delight',[30] could only antagonise the majority of his Baptist colleagues with whom his relationships were already strained. Even his most devoted supporters struggled to defend the appropriateness of this contribution to theological debate in Scotland. Alexander Wylie called it, '...a popular exposition...but without the light and shade which a precise and accurate treatment of the subject would demand.'[31] It was with hindsight, a lack of judgement that led the Baptist Union secretary to believe that even more challenging measures needed to be taken, rather than drawing back from confrontation.

The last retrograde step was the transformation of the BUS into an exclusive Morisonian body that was intended to exclude anyone who wished to retain the older Reformed opinions. At a meeting of the Baptist Union in April 1849 this transformation of the Baptist Union was complete, with the new constitution coming into place at the start of

---

[27] Baptist Union of Scotland Minutes, August 1846.

[28] Details are given in Talbot, *Search for a Common Identity*, 247-258.

[29] A more detailed discussion of Johnston's theology and the content of this book in particular, and the responses of his colleagues to it, can be found in Talbot, *Search for a Common Identity*, 265-273, and B.R. Talbot, ' "Catching the Infection of His Zeal": Francis Johnston a Baptist Voice in the mid-Nineteenth Century Scottish Evangelical Debate, in the mid-Nineteenth Century, on the Work of the Holy Spirit', *The Pacific Journal of Baptist Research*, 2.1 (April, 2006), 12-23.

[30] F. Johnston, *The Work of God and the Work of Man in Conversion* (Edinburgh: W. Innes & A. Muirhead, 1848), 112-113.

[31] Wylie, 'Francis Johnston', 47.

January 1850. In the first editorial of the Baptist Union periodical for that year William Landels, the editor and leading supporter of Johnston, made plain the significance of the step they were taking.

> We have counted the cost. Our principles we cannot renounce for friendship's sake...We calculate on the defection of those friends, with whom we differ in sentiment... We ask no favour.[32]

Scottish Baptists, horrified at such militancy, withdrew their support from the Baptist Union, which was reduced to a small association of individuals as early as the 1852 annual meeting of the Union, though it survived, in name only, until Johnston left Scotland in 1856 for a new pastorate in Cambridge. After less than a year in England the former secretary returned to Scotland, having had time to reflect on his style of leadership of the Baptist denomination in his native land. Scottish Baptists had made it very plain that an exclusive and divisive body would not gain their allegiance.

At the March 1861 committee meeting of the BHMS there was an historic motion presented with the intention of restoring the name of Francis Johnston to its Edinburgh committee.[33] Henry Dickie, BHMS secretary and James Paterson, minister of Hope Street Baptist Church, Glasgow, had spent some time with Johnston in reflecting on key theological issues and discussing the content of his sermons since his return to Scotland. In a remarkable transformation of his views Johnston made the following written statement of his new understanding of divine truth. In respect of his controversial book he stated:

> All passages which it is impossible to harmonise with the absolute necessity of the Holy Spirit's work in the faith and regeneration of the sinner, I myself renounce and blot out. This acknowledgement I freely and frankly make, and hope my brethren will accept.[34]

This change of understanding of key theological issues led to Johnston's restoration to fellowship with his colleagues. Great credit must go to Henry Dickie and James Paterson for their willingness to offer the hand of friendship to Johnston. Some contemporary supporters of Johnston denied he had changed his opinions,[35] but this is unsustainable in the light of the primary evidence from Johnston's correspondence. The

---

[32] W. Landels, 'Editorial Address', *The Evangelist*, 5.1 (January, 1850), 1-2.

[33] The details of Johnston's correspondence and the committee deliberations are given in the Appendix to the *Report of the Baptist Home Missionary Society for Scotland* (Edinburgh: D. & R. Collie, 1861), 17-18.

[34] Francis Johnston, to Henry Dickie, August 28, 1860.

[35] For example, Samuel Newnam, 'Francis Johnston', 87.

former union secretary would be involved in future attempts to unite Scottish Baptists, but with a significantly modified theology and a more conciliatory approach towards his colleagues.

It is appropriate that the man who would lay the foundations for the fourth and successful attempt to establish a union of Baptist churches in Scotland was James Paterson (1801-1880).[36] He was brought up in Dumbarton near Glasgow. The family had a connection with a Scotch Baptist cause, but it appears that they also were on good terms with Evangelical Presbyterians in that town. As a young man Paterson was quiet, keeping his own counsel, but determined to stick to his principles, leaving his first place of employment due to unreasonable demands from his employer. An office junior who politely stood his ground with the managing director revealed the strength of character that would stand him in good stead in his future pastoral ministry.[37] Paterson, having moved to Glasgow, was determined to gain a wide education, spending a short time first in serving as a teacher in a private school, then in working as a clerk in a lawyer's office, all prior to completing the medical course at Glasgow University. At that early stage it is probable that Paterson was intending to offer himself for service with the Baptist Missionary Society in India. During his time at the university he had worked as an agent of the Glasgow City Mission, in the Camlachie district of the city. Although he was a member of the Albion Street Scotch Baptist Church, the Presbyterian dominated City Mission committee had been pleased to accept this diligent worker until he was reported to have discussed the subject of baptism in a 'Kitchen meeting' on one occasion. In discussion with the two representatives appointed to meet with him, the young agent declared that 'he did not consider any truth or fact stated in the New Testament to be denominational', but in view of the paedobaptist opinions of the committee he felt it best to resign his position rather than be required to remain silent on a truth taught in the New Testament. A final resignation on grounds of principle came from the Albion Street Church. Paterson had always believed in the 'English' Baptist understanding of the pastoral office and became increasingly convinced that the Scotch practice of 'exhortations' in public worship by any male member was not conducive to building a strong Christian congregation. As a result of this decision Paterson decided to plant an 'English' Baptist cause in Glasgow with a small

---

[36] The date of his birth on current information cannot be fixed with certainty. The obituary in the *Scottish Baptist Magazine*, 6.3 (March, 1880), 38, suggests 1802, while the *Baptist Handbook* (London: Yates and Alexander, 1881), 334, in its obituary gives 1801 as the date of birth.

[37] 'The Late James Paterson, D.D.', *Scottish Baptist Magazine*, 6.3 (March, 1880), 38.

group of like-minded friends.[38] Each step of his life was carefully planned and on the basis of his personal principles, thus laying the groundwork for his future Christian ministry.

Like Francis Johnston the character of Paterson was extremely significant in determining his approach to ministry. Oliver Flett, a colleague whose theological views were much closer to Francis Johnston, though he spent three years training for the ministry under James Paterson, declared of this Glasgow minister that:

> Gifted by nature with a sound judgement and well-balanced intellect, he had carefully cultivated and disciplined his faculties, so that it might not cost him much effort to go to the root of any matter that might be under consideration...Having a clear perception of the path of duty, he kept by it steadily and unswervingly throughout... And he was where he was, altogether independently of what others might do. Not a reed shaken by the wind but a strongly rooted oak...[39]

In his earliest years of ministry when his congregation was very small and the weight of unavoidable financial debts nearly caused an end to this work there were a number of people who urged him to change direction or give up the work. To a discouraged church member he was reported as giving the following response:

> We are not wrong. We have set out right. We are only on the bar at the mouth of the harbour, where we are experiencing some breakers, and we'll not turn back. You work the sheets and I'll hold the helm; we have commenced our voyage, and we mean to follow it out.[40]

On one occasion a fellow Glasgow university student, a 'Mr Stevenson', attended one of his early services and commented afterwards: 'Paterson, this will never do; give it up. You are wasting your time and your powers in a vain attempt.' The quiet but firm response from Paterson made plain his position: 'No! This is the work I have to do, and I shall persevere;'[41] This quiet but determined Glasgow minister did not have prominent and influential Christian friends to aid him in his early years, like Jonathan Watson, or a charismatic personality with a flair for publicity like Francis Johnston, but his impact on the people who worked with him was as great as either of these two other prominent

---

[38] *Adelaide Place Baptist Church 1829-1929 The Book of The Centenary* (Glasgow: Adelaide Place Baptist Church, 1929), 6-10.

[39] Oliver Flett, contribution to 'Late James Paterson', 41.

[40] O. Flett, 'Rev. Dr Paterson's Jubilee', *Scottish Baptist Magazine*, 6.1 (January, 1880), 4.

[41] H. Bowser, 'James Paterson D.D. A Biographical Sketch', *Scottish Baptist Magazine*, 23.8 (August, 1897), 104.

Baptist ministers in Scotland. Paterson saw his life's work as the building of a strong mature Christian congregation at Hope Street Baptist Church in Glasgow. In doctrinal and ecclesiological matters he shared the same convictions as the English Particular Baptists. An unfortunate and inaccurate remark in Yuille's *History of the Baptists in Scotland,* implied that the theological basis of the Hope Street church in line with English 'General Baptists'.[42] Paterson objected to the Scotch Baptist practice of 'mutual exhortation' not the Calvinistic basis of their theology. His church was founded as a strict communion Particular Baptist church, despite the reservations of some of the founding members. William Robertson, one of those people who had worked with Paterson since the start of the church in October 1829, resigned from the membership in April 1837 'because the church continued to practice strict communion while the majority were for free communion.'[43] It is worthy of note that the pastor felt he could hold his ground and over-rule the majority opinion in the congregation on a point of principle. The stand of the pastor for this conservative Calvinistic perspective was maintained in future years.

After the collapse of the Johnstonian Baptist Union, a new group of individuals led by James Paterson formed the SBA in 1856. Out of this body emerged the 1869 Baptist Union of Scotland. The basis of this Baptist Union was not a Calvinistic or Arminian theological statement. Instead it was a declaration that the Union consisted of 'churches and individuals holding to evangelical doctrines...and who agree to promote its objects and contribute to its funds.'[44] The SBA had been founded with an evangelical Calvinistic statement of belief, but it was worded in such a way that many evangelical Arminians could also agree with its sentiments. This approach to the basis of Baptist unity in Scotland was in line with the earlier SBA in Scotland in the 1830s, supported by James Paterson as a young minister. It is important to note that though Paterson was a committed Calvinist, he was also a convinced biblicist. It appears that he was not persuaded of the necessity of using Creeds or Confessions to enforce orthodoxy, rather that the truths of the Bible

---

[42] G. Yuille (ed.), *History of the Baptists in Scotland* (Glasgow: Baptist Union of Scotland, 1926), 169. This error is repeated in D. B. Murray, 'Paterson, James', in D. M. Lewis (ed.), *The Blackwell Dictionary of Evangelical Biography 1730 1860* (2 Vols; Oxford: Blackwell, 1995), Vol. 2, 858; D. B. Murray and D. E. Meek, 'The Early Nineteenth Century', and D. Watts, 'Glasgow and Dunbartonshire', in D.W. Bebbington (ed.), *The Baptists in Scotland A History* (Glasgow: Baptist Union of Scotland, 1988), 47 n67, and 165 respectively.

[43] Hope Street Baptist Church Roll of Members 1829-1870, n.p. The MS is in the possession of Adelaide Place Baptist Church, Glasgow.

[44] *First Report of the Baptist Union of Scotland,* (Glasgow: Baptist Union of Scotland, 1869), 4.

should be self-evident to the person who truly seeks to discern an accurate understanding of biblical teaching.[45] He was, however, not ruling out the usefulness of statements of faith for guidance and indeed was willing with Henry Dickie to use James Haldane's 1832 doctrinal and practical letter to the BHMS missionaries as a means of helping Francis Johnston to return to more orthodox opinions in 1860.[46] Paterson's Presidential address to the Baptist Union assembly in 1876 was consistent with this emphasis he had maintained throughout his life. It was entitled 'The Simplicity of God's Kingdom on Earth.' Scottish Baptists were urged to accept the teaching of Scripture and put it into practice with a childlike obedience. Paterson stated: 'What we urge then, as at the very root and centre of this union, is the cultivation of the simplicity of the first age.'[47] Paterson was convinced that if his Calvinistic interpretation of the Scriptures was correct that God would reveal the same to future generations of Scottish Baptists without the enforcement of a strict confession of orthodox views. This Glasgow Baptist minister was a quiet and unassuming, but determined man, who achieved the goals he felt called of God to pursue in his ministry. His leadership of the SBA, founded in 1856, laid the foundations for the success of the Baptist Union of Scotland that was established in 1869.

Jonathan Watson, Francis Johnston and James Paterson were three Baptist ministers who were among the most prominent in Scottish Baptist ranks in the nineteenth century. Watson, the promoter of the older Reformed catholic Christianity, was a man who sought to build bridges with Baptist colleagues throughout his ministry and whose contribution to the cause of unity amongst Scottish Baptists was recognised by his appointment as the first President of the union in 1869. Johnston was an inspirational leader with a vision that showed his fellow Baptists what could be achieved if they would work unceasingly together to build God's kingdom in Scotland, yet who marred his effectiveness with the promotion of a narrow and unhelpful theological perspective that led to the collapse of a most promising work. After returning to more mainstream views and the adoption of a more gracious approach to colleagues of different opinions he too was invited to serve as the President in 1872. James Paterson, the quiet unassuming pastor was the man who built a solid foundation not only for his church but also as a basis of union in the wider Baptist family in Scotland. He

---

[45] Flett, 'Rev. Dr Paterson's Jubilee', 3-4; Flett, 'Late James Paterson', 41.

[46] Francis Johnston to Henry Dickie, May 14, 1860. James Haldane's document was printed as an Appendix to the *Report of the Baptist Home Missionary Society for Scotland* (Edinburgh: J. & d. Collie, 1832), 29-38.

[47] J. Paterson, 'The Simplicity of God's Kingdom on Earth', *Scottish Baptist Yearbook* (Glasgow: Baptist Union of Scotland, 1877), 28-34.

too was given the highest honour amongst Baptists in Scotland, the Presidency, in 1876, in which he invited fellow Baptists to maintain the vision of Baptist identity on which their union had been built.

CHAPTER 5

Evangelicals and the Establishment: Evangelical Identity in a Nineteenth-Century Market Town

Rod W. Ambler

The growing industrial towns of late eighteenth and early nineteenth century England presented a variety of opportunities for clerical employment, including openings for Evangelical clergymen of the Church of England. Some of these Evangelicals had secured livings before experiencing conversion, while the growing influence of Evangelicalism among the elite meant that there were supportive patrons for others.[1] The opportunity to serve a curacy or to take charge of a chapel of ease in the parish of a sympathetic incumbent provided routes into an Evangelical ministry within the Church of England.[2]

Anglican churches owned by individuals or trusts, and built in towns such as Hull, Birmingham, Manchester and Stockport, or churches built in fashionable areas of London and at spas or watering places, were also part of the varied pattern of 'extra-' or 'non-parochial' provision that provided opportunities for Evangelical Anglican clergymen. In Macclesfield the silk spinner Charles Roe built Christ Church at a cost of £6,000 in 1775 for David Simpson whose Evangelical views had attracted hostility when he had served a curacy in Buckingham.[3]

Further opportunities for Evangelicals to secure appointments were provided as new churches were built following the church buildings acts of 1818 and 1824: 219 by 1837, with a further 5 in the process of being built, and with grants made towards another 55. A clause in the

---

[1] H. D. Rack, 'The Providential Moment: Church Building, Methodism, and Evangelical Entryism in Manchester, 1788-1825', *Transactions of the Historic Society of Lancashire and Cheshire,* vol. 141, (1992), 236, 238-40, 253; D.W. Bebbington, *Evangelicalism in Modern Britain. A History from the 1730s to the 1980s,* (London: Unwin Hyman, 1989), 25, 31.

[2] M. Smith, *Religion in Industrial Society. Oldham and Saddleworth, 1740-1865,* (Oxford: Clarendon Press, 1994), 34-37, 41-42.

[3] G. Malmgreen, *Silk Town: industry and culture in Macclesfield 1750-1835,* (Hull: University of Hull Press, 1985), 14, 147-48.

bill for the first Church Building Act is indicative of the link that was perceived to exist between church building and patronage. Had it been passed, it would have enabled 'twelve well-disposed persons to build a church and appoint a minister' with the bishop's consent, but it was rejected after it was claimed that it would not only infringe on patrons' rights, but introduce partisan clergy into parishes.[4] There is, however, little firm evidence of the extent to which these fears were justified.

As well as those Evangelical clergymen who were dependent on the opportunities that were available to them through patronage, there were others who endeavoured to shape their own careers. Some even financed the building of the churches which they then served. Samuel Virgin sought to maximize the opportunities that were becoming available in a newly developing area when he established St George's church, Manchester. Thomas Dykes, one of Hull's leading Evangelical churchman, sank his personal fortune into building St John the Evangelist's church in the city. It opened in 1792 and was attended until 1816 by the city's Church Methodists. Despite its impeccable Evangelical credentials, the scope of Dykes' ministry there was constrained by the need to support the church by selling the rights to pews.[5]

The varied origins of the new Anglican churches of the late eighteenth and nineteenth centuries contributed to the development of the distinctive identities of particular churches. These identities were not immutably fixed, but were adapted and shaped over time, both from within the churches and in response to the circumstances of the local communities of which they were a part. There was also the possibility that tension would develop between the distinctive religious culture of a particular church and its responsibility to provide the inclusive ministry that was a mark of the parochially-based Church of England. The fact that the income of a parochial chapels was often linked to the level of support that they attracted, meant that they might take on a congregational character based on the internally defined ethos of a gathered congregation, rather than one that was related to the community that it existed to serve.[6]

In order to understand the development of Anglican Evangelical

---

[4] M. H. Port, *Six Hundred New Churches. A Study of the Church Building Commission, 1818-56, and its Church Building Activities,* (London: SPCK, 1961), 21-25, 107, 113.

[5] Rack, 'The Providential Movement', 239-40, 253; M. E. Ingram, 'The Parish Churches', in K. J. Allison (ed.), *The Victoria History of the Counties of England, A History of the County of York East Riding,* vol. I, *The City of Kingston upon Hull,* (Oxford: Oxford University Press, 1969), 293.

[6] Smith, *Religion in Industrial Society,* 41.

identity in the context of the church building movement of the late eighteenth and the nineteenth century it is, therefore, necessary to take account of the circumstances of individual churches. The position of the supporters of Holy Trinity church, which was built in the Lincolnshire market town of Louth in 1834, provides an example of the interaction between the social relations of a local community and the development of this identity. It also provides insights into the position of Evangelicals in the Church of England in the period, and the circumstances that shaped their awareness of the place that they occupied within it.

The legal and institutional structures that were the framework for the church building movement of the late eighteenth and early nineteenth centuries still remained in place when the proposal to build Holy Trinity was put forward. This meant that there was the opportunity to build a second church in Louth, under the terms of an 1824 Act of Parliament which provided for new churches to be built in places where existing church accommodation was inadequate for the needs of a parish.[7] Louth had one ancient parish church and the growth in the population of the town meant that the act could be invoked by the church builders.

Yet, although the supporters of the new church in Louth used legislation that was intended, with other church building measures of the period, to strengthen the position of the Church of England, they were perceived as constituting a challenge to the established order in the town. This meant that, as the establishment party attempted to use the limited power that they could muster to prevent a second church being built, the politics of church building became enmeshed with the wider issues of reform of church and government in a town that was already divided over these issues.

The Municipal Reform Act of 1835 marked the end of the old order in the government of Louth.[8] While the completion of Holy Trinity church in 1834 had not created a totally new order in the affairs of the Church of England, it marked a significant change in the place that the established church and its supporters occupied in the life of the town. The involvement of some of the supporters of the new church in the struggles over church rates, which were another feature of Louth in the 1830s, further enhanced what was seen as the anti-establishment character of the new church building scheme.

Yet, the support that the Louth church builders were able to attract

---

[7] *5 George IV c.103 An Act to make further provision and to amend and render more effective three acts passed in the fifty eighth and fifty ninth years of His Late Majesty, and in the Third Year of His Present Majesty, for building and promoting the building of additional churches in populous parishes.*

[8] J. E. Swaby, *A History of Louth*, (London: A. Brown and sons, 1951), 249.

was never sufficient to build well, or even to endow the church satisfactorily. Its fabric was weakened by the economies that were made to complete it, and it was rebuilt after thirty years. When the foundation stone of the new building was laid in 1864, the comments that were made by the Vicar of Louth were indicative of the tension that had developed in the town over the building of the first Holy Trinity. As he contrasted the plans for the new with those of the old church, the Vicar made a pointed reference to the way that the new building would have 'all the characteristics of a Church of England place of worship'.[9]

The Vicar went on to say how the nave and tower of Holy Trinity church contrasted 'most favourably with its predecessor' since an observer looked in vain in the old building 'for the usual features of a Church'. The 'model after which it was designed was no Church of England place of worship'. The old church had arisen 'out of a quarrel' and 'the idea of it did not originate in a desire to build a Sanctuary for God's people or from a wish to promote the glory of God'.[10] Two years after the church was rebuilt the creation of a new ecclesiastical district completed the integration of the church into the mainstream of the life of the Church of England in Louth as it began to serve officially an area of the town rather than what were seen as a particular group of people or party drawn from within the local community.

The use of the term quarrel in relation to the circumstances that surrounded the building of the new church in 1834, points up the circumstances that surrounded the building of Louth's new church. For, although the campaign to build the church occurred at a time when there was a growing commitment to the Church of England as an institution by Evangelicals within it, and although people with this commitment were among the supporters of Holy Trinity, this did not mitigate the suspicion with which the plans of the promoters of the church were regarded by Churchmen in the town. Their plans were regarded as a direct challenge to the established order in Louth, so that, although they worked within a framework of legislation that was intended to advance the position of the Church of England, the supporters of the new church were forced into confrontation with the representatives of the established order. These included the Vicar of Louth; the Archdeacon of Lincoln, who had an interest as Prebendary, and thus as patron of the living of Louth; and the bishop of the diocese, John Kaye.[11]

The qualified way in which Kaye was prepared to support church

---

[9] Lincoln Central Library [hereafter LCL], Louth Collection, *St James's Parish Magazine*, (1864).
[10] *St James's Parish Magazine*, (1864).
[11] D. Bebbington, *Evangelicalism*, 97-98.

extension was demonstrated over the proposal to build a proprietory chapel to serve the growing population of the town of Grimsby in 1851. He noted that the arrangements to vest control of the chapel in trustees would be 'the nearest approach to a dissenters' chapel to which, since the passing of the recent church building acts, a bishop can give his sanction'.[12] It was consistent with the attitude that he adopted over Holy Trinity, Louth, where fear for the position of the establishment informed his decisions, but where his active opposition was constrained by the requirements of the laws on church building. The correspondence that was directed to Kaye over the matter provides the main source on the circumstances that surrounded the building of the new Louth church. An analysis of these circumstances provides the basis of an understanding of them, and of similar local contexts, and of their significance for the development of Evangelical identity in the Church of England.[13]

Opposition to Holy Trinity was focussed on the personality of the leading protagonist for the new church, Isaac Smith. The suspicions of the Louth establishment were compounded by the way that Smith was identified with the town's reform party. This meant that when Kaye received a memorial from Smith and fourteen Louth householders in September 1833 which referred to the deficiency of church accommodation in the town, and cited the church building act of 1824 in support of their plans to provide another church, it was the beginning of the laboured and contentious process through which the prospect for church extension that was offered by Holy Trinity church was, in effect, forced on to a reluctant Church establishment.

Smith and his fellow petitioners were, of legal necessity, from the parish of Louth, but support for the new church later widened to include people from outside the town. While those from the area around Louth were relatively few, people who became supporters of the scheme included individuals who occupied a more prominent position in national Anglican Evangelical affairs. Their involvement tended to come at a later stage, but the presence in the subscription lists for the church of people sympathetic to the maintenance of position of the Church of England as a Protestant church in a Protestant nation, was expressive of a wider sense of Evangelical identity shaped by an awareness of the continuing need to sustain the parish base of

---

[12] Lincolnshire Archives [hereafter LA] Cor B5/4/104/29, Correspondence of John Kaye, Bishop of Lincoln, 1827-53.

[13] LA, Cor B5/4/69/1; Cor B5/4/86/1. All subsequent references to the Kaye correspondence relating to Louth, Holy Trinity are to this material, and will not be noted separately. Other parts of the Kaye correspondence that are cited are given their reference numbers, but are not referred to by location or title.

Evangelical Anglicanism.

Although there were signs of its growing influence from the 1820s, the relatively underdeveloped nature of Evangelical Anglican church life in Lincolnshire meant that the Louth church builders needed the support of these outside sympathisers. The growth of Evangelical influence had, however, been evident in Louth before the church was planned. In 1832 Thomas Knowles, the Evangelical rector of the nearby village of South Somercotes had felt it necessary to make Bishop Kaye aware of what he saw as the need to consider the need for more Evangelically orientated ministry in the town.

Knowles's letter came a year after Edward Mantell's appointment as Vicar of Louth in 1831. Knowles pointed out that Mantell, who was to be at the centre of the establishment opposition to Holy Trinity, did not possess 'what the more serious part of people call religious experience'. Despite his evident 'firmness and conciliation of manners' it would be impossible for him to manage these people, and to 'preserve them from seeking among the dissenters what, in this respect, they find lacking in their own clergymen'. It was a 'deficit' that could be supplied 'with a little good management ... and this class sustained in the bosom of the church to which ... they are strongly attached'

Mantell, a graduate of Emmanuel College, Cambridge, who was in his early thirties, had served a number of curacies in the south of England before going to Louth. The preferment that he enjoyed showed Mantell to be closely identified with the established order in the Church of England. He held the living in conjunction with that of Tetney, a large village on the Lincolnshire Marsh, some eight miles to the north-west of Louth. The living of Louth was in the gift of the prebendary of Louth, Charles Goddard, who was Archdeacon of Lincoln from 1817 to 1845. Tetney was in the gift of the bishop of Lincoln, and Mantell had been presented to it by John Kaye. Despite expressions of exasperation on the part of the bishop about aspects of Mantell's conduct over Holy Trinity, he continued to be favoured by the establishment in the preferment that he enjoyed, and become Prebendary of Louth, in Lincoln Cathedral, after Goddard's resignation in 1845. He held this prebend until his death in 1884, although he left Louth for the south Lincolnshire village living of Greatford, which was in the gift of the Crown, in 1859. He was also appointed rural dean and Dean of Stamford under Kaye's successor.[14]

---

[14] Biographical details of clergy are based on J. A. Venn,. (ed.), *Alumni Cantabrigienses: a biographical list of all known students, graduates and holders of office at the University of Cambridge, from the earliest times to 1900,* (Cambridge: Cambridge University Press, 1947), supplemented, where relevant, by D. M. Lewis (ed.), *The Blackwell Dictionary of Evangelical Biography 1730-1860,* 2 vols.,

Mantell's close identification with the established order was seen in his comment that the Municipal Corporation Commissioners had failed to adduce 'any proof of corruption on our truly respectable corporate body', although their enquiries could only 'but tend to spread more widely a spirit of disaffection and discontent'. It was the spirit that he associated with Isaac Smith, who had been born in 1774 at the village of Grainthorpe, some seven miles to the north-east of Louth, and had established a wholesale grocery and soap making business in the town before moving to London.[15] Smith had demonstrated his reforming principles in the complex and bitter politics of the St Marylebone Vestry, where his 'fiery eloquence' was reported to have carried away the audience at a public meeting on the issue of rates, and where he had been elected a member of the Select Vestry in 1832. He brought this reputation to Louth where he served as an elected churchwarden between 1833 and 1840.[16]

Before he returned to Louth, Smith had been associated with Whitefield's Tabernacle in Tottenham Court Road, where it was alleged that he had served as a deacon. The suspicions that this association aroused among members of the Church party in Louth were increased by the plans for Holy Trinity, since the church was to be built in the form of an octagon, the same shape as the Tabernacle.[17] These suspicions were confirmed after the church was opened, when it was described as a 'Whitefieldite place of worship', where this 'autocratic, quarrelsome man' sought to hold 'what he termed society vestry meetings' and 'extempore prayer meetings', as well as planning to 'hold forth in exhortation and prayer'.

After a minister was appointed at Holy Trinity, Smith's conduct left him in the role of 'Saul of Tarsus, sitting at the feet of Gamaliel'. Smith also planned to hold public temperance meetings – an area of nineteenth century life that alarmed those concerned with church order because of their tendency to cut across denominational boundaries – and while the public tea that he proposed to arrange for the Sunday school children with ' "lots of nice plum cakes, and fine music" ', was less threatening in this respect, it was certainly more redolent of the

(London: Blackwell, 1995), and other sources as cited; J. M. Horn and D. M. Smith (eds.), John Le Neve, *Fasti Ecclesiae Anglicanae 1541-1857, IX, Lincoln Diocese*, (London: University of London Institute of Historical Research, 1999), 11, 90.

[15] LCL, Louth Pamphlets, vol. I, 20, Obituaries.

[16] F. H. W. Sheppard, *Local Government in St Marylebone, 1688-1835: a study of the Vestry and the Turnpike Trust*, (London: Athlone Press, 1958), 279-81, 298.

[17] D. Robinson and C. Sturman, *William Brown and the Louth Panorama*, (Louth: Louth Naturalists Antiquarian and Literary Society, 2001), 41.

culture of Nonconformity than that of the Church of England.

The accusations that were made against Smith evoked long-standing fears of the threat presented to the parochial structures of the Church of England by unregulated Evangelical preaching and association with dissenters.[18] These fears were joined with concerns about the distinctively Evangelical emphasis that the involvement of the laity imparted to the movement to build Holy Trinity, fears which emerged later in arguments about the composition and powers of the trustees of the church.[19] Moreover, while their involvement in Louth parish affairs provided the opportunity for male activists such as Isaac Smith to engage with the establishment through the legal and constitutional parameters of the vestry meeting, the inclusion of significant numbers of women among the supporters of Holy Trinity, added another distinguishing feature to the identity of the group who were supporters of the church – 'weak females' according to Mantell's comments on later subscribers to the church.

The provision in the Church Building Act of 1824 that additional churches could be built in places that lacked accommodation for a fourth of the inhabitants of a parish was the legal basis on which the campaign to build Holy Trinity was based.[20] The petition to build the new church stated that the population of Louth was estimated at nearly 8,000 and the parish church would not accommodate a quarter of them. This made the question of accommodation and its provision rather than issues relating to churchmanship the central argument of the builders, although Mantell was well aware of the dangers that a church building over which he had little control would bring. Its supporters would undermine existing church order in the town by gaining 'a pulpit which they may do as they please with'. In his response to the argument about accommodation he pointed out, that at the 1831 census the population, which was in fact enumerated as 6,976, was 'returned under 7,000', and it had still not reached a sufficiently high level by 1833 to justify the application of the act. Moreover, Mantell stated, if extra accommodation was needed, it could be supplied in the parish church.

Mantell's stance on the provision of additional accommodation meant that the opponents of Holy Trinity became dependent on the politics of the town vestry meeting to provide sufficient seats in the parish church to invalidate the legal basis on which the supporters of

---

18 D. W. Lovegrove, 'Lay leadership, establishment crisis and the disdain of the clergy' in D. W. Lovegrove (ed.), *The Rise of the Laity in Evangelical Protestantism*, (London: Routledge, 2002), 120.

19 M. A. Noll, 'National Churches, gathered Churches, and the varieties of lay evangelicalism', in Lovegrove (ed.), *Rise of the Laity*, 140-41.

20 *5 Geo IV*, s.5.

Holy Trinity were proceeding. An attempt was made to use whatever strength still remained in the old order to provide additional seats with the help of a £50 grant from what was, at that stage, the still unreformed corporation. This was heavily defeated by the more representative vestry which rejected the proposal that an application be made for a faculty to undertake the work.

Petitioners for a new church under the terms of the 1824 Act were to be 'substantial householders' belonging to the Church of England who were 'desirous of building or purchasing churches or chapels, for the performance of divine service according to the rites of the Church'.[21] Mantell's attempts to characterize them as a sectarian group of outsiders was indicative of the extent to which the Louth establishment had failed as, in 1831, Thomas Knowles had predicted might be the case, to accommodate a significant and potentially influential group. It also raises the question of the extent to which the Evangelicalism of the church builders provided a sense of identity within the patterns of social relations that had developed as the town had grown.

It was alleged by Mantell that there was 'scarcely a signature of any respectability attached to the memorial' and that almost every one to whom Smith had applied to sign it were people who 'have but very recently come into the town'. Others were dissenters. Individuals who Mantell classified as 'substantial householders' and people 'of property and education' were absent from the list, although it included a solicitor who, according to Mantell, was 'always available for sectarian purposes'.

One of the male signatories of the Holy Trinity petition cannot be identified, the rest were merchants, tradesmen and craftsmen. There was also the solicitor to whom Mantell had referred. Three of the signatories were women. Most of them were resident in the new Riverhead area to the east of the town which had grown up around the canal basin of the Louth Navigation opened in 1770. Some, such as a ship owner, were dependent on the Riverhead for their livelihoods. It was according to Mantell an area of 'warehouses, stables, etc.'. Its distance from the parish church and town centre was an issue that was raised in the correspondence about Holy Trinity. This added a geographical as well as social dimension to the sense of exclusion from Church establishment in the town on the part of the church's builders.[22]

An appeal circular published in 1834, noted the need for a church to reduce the overall deficit in the accommodation provided by the Church of England in Louth, but it also referred specifically to 'the situation of the River Head'. Since its *de facto* function as a district church for the

---

[21] *5 Geo IV*, s.5.

[22] Swaby, *History of Louth*, 222.

people who lived in the area was also apparent in the local support that Holy Trinity received, it was similar to the churches and chapels of ease that were, as has been seen, established in response to the needs of newly-developing communities in other parts of the country. Although the evidence for this is based on a document that was probably drawn up by Smith himself, all the people who petitioned for it were, except for one dissenter, 'church folks'.

Throughout the campaign to build Holy Trinity, Smith constantly expressed his wish to 'keep alive some little feeling of affection towards episcopacy'. The plan for the church was, he argued, 'the only one to save the establishment in this town'. Yet it was a situation where the type of inward looking 'congregationalism' that has been noted earlier as being a characteristic of some locally supported district churches and chapels of ease could develop and so, become a further source of tension. Later, as his personal influence was challenged by the ministers appointed to the church, Smith expressed his regret that he had ever constituted the church as part of 'the starched stiff establishment', but by then Holy Trinity had become more securely embedded in it. By 1840 it attracted a £20 donation from the Bishop towards its endowment as well as a number of supporters with no obvious church party affiliations.

Smith had initially only been able to claim the support of 'several highly esteemed evangelical clergymen from the neighbourhood' as well as Samuel Emery Day, whom he claimed to be 'my present nephew', the son of the leading Bristol Evangelical, William Day, and incumbent of what had been his father's living of St Philip and St James as well as John East, of St Michael's church, Bath. But as the campaign gathered momentum this support widened. In a printed circular of 1834 which appealed for funds for the church, Smith was able to make specific reference to the support of Anglicans whose Evangelical credentials had national resonance.

They included William Marsh, one of the first Simeon trustees, who was, at the time of the Holy Trinity appeal, Rector of St Thomas's, Birmingham; Charles Mayo of Cheam School, the Evangelical Pestalozzian educationist; Nadir Baxter, of Clapham, a leading Evangelical lawyer, and member of a group of Evangelical laymen, almost all of whom were London-based lawyers linked to Alexander Haldane, the proprietor of the Evangelical newspaper the *Record*, in which Smith also appealed for funds for Holy Trinity. Haldane was deeply concerned to maintain the Protestant character of the Church of England as the church of a Protestant nation, and worked to maintain and develop voluntary societies in support of Evangelicalism, philanthropy and mission. A number of more locally based Evangelical clergy and laypeople also subscribed to the church.

There is, therefore, a degree of ambivalence about the motives of those who worked to establish Holy Trinity church, Louth, if not of its supporters, and so about the type of church that it was. The dominant role that was played by Isaac Smith and the sympathetic supporters that he gathered from outside Louth appeared to give the church a strongly Evangelical identity. It provided, like many other new churches of the period, an opportunity for Evangelicalism to develop within a parish where there had been, in the past, relatively little opportunity for this to happen. The potential role of Holy Trinity as a district church meant, however, that it was capable of being more than a place of worship where the Anglican Evangelicals of Louth gathered in preference to the parish church. Despite the opposition of the church establishment of Louth to it, Holy Trinity church attracted a widening support that included those who, while identifying with its Evangelical character, were also concerned to maintain the Church of England as the established church of the country.

An analysis of the ideals that motivated the people who built Holy Trinity church, and of the circumstances within which they realized them, provides evidence of the ways in which it was possible for Evangelicals to utilize the varied opportunities that were available to them within the Church of England. It also demonstrates the extent to which these opportunities were significant in influencing the sense that Evangelicals had of their place – their sense of identity – within the established Church.

The campaign to build the church evoked a complex set of responses, since it was subject not only to contingent local circumstances in Louth, but also, as attested by the range of people from outside the town who gave it support, to influences from the wider world of Evangelicalism. This meant that the sense of identity that was developed in these circumstances was also complex, and to some extent ambiguous, divided as it was between an inclination to establish a church which served the needs of the Evangelicals of the town, and to serve the people of the district in which it was built. Whatever the insights that can be gained from an analysis of situations such as that in Louth in the 1830s on the development of Anglican Evangelicalism, they demonstrate the value of the historical study of the communities in which Evangelicals lived, worked and worshipped as an important element in reaching an understanding the nature of this identity.

CHAPTER 6

The Eighteenth-Century Evangelical Revival and Welsh Identity

Eryn M. White

By the time of the 1851 census of religion the majority of Christian worshippers in Wales were members of Nonconformist denominations. As a result, Henry Richard, the first radical Welsh MP and one of the most prominent and influential Welsh Nonconformist politicians, was able to state with confidence that the Welsh were a nation of Nonconformists. During the nineteenth century and into the twentieth century, Nonconformity seemed almost inextricably linked to a sense of Welsh identity. Allied to Liberalism, it attained a position of pre-eminence in Welsh society and politics. The remarkable growth of Nonconformist influence came as a direct result of the eighteenth-century Evangelical Revival, which not only gave rise to a new denomination in the form of Calvinistic Methodism, but also spurred on the general growth of Dissent in Wales.[1]

It would seem, however, that the association of Calvinistic Methodism with a particularly Welsh sense of identity was largely the product of the nineteenth century.[2] An examination of the attitudes of the early eighteenth-century Methodists reveals a different set of themes and preoccupations. It is fair to say that the evangelical revival in Wales was experienced first and defined and analysed subsequently. The tendency is to date the beginning of the Welsh revival to 1735, the year when the two main leaders, Daniel Rowland and Howel Harris, went

---

[1] For nineteenth-century Nonconformity see E. T. Davies, *Religion and Society in the Nineteenth Century* (Llandybïe: Christopher Davies, 1981); Ieuan Gwynedd Jones, *Explorations and Explanations: Essays in the Social History of Victorian Wales* (Llandysul: Gomer, 1981); idem., *Mid-Victorian Wales: The Observers and the Observed* (Cardiff: University of Wales Press, 1992); R. Tudur Jones, *Faith and the Crisis of a Nation: Wales 1890-1914*, ed. Robert Pope (Cardiff: University of Wales Press, 2004).

[2] See R. Tudur Jones, 'Nonconformity and the Welsh Language in the Nineteenth Century' in Geraint H. Jenkins (ed.), *The Welsh Language and its Social Domains 1801-1911* (Cardiff: University of Wales Press, 2000).

through their conversion experience, although the Methodist movement did not really properly begin until 1737 when the first permanent societies were established and Rowland and Harris met for the first time to discuss their future collaboration. By 1742 the Association was established from the Methodist clergy, exhorters and society stewards to act as the movement's governing body. During the 1740s there was a period of gradual growth until the separation in 1750 between Howel Harris and his supporters and the bulk of the movement which remained loyal to Daniel Rowland. A reconciliation eventually ensued in 1763, by which time the movement was in the throes of a fresh outbreak of revival which reinvigorated its somewhat flagging fortunes.

In its earliest manifestation Welsh Methodism was an amorphous, fluid movement which defied too strict a definition. Its early leaders formed loose alliances with many whom they considered to be true Christians, including a number of Dissenters. All the leaders respected the Anglican minister Griffith Jones, of Llanddowror, Carmarthenshire, as 'an old and honoured soldier of Christ' and sought his advice and blessing on their endeavours. Yet, the truth is that Daniel Rowland probably gained just as much benefit from the guidance of Philip Pugh, the wise and experienced Dissenting minister in his area.[3] Several other Dissenters also gave generous advice and encouraged Methodist preachers to speak in their localities.[4] Gradually, however, it became inevitable that this group of active evangelists would have to adopt a name and a theology, along with some sort of order and strategy for the future. It soon became apparent that they would not attempt to establish a new church, but would continue to strive to revive the existing Anglican Church from within, a decision which alienated a number of their former allies among the Dissenters. The Welsh Methodists lined up on the Calvinistic side of the theological division and forged their main alliance with George Whitefield as a result. The Welsh movement was soon equated with the English Methodists to the extent that they were awarded the same nickname, despite their efforts to refer to themselves as 'society people' instead. Howel Harris in particular disliked names, divisions and categories and, as disputes arose between

---

[3] For Daniel Rowland, see Eifion Evans, *Daniel Rowland* (Edinburgh: Banner of Truth, 1985).

[4] R. T. Jenkins, 'Yr Annibynwyr Cymreig a Hywel Harris' in *Yng Nghysgod Trefeca: Ysgrifau ar Hanes Crefydd a Chymdeithas yng Nghymru y Ddeunawfed Ganrif* (Caernarfon: Calvinistic Methodist Bookroom, 1968), 9-37; Pennar Davies, 'Methodistiaeth ac Ymneilltuaeth' in E. ap Nefydd Roberts (ed.), *Corff ac Ysbryd: Ysgrifau ar Fethodistiaeth* (Caernarfon: Pantycelyn Press, 1988), 15-31; R. Tudur Jones, *Congregationalism in Wales* (Cardiff: University of Wales Press, 2004), 110-31.

the Calvinist and Arminian branches of the English evangelicals, he bemoaned the tendency to prefer such labels rather than to embrace the unifying term 'Christian'.[5] He attributed this to 'bigotry' and a 'party spirit' which seemed to revel in division and throughout the difficult period around 1741-3 was constantly reaffirming his conviction that the only distinction acknowledged should be between believers and unbelievers.[6] By urging the use of the term 'Christian' on which they could all agree he was hoping to paper over the cracks that were appearing in the evangelical movement, a move that was ultimately doomed to failure.

When attempting to formulate an identity the Methodists turned naturally to the Bible for inspiration and precedent. This is quite apparent, for example, in the first Methodist rulebook, entitled *Sail, Dibenion a Rheolau'r Societies* (The Basis, Purpose and Rules of the Societies), which was published in 1742. The rules are the third element in the title, which is an accurate reflection of the content of the book, concentrating as it does on providing scriptural basis for the system of fellowship meetings adopted by the movement. There are a number of statements regarding the usefulness of the societies and a list of questions to be used for Christian self-examination, most of which are accompanied by a scriptural reference. This is a very common pattern in Methodist writing of the time and there is little doubt that when the Methodists searched for a precedent or justification for their work that their first recourse was quite naturally to the Bible. As Howel Harris insisted, the Bible was the sole rule of faith and life for the Methodists.[7] It provided them with a framework of reference and coloured their language as they attempted to describe and analyse their spiritual experiences. There was in particular a strong tendency to identify with the Early Church of the New Testament as a faithful few who strove to keep the faith in the midst of opposition and unbelief.

The Methodists also saw themselves as part of the wider context of God's work in the world.[8] The leaders in particular reinforced the message that the evangelical revival was not confined to Wales, or indeed to the British Isles, a fact which they took to be proof of divine inspiration. News of the progress of the gospel elsewhere was

---

[5] For examples of this attitude see NLW, Calvinistic Methodist Archive (CMA), Trevecka MS 657, 23 September 1742; 658, 23 September 1742; 736, 23 November 1742; 854, 15 April 1743.

[6] For instance, Trevecka MS 447, 19 December 1741.

[7] Trevecka MS 2236, 23 October 1758.

[8] For a discussion on the international aspects of Welsh Methodism see David Ceri Jones, *'A Glorious Work in the World': Welsh Methodism and the International Revival* (Cardiff: University of Wales Press, 2004).

welcomed, as Howel Harris [illegible], 'tis natural for one part of God's Family to rejoice in hearing of y[e] other Part, and if one Member suffers, all y[e] members suffer with it'.[9] Some of the most prominent Welsh Methodists seriously considered taking their message to other countries. Harris already spent a considerable proportion of his time in England, particularly when he deputised for George Whitefield during the latter's absences in America. In addition, he felt a strong inclination to visit America himself, and, although he was invariably prevailed upon to remain in the British Isles, he was prepared to venture forth, as he wrote to his future wife, Anne or Nancy Williams, 'if He sais go beyond the sea my tender regards for Wales, for my Life & even for Nancy must all give Place'.[10] In 1746, William Williams confided in Harris that he had 'strong thoughts of going to Ireland', although again, he ultimately decided against this idea.[11] Perhaps reactions from within Wales helped convince them they still had much work to do within their own country. Joan Morgan of Abergavenny, for instance, wrote to Harris in London, stating, 'I hope that you will hasten your Return to your own native country where you are much Longed for'.[12] The leaders may well have felt that there was abundant opportunity for missionary activity within Wales itself, since Methodism was largely confined to the rural south in its early years. On one trip north in 1740, Harris's assessment was a gloomy one: 'Poor North Wales, they live here like Brutes knowing nothing'.[13] He also seemed to regard south Pembrokeshire as a benighted corner of the land, referring to its anglicised inhabitants as 'the heathenish English'.[14] It would indeed take many years for the movement to spread from its original heartland in the rural south to gain a firm hold in the north and the industrial areas of the south, therefore there was much evangelizing to be done rather nearer home than America.

It is probably the case that there were different levels of awareness of the international revival operating within the movement. The leaders displayed a greater awareness of their connections to revival movements elsewhere and a more acute sense of themselves as part of a much wider community of believers. For many of the rank-and-file members, it was natural that they identified more strongly with their own particular group or with their local network of societies. Even so, there was a sense of common cause with evangelicals elsewhere,

---

9 Trevecka MS 695, 15 October 1742.
10 Trevecka MS 769, 30 December 1742.
11 Trevecka MS 1471, 5 June 1746.
12 Trevecka MS 161, 12 May 1739.
13 Trevecka MS 219, 9 February 1740.
14 Trevecka MS 756, 14 December 1742.

manifested in contributions to Whitefield's orphan house in Georgia and to the costs of legal cases of fellow Methodists in other areas. Howell Harris advocated the cause of the orphan house at every stop on his preaching tour of the south-west between 4-20 February 1748 and succeeded in collecting the total sum of £12 18*s*. 5½*d*., including £1 3*s*. 5*d*. in Carmarthen and 3*s*. 6*d*. in Fishguard.[15] The response of ordinary members to campaigns of this kind demonstrated their sense of belonging to a wider community of saints. Yet, undoubtedly, many of them regarded God's work in their own soul and in their own locality to be a sufficient source of wonder and rejoicing, without needing to look further afield.

One of the most important printed works in terms of the philosophy of the early Methodist movement was William Williams's *Ateb Philo-Evangelius* (The Answer of Philo-Evangelius) published in 1763. Although Williams is chiefly remembered as an inspired writer of hymns, his literary contribution was much more varied than hymns alone and included elegies, epic poems and a number of prose works, mainly written with the Methodist audience in mind. *Ateb Philo-Evangelius* is written in the form of a letter from Philo-Evangelius offering guidance to a younger, less experienced Christian. It is a sequel to Williams' first prose work, *Llythyr Martha Philopur* (The Letter of Martha Philopur, 1762), in which Martha writes to her mentor, Philo-Evangelius, for spiritual guidance. This dialogue between teacher and pupil, older and younger Christian, is one of Williams' favourite devices for imparting information. On this occasion he writes during the fresh outbreak of revival which began in 1762, centred on Daniel Rowland's ministry at Llangeitho in Cardiganshire, and he outlines his view of Christian history up to that point. Central to his argument is his declaration that 'God is the sole author' of the revival and that 'it is the same as has been since the days of the apostles'. He sees proof of this in the fact that the revival is not confined to Wales and England, but as he says:

> Rhai yn Scotland hefyd a waeddasant fel utgyrn arian, nes i feirw amryw gyfodi wrth y llef. Fe dywynnodd gair y ffydd ar Loegr Newydd. Daeth yno fwrddiwnau at y Duw byw. Georgia, a gweldydd tu draw i'r moroedd mawr, a ufuddhausant i'r gwirionedd.[16]

---

[15] CMA, Howell Harris Diary 129, cover notes.

[16] G. H. Hughes (ed.), *Gweithiau William Williams Pantycelyn*, Volume II (Cardiff: University of Wales Press, 1967), 23. For a discussion in English of Williams' prose works see Glyn Tegai Hughes, *Williams Pantycelyn* (Cardiff: University of Wales Press, 1983); Kathryn Jenkins, 'Williams Pantycelyn' in B. Jarvis (ed.), *A guide to Welsh literature c.1700-1800* (Cardiff: University of Wales Press, 2000).

[Some in Scotland also shouted like silver trumpets, until many dead arose at the cry. The word of the faith shone on New England. Myriads there came to the living God. Georgia, and countries beyond the great seas obeyed the truth.]

He sets this within the context of his interpretation of Christian history as a constant, recurring cycle of revival and relapse into apathy, beginning with three hundred years full of spirit and dedication following the first Pentecost. Then, when the Emperor Constantine embraced Christianity, although Christians gained a greater measure of freedom, the result was also an increased lethargy, which, in Williams' opinion, set the foundations for what he terms 'all the errors of the Church of Rome'. During the fifteenth century, however, certain individuals were blessed with an outpouring of the spirit, including Wycliffe, Hus, and the Waldensians, as harbingers of the Protestant Reformation. Yet again, according to Williams, after the establishment of the Protestant Church, 'lukewarmness came in like a flood'. Similarly after the religious freedoms granted by the Toleration Act of 1689, apathy followed until 'around the year 1738 the light broke like the dawn in many regions of the world'.[17]

Interestingly, when Williams lists the early heroes of the Protestant faith he includes John Wycliffe and Jan Hus, but neglects the more home-grown alternatives, of which there were a number of worthy candidates. Later generations would hail John Penry as the first Welsh Nonconformist martyr, but being executed for criticising the Elizabethan Church would hardly endear him to a Methodist movement which prided itself on its loyalty to the Anglican Church, so that disqualified him from consideration.[18] However, there still remained Bishop Richard Davies, who had done more than anyone to convince the authorities of the need to use the Welsh language to convert the people of Wales; William Salesbury, the main translator of the 1567 New Testament; William Morgan, the translator who ensured that Welsh was the first stateless language in Europe to achieve a full translation of the Scriptures in the sixteenth century; and Dr John Davies and Richard Parry who revised and edited the Bible in the seventeenth century. Each and every one was a crucial pioneer in the establishment of Protestantism in the country and a vital contributor to the survival of the Welsh language. Yet, Williams and his fellow

---

[17] Ibid., 22-24.

[18] For John Penry see D. McGinn, *John Penry and the Marprelate Controversy* (New Brunswick N.J.: Rutgers University Press, 1966); Glanmor Williams, 'John Penry: Marprelate and patriot?', *Welsh History Review*, 3 (1967), 361-80; John Gwynfor Jones, 'John Penry: government, order and the "perishing souls" of Wales', *Transactions of the Cymmrodorion* (1993), 47-81.

Methodists do not sing their praises, despite their reliance on the Welsh Bible whose existence they helped ensure. Indeed, if anything the Methodists virtually completely discarded the traditional Protestant view of Welsh Christian history as it had been established since the sixteenth century.

The first attempts to introduce Protestantism in the sixteenth century had met with a very tepid response in Wales, especially with the introduction of the English Prayer Book in 1549, which for most people was as unintelligible as Latin and less familiar.[19] The overwhelming response was bewilderment and resentment of what came to be called '*ffydd Saeson*' (the English faith). If Protestantism was to be accepted in Wales, it was imperative that this perception was overturned. The most important element in this campaign was the translation of the Bible and Prayer Book, so that the Welsh could finally understand the public worship conducted in their churches. The New Testament and Book of Common Prayer first appeared in 1567 and were revised as part of the 1588 Bible translated by William Morgan. Coupled with the translation was the masterly use of history and myth by Bishop Richard Davies to present a new interpretation of Protestantism, which first appeared as a preface to the 1567 New Testament. The bedrock of Davies' argument was that the ancestors of the Welsh people had worshipped as part of a British Christian Church which preceded the influence of Rome. To this was added the traditional myth that Christianity had been introduced to the British by Joseph of Arimathea around the year 60AD. The ancestral faith of the Welsh people was therefore portrayed as the purest possible form of Christianity as conveyed by one of Christ's own followers. Davies went on to point out that the Saxons had been converted to Christianity by emissaries from Rome and had subsequently imposed this Roman Catholicism on the Welsh. Protestantism, he claimed, should therefore be regarded as a return to the pure old faith of their ancestors before it was corrupted by the influence of Rome. He urged the Welsh people to:

> Call to mind thy old privelege and thy great honour on account of the faith of Christ and God's word which thou didst receive before all the islands of the world. The religion of Christ adorned thee for thou didst obtain it true and pure as Christ taught it to his Apostles and disciples, and because thou didst keep it perfect and uncorrupt, with the price of the blood of thy blessed martyrs. This did not happen to the Saxons of old

[19] See Glanmor Williams, *Wales and the Reformation* (Cardiff: University of Wales Press, 1997).

(who today are in the right having through grace received the gospel gladly).[20]

His message was echoed in William Salesbury's preface to the 1567 New Testament:

> The best faith is the old one, which is the one that the prophets prophesised, which Christ and His Apostles taught to the people in their time and which the martyrs confirmed with their blood by testifying to it. And therefore woe to him who calleth this faith new, whether it be out of ignorance or of wilfulness to deceive himself and to beguile the people.[21]

It was a use of the past to suit the present that appealed also to Archbishop Matthew Parker as a means of providing a respectable history and tradition for Protestantism. Within Wales, it appealed to a sense of national pride and helped establish the longstanding association between Protestantism and the Welsh language and identity.

This theme was perpetuated by subsequent generations of scholars. In particular, it was taken up in the seventeenth century by Charles Edwards in his account of religious history, *Y Ffydd Di-ffuant* (The Unfeigned Faith). The first edition of this work appeared in 1667 and was based substantially on John Foxe's account of the progress of the true faith, with very little material relating specifically to Wales, other than some mention of the Welsh martyrs during Mary's reign and an appreciation of the translation of the Scriptures. The second and third editions appeared in 1671 and 1677 and gave a much more distinctively Welsh interpretation of history. Derec Llwyd Morgan has argued that Edwards became familiar with Richard Davies' account after writing the first edition and that this had a major influence on the revised work.[22] In the later editions the author was much more concerned with the salvation of the Welsh people and with their role as God's elect nation.[23] He included an account of the history of the Christian faith in Wales and attempted to demonstrate an affinity between the Welsh and

---

[20] A. O. Evans, *A Memorandum on the legality of the Welsh Bible and the Welsh version of the Book of Common Prayer* (Cardiff: William Lewis, 1925), 122-3.

[21] Ibid., 125.

[22] Derec Llwyd Morgan, *Charles Edwards* (Caernarfon: Pantycelyn Press, 1994), 12-26; idem., *Y Beibl a Llenyddiaeth Gymraeg* (Llandysul: Gomer, 1998), 59. See also Glanmor Williams, *Religion, Language and Nationality in Wales* (Cardiff: University of Wales Press, 1979).

[23] For comparisons with ideas about the English as an 'elect nation' see Patrick Collinson, *The Birthpangs of Protestant England: Religious and Cultural Change in the Sixteenth and Seventeenth Centuries* (Basingstoke: Macmillan, 1988), 1-27.

Hebrew languages. Charles Edwards urged the Welsh in majestic and stirring terms to be worthy of their glorious past:

> Oh that our nation might labour to be as lively and as warm in the Christian faith as some of our old grandfathers once were. They turned Scots, and Picts, and Germans, and other nations to Christ's faith, and shall we neglect it in our own home? they were first, and shall we be last in the causes of the kingdom of heaven? they were like eagles striving with the Sun of Justice, and shall we be like owls preferring the darkness? Let us not decline, but like Naboth cleave to the evangelical Vineyard which is the patrimony of our ancestors: and we will walk like the children of light....[24]

William Williams' version of history, however, seemed to have more in common with the first edition of Edwards' work. He did not develop the themes discussed in the later editions which emphasised the particular salvation of the Welsh people, although these themes figure prominently in the work of other religious writers of the mid-eighteenth century, such as Theophilus Evans and Griffith Jones. Theophilus Evans' *Drych y Prif Oesoedd* (The Mirror of the First Ages) was to prove to be one of the most popular historical works in Wales for the next two centuries.[25] It was first published in 1716 when Evans was twenty-three years old, but was substantially revised in its second edition in 1740. His account is set squarely in a biblical context, with an opening sentence declaring that the nation's history had been one of misfortune and tribulation ever since the confusion of languages at the tower of Babel. The founder of the British or Welsh nation was said to be Gomer, son of Japheth, son of Noah, who is listed in Genesis as one of the descendants of Noah who settled in Europe. The descendants of Gomer and his followers were claimed by Evans to have gone on to populate Britain, Ireland and part of France. Evans embraced Richard Davies' account of the introduction of Christianity by Joseph of Arimathea but elaborated further in order to claim that St Paul had also visited and preached in Britain, again emphasising the purity of the origins of the original Celtic Church, before influences from Rome were brought to bear in the British Isles.

Evans' viewpoint is obviously that of a faithful Anglican and throughout his writing he is intent on defending the Church against both the old Catholic enemy and the newer rivalry posed by Dissent.

---

[24] Charles Edwards, *Y Ffydd Diffuant* (3rd ed., 1677), 213-14.

[25] See Theophilus Evans, *Drych y Prif Oesoedd* (ed. Garfield H. Hughes , Cardiff: University of Wales Press, 1961); Gwyn Thomas, 'Two Prose Writers: Ellis Wynne and Theophilus Evans' in Branwen Jarvis (ed.), *A guide to Welsh literature c.1700-1800* (Cardiff, 2000), 54-63.

The latter threat to the unity of the Anglican Church was addressed again in Evans' *A History of Modern Enthusiasm* (1752), a fierce condemnation of secession from the Church. It is interesting to note that William Williams acted as Evans' curate in Breconshire until he resigned his benefices in 1743 to concentrate on his Methodist activities. Evans' opposition to any dissent from the Church and to the irregularities of the Methodist preachers can hardly have made for an easy relationship between vicar and curate, however. Evans' *Drych y Prif Oesoedd* proved to be enduringly popular, probably because of its patriotic appeal to a sense of pride in the antiquity of the Welsh nation and language, along with its long-established Christian tradition. Although the nation was described as having suffered numerous trials and tribulations as a result of its sinfulness, yet there is also in the work a sense that the Welsh, like the Israelites, were a nation chosen by God for a particular destiny. Such themes were by no means unique to the Welsh people in the early modern period, but they possibly proved particularly important for a nation without a state or any national institutions to uphold a sense of national identity.

The fact that the Welsh Methodists did not appeal to history in the same way did not mean that they had no special affection for their country and its people. Many of them felt that they had a particular calling or commission to work among the Welsh people. Harris was occasionally rebuked for his absences in London and reminded of his responsibility to care for the converts in Wales. It was usually on his journeys to the other side of Offa's Dyke that Harris expressed his feelings for his country in the strongest terms, referring frequently to 'dear Wales' and 'dear, dear Wales' and stating on more than one occasion that 'Wales was never so dear to me'.[26] 'I am sure', he wrote from London to Anne Williams regarding his idea of a preaching tour in America, 'tis not my choice will or Desire to go from Dear Dear Wales'.[27]

Despite these personal statements, the movement as a whole laid little self-conscious emphasis on a sense of Welshness or on an appeal to the Welsh Christian tradition. All things considered, this is perhaps not so surprising. The Methodists who saw themselves as attempting revival within a 'poor, benighted church'[28] in a land which 'lay in a dark, deadly slumber without one priest, presbyter or bishop awake'[29] were less likely to promote pride in the country's glorious Christian tradition. They were less likely also to promote the image of an elect

---

[26] For example, Trevecka MS 688, 12 October 1742; 737, 29 November 1742.

[27] Trevecka MS 627, 7 September 1742.

[28] Trevecka MS 755, 916, 934; Diary of Howel Harris, 105, 2 December 1743.

[29] N. Cynhafal Jones (ed.), *Gweithiau Williams Pantycelyn*, Volume I (Holywell, 1887), 491.

nation, since they saw the revival as an international phenomenon. They could hardly claim exclusive rights in the light of similar events and experiences in England, Scotland and America. It is probably also true to say that they did not need to appeal to the past in this way. Calvinistic Methodism was the first version of the Protestant faith which was intrinsically Welsh and was not imported from outside the country. It did not need to strive to convince people of its Welsh credentials: the majority of the members were Welsh speakers, served by Welsh-speaking preachers and provided with a wealth of Welsh hymns and printed books.[30] There was never any question but that Methodism was a Welsh faith and it could surely afford to take its Welshness for granted as a result. In the more anglicized areas of the country – along the borders and in south Pembrokeshire and the Vale of Glamorgan – it used the English language just as naturally. Unlike sixteenth-century Protestantism and early Puritanism, it had no language barrier to overcome nor any resentment of it as an alien, English innovation to combat. Early Protestantism had desperately needed to counter its image as *ffydd Saeson* (the English faith) and had to produce the propaganda to achieve this aim. A movement which emerged from within Wales did not face the same difficulties. Glanmor Williams, the leading authority on the Protestant Reformation in Wales, suggested, with good reason, that the Reformation only truly came of age in Wales in the eighteenth century, with the Methodist Revival, as substantial numbers learnt to read the Welsh Bible and began to truly understand for the first time the principles of their faith.[31]

For a while, then, it seemed that a sense of common evangelical identity superseded a sense of Welsh identity, but that was to change. One of the first histories of Methodism to be written after the movement became a denomination in 1811 was the work of Robert Jones, *Drych yr Amseroedd* (The Mirror of the Ages) in 1820. Jones's work has been looked at somewhat askance of late because he has been regarded as one of the most notorious perpetuators of what is termed 'the Methodist view of history', which portrayed Wales as a religious wilderness in the period immediately preceding the Methodist Revival. If, however, one disregards his Methodistical bias in this respect, the history he presents of the introduction of Protestantism in Wales and the main individuals and milestones he identifies in the growth of Methodism is not greatly dissimilar to any account produced in this day and age. He outlines the importance of the work of the Bible translators in the sixteenth century and their successors in the seventeenth century who ensured further

---

[30] See Geraint H. Jenkins (ed.), *The Welsh Language before the Industrial Revolution* (Cardiff: University of Wales Press, 1997).

[31] Glanmor Williams, *Wales and the Reformation*, 403-04.

revisions and editions. He refers to the groundwork of the pioneering figures in Welsh Puritanism such as Morgan Llwyd, Vavasor Powell and Walter Cradock and the major contribution of Griffith Jones in establishing the circulating schools to provide free education through the medium of Welsh. This is all standard textbook stuff. Although Jones is invariably regarded as inheriting William Williams's interpretation of history in emphasising the revolutionary nature of the evangelical revival, he differs from him in his emphasis on an exclusively Welsh context to the revival. He urges his readers to read his work because it will, he trusts, 'give them cause to wonder at the goodness of the Lord towards us poor Welsh, particularly in the present age'.[32] He has little to say about John Wycliffe and the Lollards and much about Welsh Protestant pioneers. When mentioning early nineteenth-century revivals in Wales he states that similar events were to be witnessed in Africa and America at that time, so he does not wholly ignore the international context, but his main interest is obviously in establishing the Welsh roots of Calvinistic Methodism, something which would be a recurring theme for the remainder of the nineteenth century.

It may be that this emphasis only really became important after the Methodist movement broke away from the Anglican Church and established itself as a separate Welsh denomination in 1811. It may be that it did not need to write its history within a Welsh, rather than an evangelical, context until it emerged as the Calvinistic Methodist Church of Wales in the nineteenth century. As an institution it had greater need of a history and, in order to contend with the other existing Nonconformist denominations, it perhaps had greater need of a *Welsh* history to establish its credentials. With the campaign for the disestablishment of the Church in Wales gaining force, it is possible that by then Calvinistic Methodism had to emphasise its Welshness and its Nonconformity in a way that it did not need to during the eighteenth century. For much of its earlier existence, however, it showed few signs of a self-conscious Welsh identity, despite being the first intrinsically Welsh version of the Protestant faith. Perhaps because of that inherent Welshness, it seemed content in the eighteenth century to allow defenders of the Anglican faith to make appeals on the grounds of a traditional connection with Welsh language and history. The result seems to have been a greater focus on biblical precedent and evangelical connections when seeking to define the new movement's identity.

---

[32] Robert Jones, *Drych yr Amseroedd*, ed. G. M. Ashton (Cardiff: University of Wales Press, 1958), xxxiv.

CHAPTER 7

'A Glorious Morn'?: Methodism and the Rise of Evangelicalism in Wales, 1735-62

David Ceri Jones

During spring 1735, Howel Harris, a twenty-one year old schoolmaster from Trefeca near Brecon, passed through a protracted evangelical conversion experience; at roughly the same time, Daniel Rowland, a slightly older curate in the parish of Nantcwnlle, near Llangeitho in Cardiganshire, experienced a similar spiritual awakening. These unconnected events set in motion two religious awakenings, fused together a couple of years later to create the Welsh Methodist movement. Despite its chronological precedence, the Welsh revival has not tended to figure particularly prominently in accounts of the birth of Methodism in the mid-eighteenth-century. When it has, it has often suffered at the hands of historians who, lacking a nuanced understanding of the Welsh context, have assumed that many of the processes current in other settings were present in broadly similar ways in Wales. The inaccessibility of much of the recent historiography on the Welsh revival to non-Welsh speakers has not helped but there has also been a reluctance among some historians of Welsh Methodism to engage with some of the questions which historians of Methodism and Evangelicalism elsewhere have been concerned.[1]

One of the most recent challenges to the way the events of the 1730s are interpreted stems from David Bebbington's, *Evangelicalism in Modern Britain* (1989). Bebbington has argued that while the term 'evangelical' has been applied to many groups and individuals, both before and after the Reformation, before 1730 there has never been a movement bearing

---

[1] E. Evans, *Daniel Rowland and the Great Evangelical Awakening in Wales* (Edinburgh: Banner of Truth Trust, 1985) is a good example of this. There has also been a tendency to reprint nineteenth-century hagiographical works such as W. Williams, *Welsh Calvinistic Methodism: a historical sketch of the Presbyterian Church of Wales* (Bridgend: Bryntirion Press, 1998 [1872]); H. J. Hughes, *Life of Howell Harris: the Welsh Reformer* (Stoke-on-Trent: Tentmaker Publications, 1996 [1892]).

the name Evangelicalism.[2] The evangelical movement, birthed in the religious revivals in Britain, parts of Continental Europe and the American colonies, eschewed traditional confessional allegiances, in favour of a more fluid set of core beliefs corresponding to a quadrilateral of convictions encompassing biblicism, conversionism, crucicentrism and activism. This allowed a diverse mix of individuals, groups and churches to style themselves evangelicals.[3] Being an evangelical was, therefore, as much about self-identification[4] as it was about any particular theological or cultural outlook and in this it reflected the cultural ethos of the Enlightenment, which placed such a premium on the integrity of individual inquiry.[5]

Mark Noll has offered a further layer of definition by arguing that Evangelicalism was shaped as much by the social and cultural milieu of the mid-eighteenth century Atlantic world as it was by the evangelical's core convictions. Major advances in literacy, the expansion of a cheap print and a popular press, a consumer revolution which brought more goods within the reach of more people, the opening up of trade around the north Atlantic basin, more efficient and safer methods of travel, increased social mobility and an openness to new ideas, created a climate in which evangelists like George Whitefield, John Wesley, Jonathan Edwards and Howel Harris could spread their message with relative ease. These developments led Noll to argue that Evangelicalism was actually made 'by the individuals, associations, books, practices, perceptions, and networks shared by the promoters of the eighteenth-century revivals and their descendents'.[6] With it's pared down theological framework and formidable publicity machine, Evangelicalism was a modern recasting of the Protestant spirit, and one that in many instances had more success in reaching the wider population than any of its predecessors. While this is not the place to embark on a full-scale analysis of how closely early Methodism in Wales correlates with the paradigm popularised by Bebbington and

---

[2] M. A. Noll, *The Rise of Evangelicalism: The Age of Edwards, Whitefield and the Wesleys* (Leicester: Inter-Varsity Press, 2004), 13-15.

[3] D. W. Bebbington, *Evangelicalism in Modern Britain: a History from the 1730s to the 1980s* (London: Unwin Hyman, 1989), 1-19.

[4] A. McGrath, *Evangelicalism and the Future of Christianity* (London: Hodder and Stoughton, 1993), 49.

[5] For the close correlation between Evangelicalism and the Enlightenment, see David W. Bebbington, 'Revival and Enlightenment in Eighteenth-Century England', in Randall Balmer and Edith L. Blumhofer (eds.), *Modern Christian Revivals* (Chicago: University of Illinois Press, 1993), 17-41.

[6] Noll, *The Rise of Evangelicalism*, 15-16.

Noll, it is possible to make some general observations.[7]

Firstly, perhaps one of the most controversial aspects of the Bebbington thesis is the way that it introduces a sharp discontinuity between the revivals of the 1730s and the development of indigenous Protestant traditions following the Reformation. In Wales, it is possible to argue that there was a natural continuity between the activities of the godly in the sixteenth and seventeenth centuries and the Methodists. Initially, Protestantism had been regarded as the *ffydd saeson* (the English faith), and it had taken the activity of a dedicated band of Churchmen and scholars that included Richard Davies, William Salesbury and William Morgan, to make Protestantism intelligible to the monoglot Welsh-speaking population.[8] By the end of the sixteenth century, largely as a result of their efforts to get the Bible and Prayer Book translated into Welsh and the conditions imposed by the Act of Uniformity (1559), the majority had become at least nominal members of the Church of England. However, they were far from enthusiastic Protestants, their loyalty born more of their loyalty to the Tudors than any spiritual commitment. During the seventeenth century, the Puritans fared little better. Despite the establishment of the first separatist congregation in Wales at Llanfaches, Monmouthshire, in 1639, this hotter sort of Protestantism did not go down well in rural Welsh communities where illiteracy and innate conservatism remained formidable barriers.[9] Protestantism was a word-orientated faith and it should come as no surprise that the largely illiterate Welsh remained, on the whole, unmoved by the passionate endeavours of radical reformers and evangelists of the calibre of Vavasor Powell and Morgan Llwyd. Even the Rump Parliament, which passed the Act for the Better Propagation for the Gospel in Wales in 1650 in an attempt to provide a godly preaching ministry in Wales, failed to win them to a more thorough-going devotion to the Protestant faith.[10]

It was not until the Restoration in 1660, that a concerted effort to win

---

[7] This has been attempted in greater detail in D. C. Jones, *'A Glorious Work in the World': Welsh Methodism and the International Evangelical Revival, 1735-1750* (Cardiff: University of Wales Press, 2004).

[8] R. G. Gruffydd, 'The Renaissance and Welsh Literature', in G. Williams and R. O. Jones (eds.), *The Celts and the Renaissance: Tradition and Innovation* (Cardiff: University of Wales Press, 1990), 31-3; G. Williams, *Wales and the Reformation* (Cardiff: University of Wales Press, 1997), *passim.*

[9] G. Williams, 'Wales and the Reformation', *idem., Welsh Reformation Essays* (Cardiff: University of Wales Press, 1967), 27-30.

[10] See A. M. Johnson, 'Wales during the Commonwealth and Protectorate', in D. Pennington and K. Thomas (eds.), *Puritans and Revolutionaries: Essays in Seventeenth-Century History Presented to Christopher Hill* (Oxford: Oxford University Press, 1978), 233-56.

the Welsh to a more thorough commitment to Protestantism occurred. Through Thomas Gouge's Welsh Trust and the Society for Promoting Christian Knowledge (SPCK), the number of godly books in Wales began to increase, as did the numbers able to read them, albeit at first only in English.[11] But it was Griffith Jones, inspired by the example of Pietists like August Herman Franké and Jacob Böheme who, through his circulating schools, prepared the way for the more enthusiastic acceptance of the Protestant message. Conducted through the medium of Welsh, and complementing the seasonal patterns of life in rural communities, Jones's schools used the Bible, Prayer Book and Catechism to provide men, women and children with the basic tools of literacy. Between the establishment of his first school in 1731 and his death in 1761, it is likely that well over 250,000 pupils passed through the doors of his schools;[12] they became fertile ground for the evangelism of the Methodists. On the basis of these developments, Geraint H. Jenkins has argued that the Welsh revival did not suddenly burst on the scene in 1735, but emerged as the result of the major advances in printing, publishing and education during these years of gestation. Methodism, according to Jenkins, was an evolutionary phenomenon, it 'grew from roots laid in this period' and, consequently, did not really represent an awakening at all.[13]

By the eve of the Methodist revival, Wales could boast an embryonic Protestant tradition, but its sophistication and confidence was hampered by frustration and low morale, the consequence of repeated failure to win the Welsh over to a more intelligent commitment to the faith. On the surface there was a strong measure of continuity between the pioneer Methodists and previous generations of Protestants in both Wales and further afield. Howel Harris, for example, frequently placed his Methodists in direct succession to the 'good old Reformers and Puritans'[14], while William Williams later boasted to Thomas Charles of Bala, that 'the books of Dr Goodwin, Dr Owen, Dr Gill, Marshal,

---

[11] E. M. White, 'Popular Schooling and the Welsh Language, 1650-1800', in G. H. Jenkins (ed.), *The Welsh Language before the Industrial Revolution* (Cardiff: University of Wales Press, 1997), 318-24.

[12] G. H. Jenkins, *The Foundations of Modern Wales, 1642-1780* (Oxford: Oxford University Press, 1993), 377.

[13] G. H. Jenkins, *Literature, Religion and Society in Wales, 1660-1730* (Cardiff: University of Wales Press, 1978), 307.

[14] National Library of Wales, Calvinist Methodist Archive (Trevecka Group); The Trevecka Letters (hereafter Trevecka), 1295; Howel Harris to James Erskine, 19 February 1745.

Hervey, Usher and others',[15] all staunch defenders of Calvinistic orthodoxy, had played a vital role in his theological development. Furthermore, there is plenty of evidence to suggest that the pioneer revivalists in Wales used a wide array of adjectives to define themselves. Although he stated on many occasions that he did not like the term 'Methodist' and only advocated the term 'Christian',[16] Howel Harris referred to himself as a Christian, a Methodist, an Anglican and an evangelical without any apparent hint of contradiction. As elsewhere, the term evangelical had a long lineage in Wales, and the Methodists were certainly not the first to use it.[17] There is evidence to suggest that the Welsh Cistercians, as well as some of the Celtic Saints, may have styled themselves evangelicals,[18] and there are plenty of examples of its use by some of the early Welsh Protestants and the Puritans.[19]

It is also possible to argue, that the first generation of Methodists in Wales, as elsewhere, were conscious that their revivals marked a decisive break with the past. The early Methodists and evangelicals were skilled propagandists and devoted considerable attention to the re-writing of Welsh Christian history to service their own requirements. William Williams, Pantycelyn, developed a Methodist-orientated interpretation of the whole sweep of Christian history that drew attention, in stark terms, to the marked discontinuity between the Methodists and their immediate predecessors. Williams argued that the outbreak of revival in Wales in 1735 was like a new dawn following a long, dark and cold winter's night. In the decades before 1735, Wales had been trapped in spiritual darkness, a gloom only dispelled by the clarion call of Harris and Rowland. In *Atteb Philo-Evangelius* (1763), Williams evocatively used the metaphors of darkness and light to convey the impact of the pioneer revivalists. He wrote that before 1738:

---

[15] Quoted in R. T. Jones, 'The Evangelical Revival in Wales: A Study in Spirituality', in J. P. Mackey (ed.), *An Introduction to Celtic Christianity* (Edinburgh: T & T Clark, 1989), 243.

[16] T. Beynon (ed.), *Howell Harris, Reformer and Soldier, 1714-1773* (Caernarfon: Calvinistic Methodist Bookroom, 1958), 156.

[17] The history and various uses of the term are discussed in Noll, *The Rise of Evangelicalism*, 13-18; M. A. Noll, 'The Future of Protestantism: Evangelicalism', in A. McGrath and D. C. Marks (eds.), *The Blackwell Companion to Protestantism* (Oxford: Blackwell Publishing, 2004), 421-6.

[18] This claim is made in M. Stephens (ed.), *The New Companion to the History and Literature of Wales* (Cardiff: University of Wales Press, 1998), 225-6.

[19] Some of these occurrences have been traced by D. D. Morgan, 'Continuity, Novelty and Evangelicalism in Wales, c.1640-1850', in M. Haykin and K. J. Stewart (eds.), *Continuities in Evangelical History: Interactions with David Bebbington* (Leicester: Inter-Varsity Press, forthcoming).

> Ignorance covered the face of Wales; hardly any gospel privilege could stand against the corruptions of the day, until about 1738 light broke forth as the dawn in many parts of the world [. . .] and O glorious morn! The sun shone on Wales.[20]

He then fleshed out a cyclical view of Christian history by arguing, in a way which anticipated Jonathan Edwards's *A History of the Work of Redemption* (1774),[21] that the sun which had shone so brightly on the Apostolic Church had faded dramatically over subsequent centuries, only being kept alight by radical sects like the Waldensians, Albigensians and Lollards. Since the Reformation a series of shorter cycles had been completed, and there had been a succession of false dawns for the cause of the Gospel in Wales. The emergence of the Methodists was interpreted as the full flowering of the Reformation spirit, and possibly even represented the dawn of the millennial reign of Christ. Williams's interpretation of history came to hold a powerful sway over many of the historians of Welsh Calvinistic Methodism, writing, by the nineteenth century, from within the context of a hegemonic Nonconformist religious establishment. This so-called Methodist view of history has recently come in for criticism, particularly from Geraint H. Jenkins, whose *Literature, Religion and Society in Wales, 1660-1730* (1978) argues that the Methodist revival would never have occurred without the prior achievements of Dissenters and Churchmen between 1660 and 1730; and that the Methodist Revival, in its first three decades at least, experienced only fitful growth, and was riven by tensions and personality clashes.[22] While there is little doubt that the early Methodists exaggerated their initial impact, Jenkins' criticisms do not appreciate the extent to which the Methodist movement was distinct from the modes of piety which had gone before. Glanmor Williams hints at this discontinuity when he comments that the evangelicals were advocating a different, even new, way of experiencing God. It is hard to get away from the impression that the Methodist message did indeed appear to be a clarion call, especially to those pious middling sorts whose spiritual hunger had not been satisfied by the kind of moralistic devotional literature which had begun to appear in the Welsh language in the years following the Restoration.[23] The Bebbington thesis is clearly

---

[20] English translation quoted in Evans, *Daniel Rowland*, 75.

[21] For discussion of Edwards's work, see J. F. Wilson, 'History, Redemption and the Millennium', in N. O. Hatch and H. S. Stout (eds.), *Jonathan Edwards and the American Experience* (New York: Oxford University Press, 1988), 133-41.

[22] Jenkins, *Literature, Religion and Society in Wales, 1660-1730*, 307.

[23] See G. Williams, 'Fire on Cambria's Altar: the Welsh and their Religion', in *idem., The Welsh and their Religion: Historical Essays by Glanmor Williams* (Cardiff: University of Wales Press, 1991), 50-3.

not a contemporary recasting of the Methodist view of history, but both views do, nonetheless, share an emphasis on the discontinuity that existed between the emergence of Methodism and previous generations of Christian development in Wales.

However, a more accurate assessment of the situation might lie in a combination of these two somewhat polarised points of view. Elements of continuity between evangelicals and the native Protestant traditions that preceded them are readily discernible, and have been traced in detail elsewhere.[24] While an awareness of the tendency of all 'new' religious movements to refer to their origins in the most dramatic terms possible should warn the historian to treat their claims with a measure of scepticism,[25] disregarding their perspective altogether would be a mistake. Indeed it is quite possible that William Williams, Pantycelyn, had a much more sophisticated view of the Methodists' place within the development of Welsh Christianity than some of his critics have been prepared to accept. Part of the problem with the Methodist view of history, as it was adopted by denominational historians in the nineteenth century, and in the form that it has been criticised more recently historians, is that both groups have focused on only one aspect of Williams's interpretation.

Alongside his historical perspective, stressing successive cycles of revival and declension, Williams adopted an international perspective. When talking of the dawning of the revival in 1735, he talked about the dawn encompassing 'many parts of the world'.[26] Similarly, after the death of Whitefield in 1770 he penned a long elegy demonstrating his familiarity with the many communities in which Whitefield had worked and the revival taken root:

> To thousand souls within the western land.
> Thro' Pennsylvania, and each country round,
> Great Philadelphia his blessed mission own'd;
> New England where the pious Boston rise
> Her stately towers to the vaulted skies:
> And Newbury, where the blessed seraph dies,
> And Caroline's, the Jersies, and Long Isle,
> And on New York, his glorious doctrines smile;
> All the plantations heard the Gospel sound,
> From those pure lips that moulder in the ground . . .

---

[24] See Morgan, 'Continuity, Novelty and Evangelicalism in Wales, c.1640-1850'.

[25] R. E. Richey, 'Methodism and Providence: A Study in Secularisation', in K. Robbins (ed.), *Protestant Evangelicalism, Britain, Ireland, Germany and America c.1750-c.1950: Essays in Honour of W. R. Ward* (Oxford: Basil Blackwell, 1990), 55.

[26] English translation from Evans, *Daniel Rowland*, 75.

Old England mourn, if any love remains,
A Gloomy grave thy WHITEFIELD now contains;
Who once invited to the Gospel feast
The British Isle from western shore to east;
Wales, England, Scotland, and the Irish isle
Should not forget that blessed man awhile.[27]

But this community was far more than a loose confederation of broadly similar religious awakenings. For its first fifteen years, it was underpinned by a fairly sophisticated communications network that included the exchange of personnel between the individual awakenings, a letter-writing network and a publication programme that included books and sermons as well as three evangelical magazines carrying news of the progress of the revival.[28] By locating the Welsh Methodist revival within the context of these trans-national and trans-Atlantic religious revivals and analysing its participation in the communications network that made it a reality, thereby doing justice to the totality of Williams's historical analysis, it is possible to make the case for the revival being part of a major reconfiguration within Protestantism, a shift which, in the words of Nathan Hatch, brought about the democratisation of Christianity.[29]

For almost fifteen years the Welsh revival occupied a central place in the larger evangelical enterprise. Their involvement operated on a series of levels. Initially the Welsh Methodist awakening, in common with awakenings elsewhere, had begun under its own head of steam. Introduction to the wider evangelical movement did not take place until early 1739 when Harris received a letter from Whitefield,[30] who at this stage was the undisputed leader of the English revival. At a hastily arranged meeting, Whitefield travelled to Cardiff to meet Harris in early March, and the meeting proved crucial in the development of the Welsh revival, and what was soon to become the English Calvinistic Methodist movement. Having already read Jonathan Edwards's, *A Faithful Narrative of the Surprising Work of God ... in Northampton* (1737),[31] Harris's first-hand acquaintance with the English revival now began to alter his

---

[27] W. Williams, 'An Elegy on the Reverend Mr G. Whitefield, A. M.', in N. Cynhafal Jones (gol.), *Gweithiau Williams Pantycelyn, I* (Treffynon, 1887), 656-7, 658.

[28] For the lineaments of this network, see S. O'Brien, '"A transatlantic community of saints": the Great Awakening and the first Evangelical network, 1735-1755'. *American Historical Review*, 91 (1986), 811-32.

[29] Nathan O. Hatch, *The Democratisation of American Christianity* (New Haven: Yale University Press, 1989).

[30] Trevecka 133, George Whitefield to Howel Harris, 20 December 1738.

[31] National Library of Wales, Howel Harris's Diary 35, 27 November 1738.

perception of the significance of events in Wales. In his diaries and correspondence he began increasingly to talk about 'the glorious work [. . .] going on in the world',[32] and to tell his converts about the progress of the gospel in 'Scotland, Yorkshire, Lincolnshire, Warwickshire, Wiltshire, Germany, Prussia, New England, Pennsylvania and many other provinces'.[33] By the time of Whitefield's second visit to Wales, a month later, he and Harris 'agreed on such measures as seemed most conducive to promote the common interest of our Lord',[34] beginning the process whereby the fortunes of their respective revivals were to become more closely entwined.

Impressed with what he had seen in Wales, Whitefield made a concerted effort to publicise the Welsh revival throughout the international revival movement.[35] As if to confirm the Welsh Methodists' participation in the wider evangelical enterprise, Whitefield invited Harris to return with him to London in April 1739. Harris stayed for almost three months and met the Wesley brothers, the Countess of Huntingdon, John Cennick and some of the leading the Moravians, all of whom were still contained within the Fetter Lane Society. Despite initially being intimidated by the 'ripe saints'[36] at Fetter Lane, Harris quickly carved out a niche for himself as an inspirational exhorter, perceptive pastor and trusted confidant of a wide range of London evangelicals. The connections made during these months cemented the relationship between the Welsh and English Methodist movements, and on its basis Harris and Whitefield began to pool their resources. Whitefield became a frequent visitor to Wales and a trusted advisor and Harris, to the irritation of his fellow Welsh Methodists,[37] began to split his time more or less equally between the English and Welsh revivals, becoming the *de facto* leader of English Calvinistic Methodism by the end of 1745.

Between 1739 and 1741, the Welsh revival enjoyed a period of steady, if unspectacular growth, closely superintended by Harris and Rowland. In England, Whitefield had been joined by the Wesley brothers in the spring of 1739, and for a time they worked harmoniously together, until

---

[32] Trevecka 708, Howel Harris to Marmaduke Gwynne, 22 October 1742.

[33] Trevecka 2803, Howel Harris to Herbert Jenkins, 22 November 1742.

[34] I. H. Murray (ed.), *George Whitefield's Journals* (London: Banner of Truth Trust, 1960), 230.

[35] George Whitefield to Daniel Abbot (13 April 1739), G. C. G. Thomas (ed.), 'George Whitefield and Friends: the Correspondence of some Early Methodists', *National Library of Wales Journal*, vol. 27, no. 3, 291–2; William Seward to Joseph Stennett (17 April 1739), *ibid.*, 292–3 and Murray (ed.), *George Whitefield's Journals*, 229–30.

[36] Howel Harris' Diary, no. 43, 25 April 1739.

[37] Trevecka 705, Daniel Rowland to Howel Harris, 20 October 1742.

Whitefield's absence in the American colonies for much of 1740 and part of 1741, allowed John Wesley to fill the leadership vacuum that Whitefield's departure had created.[38] By the time of Whitefield's return to England in March 1741, a highly damaging division between the followers of Whitefield and Wesley over the relative merits of Calvinism and Arminianism was unavoidable. Harris and his followers in Wales sided with Whitefield, largely on account of their shared Calvinism, a decision that forced Whitefield to pursue the even closer integration of the English and Welsh Calvinistic awakenings. The Welsh Methodists did much of the spade-work; Harris developed a system of monthly and quarterly gatherings of society leaders, who reported to a group of superintendents, who were in turn accountable to the governing body of the movement, the Association. Whitefield's counsel was sought at strategic points, but discussions came to fruition at the first 'Joint Association of English and Welsh Calvinistic Methodism', at Watford near Caerphilly in south Wales during January 1743. In what closely resembles a quasi-presbyterian structure, both revivals were united under the government of a single Association. Whitefield was appointed Moderator and Harris, General Superintendent, with responsibilities split between Wales and Whitefield's Tabernacle at Moorfields.[39]

The months immediately following were very different from those which had preceded the Watford meeting. For most of 1743, Whitefield had kept a close eye on events in Wales and Harris ensured, through his correspondence, that events in Wales were kept in the minds of the English Methodists.[40] However, Whitefield subsequently enjoyed a lower profile in Wales, especially after his departure to the American colonies in 1744. In Whitefield's absence, the role of Moderator was taken on, as arranged by Harris, which gave him a higher profile among the English Calvinistic Methodists also. The inter-dependence of the two revivals continued unabated, but the exact balance of the relationship changed, largely due to the contrasting fortunes of both awakenings. The revival in Wales flourished under its new organisational structure at precisely the same time as the English revival, in the face of an aggressive Wesleyan movement and divisive internal disagreements, was forced to fight for its very survival.

---

[38] See H. D. Rack, *Reasonable Enthusiast: John Wesley and the Rise of Methodism* (London: Epworth Press, 1989), 198-202; H. B. McGonigle, *Sufficient Saving Grace: John Wesley's Evangelical Arminianism* (Carlisle: Paternoster Press, 2001), ch. 5.

[39] Jones, '*A Glorious Work in the World*', 214-17.

[40] See, for example, J. Lewis (ed.) *An Account of the Most Remarkable Particulars Relating to the Present Progress of the Gospel*, vol. II, no. I, *passim*.

Howel Harris was drafted into the leadership of the English Calvinistic revival on a much more regular basis. His visits to London became longer and while there his time was increasingly taken up with shuttle diplomacy between the various factions that constituted English Methodism. In Wales, Harris had become an increasingly controversial figure, whose belligerence and theological aberrations had begun to disrupt the unity of the revival.[41] But in London he remained on friendly terms with Calvinists, Arminians and Moravians, a position that enabled him to keep the channels of communication open. On a number of occasions he brought the three groups to the brink of agreement through which each would have been able to bury some of their differences and commit themselves to meaningful co-operation, based on an inclusive definition of what it meant to be a Methodist. But each time he thought he had made a breakthrough, his efforts were thwarted when one or other party pulled out at the last minute.[42]

The most obvious reason for Harris's failure to secure a pan-Methodist unity was the precarious state of the English Calvinistic revival by the late 1740s. The movement had struggled to carve out a distinct niche for itself following the division with the Wesley's – a position compounded by Whitefield's decision to leave England in 1744 for what turned out to be a four-year visit to the American colonies. In his absence, the Tabernacle society lurched from one crisis to another. John Cennick defected to the Moravians with over 400 Calvinistic Methodists at the end of 1745.[43] Harris was therefore forced, almost by default, to assume the sole leadership of English Calvinistic Methodism and to guide the revival through a series of further smaller, but lesson less damaging, losses. By the time that Whitefield returned to England in 1748, morale within the Calvinistic revival was at an all time low. But rather than commit himself to reinvigorating his revival Whitefield, reluctant to get too closely involved in the quagmire of London Methodism, revealed his desire to relinquish his leadership altogether.[44] After a number of eligible candidates declined the leadership, he reluctantly turned to Harris and persuaded him to become the outright leader of English Calvinistic Methodism, an ill-judged decision that

---

[41] G. Tudur, *Howell Harris: From Conversion to Separation, 1735-1750* (Cardiff: University of Wales Press, 2000), chs. 7 and 8.

[42] These discussions are dealt with in D. C.Jones, '"The Lord did give me a particular honour to make [me] a peacemaker": Howel Harris, John Wesley and Methodist Infighting, 1739–1750', *Bulletin of the John Rylands University Library of Manchester*, vol. 85, nos. 2 and 3 (Summer and Autumn, 2003), 73-98.

[43] Podmore, *The Moravian Church*, 89-92.

[44] B. S. Schlenther, *Queen of the Methodists: The Countess of Huntingdon and the Eighteenth-Century Crisis of Faith and Society* (Durham: Durham Academic Press, 1997), 39.

failed to take into account the mounting criticism of Harris in Wales, as a result of his embarrassing relationship with the self-styled prophetess, Mrs Sidney Griffith.[45]

Much of what I've discussed has concentrated on some of the ways in which the leaders of the Welsh revival, and Howel Harris to a greater degree than either Daniel Rowland or William Williams, actively participated in the wider evangelical movement. But their participation should not be allowed to disguise the extent to which many of the ordinary members of the Welsh revival responded enthusiastically to the news of the existence of awakenings in other places. Throughout the 1740s many of them took full advantage of the opportunities for interaction with some of their widely-scattered fellow Methodists and evangelicals. This was made possible by the communications network that Whitefield, with the help of a group of printers and booksellers, had established in order to create a sense of mutual dependence between evangelicals throughout the British Atlantic world. It was a network made up of a letter-writing exchange, from which developed an evangelical magazine, *The Weekly History*, which carried regular updates of the progress of the revival, and which spawned sister publications in Scotland and the American colonies.[46] Once the revival had become more established, the revivalists also sustained an ambitious publication programme, reprinting the classics of Reformation and Puritan spirituality as well as some of their own theological works.

An analysis of some of the ways in which rank-and-file Methodists in Wales participated in this evangelical community can be used not only to delineate some of the main features of early evangelical spirituality, but also to show their commitment to participation in the broader evangelical enterprise. We know that they utilised the network to closely follow the progress of the awakenings in other countries; to relate and test the reality of their experiences against the models that were circulated by letter and in *The Weekly History*. They also discovered that the network could operate as a primitive counselling forum in which many of the problems and difficulties associated with membership of the evangelical movement could be regularly aired. Among the problems discussed was the very real threat of persecution that Methodists in Wales, as elsewhere, faced during the mid 1740s.[47] In

[45] G. Tudur, 'The King's Daughter: A Reassessment of Anne Harris of Trefeca,' *Journal of Welsh Religious History*, 7 (1999), 55–75;.
[46] S. Durden, 'A study of the first evangelical magazines, 1740-1748', *Journal of Ecclesiastical History*, 27, 3 (1976), 266-75.
[47] The Methodist experience of persecution has been examined in J. D. Walsh, 'Methodism and the mob in the eighteenth century', in G. J. Cuming and D.

its early phase, evangelicalism, particularly in its Methodist variety, was regarded with deep suspicion by the authorities. Its tendency to enthusiasm and its network of small cell-groups seemed to hark back to the chaotic days of the mid-seventeenth century when enthusiastic religious belief had contributed to the execution of the King. When the threat from the Jacobites was at its most acute, the pages of the evangelical magazine became a useful public outlet for the Welsh Methodists to proclaim their loyalty to the British state, the King and the Established Church. This was a far-sighted policy that resulted in the easing of some of the more extreme forms of persecution, but it also contributed in no small way to the close association of Welsh evangelicalism with British Protestant nationalism.[48]

For a while during the earliest months of the revival the network, particularly through the first evangelical magazine, *The Christian's Amusement*, also facilitated a primitive 'community of goods' in which shopkeepers and trades people advertised their services for the benefit of their fellow evangelicals. Among those who responded was the proprietor of a clothes shop and a watch and clock maker. But once the English revival had splintered in 1740 and 1741 this sharing of resources came to an abrupt end. Later in the 1740s, Methodists in Wales were able to use the network to keep track of the uses to which the financial contributions they made to Whitefield's Orphan-house in Georgia were being put, a venture that gave them a stake in the success of the Gospel in foreign parts.[49]

For most Welsh evangelicals, participation in this network, but not in the wider evangelical enterprise, came to an abrupt end in 1750, when Howel Harris was first dismissed from the leadership of the London revival and then ousted from the leadership of the Welsh revival for a number of reasons, both doctrinal and personal.[50] In his absence the Welsh revival went through a period of quiet consolidation. But in England, Whitefield, anxious to divest himself of the burden of leading the Calvinistic revival, turned increasingly to the Countess of Huntingdon, who more or less assumed control over the movement, opening her own chapels during the 1760s and beginning what Alan

---

Baker (eds.), *Popular Belief and Practice, Studies in Church History*, 6 (Cambridge: Cambridge Press, 1972), 215-27. See also Jones, *'A Glorious Work in the World'*, 313-28.

[48] G. Williams, 'Some Protestant Views of Early British History', in *idem., Welsh Reformation Essays*, 207-20; E. M. White, '"The People called Methodists": Early Welsh Methodism and the Question of Identity', *Journal of Welsh Religious History*, 1 (2001), 1-14.

[49] For the Welsh Methodists' contributions to the orphan-house, see Jones, *'A Glorious Work in the World'*, 294-302.

[50] For a discussion of these reasons, see Tudur, *Howell Harris*, chs. 7 and 8.

Harding has called 'Connexional work'.[51] Opportunities for interaction between the Welsh revival and the wider evangelical movement became less frequent, although both Whitefield and Wesley travelled to Wales on a number of occasions during the 1750s.[52] Harris, meanwhile, devoted himself to the establishment of his religious community at Trefeca[53] and, later to serving in the Breconshire militia during the Seven Year's War.[54] The fortunes of Welsh Methodism stagnated, not reviving again until 1762 when a new outbreak of revival at Llangeitho,[55] that almost eclipsed that of the later 1730s, precipitated both the reintegration of Harris, and the beginning of the rapid growth of Welsh Methodism. Contacts with the wider evangelical movement remained, and the close links between English and Welsh Calvinistic Methodism saw the establishment of a training college for the Countess of Huntingdon's preachers at Trefeca in 1768 and the regular deputation of Welsh Methodist preachers in the Countess's London chapels.

It was the Methodists' decision to engage in a fresh attempt to win over parts of north Wales that set in motion the rapid growth of Methodism, and by consequence evangelical religious forms, throughout Wales. So successful were their evangelistic efforts that by the end of the eighteenth century the balance of power within the Methodist movement had shifted from Llangeitho to Bala. A new generation of leaders emerged, taking full control of the movement by the deaths of Daniel Rowland and William Williams in the early 1790s. It was under the dynamic leadership of Thomas Charles and John Elias that the Methodists finally mustered sufficient confidence to sever their links with the Established Church, ordaining their own ministers for the first time in 1811.

By the second half of the eighteenth century, the evangelicalism of the Methodists had begun to impact the other Nonconformist bodies in Wales. It is here that Geraint H. Jenkins' stress on the limited effects of the revival, especially in its first thirty years, requires some qualification. While the early Methodists did not sweep all before them,

---

[51] A. Harding, *The Countess of Huntingdon's Connexion: a Sect in Action in Eighteenth-Century England* (Oxford: Oxford University Press, 2003), 62.

[52] E. Evans, *Howel Harris, Evangelist 1714-1773* (Cardiff: University of Wales Press, 1973), 58-9; A. H. Williams, *John Wesley in Wales 1739-1791* (Cardiff: University of Wales Press, 1971), 42-61.

[53] The fullest study remains the unpublished thesis of A.W. Owen, 'A study of Howel Harris and the Trevecca "Family" (1752-1760) based upon the Trevecca letters and diaries and other Methodist archives at the National Library of Wales' (MA thesis, University of Wales, 1957).

[54] Beynon (ed.), *Howell Harris: Reformer and Soldier*, 58-146, *passim*.

[55] R. G. Gruffydd, *The Revival of 1762 and William Williams of Pantycelyn* (Bridgend: Evangelical Library of Wales, 1981).

they certainly enjoyed considerable success. By 1750, over 420 Methodist societies had been established in south Wales.[56] Accepting an average membership of between twenty and twenty-five in each society, there is likely to have been somewhere in the region of 10-12,000 members of the Methodist movement in Wales by this date. But this figure does not do justice to the number of people who would have been influenced by the preaching of Harris or Rowland, but who did not actually take the step of joining a Methodist society. Although Harris could be guilty of wildly exaggerating the size of his congregations, there can be little doubt that some of the thousands who listened to him were affected by what they heard, and that their religious commitment was revived and reinvigorated, even though they may have preferred to continue attending their local parish church or dissenting meeting house, rather than join a Methodist society. Judging the impact of the Methodists on statistics alone can therefore be misleading; the Methodists' impact reached far beyond the members of their societies, and there can be no question that they successfully communicated Protestant piety to large sections of the population of Wales, something that had evaded Welsh Protestants for well over two centuries.

The startling success of the Methodists, especially by the second half of the eighteenth century soon roused the Dissenters to jealous imitation. They were gradually weaned away from the introspective piety that had blunted their effectiveness for much of the eighteenth century, and were inspired by the Methodists to adopt a more outgoing evangelicalism, whose keynote became the vibrant communal religious revival. Led by charismatic preachers of the calibre of John Elias, Christmas Evans and William Williams of Wern, these revivals fuelled the growth of evangelical Nonconformity in Wales. It has been calculated that between 1762 and 1862, Wales experienced at least fifteen national religious awakenings as well as countless other local revivals.[57] Frequent religious revivals brought a regular influx of new people into the Nonconformist denominations who could be accommodated in new chapel buildings which were built quickly and cheaply, without recourse to the cumbersome legislative process that hampered the ability of the Anglicans to respond to the challenges presented by the new urban and industrial communities of south

---

[56] E. M. White, '"The World, the Flesh and the Devil" and the Early Methodist Societies of South West Wales', *Transactions of the Honourable Society of Cymmrodorion* (1990), 60.

[57] D. Geraint Jones, *Favoured with Frequent Revivals: Revivals in Wales, 1762-1865* (Cardiff: The Heath Christian Trust, 2001), 7.

Wales.[58]

By the early part of the nineteenth century, evangelical religion had made significant inroads into both south and north Wales. Precise figures for this growth are startling, but they could conceivably only represent the tip of the iceberg since figures of church membership do not include the large numbers of adherents and casual listeners that made up most Nonconformist congregations. By 1815 it was estimated that the Independents alone could boast 257 congregations;[59] while the Baptists had increased their membership six-fold from 1,601 in 1760 to 9,232 in 1800.[60] By the time of the 1851 religious census, over three-quarters of the population of the country could be comfortably accommodated within Welsh places of worship, and the overwhelming majority of the church-going population preferred to attend a Nonconformist chapel than the local parish church.[61] But these figures tell only half the story, and do not reflect the cultural hegemony of Nonconformity. The report of the Education Commissioners in 1847, the notorious 'Blue Books', accused the Welsh of being ignorant, lazy and immoral laying the blame for this squarely at the door of the Welsh language and Nonconformity. This spurred the Nonconformists into action and brought about the forging of an image of Wales that was, on the surface at least, peaceful, pious and well-ordered. Biblicism, Sabbatarianism, temperance, hymn-singing and the like became the abiding images of Welshness,[62] fusing seamlessly with the badges of nationhood that had already been created by the Romanic revivalists.[63] All of these developments gave rise to the impression that Wales was in fact a Nonconformist country, and became the basis on which Liberal politicians launched their attack on the political establishment in the wake of the 1868 election.

Unlike the historiography of Methodism in England, which has benefited from a considerable amount of detailed work on its initial

---

[58] E. T. Davies, *Religion in the Industrial Revolution in South Wales* (Cardiff: University of Wales Press, 1965), ch. III.

[59] R. T. Jones, *Congregationalism in Wales* (Cardiff: University of Wales Press, 2004), 149.

[60] T. M. Bassett, *The Welsh Baptists* (Swansea: Illston House, 1977), 93.

[61] I. G. Jones, 'Denominationalism in Caernarfonshire', in *idem., Explorations and Explanations: Essays in the Social History of Victorian Wales* (Llandysul: Gwasg Gomer, 1981), 21.

[62] D. Hempton, *Religion and Political Culture in Britain and Ireland: from the Glorious Revolution to the Decline of Empire* (Cambridge: Cambridge University Press, 1996), 56-7.

[63] P. Morgan, *The Eighteenth Century Welsh Renaissance* (Llandybië: Christopher Davies, 1981).

phase of rapid growth and expansion,[64] little attention has been paid to the even more spectacular expansion of evangelical Nonconformity in Wales. Despite the abundance of source material, the chief studies of the leaders of Welsh Nonconformity are, with a few exceptions, hagiographical studies that do not really address the questions that concern professional historians. For a variety of reasons, mostly to do with Welsh historians' traditional preoccupations with issues of language, cultural nationalism and popular radical politics during this period, Welsh Nonconformity has been regarded as a deeply conservative force, whose other-worldy preoccupations bred in its followers a supine acceptance of the inequalities of the social order, and an antipathy for many of the traditional elements of popular Welsh culture.

While the religiosity of Victorian Wales can, and indeed has been, exaggerated, there can be little doubt that the revivals which occurred regularly in the two hundred years between the Methodist awakening and the last national religious revival in 1904-5, were the engines that drove the transformation of many parts of Wales into a sober-minded godly nation, every aspect of whose national life, it appeared, was permeated by the influence of evangelical religion.[65] But the remarkably close correlation between evangelical religion and Welshness in the nineteenth century has to be traced back the mid 1730s when a small group of enthusiastic evangelicals, in close contact with renewal movements throughout the British Atlantic world, launched the first concerted, and successful, attempt to evangelise their fellow countrymen and women. That evangelisation turned out to be a long and fitful process, but Methodism, and the Evangelicalism that it spawned, turned out to be the means by which many in Wales were finally won over to the kind of committed allegiance to the Protestant faith for which the Elizabethan martyr, John Penry, had petitioned so passionately two centuries earlier.

---

[64] A good way into this historiography is D. Hempton, *Methodism: Empire of the Spirit* (New Haven: Yale University Press, 2005).

[65] The close correlation between Welshness and Nonconformity has been explored in R. T. Jones, *Faith and the Crisis of a Nation: Wales 1880-1920* (Cardiff: University of Wales Press, 2004).

CHAPTER 8

Evangelical Identity and the Writing of Evangelical History in Northern Ireland*

Andrew R. Holmes

In comparison with the rest of the British Isles, the evangelicals of Northern Ireland are a peculiar people. Three differences in particular relate directly to the themes of this volume. First, the number of evangelicals is proportionately greater than elsewhere, estimated to comprise between twelve and eighteen percent of the total population of Northern Ireland.[1] Second, Northern Irish evangelicals are more self-consciously British. Michael Ignatieff has suggested that 'a visit to Ulster is to travel down through the layers of historical time that separate mainland Britain from a Britishness that was once its own'.[2] Third, evangelicals in Ulster are much more inclined to describe their identity in historical terms. In Northern Ireland, certain interpretations of the past remain powerful forces in determining political allegiance and shaping relationships between nationalists and unionists. By contrast, other parts of the United Kingdom often display either signs of forgetfulness or encounter a sanitised view of the past through the heritage industry.[3] Yet there are indications, including the cultural and religious pluralism implicit in the Belfast Agreement, that forgetfulness is becoming a virtue amongst sections of Northern Irish society.

The interplay between evangelicalism, national identity, and history in Northern Ireland provides an opportunity to explore the general theme of evangelical identity and the use and interpretation of the past

---

* I am most grateful to Andrew Brown, David McMillan, Alwyn Thompson, and Stephen Williams for comments upon an earlier draft of this essay. The author is alone responsible for any errors of fact or interpretation.

[1] Evangelical Contribution on Northern Ireland [ECONI], *A future with hope: biblical frameworks for peace and reconciliation in Northern Ireland* (2nd ed., Belfast: ECONI, 1998), 9.

[2] Cited in, Alwyn Thomson, *Fields of vision: faith and identity in protestant Ireland* (Belfast: Centre for Contemporary Christianity in Ireland, 2002), 4.

[3] C. R. Trueman, 'Reckoning with the past in an anti-historical age', *Themelios*, 27 (2002), 28-44.

in this process. The term 'evangelical history' in the title of this essay has two meanings: the history of the evangelical movement and a distinctive evangelical historiography, and both will be examined in due course. Part one begins by outlining how evangelicalism became associated with unionism in Ulster. It then examines how the complex nature of the community itself, and the sense of insecurity felt by many of its adherents, highlight the problems associated with the exclusive concentration upon the political dimensions of evangelicalism. The second section suggests how, in broad terms, some of the principles held by evangelicals may address the problems and shortcomings of both academics and evangelicals in their respective approaches to the past. This essay will determine whether the theological and historical resources of evangelicalism have anything to offer both of these groups, and whether an evangelical approach to history can provide a better way of examining the identity of the movement more generally.

I

The past continues to have a relevance in Ireland that others in the western world find hard to understand. The bitterness of the Northern Ireland conflict is usually explained as a product of at least four centuries of conflict. Irish political and religious groups, whether legitimate or otherwise, rely upon certain interpretations of historical events to justify their existence and aspirations. More particularly, both nationalists and unionists in Northern Ireland have used history to support their present day political objectives. These histories are mutually exclusive and teleologically distinct. The historian Ian McBride has suggested that the nationalist and loyalist understanding of history may be described as redemptive and providential respectively.[4] Nationalist history extols the centuries-long struggle against British rule and the heroic martyrdom of a phalanx of Irish patriots. This is a story of martyrdom and redemption, of the blood sacrifice that will free Ireland. By contrast, the loyalist vision of the past is the story of providential protection that finds its ultimate symbol in the besieged city of Derry, defended against the Catholic army of James II by honest hardworking Ulster protestants. The main themes of this unionist history are cast in terms of siege, defence, and the ever-present threat of treachery.[5] The cardinal dates are as follows: 1641, the

---

[4] I. R. McBride, 'Memory and national identity in modern Ireland', idem. (ed.), *History and memory in modern Ireland* (Cambridge: Cambridge University Press, 2001), 15-36.

[5] Alvin Jackson, 'Unionist myths 1912-1985', *Past and Present*, no. 136 (1992), 164-85; idem., 'Irish unionism', D. G. Boyce and Alan O'Day (eds), *The making of*

massacre of protestants by Catholics in Ulster; 1689, the siege of Derry; 1690, the defeat of James II by William of Orange at the Battle of the Boyne; 1912, the Ulster Covenant; 1916, the Battle of the Somme and the decimation of the 36th 'Ulster' Division, the Ulster protestant blood sacrifice to rival that of Patrick Pearse and the rebels of the Easter Rising. Until recently in Northern Ireland, the teaching of Irish history was sidestepped in schools and museums shied away from exhibitions dealing with the Troubles. The significance of these dates is therefore learnt on the streets, in Orange Halls, through various populist publications, and sometimes from the pulpit.[6]

It was during the nineteenth century that evangelicalism became inextricably bound with this historical understanding, a strong sense of Britishness, and opposition to Irish independence.[7] Evangelicalism did not create the deep fissures in Ulster society but it did exacerbate the tensions caused by the massive transfer of land in the seventeenth century.[8] During the second half of the eighteenth century, evangelicalism in the form of Methodism and Scottish Seceder Presbyterianism increased rapidly in the southern counties of the ancient province of Ulster. As in other areas of the Atlantic world, evangelicalism in Ulster fed off the religious and economic insecurity of the frontier in south Ulster and the upheaval that surrounded the United Irish rebellion of 1798, which resulted in the deaths of some 30,000 individuals.[9] According to David Hempton, these developments focused the minds of a substantial cross section of Irish protestant opinion 'on the potential of [evangelicalism's] moral creed and its anti-Catholicism to act as compelling antidotes to civil and political unrest'.[10] During the nineteenth century, evangelicalism continued to thrive in areas of sectarian and economic competition, particularly in Belfast whose population mushroomed from around 20,000 persons in 1800 to

---

modern Irish history: revisionism and the revisionist controversy (London: Routledge, 1996), ch.7; Brian Walker, *Dancing to history's tune: history myth and politics in Ireland* (Belfast: Queen's University Belfast Institute of Irish Studies, 1996), ch.1.

[6] Elizabeth Crooke, 'Confronting a troubled history: which past in Northern Ireland's museums?', *International Journal of Heritage Studies*, 7 (2001), 119-36; B. W. Walker, *Past and present: history, identity, and politics in Ireland* (Belfast: Queen's University Belfast Institute of Irish Studies, 2000), 106-8.

[7] David Hempton, *Religion and political culture in Great Britain and Ireland from the Glorious Revolution to the decline of empire* (Cambridge: Cambridge University Press, 1996), ch. 5.

[8] David Hempton and Myrtle Hill, *Evangelical Protestantism in Ulster society 1740-1890* (London: Routledge, 1992).

[9] R. F. Foster, *Modern Ireland 1600-1972* (London: Penguin Books, 1989), 280.

[10] Hempton, *Religion and political culture*, 95.

375,000 in 1901.[11] After receiving a boost in morale from the 1859 revival, the relationship between evangelicalism and Britishness in Ulster was fused during the three Home Rule crises of 1885-6, 1892-3, and 1912-14, which saw a gradual refocusing of unionist opposition from the whole of Ireland to the predominantly protestant six counties of the north-east.[12]

Then as now, the opposition of Ulster protestants to the claims of Irish nationalism are predicated on a number of interlocking arguments.[13] Yet for religiously minded protestants the issue was more profound than national identity, economic gain, and constitutional questions: Home Rule was synonymous with Rome Rule. Evangelicalism fostered the age-old distinction between protestant liberty and Catholic tyranny; a distinction given added urgency by the prospect of Catholic dominance in an independent Irish state.[14] Though religiously committed evangelicals do not make up the majority of protestants in Ulster, its values, symbols, and rhetoric have influenced the community more generally.[15] Present-day loyalists openly demand their civil and religious freedoms, but they rarely read the Bible or darken the door of a church for themselves. As one prominent unionist politician and Presbyterian minister said of the inhabitants of Sandy Row; 'They are Bible lovers even if not Bible readers.'[16] Yet, until recently, evangelicalism has continued to act as a class and denominational solvent by uniting a diverse protestant community behind its anti-Catholicism and, perhaps less significantly, its moral seriousness.

As noted, a distinctive version of the past has constantly underpinned the religio-political case of northern Protestants against an independent all-Ireland state. Patrick Mitchel has laid bare the obsession of 'closed' forms of evangelicalism with the past and the historical struggle for protestant freedoms.[17] A commemorative

---

[11] Leslie Clarkson, 'The city and the country', J. C. Beckett et al., *Belfast: the making of a city 1800-1914* (Belfast: Appletree, 1988), 153.

[12] Alvin Jackson, 'Irish unionism, 1870-1922', D. G. Boyce and Alan O'Day (eds), *Defenders of the Union: a survey of British and Irish Unionism since 1801* (London: Routledge, 2001), ch. 6.

[13] Ibid.; James Loughlin, 'Imagining "Ulster": the north of Ireland and British national identity', S.J. Connolly (ed.), *Kingdoms united? Great Britain and Ireland since 1500: integration and diversity* (Dublin: Four Courts Press, 1999), 109-22.

[14] Hempton, *Religion and political culture*, 106-13.

[15] Ibid., 108; Frank Wright, 'Protestant ideology and politics in Ulster', *Archives Européenes de Sociologie*, 14 (1973), 243-7.

[16] Wright, 'Protestant ideology and politics', 245.

[17] Patrick Mitchel, *Evangelicalism and national identity in Ulster, 1921-1998* (Oxford: Oxford University Press, 2003), chs 5&6.

publication celebrating the two-hundredth anniversary of the Orange Order in 1995 called on its members to remember 1795 as 'many lessons learnt by our forefathers are true for us in this age'. It continued: 'It is important that we learn from our past and even more as we celebrate this occasion we must keep clearly in mind and in view the enemy that we face in this age and be prepared to make the same defence of all we hold dear to us.'[18] The symbols, rituals, and parades of the Order are also deeply imbued with a providential view of the past. They portray a chosen people in a heathen land, 'contending against alien peoples and false Gods eventually to reach, with faith, the Promised Land and the blessing of God'.[19] This is not, however, a vision of hope. McBride observes that 'In remembering 1690, loyalists implicitly recall the lessons of 1641: the need for eternal vigilance, the dangers of backsliding, and the implacability of Roman Catholic vengeance.'[20] Protestants not only fear a united Ireland but also of letting the side down, of betraying their British and protestant heritage.[21]

Since the imposition of direct rule in 1972, Ulster protestants have exhibited all the signs of a besieged and insecure people. Unionist hegemony from 1922 to 1972 has been replaced by political accommodation orchestrated from London. Protestants feel that the equality agenda since the Belfast Agreement has solely benefited nationalists and a recent survey concluded that since the mid-nineties the number of protestants who feel that community relations are degenerating has risen significantly.[22] This is partly a result of a well-managed republican campaign against the routing of Orange marches through predominantly Catholic areas. Another factor is the alienation of working class loyalism from the two main Unionist parties. Yet evangelical commitment, language, and symbolism remain inextricably linked with various forms of unionism because it has tended to feed off the frontier and the attendant sense of fear. The close relationship forged in Ulster between evangelicalism and local expressions of Britishness does place the region out of step with the predominant expressions of evangelicalism in the rest of the United Kingdom.

Despite the close relationship between religion, identity, and history

---

[18] Cited in ibid., 139.

[19] Ibid., 154. For a further elucidation of these themes see A. D. Buckley, '"We're trying to find our identity": uses of history among Ulster protestants', Elizabeth Tonkin, Maryon McDonald, and Malcolm Chapman (eds), *History and ethnicity* (London: Routledge, 1989), ch.12.

[20] McBride, 'Memory and national identity', 21.

[21] R. A. Wells, 'A fearful people: religion and the Ulster conflict', *Eire-Ireland*, 28:1 (1993), 66-7.

[22] Mitchel, *Evangelicalism and national identity*, 87-98.

in Ireland, one of the key weaknesses of the enormous literature on Northern Ireland is the neglect or misinterpretation of a significant religious dimension.[23] This is particularly true of social scientists who routinely dismiss the influence of religion because of a rigid understanding of religious belief as purely a matter of private faith.[24] Commentators reflecting the secular and pluralist values of the university system find it hard to comprehend how privatised religion could influence political behaviour and how anything but a religious solution to the Northern Ireland issue could be achieved if the importance of religion is granted. Political problems, it seems, should only be solved by political solutions. Others have acknowledged the importance of religion, particularly of evangelicalism, in providing the religious motivation and symbols for the mobilisation of Ulster protestant opinion against the demands of Irish nationalists.[25] Disappointingly, however, those who have taken religious motivations seriously have tended to focus solely on political issues and the right-wing fringes of evangelicalism.[26]

In reality, political allegiance, social class, ecclesiology, theology, and geography, especially between rural and urban areas, divide Northern Irish evangelicals.[27] As Patrick Mitchel has recently demonstrated, evangelicals display a wide variety of approaches to the relationship between faith and national identity. The Orange Order and Paisleyism are examples of 'closed' evangelicalism: that is, they are deeply embedded in the particular political and cultural circumstances of Northern Ireland and deny the legitimacy of other ways of conceptualising religious identity. Sections of the Presbyterian Church

---

[23] For a discussion see, R. A. Wells, 'Decoding conflicted history: religion and the historiography on Northern Ireland', idem. (ed.), *History and the Christian historian* (Grand Rapids, Mich.: Eerdmans, 1998), 178-201; Thomson, *Fields of vision*, ch. 3.

[24] A notable exception is Claire Mitchell, *Religion, identity, and politics in Northern Ireland: boundaries of belonging and belief* (Aldershot: Ashgate, 2006). See also, R. A. Wells, 'Decoding conflicted history: religion and the historiography on Northern Ireland', idem. (ed.), *History and the Christian historian*, 178-201.

[25] Wright, 'Protestant ideology and politics in Ulster' and the work of Ronald Wells cited above.

[26] The most influential analysis of religious conservatism remains Steve Bruce, *God save Ulster: the religion and politics of Paisleyism* (Oxford: Clarendon Press, 1986).

[27] Fred Boal, J. A. Campbell ,and D. N. Livingstone, 'The protestant mosaic: a majority of minorities', P. J. Roche and Brian Barton (eds), *The Northern Ireland question: myth and reality* (Aldershot: Avebury, 1991), ch. 5; Glenn Jordan, *Not of this world? Evangelical protestants in Northern Ireland* (Belfast: Blackstaff Press, 2001).

and the Church of Ireland, and groups such as the Evangelical Contribution on Northern Ireland (ECONI), recently rebranded the Centre for Contemporary Christianity in Ireland (CCCI), are more 'open' in their attitude towards national identity and seek to create a sense of distance from their environment. To further complicate matters, one commentator has recently claimed that the majority of evangelicals are proudly ignorant of politics.[28]

Differences between evangelicals extend to their understanding of history. Many consciously or otherwise adopt the traditional Ulster protestant reading of the past that emphasises their forefathers defence of both the protestant way of life and the union with Great Britain. Followers of Ian Paisley construct an historical narrative that emphasises their role as God's chosen people, instruments in his hand for the promotion of godliness and the suppression of error and immorality. Pietists concentrate upon the history of revivals, mission halls, and prominent evangelical heroes, or utilise dispensationalism or a charismatic experience to situate themselves within God's plan. At the other end of the theological and political spectrum, liberal evangelicals attempt to counter such views by focusing upon those events that do not fit easily into the traditional account. Mediating groups such as ECONI/CCCI seek to affirm that God is indeed active in the affairs of the world but that discerning his activity is problematical both practically and theologically. Also an increasingly significant number of evangelicals are disgruntled with the alleged parochialism of Northern Irish church life and display little interest in sectional views of the past. The variety of evangelical experience casts serious doubt upon the over-concern of scholars with the political implications of evangelical belief. It suggests that more attention ought to be devoted to the internal workings of this diverse and often divisive community. It is obvious that without an appreciation of this background, the relationship between religion and politics in Northern Ireland will continue to be misrepresented or neglected.

II

The founders of modern Irish historical scholarship in the 1930s sought to disable the historical myths that sustained republican and loyalist terrorism by employing the methods of scientific history.[29] That 'noble dream' of objectivity has had a salutary impact at some points but has not significantly altered the popular appropriation of the past and has

---

[28] Jordan, *Not of this world?*, ch. 7.

[29] Ciaran Brady (ed.), *Interpreting Irish history: the debate on historical revisionism 1938-1994* (Dublin: Irish Academic Press, 1994).

led to the neglect of religious themes. Furthermore, contemporary commentators argue that the multiplicity of particular views of the past seems to be limited only to the number of autonomous individuals who care to think about it. Indeed, the possibility of producing an accurate and agreed account of the past is increasingly rejected. This situation is the product of the growth of religious and cultural pluralism within society and the post-modern denial of the possibility of accurate, objective knowledge. The pluralist agenda raises all sorts of philosophical issues about the possibility of historical knowledge and practical questions concerning the mechanisms that might transmit a new understanding of the past to those whom it is intended to influence.

Recognising the 'situatedness' of all scholarship, yet rejecting the claims of post-modernists, I want to propose that the theological and historical resources of evangelicalism provide a way of dealing with the concerns of those academics who continue to ignore the influence of religious ideas and evangelicals in Northern Ireland who are insecure. Evangelicalism contains within itself a number of principles and potential approaches to the past that may be employed for the enrichment of both an evangelical historiography and the history of evangelicalism. These include the following affirmations: that God created and sustains the world; the twofold character of humanity as both special, because they are made in God's image, but also finite and sinful; a commitment to truth and humility; that the Word became flesh in history with universal implications; the global character of the church; and the possibility of forgiveness and redemption within history. The subjects for study suggested by the evangelical movement itself include the religion of the people, spirituality, missionary activism, and the influence of evangelical attitudes on a range of economic, political, and cultural issues.

It should be stressed that despite the religious assumptions that underlie this framework, a commitment to ethical scholarship is not the preserve of believers alone, but may be common ground upon which scholars from different faith commitments or none may explore the past.[30] The careful application of the above affirmations ought to lead to a sympathetic yet rigorous examination of evangelicalism and not a simplistic reading of the past immune from the normal standards of scholarship.[31] In that regard, an evangelical historiography may manifest itself in the subjects chosen for study rather than underlying

[30] G. M. Marsden, *The outrageous idea of Christian scholarship* (New York: Oxford University Press, 1997).

[31] John Wolffe, 'Historical method and Christian vision in the study of evangelical history', *Christianity and History Newsletter*, no. 18 (1999), 46-63.

principles, which, at any rate, are derived from orthodox Christianity.

Evangelicals share with other Christian traditions the conviction that God created and continues to sustain the world. According to Mark Noll, this principle leads to epistemological and ontological confidence because our knowledge of the world, and the past, depends ultimately upon God's sovereignty and grace and not ourselves.[32] Yet, because humans are affected by sin, our knowledge of the past is finite and often inaccurate. All our interpretations are to some extent provisional and open to criticism, yet they can and must convey truth because God created us. The tendency of all humans to view and write history from their perspective tells us something important about human nature and what it means to be made in the image of God. What humans do presupposes who they are; in this case creative and imaginative beings made in the image of the Creator. It can therefore be suggested that humans re-create rather than create the past out of nothing. Furthermore, because God is sovereign and sustains the cosmos, Christians ought to be wary of privileging a providential reading of the fortunes of a particular national group or religious community in the present.

The finitude of humanity and the provisional nature of our understanding reinforce the evangelical commitment to the humble search for truth. Evangelicals ought to have a passion for truth as their salvation depends upon the truthfulness of the gospel and its author. There is an onus on truth-loving evangelicals to identify and challenge errors of fact and interpretation and the presuppositions at the root of erroneous and misleading historical interpretations. The implications of this for theological disagreement between protestants and Catholics in Northern Ireland and the possibility of a 'truth and reconciliation' process must be faced squarely and not sidestepped. Yet, the evangelical commitment to truth should be inseparable from holiness and ethical behaviour. Truth telling is not only about the facts, but also the manner in which we present them. There must be a commitment to certain moral virtues as they apply to intellectual endeavour and the use of appropriate modes of argumentation and interpretation. Jay Wood helpfully expresses the point: 'Like so much of the virtuous life, seeking the truth appropriately is a matter of seeking it in the right way, for the right reason, using the right methods for the right purposes.' The intellectual virtues he highlights are 'wisdom, understanding, prudence,

---

[32] The argument of the following paragraph is indebted to M. A. Noll, 'Traditional Christianity and the possibility of historical knowledge', Bruce Kuklick and D. G. Hart (eds), *Religious advocacy and American history* (Grand Rapids, MI.: Eerdmans, 1997), 28-53.

studiousness, intellectual honesty and love of truth'.[33] For Christians, our primary allegiance to Christ has significant implications for how the historical task should be approached. We ought to be as wise as serpents and as innocent as doves. We ought to be generous to those with whom we disagree but rigorous and utterly professional in weighing evidence and constructing arguments. Above all, an evangelical approach to the past should display a humility based upon the realisation that we are finite, fallen beings that are not given privileged access to God's plans. Any judgements we make on others are equally self-judgements.

Another characteristic of evangelicalism that may be employed is the conviction that redemption happens in history. Christianity is an historical religion. It is claimed by evangelicals that both the Old and New Testaments chart God's gracious efforts to redeem fallen humanity.[34] Crucially, redemption occurred in history with the life, death, and resurrection of Jesus the Christ. The implications of the Messiah, the Christ, appearing in a particular culture at a particular time have been elucidated by Andrew Walls.[35] Surveying the history of global Christianity, Walls concludes that the incarnation was a paradigmatic moment in which the Word became translated into recognisable human categories. 'So the process of Christian expansion is the story of various re-translations of that original into other cultural media as Christ is received among people of different languages and cultures.'[36] According to Walls, the 'proper response' to this divine act of translation is conversion to Christ within a particular culture. Therefore, the human understanding of the gospel cannot be expressed outside of the culture into which it is brought.

This translation principle has implications for both academics and evangelicals. Though evangelicals would want to stress the importance of religious motivations, secular historians should not see this as a form of Gnosticism. Because of the cultural embedded-ness of the gospel, evangelical historians will seek to situate religious belief within its proper social, cultural, political, and economic context. Evangelicals

---

[33] W. J. Wood, *Epistemology: becoming intellectually virtuous* (Leicester: Apollos, 1998), 57, 73.

[34] R. E. Frykenberg, *History and belief: the foundations of historical understanding* (Grand Rapids, Mich.: Eerdmans, 1996), ch. 7.

[35] A. F. Walls, *The missionary movement in Christian history: studies in the transmission of the faith* (Edinburgh: T.&T. Clark, 1996); *The cross-cultural process in Christian history: studies in the transmission and appropriation of the faith* (Edinburgh: T.&T. Clark, 2002).

[36] A. F. Walls, 'Eusebius tries again: the task of reconceiving and re-visioning the study of Christian history', W. R. Shenk (ed.), *Enlarging the story: perspectives on writing world Christian history* (Maryknoll, N.Y.: Orbis Books, 2002), 19.

would wish to practice a chastened social history of ideas – to examine any ideas, whether religious or otherwise, within the social and cultural context from which they emerge, without regarding them as being determined by that context or blindly accepting an unsatisfactory relativism. Such an approach would facilitate a sympathetic yet rigorous examination of those aspects of evangelicalism that are often ignored by historians of the movement, never mind historians more generally. It would allow for a serious study of lay religious experience and a sympathetic examination of the religious motivations of historical figures.[37] Other topics may include how believers interacted in their various church fellowships, or neglected aspects of social and missionary endeavour. This focus on the particular ought to save evangelicals from overtly pietistic and eschatological readings of the past. In some cases, it would also allow the focus to be narrowed from broader developments within evangelicalism towards local history and biography. Local history in particular is very popular in Northern Ireland and some have suggested that it provides the space necessary for both communities to explore topics of common historical concern.[38]

As Walls points out, there is a paradox at the heart of Christianity: 'the twofold affirmation of the utter Jewishness of Jesus and of the boundless universality of the Divine Son'.[39] The Incarnation was at once a particular event and an event of universal significance. God identifying with humanity in such an intimate and culturally sensitive manner was the supreme way he could express his love for the whole of humanity. Consequently, Christians are members of a multiethnic, trans-national family, inheritors of an 'adoptive past' that links them to generations of believers and to Israel to whom God first revealed himself.[40] An awareness of the heritage into which we have been engrafted allows us to become aware of our own situatedness, that we are but one expression of a process that has been ongoing since Abraham. It should help us to appreciate that though we belong to a certain cultural expression of faith in the universal Christ, our ultimate citizenship is in heaven. Furthermore, if evangelicals, especially in Northern Ireland, adopted this perspective upon the shape of history, it would allow them to think of the land in which they live as a gift rather than a covenantal inheritance.[41]

Recent discussion about the possibility of writing a global history of

---

[37] Wolffe, 'Historical method and Christian vision'.

[38] W. A. Maguire, 'Past and present: the study of local history as an agent of reconciliation', PACE, 12, no. 3 (1980/1), 9-11.

[39] Walls, *The missionary movement in Christian history*, xvi.

[40] Ibid., 9.

[41] For a discussion of this theme see, Thomson, *Fields of vision*, ch. 5.

Christianity points to another aspect of evangelicalism that may provide a way out of both an overtly politicised view of the Irish past and the pessimism expressed by certain sections of evangelicalism in Ulster.[42] Northern Ireland has an enviable reputation for its support of missionary activity, both in terms of money and manpower. Despite this, Northern Irish evangelicalism is in many respects a closed system, or at any rate a system that assimilates only that which reinforces its core beliefs and prejudices. This in part explains why unionists do not like Northern Ireland being compared with other parts of the world, which is often understandable when the two favoured comparative societies are apartheid South Africa and Israel.[43] It also explains hostility towards the political process that has garnered support from those sections of unionism that stress its civic nature and are more sympathetic to a pluralist understanding of modern society. Placing Ulster evangelicalism within a global perspective may create a sense of distance for evangelicals that would allow them to look beyond the Northern Ireland situation to the faithfulness and sovereignty of God in other parts of the world. Awareness of their adoptive past and the global spread of Christianity would allow evangelicals to take heart from the promise of Christ that he will build his church.

The occurrence of redemption in history raises the possibility of redemption from history. This has particular relevance in Northern Ireland where the conflict is sustained by partial and partisan understandings of the past. A flaccid attitude of 'forgive and forget' is routinely heard from well-meaning commentators while public institutions try to avoid the 'difficult issues' in an effort to create a common past.[44] There are a number of serious problems with this approach: psychologically, we cannot choose what we wish to remember; morally, the wrongs of the past may be repeated and we lose perspective on the nature of sin; theologically, it minimises how seriously God took the reality of sin by sending his son to die on the cross.[45] An evangelical understanding of history and redemption cannot ignore those issues that remain sources of pain and division. A robust understanding and outworking of the Gospel entails that we remember the wrongs done to us and learn to remember them differently. We do so because Christ suffered on our behalf. If forgiveness cost God so much, the cost for finite, frail humans is also considerable. Forgiveness is not a momentary decision but a long term, practical process that

---

[42] See the essays in Shenk (ed.), *Enlarging the story*.
[43] For example, D. H. Akenson, *God's people: covenant and land in South Africa, Israel and Ulster* (Ithaca, N.Y.: Cornell University Press, 1992).
[44] Crooke, 'Confronting a troubled history'.
[45] L. G. Jones, *Embodying forgiveness* (Belfast: ECONI, 2002), 25-6.

recognises and examines the real character and nature of the offence. This means that historians of evangelical sympathies should endeavour to produce as accurate an account of the past as possible, exercising understanding, grace, and modesty. It should not result in the production of bad history coupled with poor theological reflection with the unintentional result of rendering meaningless the heritage of violence and hurt.[46] For the past to become the past, forgiveness must occur; and for forgiveness to be psychologically, morally, and theologically satisfying, the nature and extent of the hurt caused must be adequately acknowledged and dealt with.

The issues discussed throughout this essay have implications for the broader themes of this volume. In conclusion, three in particular will be highlighted. First, there is an obvious need for any debate about evangelical identity to be informed by a sufficient understanding of the history of the movement. After all, the study of the past is fundamentally about identity.[47] An historical approach along the lines suggested in this essay would allow evangelicals to situate their particular expression of the faith within a global perspective and in that of their adoptive past. A greater sensitivity to temporal and spatial variations will lead to a better understanding of the distinctive features of the movement and the inadequacy of catch-all definitions.

Second, in attempting to understand the distinctive identity of evangelicalism it will be imperative to look beyond issues of nationality and formal theological statements. For a movement that has done so much to empower the laity, it is regrettable that until recently little scholarly attention has been devoted to how ordinary believers expressed their faith through public worship, personal devotions, and in their daily lives.[48] The tendency to focus upon the leaders and theologians of the movement distorts the true influence of evangelicalism upon society. Evangelicals have approached a host of issues in distinctive ways and it may be that in the examination of these practical outworkings of theological principle a better, more sophisticated understanding of evangelical identity may emerge. It is time to devote attention to the contribution of evangelicals to other fields of economic, cultural, social and political life. In that regard it may be worth including distinctive Irish expressions of evangelicalism in this process as it would offer a perspective on a range of issues including the

---

[46] This is the unfortunate tendency of an important study by J. D. Brewer and G. I. Higgins entitled, *Anti-Catholicism in Northern Ireland, 1600-1998: the mote and the beam* (Basingstoke: Macmillan, 1998).

[47] Noll, 'Traditional Christianity and the possibility of historical knowledge', 33.

[48] D. W. Lovegrove (ed.), *The rise of the laity in evangelical Protestantism* (London and New York: Routledge, 2002).

origins of Pentecostalism, millennialism, foreign mission, and a particular form of Ulster fundamentalism.

Finally, it is obvious that many of the principles highlighted in this essay are shared by other Christian traditions, at least with regard to historical scholarship. Evangelicals ought to be proud of their commitment to biblical truth, the person and work of Christ, and activism in all its expressions. Yet, there is a natural tendency, especially amongst evangelicals in Northern Ireland, to define ourselves in negative terms rather than by what we cherish and love. It seems that the recurring challenge is to learn to live in the relative stability of the heartland rather than to feed-off the fear and insecurity of the frontier. By adopting a global perspective and regaining a sense of our adoptive past, evangelicals should affirm their essential orthodoxy and then establish what distinguishes them from others. An evangelical approach to the past will be a vital part of this process.

CHAPTER 9

Black Evangelicals in Darkest Britain 1770s-1930s

David Killingray

Sometime in the late 1740s a black slave in New England named James Albert Ukawsaw Gronniosaw had a conversion experience. In his *Narrative* he wrote: 'The peace and serenity which filled my mind after this was wonderful, and cannot be told. I would not have changed my situations, or been anyone but myself for all the world... I seemed to possess a full assurance that my sins were forgiven me.'[1] Gronniosaw became a sailor and eventually arrived in London in the late 1760s where he was baptised in a particular Baptist church. He married a white wife and his *Narrative* concludes by describing their search for work and harsh poverty in Colchester, Norwich, and Kidderminster. His book, the first slave narrative published in Britain, appeared in 1772 the same year in which the Mansfield decision stated that a slave could not forcibly be removed from England.

Several later slave accounts contain a conversion narrative. Most early Afro-British writers – Gronniosaw, Phillis Wheatley, Olaudah Equiano, and John Marrant, were imbued with a deep evangelical faith, the latter three being 'Methodist[s] ... embracing the predestinarian Calvinism preached by George Whitefield and the clergymen associated with his aristocratic patron, the Countess of Huntingdon'.[2] Potkay and

---

[1] James Albert Ukasaw Gronniosaw, *A Narrative of the Most Remarkable Particulars In the Life of James Albert Ukawsaw Gronniosaw, An African Prince, As related by Himself* (Bath, 1770), 42. References are to the edition by Vincent Carretta (ed.), *Unchained Voices. An Anthology of Black Authors in the English-Speaking World of the 18th Century* (Lexington: University Press of Kentucky, 1996.)

[2] Carretta, *Unchained Voices*, 7. For Wheatley see Carretta, *Phillis Wheatley: Complete Writings* (London: Penguin Classics, 2001); for Olaudah Equiano see his autobiography, *The Interesting Narrative of the Life of Olaudah Equiano, or Gustavus Vassa, the African. Written by Himself* (London, 2 vols, 1789), Carretta (ed.), *Olaudah Equiano, The Interesting Narrative* (London: Penguin Classics, 1995); and John Marrant, *A Narrative of the Lord's Wonderful Dealings with John Marrant, a*

Burr argue that 'surely it was evangelicalism that gave these Africans an English voice; but, conversely, these voices gave evangelicalism a new resonance, by making it clear that each Christian self is rooted in cultural pasts that cannot and ought not to be forgotten'.[3]

A century later, in July 1878, the African American evangelist Amanda Berry Smith addressed and sang at an after meeting at the Keswick Convention and spoke at evangelistic gatherings and Bible readings in England, Scotland and Ireland.[4] Undoubtedly she was known, at least by name, to a fellow African American who had been born into slavery, Thomas L. Johnson, erstwhile worker for the YMCA in Manchester, student at Pastor's College, missionary to West Africa, and thereafter 'evangelist in England'.[5] Another ex-slave, but from Arabic slavery in the Sudan, was Salim Wilson, who also served as a missionary in Africa but then became widely known as the 'black evangelist of the north' – northern England that is, where he died in 1946.[6]

People of African Origin and Descent in Britain

Britain has had a small black population of people of African origin and descent since the mid sixteenth-century. By the mid-seventeenth century some were Christians and, by the end of the next century, a few were active as evangelists and also eager for missionary service in Africa. During the 'age of discovery' black people in increasing number came to Britain and by the 1590s formed a noticeable minority in London. With the expansion of the trans-Atlantic slave trade in the seventeenth and eighteenth centuries the black population of Britain increased, men outnumbering women.[7] Most black people lived in the

---

Black (London 4th edn, enlarged, London, 1785) in Carretta, *Unchained Voices*, 110-33.

3 Adam Potkay and Sandra Burr (eds), *Black Atlantic Writers of the Eighteenth Century: Living the New Exodus in England and the Americas* (Basingstoke: Macmillan, 1995), 3.

4 M. H. Cadbury, *The Life of Amanda Smith 'The African Sybil, the Christian saint* (Birmingham, 1916).

5 Thomas L. Johnson, *Twenty-Eight Years a Slave or the Story of my Life in Three Continents* (1882; 7th edn, Bournemouth, 1909).

6 Salim Wilson, *I Was a Slave* (London, nd. *c.*1939). Douglas H. Johnson, 'Salim Wilson: The Black Evangelist of the North', *Journal of Religion in Africa* XXI, 1 (1991), 26-41.

7 See Peter Fryer, *Staying Power. The History of Black People in Britain* (London: Pluto Press, 1984); James Walvin, *Black and White. The Negro and English Society 1555-1945* (London: Allen Lane and Penguin Press, 1973); Folarin Shyllon, *Black*

major Atlantic trading ports of London, Bristol, and Liverpool. The majority worked as servants, seamen, labourers, and artisans, with a handful being literate, the total numbering *c.*10,000 by the 1770s.[8] As Britain's overseas trade and empire expanded through the nineteenth-century, so the number of black people coming to live in the country increased. Most black immigrants came from the Caribbean and West African colonies and the Cape, plus a small number of African Americans from the United States and Canada. In addition to seamen, labourers, servants and skilled workers, there were also entertainers and those who came for commercial reasons or in pursuit of education and training.

A good number of these immigrants, especially those who were literate, had a Christian background provided by churches in the Americas or the relatively new missions in Africa. For escaped and former slaves the Christian Gospel offered a radical message of freedom. Britain provided a more liberal environment where large and enthusiastic crowds flocked to hear demands for emancipation from articulate black men and women many of whom had been slaves. Black Christians in 1846 opposed an international Evangelical Alliance (EA) to include American churches containing slave owners.[9] While some white proponents of the EA sought to demolish walls of denominational and national separation, African American abolitionists were intent on building an anti-slavery wall in Britain.[10] Many of the people of African origin and descent who came to Britain in the period 1770-1920 were profoundly Christian. Some came with an idealistic view of a Christian Britain that invariably was sorely shattered shortly after arrival. Others had their eyes set upon return to Africa either as settlers but more often as Christian agents and missionaries.[11] Britain was not only an imperial cross-roads but its Christian constituency served as a source of hope and inspiration to many black people living within the compass of the Atlantic world.

People in Britain 1555-1833 (London: Oxford University Press, 1973); and *Black Slaves in Britain* (London: Oxford University Press, 1974).

[8] Norma Myers, *Reconstructing the Black Past. Blacks in Britain 1780-1830* (London: Frank Cass, 1996), ch. 2. See further Kathy Chater, 'Úntold histories: Black people in England, 1660-1812', PhD thesis, University of London, 2007.

[9] See *Report of the Proceedings of the Conference Held at Freemasons' Hall, London, From August 19th to September 2nd Inclusive, 1846* (London, 1847), 485-7.

[10] J. R. M. Blackett, *Building an Anti-Slavery Wall: Black Americans in the Atlantic abolitionist movement, 1830-1860* (Baton Rouge: Louisiana State University Press, 1983), 97-104. See also J. F. Maclear, 'The Evangelical Alliance and the Antislavery Crusade', *Huntington Library* Quarterly, XVII, 2 (1978-9), 141-64.

[11] See David Killingray, 'The Black Atlantic Missionary Movement and Africa, 1780s-1920s', *Journal of Religion in Africa* 33, 1 (2003), 3-31.

Few researchers on the history of black people in Britain have paid much attention to the Christian constituency, which was considerable. This is clear from missionary society records and the burgeoning local and religious press of the nineteenth-century.[12] For example, a survey of the *Chatham News* and the *Chatham Observer* reveals that between 1859 and 1935 the following black evangelicals preached or conducted missions in the lower Medway area of Kent, several on more than one occasion: J.C. Taylor, Samuel Ajayi Crowther, Henry Johnson, James Quaker, T.C. John, Peter Hazely - known as the 'Apostle to the Limbas', Joseph Fuller, Isaac Dickerson, S.C. Gordon, Harold Moody, and a good number of Salvationists.[13]

The Focus of this Essay

This chapter attempts to analyse the role of a number of little-known black evangelicals in Britain's recent past, many of them found in a range of disparate sources. Besides the obvious readership, it is hoped that the chapter will be read by the following groups: those British historians largely unaware that Britain had a black population before 1950; and that small number of people who research and write about peoples of African origin and descent in Britain but who, for the most part, ignore the fact that a significant number were Christians. The wider aim of this chapter, then, is to place more firmly in the historical frame the role of a certain black Christians who helped to shape popular perceptions of black people and thus, possibly, the nature of race relations within Britain during the past 250 years.

Black British Evangelicals

Today when the spectrum of evangelicals is wider than it has been before, it is not always easy to identify and label people's religious affiliations in the past. Bebbington's four 'enduring priorities' are vital but it is not always possible to push the identification when extant texts or letters are few.[14] Of course, texts alone may not be a reliable guide to a writer's theology. The sanctified language and emphasis on divine providence, common in many late eighteenth and nineteenth century biographies, cannot always be accepted at face value. Typical is Briton Hammon, a black seaman who was captured by Native Americans, and

---

[12] See David Killingray and Joel Edwards, *Black voices: The shaping of our Christian experience* (Nottingham: IVP, 2007).

[13] I am grateful to Mr Brian Joyce for these references.

[14] David Bebbington, *The Dominance of Evangelicalism: The Age of Spurgeon and Moody* (Leicester: IVP, 2005), 21-36.

who briefly visited England in the late 1750s:

> And now, That in the Providence of that GOD, who delivered his Servant David out of the Paw of the Lion and out of the Paw of the Bear, I am freed from a long and dreadful Captivity, among worse Savages than they; And am return'd to my own Native Land, to Shew how Great Things the Lord hath done for Me; I would call upon all Men, and Say, O Magnifie the Lord with Me, and let us Exalt his Name together! – O that Men would Praise the Lord for His Goodness, and for his Wonderful Works to the Children of Men![15]

A good number of black servants (few contemporary sources call them 'slaves') brought to England were baptised, the earliest references dating from the late sixteenth-century. Baptisms were often at the whim of a white master, the ritual sometimes being a naming ceremony for entry into 'civilised' society. Certain masters hoped that adoption of Christianity would make slaves more docile and accepting of their condition. Some slaves entering Britain also entertained the false idea that embracing Christianity and being baptised would protect them from being returned to the colonies.[16] Ottobah Cugoano, wrote in his condemnation of the slave trade, that in 1772: 'I was advised by some good people to get myself baptized, that I might not be carried away and sold again'.[17] Baptism by the rites of the Church of England, even when administered for an older child or adult as was common with many blacks in Britain, did not necessarily indicate firm Christian belief. Nevertheless, it is fairly clear from Cugoano's book, in which he used many arguments based on biblical texts to denounce both the slave trade and slavery, that his was a soundly evangelical faith.[18] We can be more certain of the commitment of a 'Blackymore maide', named Francis, who, in the 1640s, is recorded at Broadmead Baptist church in

[15] Briton Hammon, *Narrative of the Uncommon Sufferings and Suprizing Deliverance of Briton Hammon, a Negro Man ...* (Boston MA, 1760), in Carretta, *Unchained Voices*, 24. Robert Desroches Jr., '"Surprizing deliverance"? Slavery and Freedom, Language and Identity in the *Narrative of Briton Hammon, "A Negro Man"*', in Vincent Carretta and Philip Gould (eds), *Genius in Bondage: Literature of the Early Black Atlantic* (Lexington: University of Kentucky Press, 2001), 153-74.

[16] An English legal ruling in 1729 stated that 'baptism doth not bestow freedom on him [the black slave] nor make any alteration in his temporal condition in these kingdoms'.

[17] Quobna Ottobah Cugoano, *Thoughts and Sentiments on the Evil and Wicked Traffic of the Slavery and Commerce of the Human Species ...* (London, 1787); Carretta (ed., *Thoughts and Sentiments* (London: Penguin edition, 1999), 7.

[18] On Cugoana see David Killingray, 'Britain, the slave trade and slavery: An African hermeneutic', *Anvil*, 24 no. 2, (2007), 121-36.

Bristol 'to be truly Convinced of Sin and to be truly Converted to ye Lord Jesus Christ'.[19] Most baptismal records are brief single lines in a parish register. Occasionally there is further evidence. In December 1793, John Newton wrote of Anthony, the 'faithful black servant' of Walter Taylor, the naval block maker at Portsmouth:

> It was a pleasing sight to see this poor man and his white wife, dedicating their child in baptism; he having renounced idolatry, and professing himself to be a believer in the one God – Father, Son, and Holy Ghost, in a confession of his faith by answering questions put to him by the Rev. Wm. Kingsbury ... .[20]

Records may have to be taken at face value but where possible it is helpful to look at lives and words, associates and attributions for firmer signs of evangelical belief and practice. For example James Ramsay, the evangelical abolitionist vicar of Teston in Kent, inscribed on the tomb of his Black servant, Nestor, that 'From his humble state he fixed his faith in Christ and looked up to heaven for happiness'.

There were, of course, those who *were* evangelicals and then ceased to be so, some indeed abandoning their early Christian faith. An interesting possible example is Theophilus Scholes, the Jamaican born evangelist and medical missionary. Scholes engaged in evangelistic work in Britain in the mid 1880s and went as a medical missionary first to Congo and then to southern Nigeria. By the late 1890s he returned to live in Britain where he wrote works critical of European colonial rule and racism.[21] Scholes is an important but neglected figure in black British history but little is known of his later life, even the date and place of his death. Undoubtedly more on his earlier evangelical life can be gleaned from the Christian press, a source largely ignored by those few scholars who have written about his political literary activities.

Significance and Context

An inevitable question that needs to be raised is the significance of the history of black people in Britain. If they are part of British history then

---

[19] Roger Hayden (ed.), *The Records of A Church of Christ in Bristol, 1640-1687* (Bristol, 1974), 101-2.

[20] John Newton, *The Aged Pilgrim's Triumph Illustrated in a Series of Letters Never Before Published by the Rev. John Newton, of St. Mary Woolnoth. Written During the Decline of Life, to Some of His Most Intimate Friends* (London, 2nd edn, 1825), 133.

[21] Scholes (c.1858-c.1940) wrote *British Empire and Alliances: Britain's Duty to Her Colonies and Subject Races* (London, 1899), and *Glimpses of the Ages, or the 'Superior' and 'Inferior' Races so-called, Discussed in the Light of Science and History* (London: John Long, 2 vols, 1905 and 1908).

why single them out and, indeed, why do this with black evangelicals? Is their role and place in the history of evangelicalism sufficiently distinctive to demand special attention? There are several issues here worth discussing.

The study of black evangelicals in the past presents certain problems. They did not form a large or cohesive group and their impact on the British church scene was decidedly limited until post 1950. Before then black evangelicals have to be seen as individuals, sometimes working with other black people, as in the anti-slavery protests of the late eighteenth and nineteenth centuries, but for the most part often acting alone. A few black evangelicals wrote about their lives or had biographies written about them. Isolated biographies of relatively obscure people offer untidy and inconclusive material for the historian to work with. Certainly some of the people concerned are major figures in other contexts. For example the west African clerical nationalist James 'Holy' Johnson spoke at the Keswick convention in 1887 and again in 1899, but more importantly, as his biographer argues, by appearing there and on other public platforms he impressed European audiences by demonstrating that Africans possessed 'virtues and merit' thought by many to be 'beyond the reach of a Negro'.[22] So in many cases the historian has to read the available sources and texts and attempt to see the significance of the figure concerned and how they fit on to the broader canvas of the evangelical British past.

As black people have been ignored or been 'invisible' to many historians, drawing them into the broader picture helps provide a more balanced account of Britain's past. There is also the question of the exceptionalism of black people in a white society. In most instances people of African origin and descent could be readily identified by their colour and labelled as outsiders. By the mid-eighteenth century, when Britain dominated the trans-Atlantic trade in African slaves, black people were widely regarded as inferior and fit only for servile employ. Black children were often treated as lap pets, as is evident from many seventeenth and eighteenth century portraits, but usually dismissed as they reached adolescence. Of course, there were other ideas current about black people: that in their primal state they were 'noble savages', or that it was good luck to encounter a black person. There is debate about the origin of racism but it had a wide and growing currency by the mid-eighteenth century. Despite the ending of slavery it gained greater weight from 'pseudo-scientific' racist ideas in the following

---

[22] Ayendele, *Holy Johnson*, 307. Evan Hopkins, *The Keswick Week 1899* (London: Life of Faith, 1899), 178.

century.[23]

Certain free blacks in eighteenth century Britain were not only Christian but also literate. The former slave Quobna Ottobah Cugoano relied heavily on Scripture to denounce the 'wickedness and evil' of the slave trade in his book published in London in 1787.[24] He also helped to prevent a slave named Green being returned to the American colonies. Another ex-slave, Olaudah Equiano, was more directly involved in the British political campaign to abolish the slave trade. His *Interesting Narrative,* published in 1789, clearly proclaimed his evangelical conversion, of how 'I saw clearly with the eye of faith, the crucified Christ bleeding on the cross on Mount Calvary ... in his humiliation, loaded and bearing my reproach, sin, and shame'.[25] The autobiography was sold by subscription – Equiano was a redoubtable and successful entrepreneur – and the list of subscribers included a good number of prominent evangelicals. On the title page Equiano proudly announced that he was 'the African' and this is accompanied by a frontispiece picture of him holding a Bible open at Acts ch. 4 v.12 which firmly stated his faith. Christian awareness and enlightenment thinking, along with his personal experience of being possessed as a chattel, all combined to make Equiano a sturdy opponent of the slave trade. This political activism was further sealed by his membership of the London Corresponding Society in the early 1790s.[26] In the next century former slaves and slaves from the United States, some being evangelicals such as James Pennington and John Sella Martin, were active in the political campaigns in Britain for abolition of U.S. slavery.[27]

Pulpits and Black Preachers

For white audiences black people represented the exotic. Black entertainers, boxers, and evangelical preachers all had a pulling power.

[23] See further Philip D. Curtin, *The Image of Africa: British Ideas and Action, 1780-1850* (London: Macmillan, 1965); Christine Bolt, *Victorian Attitudes to Race* (London: Routledge & Kegan Paul, 1971); Douglas A. Lorimer, *Colour, Class and the Victorians: English Attitudes to the Negro in the Mid-Nineteenth Century* (Leicester: Leicester University Press, 1978).

[24] Cugoano, *Thoughts and Sentiments,* Carretta edn, 10.

[25] Equiano, *Interesting Narrative,* Carretta edn, 190.

[26] James Walvin, *An African's Life. The Life and Times of Olaudah Equiano, 1745-1797* (London: Continuum, 1998), 177. Vincent Carretta, *Equiano the African: Biography of a Self-Made Man* (Athens GA: University of Georgia Press, 2005), 349-50.

[27] For Pennington and Martin see R. J. M. Blackett, *Beating Against the Barrier: The Lives of Six Nineteenth-Century Afro-Americans* (Ithaca: Cornell University Press, 1986), chs I and IV.

John Sella Martin preaching in the Weald of Kent and in East London, James Newby with a tent mission in the Scottish midlands, Alexander Crummell as curate at St Stephen's, Ipswich in the early 1850s, John Piper in his churches at East Grinstead and St Albans, and the Fisk Jubilee Singers touring the country in the 1870s, were all aware that they attracted an audience because of their colour.[28] Black women preachers and speakers in the nineteenth century, although sometimes bidden not to preach, nevertheless were helped by their colour in securing an interested audience, for example the African American Zilpha Elaw who, in 1840-6, preached in chapels up and down the country.[29]

At times black preachers deliberately played to popular stereotypical images. Dramatic presentation was a common feature of black abolitionist speakers on the anti-slavery circuits that covered the country from London's Exeter Hall via various town halls and corn exchanges to unimposing churches and chapels. The personal experience of slavery offered ready illustration for a number of black evangelical preachers, Boston King[30] in the eighteenth century, and John Jea[31] and the African Americans Zilpha Elaw, James Newby, and Thomas L. Johnson in the nineteenth century. All had graphic and gripping stories to tell that they could variously illustrate by showing and describing the shackles of slavery and the verbal sound of the master's brutal whip. The power of the Gospel could thus be seen to triumph not only over sin and degradation but also in rescuing black people from heathendom and wretched enslavement. The language employed by nineteenth century black speakers and writers frequently

---

[28] For John Sella Martin in the Weald: *Kentish Independent*, 28 March 186; James Newby: E. McHardie (Elizabeth Taylor) and Andrew Allan, *The Prodigal Continent and Her Prodigal Son and Missionary* (London, 2nd edn., 1885); Revd John Piper: *The Earthen Vessel and Gospel Herald* XLIV, (September 1888), 261-4, and (November 1888), 331-4; and the Fisk Jubilee Singers: Andrew Ward, *Dark Midnight When I Rise* (New York: Farrar, Strauss & Giroux, 2000).

[29] Zilpha Elaw, *Memoirs of the Life, Religious Experience, Ministerial Travels and Labours of Mrs. Elaw, an American Female of Colour* (London, 1846).

[30] Boston King (1760?-1802), 'Memoirs of the Life of Boston King, a Black Preacher. Written by Himself, during his Residence at Kingswood School', *The Methodist Magazine*, (March 1798).

[31] John Jea (1773-18??), *The Life, History and Unparalleled Sufferings of John Jea, The African Preacher* (Portsea, 1815); also *A Collection of Hymns, Compiled and Selected by John Jea, African Preacher of the Gospel* (Portsea, 1816). Taken from Africa as a child, Jea was converted, gained his freedom, went to sea and eventually settled in Portsea, near Portsmouth; nothing is known of him after 1817. See Graham Russell Hodges, ed., *Black Itinerants of the Gospel. The Narratives of John Jea and George White* (New York: Madison House, 1993; 2nd edn, New York: Palgrave, 2002).

drew on the imagery of Bunyan's *Pilgrim's Progress* so familiar to white audiences - of a journey of endurance in the face of much suffering, of evils fled, dangerous obstacles overcome, and arrival at the Celestial City by God's grace. The heathen black enslaved and lost without hope, burdened with chains, and then redeemed provided rich illustration for an evangelical message.

Certain black preachers directly challenged white audiences to acknowledge that the Gospel message condemned racial inequality and discrimination. J. S. Celestine Edwards from Dominica, arrived in Britain in the early 1880s and soon established a reputation as a Primitive Methodist temperance evangelist. He preached in the open air and ran regular Bible study groups for men at St Andrew's Hall, Cambridge Road, in East London. In March 1888 Edwards became editor of *Anti-Caste,* a Quaker monthly 'Devoted to the Interests of the Coloured Races', and then its successor *Fraternity.* In 1892 he was also editing *Lux,* the journal of the Christian Evidence Society, and speaking at large meetings for the Society mainly in the north and midlands. He appeared on platforms with John Kensit who also published some of his apologetic tracts refuting atheism. Ill with consumption Edwards went back to the West Indies to recover but died there aged 37 in 1894.[32] Edwards' addresses and writings robustly denounced colonial conquest and misrule, the lynching of blacks in the United States, and racial discrimination in Britain and in the Empire.

Another example of a black preacher not afraid to speak directly to white audiences on racial and political issues was Dr Harold Moody. He came from Jamaica in 1904 to study medicine at King's College London where he was active in the Christian Union. Moody married a white British wife and established a medical practice in south London. In 1931 he founded the multi-racial League of Coloured Peoples (LCP) which was led by black people. Moody saw the LCP as a Christian pan-African body, its major aim being to end the prevailing 'colour bar' in Britain and the colonies. It became more politically radical following the Italian invasion of Ethiopia in 1935. As a leading Congregationalist lay preacher, active in the Bible Society, national president of Christian Endeavour, and, towards the end of his life, chairman of the London Missionary Society, Moody had access to pulpits up and down the

---

[32] I am not sure that Edwards (1865-94) was an evangelical, or remained so; he is described as such at various times. His biography appeared in *Lux* between 15 Sept 1894 and 26 January 1895. See Jonathan Schneer, *London 1900: The Imperial Metropolis* (New Haven, CN: Yale University Press, 1999), 204-12; also Schneer's entry in the *Oxford Dictionary of National Biography* (Oxford, 2004), vol. 17, 912-13.

country.[33] His sermons and talks, invariably based on a biblical text, wove in denunciations of racial discrimination at home and overseas along with demands for a colour-blind colonial Empire. Inevitably some critical white fellow Christians accused Moody of having a chip on his shoulder; they argued that he was diluting the Christian message and promoting a social gospel. Like most whites they were slow to understand the experience of constant racial slights, being quick to criticise sensitivities that they could not appreciate.

Black preachers in Britain addressed white audiences and congregations. This could put them in a vulnerable but also an influential position. A friend of Celestine Edwards remembered:

> There was something so unique in a black man teaching Christianity, and in knowing more about it than themselves, that at first one would feel inclined to be angry and resent it, but you could not. He [Edwards] was so happy in his method, so agreeable in his manner, so witty in his argument, so choice in his illustrations, so scathing in his remarks, that he insensibly won you to his side.[34]

White ignorance about black people was profound. Harold Moody, as no doubt other black speakers, endured frequent comments on his fluency in English.[35] When black preachers were lent platforms by white patrons there was the weight of white expectation and apprehension to be endured. Black men and women were often seen as role and race models and white patrons hoped that they would be exemplary in word and deed, deportment and sensitivity. Those who met these exacting standards were applauded; those who fell short were likely to meet criticism more severe than those accorded to their white counterparts. Black preachers and evangelists had to survive in a highly critical climate where their words and actions were often closely observed. Some whites in the nineteenth century preferred black speakers to be very black, not mulatto, their blackness being a vivid demonstration that the savage children of Africa were capable of redemption and 'civilisation'. Catherine Clarkson, daughter of the great abolitionist Thomas Clarkson, wrote of the light coloured Frederick Douglass in 1846: 'I wish he were full blood black for I fear pro-slavery people will

---

[33] David Killingray, 'Race, Faith and Politics: Harold Moody and the League of Coloured Peoples', an inaugural lecture, Goldsmiths College London, 23 March 1999.

[34] Revd W. Horan, in *Lux*, (15 December 1894), 313.

[35] For example, *Bulletin* [Glasgow], (5 May 1933). 'African Native Startles Assembly' - 'Speaking faultless English, Dr. Moody told the [Baptist] Assembly...'.

attribute his preaching abilities to the white blood that is in his veins'.[36]

Relatively little is known about the impact that black preachers and speakers had on the white audiences that came in great numbers to hear them. To what extent did these exposed figures help to shape attitudes to race in Britain in the nineteenth and early twentieth centuries? Without their presence would racial antipathy have been greater? And to what extent were racially discriminatory ideas tied to social class? What were the racial ideas and attitudes of the British white working class? Certainly black anti-slavery speakers attracted crowds that included a sizeable number of working class men. And black ministers were appointed to lead congregationally organised churches in working class areas of the West Midlands, George Cousens at Cradley Heath in the late 1830s, and then at Brierley Hill, and Netherton (earlier he had been briefly at Aylesbury), and Peter Stanford at Hope Street Baptist Chapel in Birmingham in 1889.[37] Certainly more needs to be known about the life and Christian activities of the Gold-Coast businessman T. Brem Wilson who led a Pentecostal church in London from 1906 to 1929.[38]

The Variety of Black Evangelicals

There was great variety among black men and women who were evangelicals: missionaries; evangelists; poets; apologists; students; those that were quiet and also the occasional rabble-rouser. A few examples will illustrate this variety. Phillis Wheatley (*c*.1753-84), taken from Africa as a child, was the first woman of African descent to be published in the western world. She enjoyed the patronage of the Countess of Huntingdon and among her poems was one 'On the Death of the Rev. Mr. George Whitefield. 1770'.[39] Numerous young men (and a few women also) came to Britain from Africa and the Americas in order to study from the late eighteenth century. Some were brought by missionaries, the intention being that they should train and then return to Africa as agents of Christianity and 'civilisation'. In 1816 Edward Bickersteth returned from a brief visit to Sierra Leone accompanied by a young African, Simeon Wilhelm, who was anxious to be educated so

---

[36] Catherine Clarkson to Maria Weston Chapman, 2 August 1846, quoted in William S. McFeely, *Frederick Douglass* (New York, 1991), 132.

[37] David Killingray, 'Black Baptists in Britain 1640-1950', *Baptist Quarterly* 40, 2 (2003), 78.

[38] Desmond Cartwright, 'Black Pentecostal churches in Britain', *Journal of European Pentecostal Theological Association*, XXVII, 2 (2007), 128-37.

[39] *Phillis Wheatley: Complete Writings*, edited and with an introduction by Vincent Carretta (London: Penguin Books, 2001), 15.

that he could return to help evangelise his own Susu people. Wilhelm studied in Suffolk and then in London but died in 1817 aged 17. Bickersteth wrote an eighty-page *Memoir* of Wilhelm's later life which includes observations on his piety and devotion with lengthy accounts, often using words credited directly to the young man, of his faith as a Christian. Wilhelm may not have publicly evangelised, preached profound sermons or written theological texts but his young life of faith clearly impressed Bickersteth and others of his fellow evangelicals.[40]

Bickersteth's *Memoir* was in a similar vein to other contemporary tracts that used black conversion narratives, for example, Legh Richmond's *Annals of the Poor* which included the three part 'The Negro Servant'.[41] It would be interesting to know the extent to which these booklets and pamphlets were read and the impact that they had on their white readers' perceptions of black people. Samuel Barber, the son of Frances, the Black servant of Dr Johnson, is mentioned as being 'coloured', but there seems to have been little if any attempt to exploit his race for gospel purposes. He was converted around 1805 and became a Primitive Methodist local preacher on the Tunstall circuit, handing out tracts, talking of Christ to those who would listen.[42] In a slightly different category is Christopher Davies, from Barbados. He was a medical student at Aberdeen University in the 1860s and belonged to the Christian Brethren on whose behalf he evangelised in the city. He died of small-pox while treating Bavarian soldiers wounded at the battle of Sedan in 1870. At his funeral service he was described as *le bon docteur noir*.[43]

Black missionaries are also numerous but it would be helpful to know more about their activities in Britain. Again the ecclesiastical journals and press, and also church records, may indicate their movements and contacts. A few examples are given here. Thomas Birch Freeman (1809-90), who was born in Hampshire and converted as a young man, became the premier Wesleyan Methodist worker in West Africa where he spent most of his adult life. Another is Alexander Crummell (1819-98), African American, Cambridge graduate and active in mission work in three continents. Then there is the gentle African ex-slave Samuel Ajayi Crowther (*c*.1806-91), the first black Anglican

---

[40] Edward Bickersteth, *Memoirs of Simeon Wilhelm A Native of the Susoo Country, West Africa ...* (New Haven, 1819).

[41] Legh Richmond, *Annals of the Poor* (London, *c*.1809).

[42] John Smith, 'Memoir of Samuel Barber, a local preacher', *The Primitive Methodist Magazine*, X (1829), 81-90, 118-28.

[43] See obituary in *The Aberdeen Free Press*, 9 December 1870, and John D. Hargreaves, 'The Good Black Doctor: Christopher J. Davis, 1840-1870', *ASACHIB Newsletter* (London) 16 (1996), 6-7.

bishop, appointed to the Niger region in 1864, who in later life graciously bore the racial criticism and unkind treatment handed out by his fellow white missionary evangelicals. Tiyo Soga (c.1829-71) studied in Scotland, the first black South African to be ordained; he returned to work among his Xhosa people accompanied by his redoubtable white Scottish wife. Joseph Jackson Fuller (1825-1905), from Jamaica, was a long-term Baptist missionary in West Africa who retired to north London.[44] One group of missionaries in reverse were the black students who attended the Colwyn Bay Institute in North Wales established by William Hughes, a former Baptist missionary, in order to train Africans for mission from 1887-1911.[45] Many of the students preached throughout Wales, in both English and Welsh, and undoubtedly their progress could be traced from the local and the evangelical press. And there is also a rabble rouser, one John S. Orr from British Guiana, undoubtedly evangelical in theology although probably deranged – he called himself the 'Angel Gabriel', carried a brass trumpet, and was implacably hostile to Roman Catholicism which he harried at every opportunity in Scotland, in the United States, and in his own country.[46]

Several evangelists have already been mentioned. The Fisk Jubilee Singers provide a few more. The Singers, from Fisk University, Tennessee, first toured Britain in 1874-75 to raise money for the school. Each member of this original company 'was a professing Christian, one or two having been converted in connection with the religious influences that had, through the Divine blessing, ever attended the work'.[47] They sang at the Moody and Sankey revival meetings where they injected a new and dramatic form of music into evangelical worship, Moody, so it was claimed, prizing 'their services of song as an effective ally in gospel effort'.[48] Several choir members preached at various places while Isaac Dickerson, an accomplished tenor, studied theology in Edinburgh and engaged in evangelistic work in France.

[44] All of these have the imprimatur of being included in Donald M. Lewis (ed.), *Dictionary of Evangelical Biography 1730-1860*, 2 vols (Oxford: Blackwell, 1995).

[45] Ivor Wynne Jones, 'Hughes the Congo: The Rise and Fall of the Congo Institute', in Charlotte Williams, Neil Evans and Paul O'Leary (eds), *Tolerant Nation? Explaining Ethnic Diversity in Wales* (Cardiff: University of Wales Press, 2003).

[46] John Wolffe, *The Protestant Crusade in Great Britain 1829-1860* (Oxford: Clarendon Press, 1991), 194. Nathaniel Paine, *An Episode of Worcester History* (Worcester MA, 1884). Interestingly Wolffe does not identify Orr as black while Paine calls him a 'Scotchman'. Orr died in prison in his home colony in 1856.

[47] J. B. T. Marsh, *The Story of the Jubilee Singers* (London: Hodder & Stoughton, 1885 edn), 102.

[48] Marsh, *Jubilee Singers*, 96. See also *The Christian*, (3 June 1875), 9-11, 12, and (24 June 1875), 9.

The individuals mentioned above are some of the black evangelicals that can relatively easily be identified. They were literate, spoke on public platforms, and a few left some correspondence or wrote about their activities. Some were the subjects of biographies. But surely in addition there must be many more black men and women who lived in Britain, anonymous to history and unlikely ever to be known, who quietly went about their lives and practised their evangelical faith.

Conclusion

Some of the black evangelicals that have been discussed in this chapter acted in ways very little different from fellow white evangelicals. They were members of churches, preached, taught, held office of one kind or another, and lived lives of evangelical purpose. Few, however, despite the silence of their texts and the occasional disavowal, can have been unaware that they were viewed as 'different', condescended to, patronised, and were the victims of overt and covert racist comments and actions. This occurred in the public sphere as well as within the churches. A small number spoke out and argued for acceptance and equality of treatment. Those who wrote slave narratives in the late eighteenth and nineteenth centuries often argued from scriptural foundations for an end to the slave trade and to slavery. Black women evangelists such as Zilpha Elaw and Amanda Smith boldly stood for the right of women to proclaim the Gospel. Celestine Edwards, Theophilus Scholes, and Harold Moody refused to accept discrimination against black Britons or a world where white overlords ran racially structured empires. Their deepest frustration was often directed at fellow white Christians who seemed oblivious to, or simply could not understand what black people endured in a church and a wider society permeated by racist action and rhetoric. A strand running through these black protests over the last 250 years is that it was not sufficient for Christians just to have orthodox beliefs and to lead pious lives. Faith had to be demonstrated in personal relationships and in a commitment to spiritual and social change.

CHAPTER 10

Ministry, Marriage and Celibacy: The Impact of Marriage on the Public Ministry of Women in British Evangelical Churches from 1900-1959

Rachel Jordan

This paper examines the choices surrounding marriage and celibacy faced by women in full-time evangelical ministry between 1900 and 1959. It looks at the consequences of both their marriage on their work, and of their work on their opportunities to marry. The vast majority of women who entered full-time ministry during this period were single; and as a result of their decision to enter ministry many remained unmarried. A considerable proportion of those who married, married men in full-time ministry, pastors, Salvation Army officers and ministers. Of these women some were able to continue their public ministry whilst others, either choose to withdraw, or found that their circumstances dictated it. Some of the women resigned from their public ministry on marriage, in particular those who married men in secular employment. This resulted in a difficult decision for some of the women between their calling or marriage and family life; as a result many women in full-time ministry choose to remain celibate. This paper argues that although the difficulties faced by these women with regard to marriage appear discriminatory from a twenty first century view point, the church at the time was following the employment patterns prescribed for women within secular society. It was neither a radical initiator of new ways nor an ardent chauvinist in its attitude to women's employment, but was swept along by the currents that shaped the society of which it was a part.

The census of 1911 was the first to present data on married women workers, and from this and later census data it can be deduced that from 1911 to 1931 'the proportion of married women who worked remained steady at about ten percent'.[1] Although many women were

[1] J. Lewis, *Women in England 1870-1950* (New York and London: Harvester, Wheat Sheaf, 1984), 150.

called upon to work during the First World War there was a mass exodus out of paid employment, especially by married women, once the war ended. This was due to 'the intense pressure exerted by the press, government committees and trade unionists for married women to give up their jobs for the sake of returned men',[2] and the fears created by the falling birth rate. The war work of women did little in general to change the dominant ideas 'about gender roles'.[3] In the depressed 1920s and 1930s the marriage bar, which had been 'introduced in the last quarter of the nineteenth century',[4] became more significant; forcing women to resign upon marriage from many professions, in particular from teaching and the civil service.[5] In the 1930s, both working class and middle class women, frequently worked prior to marriage but 'seemed keen to abandon their jobs' on marriage.[6] It was not until the Second World War that changes began to take place in women's employment due once again to the need for women workers to replace the enlisted men.[7] Even after this there remained little change in the dominant thinking and practice within society about the conflict between marriage and employment and still in the 1950s; 'the idea that women should not necessarily have to choose between paid work on the one hand and unpaid work and motherhood on the other was potentially radical.'[8]

The Salvation Army

Within the Salvation Army officers were only to marry fellow officers. This was to ensure that the ministry of both continued. The reality was all too often that once married, the wife ended up doing all the domestic chores and did not have the time or opportunity to develop her public ministry. Working class women with a small family budget could not afford help in the home, or, before the 1940s, domestic gadgetry to

---

[2] Lewis, *Women in England*, 151.

[3] M. Pugh, *The March of the Women. A Revisionist Analysis of the Campaign for Women's Suffrage* (Oxford: Oxford University Press, 2000), 286.

[4] J. Humphries, 'Women and paid work', in J. Purvis (ed.) *Women's History; Britain 1850-1945; An Introduction* (London: UCL Press 1995), 100.

[5] H. L. Smith, *British Feminism in the Twentieth Century* (Aldershot: Edward Elgar, 1990), 53.

[6] M. Pugh, 'Domesticity and the Decline of Feminism, 1930-1950', in H. L. Smith (ed.), *British Feminism in the Twentieth Century* (Aldershot: Edward Elgar, 1990), 152.

[7] Pugh, 'The Decline of Feminism', 158.

[8] J. Lewis, 'Mydral, Klein, Women's Two Roles and Postwar Feminism 1945-1960', in H. L. Smith (ed.), *British Feminism in the Twentieth Century* (Aldershot: Edward Elgar, 1990), 167.

alleviate the arduous and monotonous tasks of housework.[9] Added to this there was the slow acceptance and availability of birth control.[10] The life of an officer wife for much of this period was not an easy one.

The problem of the officer wives was recognised by those in command in the Salvation Army. In the staff review in 1922 the following article discussed their predicament;

> In some cases, doubtless, the fact that a Staff Officer's wife is not actively employed is due to the limitations imposed by impaired health, or because the claims of home and family prevent her undertaking any large responsibility. To those who before marriage held commands of their own, or even since marriage were able, in more favourable circumstances, to take a prominent part in the work of their husband's command, this is a very considerable trial.[11]

In another article in 1931 the place of women in the Salvation Army is under scrutiny and rather than seeing the limitations of marriage as a trial for the women, their choice to marry is blamed for their lack of professional progress. In 1944 the issue had not gone away as is explained in the following:

> In some territories there is an increasing inclination for the wife, especially if she has children, to sit in the Hall during the public meetings. ....It becomes easy to an Officer-wife who is permitted to slip out of the position of Officership to lose desire, and in time the ability to take her rightful place... there are others who do little more than keep house.[12]

Yet again the women are seen as the problem but it is never suggested that a radical rearrangement of the domestic work between officer husband and officer wife would free the women to be involved in the public work of the Army.

The Salvation Army's ideal of a ministry partnership where both the husband and the wife led in the work and preached was born and put into practice in the late nineteenth century by Catherine and William Booth.[13] Yet it was not to undermine the role of the wife as the key

---

[9] For a good description of the drudgery of domestic work for the average 1930's/1940's housewife see M. Forster, *Hidden lives* (London: Penguin, 1996) A good example is wash day described on p. 99.

[10] See S. Bruley, *Women in Britain since 1900* (Basingstoke: Macmillan, 1999), 87.

[11] *The Staff Review* (London: Salvation Army, 1922), 111.

[12] Mrs General Carpenter, 'Women's Sphere and influence in the Salvation Army' (A paper given at the commissioners' conference: Salvation Army, 1944), 10.

[13] R. J. Green, *Catherine Booth; A Biography of the Cofounder of the Salvation Army* (Grand Rapids, Michigan: 1996).

domestic overseer, these dual roles sometimes stretched Catherine to her limits.[14] Catherine achieved a public ministry and yet the domestic duties of the home were not shared between her and William.[15] Those that followed her were mostly working class women on a budget that precluded paid help and therefore to fulfill their domestic role they often had to sacrifice their public one.[16] They also didn't all have husbands as willing as William to encourage them in their public preaching role. By the 1920s the prevalent idea in middle and working class society, that married women should retire from their public work and concentrate on the home, appears to have been stronger than the Salvation Army's original intention of public ministry for women.

Other Salvation Army women were single and therefore continued in public ministry for the whole of their working lives but had to remain celibate. For them it was often a choice between ministry and marriage. From the 1905 to 1955 women made up on average 67% of the commissioned cadets,[17] and as marriage to a non-officer meant resignation, a proportion of the women faced a difficult decision between marriage or their ministry, not unlike the choice faced by the working women of the day between marriage or their career.

The Elim Church

Husband and wife preaching partnerships were a feature of the early Pentecostal churches. Mr and Mrs George Kingston, who led the burgeoning Pentecostal work in the South East of Essex, planted several churches that were later joined to the Elim Alliance; they were both preachers and pastors who frequently spoke at Elim conventions from 1921.[18] They are even listed as the pastors of two separate churches in the *Elim Evangel*.

The freedom Mrs George Kingston enjoyed to pastor a church was also shared by other women in the new Elim Evangelistic band. This band of evangelists led by George Jeffreys had female evangelists as members from its early days.[19] These women functioned as evangelists at missions, and as pastors of the new churches. From this group of evangelists and pastors many ministry partnerships of husband and wife were formed. Two noticeable examples were Miss Streight and

---

[14] Green, *Catherine Booth*, 95.

[15] A.M. Eason, *Women in God's Army: Gender and Equality in the early Salvation Army* (Ontario: Wilfred Laurier University Press, 2003), 55.

[16] Eason, *Women in God's Army*, 55.

[17] Figures taken from the records at the Salvation Army Heritage Centre.

[18] *The Elim Evangel*,2.5 (December, 1921), i.

[19] Elim Evangelistic Band Minute Book, 1915 (Unpublished).

Miss Adams, who both married prominent pastors,[20] Miss Streight after fifteen years of ministry as a single woman and Miss Adams after seven. In both cases they continued in full-time public ministry after marriage. A few married Elim women preachers appear on the lists of convention speakers,[21] and their husbands are not listed or mentioned as preachers or pastors. It was rare, but married women could have a preaching ministry within the Elim church independently of their husbands.

The success of married women in public ministry was determined by two factors, the attitude of their husbands and whether or not they had children. For example Miss Edwards, another full time Elim pastor evangelist who married Pastor Arthur Gorton, in 1934, praised her husband for actively encouraging her to continue in public ministry. She said;

> Arthur encouraged me. He deserves a lot of praise because if you had married a man who didn't want you to preach, I probably wouldn't have had the experience that I've had but he always used to encourage me. So we were together in the pulpit, ...right up until we retired.[22]

If a couple had children the woman's domestic load increased often forcing her to retire from active ministry at least for a time. Mrs Gorton explained this clearly as follows; 'We've never had any children, and because of me not having any children I kept up the ministry with Arthur.'[23] Some women did obviously manage to marry, have children and preach, for example Mrs Tweed, an evangelist who married a pastor, had two daughters and continued to be active in ministry.[24] Other women were free to minister because they were older and their children had grown up, for example Mrs George Kingston.

This freedom was greatest in the initial years of the movement but by the mid 1930s women were not entering into the ministry due to new regulations, only men were being ordained. As explained by Desmond Cartwright:

> As the emerging groups developed their organisational structures, women were given a lesser role. Behind the scenes some of them continued to

20 *The Elim Evangel*, 7.1 (January, 1926), 11.

21 For example Mrs Crisp a speaker at various events, including the Belfast Christmas Convention in 1919, see The Elim Evangel, 1.2 (March 1920), 24-26.

22 Mrs Gorton, interviewed on 4 April 2001.

23 Mrs Gorton, interviewed on 21 November 2000.

24 For example she is listed as leading a waiting meeting with her husband in 1926 see, *The Elim Evangel*,7.17 (September, 1926), 200.

> exert considerable influence but in public at least, they assumed a more subservient position.[25]

This not only conforms to the pattern often seen in history with the institutionalisation of new denominations limiting the public role of women, but also to the trends within society. Some of the original women preachers did continue in active ministry throughout this period, like Mrs Gorton, but new ministers were male.

The Assemblies of God

Desmond Cartwright's observation is relevant for the British Pentecostal movement as a whole. The Assemblies of God as the Elim church had notable women preachers and pastors in its early years. In the 1928 list of associated churches and presbyters out of the one hundred churches listed seven have women as presbyters.[26] Not a very high proportion but it was permissible for a woman to lead an Assemblies of God Church within England. There are no women mentioned as presbyters of any churches in Wales, Ireland or Scotland. Of the seven women listed three were married and four single. Therefore, it was possible for a married woman to hold a position as a pastor in an Assemblies of God church independently of her husband in a similar way to Mrs George Kingston. Not all the women preachers, within the assemblies of God, were pastors some were evangelists. This group included both men and women, who were itinerant preachers. Out of a list of seventeen recognised evangelists in 1929, five were women, of whom three were married and two single.[27] Also, as in the Elim church, the opportunity existed within the Assemblies of God for women to be preachers independently of their husbands. One married evangelist who had a very prominent role was Mrs Wall. Her husband and son often worked with her and were even sometimes listed as 'her assistants'[28] rather than *vice versa*.

During the early years of the Pentecostal movement a small group of notable women had considerable freedom in the two branches of the Pentecostal church in Britain but with denominational institutionalisation and the rising prominence in society of conservative views concerning women's public roles these women were not followed

---

[25] D. Cartwright, 'Your daughters shall prophesy: The contribution of Women in early Pentecostalism' (unpublished paper given at the society for Pentecostal Studies Conference, Gaithersburg, Maryland, 15 November 1985).

[26] *Redemption Tidings* 4.7 (July, 1928), 15.

[27] *Redemption Tidings* 5.9 (September 1929), 14.

[28] *Redemption Tidings* 5.11 (November ,1929), 20.

by a second generation.

The Methodist and Baptist Deaconess Orders

For many of the women entering into full-time ministry there was no option of marriage. The deaconess orders made it clear to their new recruits that they were dedicating themselves to a celibate life.[29] The Methodist deaconesses had to sign on entry into the order that they were 'free for this work, from all home duties and ties, and from any matrimonial engagement'.[30] For many this must have been a difficult choice, they joined the order in the years when most women were likely to choose to marry. If a Methodist deaconess decided to marry she would have to resign from the order and the same rule applied within the Baptist Order. Deaconesses were left with an agonizing choice, ministry or marriage.

One Baptist deaconess married when she retired and explained that it was still quite a struggle to overcome her qualms because celibacy had been 'engrained' in her.[31] If deaconesses choose to resign and marry they could face disapproval, this is seen in the way their resignations were described by others, 'and then she married and that was that,'[32]or 'she only lasted a few years and then she married'.[33] Yet the disapproval appears to have relaxed over time and some of the later deaconesses married after only a few years in ministry.[34] What to do with those Baptist deaconesses who did marry but still felt part of the order was a difficult question and in 1941 the idea of an associate membership list was suggested. This would mean that on marriage deaconesses might be able to keep in touch with the order by coming to the conference but would no longer be listed as official deaconesses. It wasn't until 1952 that a decision was made and this scheme of associate membership was introduced. Resignation on marriage was still being discussed in 1955, and in 1957 two women were given special permission to continue as full status deaconesses on marriage, for an extra year.[35] The crucial factor like the other women in ministry appeared to be that of children, one Baptist deaconess married when she was fifty, she married a pastor and continued as an active deaconess until her retirement. Those that

---

[29] Blanche Baker, interviewed on 17 January 2002.

[30] Form for entry into the order. (no date on form).

[31] Mabel Ingram, interviewed by R. Goldbourne on 23 May 2000.

[32] Sister Winifred Waller interviewed by the Revd V. Lassatter on 21 January 1998.

[33] Mabel Ingram interviewed by R. Goldbourne on 23 May 2000.

[34] Mabel Ingram, interviewed by R. Goldbourne on 23 May 2000.

[35] Notes from the Deaconess Annual Business Meeting, (22 October 1957).

married at a younger age tended to resign from the order. This did not necessarily mean that the women retired from ministry; a number married Baptist pastors and continued in some public ministry as the Pastor's wife. It was not until 1967 that the rule of resignation on marriage was lifted from the Baptist order.[36]

A detailed questionnaire was compiled in 1947 for the World Council of churches on 'the life and work of women in the church.' The responses sent in summarising the position of the Methodist church were focussed around the issue of married women. It states that the only real objection within the Methodist church to ordaining women was the difficulty of what to do when they married;

> There is no Theological or Biblical difficulty in women being ordained, it is all connected with administration and the question as to whether they should 'retire' or 'resign' on marriage.[37]

It goes on to explain that this question was one that also troubled the Wesley deaconess order as well as the Methodist Missionary Society. Secular society's precedent of resignation on marriage for professional women was a greater issue for the Methodist churches than their own interpretation of the Bible or their own traditions.

The Methodist and Baptist deaconesses therefore remained single to enable them to pursue their calling; their career. It was not unlike the dilemma faced by other women in society as a whole. Most women of this period were faced with the same choice, 'between either marriage and motherhood, or a career'.[38] It was not that the church was being unreasonably harsh in expecting the resignation of deaconesses upon marriage it was simply following a precedent of society.

The Unofficial Stories

The history of the women who left the deaconess orders to marry is for the most part left unrecorded. Yet resignation on marriage did not necessarily mean the end of a woman's ministry. The story of a Joyful News Evangelist, whose recorded ministry began at the close of the nineteenth century, illustrates this point. The Joyful News Mission trained and paid lay evangelists, in particular from working class

[36] J. H. Y. Briggs, 'She Preachers, Widows and other Women: The Feminine dimension in Baptist Life since 1600', *Baptist Quarterly*, 31.7 (July, 1986), 346.

[37] *The Scottish Report on the Life and Work of Women in the Church*, (Compiled in response to a questionnaire for the World Council of Churches, February 1947), 35.

[38] Lewis, 'Women's Two Roles', 167.

Methodism to work both on the foreign mission field and in Britain.[39] In 1891 the mission opened its doors to women. In 1894 Mary Ann Dixon became a Joyful News Evangelist,[40] but in 1897 she had to leave the work when she married. This choice is only reflected officially in her disappearance from all records of the mission from 1897 onwards.[41] Ordinarily the story of her ministry would have stopped at this junction yet due to her family keeping her history it is clear that Mary Ann Hills (nee Dixon) far from ended her ministry.[42] She married a postman called Frank Hills on Boxing Day in 1897. They lived in Walkern near Stevenage (where Mary Ann had first met Frank when conducting a mission at the Wesleyan Methodist Chapel in 1895). Here Mary Ann began to work alongside the minister at the local Methodist Chapel, using her evangelistic and teaching gifts. Yet when problems arose in the Methodist chapel she and Frank left with a devoted following and set up an independent chapel in 1907/8. Frank was not a natural leader and although he worked hard to renovate their new premises it was Mary Ann who was the pastor and superintendent of the new 'Walkern Mission' from 1908 till her death in 1946. Statistically she is a woman who left the ministry on marriage but that could not be further from the truth. The unofficial work of women like Mary Ann Hills is hard to quantify with no data it can only be imagined that some of the women who resigned on marriage from official ministry, like her, continued unofficially for many years but this cannot be proved.

Conclusion

The women who followed their calling into full-time ministry in Britain during this period often remained single as a consequence. Within the Salvation Army from the 1930s onwards many could not marry fellow officers due to the unequal numbers of male and female officers, leaving them with an awkward choice between marriage and ministry. Those that did marry fellow officers, although they were supposed to be equal partners with their husbands often ended up following the patterns of society in fulfilling domestic responsibilities at the cost of their public ones. Celibacy was a rule within the Methodist and Baptist deaconess orders, the women were once again forced to choose between their ministry or marriage. This was not unlike many women in secular employment who faced the same sort of choice between a career or

---

39 E. Champness, *The Life Story of Thomas Champness*, (C. H. Kelly, London, 1907).

40 Joyful News (20 Sept 1894). The first recorded entry of Mary Ann Dixon.

41 Joyful News (1 April 1897). The last recorded entry of Mary Ann Dixon.

42 B. Hills, 'Mary Ann Hills (nee Dixon) 1864-1946: some brief notes on her background, life and work' (unpublished work written by family member).

marriage especially after the introduction of the marriage bar. The Elim Church and the Assemblies of God offered women the opportunity to marry and continue in ministry if they married an understanding pastor. Yet these partnerships did not lead to a radical re-arrangement of domestic responsibilities, and the women who did not have children, or whose children had grown up, were obviously freer to exercise their public gifts. The freedom for a married woman to minister was significant and these women are therefore notable exceptions but still only few found this freedom and no second generation followed. Overall the patterns of married women's employment in public ministry in the denominations studied from 1900 to 1959 mirrored those of the surrounding dominant culture.

CHAPTER 11

Making Men Men: Masculinity and Contemporary Evangelical Identity

Kristin Aune

The significance of men and masculinity to evangelical identity would surely be apparent to an outsider after visiting a few evangelical churches. Men constitute the vast majority of church leaders, yet the minority of members. They preach more frequently than women, lead more services and make most decisions about church strategy and function. Yet, at the grassroots levels of the church, the day-to-day less public activities that keep the community working – praying, preparing refreshments, running the crèche, writing the newsletter – are generally women's domains. Although men are in short supply in the church's social life, they are esteemed because of the public positions of influence they tend to hold.

But masculinity is about more than being (genetically, hormonally, physically etc.)[1] male, as sociologists, psychologists, anthropologists and historians demonstrate. From the things that men do, the roles they play, the characteristics they are encouraged to develop, the interactions they choose to participate in and the historical ideas that have developed around them, come beliefs about and practices of masculinity. Leading a church, preaching, playing with their sons, earning more money than their wife and watching football matches

---

[1] These 'biological' markers of sex are not straightforward either. There is some evidence that the notion of two diametrically opposite male and female sexes is a recent development, dating from the late eighteenth century. See Thomas Laqueur, *Making Sex: Body and Gender from the Greeks to Freud* (Cambridge, MA: Harvard University Press, 1990). Intersex conditions pose a further challenge to the sex binary recent western cultures have become so accustomed to. See Anne Fausto-Sterling, *Sexing the Body: Gender Politics and the Construction of Sexuality* (New York: Basic Books, 2000). And as poststructuralist theorist Judith Butler reminds us, the phenomenon of sex is a linguistic construct that bodies respond to: we create ourselves as male and female in obedience to cultural discourses about sex and gender. See Judith Butler, *Gender Trouble: Feminism and the Subversion of Identity* (London and New York: Routledge, 1990).

with male friends become, in this context, markers of masculinity.

One of the questions facing evangelical Christians is how far their expressions of masculinity should reflect those of their non- or less religious peers. What does 'godly manhood' look like? Should Christians adopt their culture's behaviours in order to be 'relevant' and gain opportunities to evangelise? Should they aim for a totally 'counter-cultural' masculinity? These are difficult questions that are only sometimes answered, are answered in diverse ways, or that find implicit responses in the manifestations of masculinity and humanity Christians end up, by default, portraying to others. Whatever forms of masculinity result are all created, constructed, performed or effortlessly imitated; they may feel natural, but they are not.

This makes masculinity an important topic of investigation for those interested in evangelical identities, whether past, present or future. Historically in the West, the development of evangelical identity has been closely tied to middle-class ideas about gender that dominated in the late eighteenth and nineteenth centuries.[2] Industrialising countries underwent profound changes, as work moved from the household (where all were involved, including children) out into what became known as the public sphere. The separation of society into the male, public workplace and the private female sphere of domesticity encouraged the development of opposite notions of gender.[3] If the family could manage financially without a second wage, a feat

---

[2] Unless otherwise stated, sources for the material in this and the following paragraph include: Deborah M. Valenze, *Prophetic Sons and Daughters: Female Preaching and Popular Religion in Industrial England* (Princeton, NJ: Princeton University Press, 1985); Leonore Davidoff and Catherine Hall, *Family Fortunes: Men and Women of the English Middle Class, 1780-1850* (London: Hutchinson Education, 1987); Mary Poovey, *Uneven Developments: The Ideological Work of Gender in Mid-Victorian England* (Chicago: The University of Chicago Press, 1988); Wally Seccombe, *A Millennium of Family Change: Feudalism to Capitalism in Northwestern Europe* (London and New York: Verso, 1992); Wally Seccombe, *Weathering the Storm: Working-Class Families from the Industrial Revolution to the Fertility Decline* (London and New York: Verso, 1993); Anna Clark, *The Struggle for the Breeches: Gender and the Making of the British Working Class* (Berkeley, CA: University of California, 1995); Callum G. Brown, *The Death of Christian Britain: Understanding Secularisation 1800-2000* (London and New York: Routledge, 2001); and Rosemary Radford Ruether, *Christianity and the Making of the Modern Family* (London: SCM Press, 2001), 83-106.

[3] This 'separate spheres' thesis is challenged by some historians. See Robert B. Shoemaker, *Gender in English Society, 1650-1850: The Emergence of Separate Spheres?* (Harlow: Addison Wesley Longman, 1998) and Amanda Vickery, 'Historiographical Review: Golden Age to Separate Spheres? A Review of the Categories and Chronology of English Women's History', *Historical Journal*, 36.2 (1993), 383-414.

impossible for many working-class families, women's role shifted to domesticity and childcare in the home. As 'angels in the house' they were expected to provide a harmonious, supportive environment for their husbands to return to at the end of the day. Men, meanwhile, took on the role of breadwinner and household head, carrying the weight of responsibility for providing for and leading their wives and children. The evangelical middle class took a leading role in promoting these gendered ideals and practices, claiming them as biblical mandates for social stability.

These roles carried through to the church. Since the church was regarded as a reflection of the family, it was judged proper for its leaders to be male. Priests, preachers and ministers were almost exclusively men. The new opportunities the eighteenth-century Evangelical Revival produced for (particularly working-class) women as preachers in dissenting groups like Methodism fell away in the nineteenth century as cottage religion became institutionalised and support for separate spheres gathered momentum. The belief that Christians were 'all one in Christ Jesus' did provide a 'base line' of spiritual equality between women and men.[4] But though laywomen gained new opportunities for church work that was not simply domestic, these roles – visiting the sick, teaching children in Sunday schools, writing and informal evangelism – often accorded with separate spheres conceptions of nurturing, maternal femininity. The feminisation of piety that occurred alongside the separation of the spheres contributed to the church's declining ability to appeal to men, a legacy that remains today. While there is surprisingly little data on the gender dimension of church membership, Clive Field's research on attendance among Nonconformists suggests that as industrialization and separate spheres advanced, the gender disparity became more exaggerated. Field reveals a female-majority in membership between 1750 and 1800, rising to a two-thirds majority after 1800; between 1826 and 1950 this two-thirds majority barely changed.[5] By endorsing separate spheres evangelicals in effect signalled acceptance of the inevitable lower male church attendance. At various times since then attempts have been made to reclaim Christianity as 'manly' through promoting male authority based on a Calvinist theology of 'God's created order' of male leadership and female submission.[6] Indeed, as

[4] Davidoff and Hall, *Family Fortunes*, 107.

[5] Clive D. Field, 'Adam and Eve: Gender in English Free Church Constituency', *Journal of Ecclesiastical History* 44.1 (1993), 63-79.

[6] This strategy is probably self-defeating. Asserting men's public, work-oriented identity almost inevitably pushes men away from the more private sphere of the church.

historian Margaret Lamberts Bendroth has shown,[7] this emphasis on male leadership has continued to be an important feature of fundamentalism. Thus from their origins, masculinity has been of great significance to evangelicals.

But what about evangelicals today? To be sure, evangelicals' views about gender are now more diverse. Evangelicals occupy a spectrum of gendered beliefs and practices that range from the conservative to the radical – often in the same denomination, congregation or even family. Although evangelicals vary, it is possible for researchers to conduct studies that reveal valuable and useful findings. Some researchers conduct quantitative research to enable them to formulate statistics and generalisations about what evangelicals think and do. From this research we have learned, for example, that British church leaders are more positively than negatively disposed towards women in leadership,[8] even if this support for female leaders is not reflected in the actual numbers of women who attain leadership positions.[9] Other researchers conduct qualitative, in-depth studies of particular evangelical groups, uncovering not only what these groups believe and do, but also how what they say matches (or does not match) what they actually do.[10]

---

[7] Margaret Lamberts Bendroth, *Fundamentalism and Gender, 1875 to the Present* (New Haven and London: Yale University Press, 1993). See also Betty A. DeBerg, *Ungodly Women: Gender and the First Wave of American Fundamentalism* (Minneapolis, MN: Fortress Press, 1990).

[8] Research reported by Heather Wraight involved 478 members of the Christian Research association (not all evangelical). Nearly half (47%) reported enjoying working with or for a woman or women working for them. A similar number were not bothered either way. 87% agreed with the statement 'I welcome women in leadership and value their contribution' and 61% with 'The church has been influenced by society to undervalue the gifts of women', indicating strong support for women's ministry. Furthermore, 68% disagreed with the statement 'Women can be church leaders, just so long as they are subordinate to men,' and 76% with 'The Bible makes it clear that women should never be church leaders'. See Heather Wraight, *Eve's Glue: The Role Women Play in Holding the Church Together* (Carlisle: Paternoster, 2001), 141-43.

[9] In 2000, only a tenth (10.4%) of Christian ministers were female. Moreover, the denominations containing the lower percentages of female ministers were often evangelical, meaning that the proportion of female evangelical ministers is closer to 5%: in 2000 8.1% of New Church ministers were female, 6.1% of Pentecostal, 4.6% of Baptist and 2.6% of Independent ministers. See Peter Brierley (ed.), *UK Christian Handbook: Religious Trends No.3 2002/2003* (London: Christian Research, 2001), 2.21.

[10] Qualitative analyses of the gendered nature of contemporary British evangelicalism include: Myfanwy Franks, *Women and Revivalism in the West: Choosing 'Fundamentalism' in a Liberal Democracy* (Basingstoke: Palgrave

Masculinity in New Frontiers International

This essay is based on an in-depth qualitative study of beliefs and practices of gender in the New Frontiers International movement (NFI).[11] With 28,000 members in approaching 250 UK churches, NFI is the largest surviving network of what was labelled the House Church movement or Restorationism and are now more often called New Churches.[12] Worldwide, nearly 500 NFI churches exist.[13]

The House Church movement began in the 1970s in the UK as small groups meeting in homes and grew rapidly through the 1980s. Its theological roots lie in the nineteenth-century Brethren movement and Catholic Apostolic Church, and in twentieth-century Classical Pentecostalism. Like earlier Pentecostals, NFI see being 'born again' as essential and practice believers' baptism in water and 'of the Holy Spirit' and spiritual gifts such as tongues-speaking, a feature they share with the charismatic movement.

Three features, which largely remain within NFI, distinguished the House Churches from their Pentecostal forerunners. First, they believed denominations should not exist and should be replaced by the Church or 'kingdom'. The second feature is their ecclesiology. They aimed to 'restore the church' to what they perceive as the New Testament pattern for church life. This led Andrew Walker to name them 'Restorationists.'[14] Their literal interpretation of the Bible shares similarities with fundamentalism. In their leadership structure men known as apostles, around whom house churches gathered, oversee networks of churches, which are led by elders. The third is the (sometimes criticised) doctrine of discipleship or 'shepherding', in which Christians submit themselves to leaders' guidance and authority.[15]

NFI's mission is five-fold: 'Restore the Church; Make Disciples; Train

---

Macmillan, 2001); Sandra M. Baillie, *Evangelical Women in Belfast: Imprisoned or Empowered?* (Basingstoke: Palgrave Macmillan, 2002); and Fran Porter, *Changing Women, Changing Worlds: Evangelical Women in Church, Community and Politics* (Belfast: Blackstaff Press, 2002).

[11] In late 2002, a year after I finished my research, NFI dropped 'International', becoming Newfrontiers. Because the material to which I refer dates from before this change, and because 'NFI' has remained common parlance for the network, I do not reflect this name change in this essay.

[12] Andrew Walker, 'Crossing the Restorationist Rubicon: From House Church to New Church', in Martyn Percy and Ian Jones (eds), Fundamentalism, Church and Society (London: SPCK, 2002).

[13] Figures obtained from NFI in June 2004.

[14] Andrew Walker, *Restoring the Kingdom: The Radical Christianity of the House Church Movement* (Guildford: Eagle, rev. edn, 1998).

[15] Walker, *Restoring the Kingdom*.

Leaders; Plant Churches; Reach the Nations.'[16] A large church-planting program exists, with groups of NFI Christians moving, sometimes across the country, to begin new congregations. Church planting accounts for just under half of NFI's continued growth, a rate of growth that sets it apart from other New Church networks.[17] 'House' or 'cell' groups of around a dozen people which meet weekly to pray, study the Bible, sing and develop close friendships have always been key within NFI in addition to Sunday services.[18]

As well as studying the publications and public events of the movement as a whole, I paid close attention to one NFI congregation who, to preserve their confidentiality and anonymity, I gave the pseudonym Westside. My primary research methods were participant observation over a fifteen-month period and follow-up visits and structured interviews[19] with twenty members of the congregation. These methods were augmented by detailed study of published literature and audiotaped talks from NFI's yearly summer festival Stoneleigh Bible Week, which I attended for a day in 2000 and a week in 2001. I also attended two two-day leaders Prayer and Fasting events, where I interviewed twenty leaders, and attended about thirty services at other NFI congregations in various parts of the UK. This essay concentrates particularly on NFI's public discourse about masculinity.

Three months into my fieldwork at Westside, a friend of Westside's leader Chris (also a pseudonym) was visiting and Chris introduced him to me. 'Kristin's doing her Ph.D. on the role of women in New Frontiers,' Chris explained. Wanting to correct this perception that 'gender' meant 'women', I added, 'I'm doing it on gender, so men as well.' Chris seemed surprised. 'Men?' he questioned, 'What do you want to know about men? Whether they're proper men?'

Chris' response generated many questions for me. What did he mean by 'proper men'? Was there a standard, an ideal, of masculinity which he believed men should live up to? If so, what did it consist of? And did

---

[16] www.newfrontiers.xtn.org/our-mission/category_index.php?id=3 (accessed 9 March 2004).

[17] The rest of NFI's churches are 'adopted' – that is, NFI take on oversight of already-existing congregations. See Colin Baron, 'Church Planting', NFI Magazine 9 (2000), 22.

[18] For more information about the history of NFI see founder Terry Virgo's (2001) autobiography, especially chapter 27 which lists areas where NFI differ from some evangelical churches.

[19] Participant observation occurs when researchers enter and participate in the social world of those they are studying (to a lesser or greater extent depending on the access they negotiate) with the aim of understanding things from their perspective and rendering that perspective intelligible to an outside audience. In structured interviews the same questions are asked to each participant.

others in NFI and Westside share that ideal? What lay behind his suggestion that I was interested in how 'proper' men in Westside were? Did he fear that they would not measure up?

In NFI masculinity is important. NFI possess a clear conception that men are not simply people: they are men. Their masculinity has meanings attached to it. It is considered natural, existing in a raw state through the male body and its desires and inclinations. But it is also to be made, improved, constructed under the guidance of God, the Bible and through social relations with other Christians. The making of masculinity in NFI is also done in (conscious and unconscious) negotiation with British culture; it feeds off, takes on, rejects and transforms popular notions of masculinity in contemporary, and historical, British society. Masculinity in NFI may be understood with reference to this culture.

Masculinity is a central arena where not only gender but also NFI's identity as a movement is displayed. This is so, I suggest, because of their social and historical context. The House Church movement from which NFI grew began at a time of social upheaval in which it became necessary to make decisions about where to place allegiance. The counter-cultural expressive, left-wing, environmentalist, anti-nuclear, sexual liberationist, anti-racist and feminist movements of the 1960s and 1970s had issued profound challenges to British structures and traditions. Although many churches associated with both the Charismatic Renewal and the developing House Church movement mirrored the counter-culture stylistically, promoting free expression in worship, tongues-speaking, prophesying and praying for healing, House Church leaders perceived the counter-culture as a threat to the family and society.

One notable occasion accelerated the House Churches' emergence and, I suggest, crystallised their developing pro-family, anti-feminist stance. The 1971 and 1972 London Festivals of Light were mass demonstrations against the 'permissive society' organised by a House Church leader and supported by figures including Mary Whitehouse. Closely linked to the emergence of a political 'New Right' that vocally opposed the sexual revolutionaries and the developing women's liberation movement, the Festival was the first event to assemble and make visible, to each other and outsiders, the substantial numbers of House Church members.[20]

At this time of polarisation between the counter-culture and their more conservative opponents, the House Church attendees who later became NFI became located within the developing New Right backlash against feminism (which the New Right tended to conflate with sexual

---

[20] Walker, *Restoring the Kingdom*, 66-86.

liberationism). Various scholars have traced this backlash through the 1970s to the 1980s and beyond.[21] As feminism gathered pace during the 1970s, opposition strengthened. One strand of the backlash involved the reinstatement of a more 'traditional' masculinity against the new egalitarian and anti-sexist forms of masculinity that women's liberationists had advocated. The idea that masculinity was 'in crisis' was evoked to justify this return to tradition.[22]

At its foundation in the 1970s and again as part of a recent backlash against evangelical feminism[23] visible in organisations like the Council on Biblical Manhood and Womanhood and Reform, NFI concentrated on 'restoring' an allegedly lost masculinity. Two particular passages, from writings by John Piper (co-editor of backlash text *Recovering Biblical Manhood and Womanhood*) and evangelical psychiatrist John White, appear several times in NFI's books, magazines and sermons and were recounted to me as I talked with NFI members and leaders. A third, which I also consider key to NFI's view of masculinity, comes from a talk by NFI's David Holden in a men's seminar:

> If I were to put my finger on one devastating sin today, it would not be the so-called women's movement, but lack of spiritual leadership by men at home and in the church. Satan has achieved an amazing tactical victory by disseminating the notion that the summons for male leadership is born of pride and fallenness, when in fact pride is precisely what prevents spiritual leadership. The spiritual aimlessness and weakness and lethargy and loss of nerve among men is the major issue, not the upsurge of interest in women's ministries.[24]

---

[21] Susan Faludi, *Backlash: The Undeclared War Against Women* (London: Chatto and Windus, 1992); Martin Durham, *Sex and Politics: The Family and Morality in the Thatcher Years* (Basingstoke: Macmillan Education, 1991); Ann Oakley and Juliet Mitchell (eds), *Who's Afraid of Feminism? Seeing through the Backlash* (London: Hamish Hamilton, 1997); Sylvia Walby, '"Backlash" to Feminism', in Sylvia Walby, *Gender Transformations* (London and New York: Routledge, 1997); William Thompson, 'Britain's Moral Majority' in Bryan Wilson (ed.), *Religion: Contemporary Issues: The All Souls Seminars in the Sociology of Religion* (London: Bellew, 1992); William Thompson, 'Charismatic Politics: The Social and Political Impact of Renewal' in Stephen Hunt, Malcolm Hamilton and Tony Walter (eds), *Charismatic Christianity: Sociological Perspective* (Basingstoke: Macmillan, 1997).

[22] Jeff Hearn, 'A Crisis in Masculinity, or New Agendas for Men?', in Sylvia Walby (ed.), *New Agendas for Women* (Basingstoke: Macmillan, 1999).

[23] British evangelical feminism began in the mid 1980s.

[24] John Piper, 'A Vision of Biblical Complementarity: Manhood and Womanhood Defined According to the Bible', in John Piper and Wayne Grudem (eds), *Restoring Biblical Manhood and Womanhood: A Response to Evangelical Feminism* (Wheaton, IL: Crossway, 1991), 3.

> Men and women need one another *as* men and women. They need real men and women, *healed* men and women. And the day has come for manliness and womanliness to be restored. Yet I shall talk more about manliness than about womanliness. Why? Because I believe that when men are men, women will find much less difficulty entering into their own identity.[25]

> I think the crisis we're facing, not only in the church but also in society at the moment – and there are more and more sort of articles now coming out, because the pendulum swings, doesn't it, so there's more coming out saying 'What about us guys? What's our role? What's a father? What is it to be taking leadership? Do we have any role at all? Are we obsolete, dinosaurs?'...Because actually the crying need it seems to me in a lot of people, men particularly, is we need to have these issues addressed as well...The whole issue addressing the role of women and femininity is absolutely right and it's been brilliant that the last three decades of the last century, in the church as well as society, have done that and I applaud all of that...but how much has been neglected in the process? As I travel around talking to men about their role, how to be a good father, how to be a good husband...it's like 'well, I've never heard anything about it, I've never read anything about it, I've never heard anyone preach on that before.' Because in our desire to align ourselves with one need we've often neglected the other.[26]

These passages, though not wholly critical of feminism, represent a pendulum swing away from women and towards masculinity. For NFI, gender identity revolves not around women or femininity but around making men men.

While NFI and Westside's discussions of masculinity encompassed many themes – the husband's role, work, fatherhood, sport, sexuality, the uneasy relationship between masculinity and religion – two predominated: fatherhood and sexuality. I will confine my discussion here to fatherhood, outlining the secular backlash's treatments of fatherhood and then showing how backlash ideals are uttered within NFI's fathering discourse.

Fatherhood in the UK Backlash

The backlash against feminism represented an attempted return to the late eighteenth- and nineteenth-century gender ideology of separate

---

[25] John White, cited in David Devenish, *Demolishing Strongholds: Effective Strategies for Spiritual Warfare* (Milton Keynes: Word, 2000), 276.

[26] David Holden, 'Man in the New Millennium: In the Home', audiotape of a talk given at Stoneleigh Bible Week (Hove: New Frontiers International, 2000).

spheres that paralleled the development of industrial capitalism. Within separate spheres, three dominant concepts associated with fatherhood were authority, the breadwinner role and absence.[27] These were reasserted from the late 1970s in opposition to the second-wave feminist movement. Feminists had argued for men's equal participation in childcare and housework, critiqued the separation of home and work hindering co-parenting and raised concern about some men's violence towards their partners and children. However, a flight from these feminist views and towards a restoration of a breadwinning father occurred in the backlash period. State, media and 'fathers' rights' discourse claimed to solve – though arguably also discursively created – a 'crisis' of uncertain and unstable masculinity. Right-wing commentators like 'underclass' theorist Charles Murray pointed to father-absence and illegitimacy as the major reason for a perceived crisis around young men, unemployment and urban crime.

Other manifestations of the backlash were fathers' rights groups like Families Need Fathers and Dads After Divorce (and recently, Fathers 4 Justice), who appeared from the mid 1970s claiming that feminists' focus on women's rights led to men's being ignored. They pushed for joint custody and equal decision-making responsibility after divorce even if the child resided with its mother and argued that retaining contact with the father was best for the child, even if the father had previously been violent.

As Thatcher and Major's governments promoted breadwinner fatherhood, a moral panic vilified single mothers and absent fathers as epitomising troubled parenting. A state discourse about 'feckless fathers' or 'Deadbeat Dads' who became absent after relationship breakdown emerged from a government concerned that, as well as producing inadequately brought up children, father absence increased its financial burden, forcing it to act as surrogate breadwinner father. This concern had its basis in the rapid increase in non-resident fathers during the 1980s and 1990s.[28]

Wanting to reduce expenditure, in the wake of the 1991 Child Support Act the government created the Child Support Agency to force non-resident fathers to support their children financially. New legislation (the Children Act, the Child Support Act and the Family Law Act 1996) required fathers to be economically responsible for their first family and have joint accountability for parenting after divorce; this

[27] Leonore Davidoff, Megan Doolittle, Janet Fink and Katherine Holden, *The Family Story: Blood, Contract and Intimacy, 1830-1960* (Harlow: Longman, 1999), pp. 135-57.

[28] Jonathan Bradshaw, Carol Stimson, Christine Skinner and Julie Williams, *Absent Fathers?* (London and New York: Routledge, 1999).

represented a new assumption that shared parenting was best for the child.[29]

This fatherhood discourse can be interpreted as a backlash against feminist critiques of fatherhood and the nuclear family and as a fear of women's increasing autonomy. It represents a return to separate spheres notions of fathers as necessarily *authoritative* (leading their family and disciplining their children), *breadwinners* and *absent*.

Fatherhood in NFI

Leaders in NFI perceive father absence as a primary social problem. Two talks at their summer Stoneleigh Bible Week illustrate this. In a seminar on masculinity in 2000 leader David Holden argues that fathers' involvement in their homes is central to 'true manhood'. He believes society is here 'at loggerheads' with the Bible. He says 'our culture seems to be saying that this is somewhat archaic, this idea of a man in the home who takes responsibility and maybe takes some form of leadership.' As society has rejected and neglected fatherhood, as fathers have become passive and distracted, 'suffering' has resulted. Undefined, absent, 'emasculated' fathers are unacceptable above all because human fatherhood is designed to reflect God's fatherhood:

> The very root of society, of what we are, is being undermined because nobody's taking responsibility. The whole point was: I am a reflection of the father-heart of God...That's why he created families where our heavenly father could be displayed through earthly fathers. And for us when we become absent – you know what I mean by that: you can be in your home and yet be an absent father because you're not taking the responsibility of true fatherhood. So when I'm tired and I'm fed up and I think 'oh I just wanna have some quiet time, I just wanna get away from everything'... something inside me says 'now come on, if you do that you are not reflecting God's fatherhood'. Because God's fatherhood – God's not like that with me.... He doesn't say 'I'm too busy, I can't sort you out'...It's like when you discipline your children. You think 'I can't be bothered to bring a line...with my kids or discipline my children when they're younger'. Every time you do that you are undermining the very purpose of God's relationship with us. The Bible says 'God disciplines us for our good.' So every time I usurp that, I say 'my wife's good at that, my wife's good at that bit, in fact my wife's good at most things about parenting.' So many guys seem to think parenting's left to the wife. Raising the kids? 'Oh, that's my wife's interest.' Instructing them? 'That's what my wife does'. Disciplining them? 'That's what my wife does.' Loving them? 'That's what my wife does.' Being affectionate to them?

[29] Carol Smart, 'Wishful Thinking and Harmful Tinkering? Sociological Reflections on Family Policy', *Journal of Social Policy*, 26.3 (1997), 301-21.

'That's what my wife does.' And every single one of those things it's the major responsibility of us as fathers to do...Why are there so many overbearing mothers today? I suggest to you that sometimes it is because of the neglect of the father. It's time to change. God never intended the father's role to be taken over by the mother. It is part of the function, the responsibility of the man in the home.[30]

Greg Haslam's 2001 seminar on Malachi chapter four was a passionate and poignant call for fathers to eschew passivity and absence and take a central role in their children's lives. Haslam believes that post-war Britain, like post-exilic Judah, rejected Christianity, with countless negative results he documents statistically: hopelessness, poverty, crime, violence against women, divorce, single parenthood and sexual experimentation. Haslam considers father absence the major cause of social disintegration in the West and 'evidence of a curse on our land.' Britain, he believes, needs revival: widespread return to faith in God that transforms social behaviour. This ethos dovetails with New Right individualism; social change happens through individuals deciding to alter their behaviour, but within a prescribed framework.

What will bring this much-needed revival? Haslam asks rhetorically. His answer equates spiritual vitality and social reform with more active fatherhood:

The Bible would give this simple answer to one of the greatest things we could see in our nation today: better fathers. Better fathers. Here it is in Malachi 4 verses 5-6: 'Behold, I will send you the prophet Elijah before the great and dreadful day of the Lord comes. And he will turn the hearts of the fathers to their children and the hearts of the children to their fathers, or else I will come and strike the land with a curse.' Now that's a statement that will ring long in your ears once you have truly heard it. If you like, it's God's final word to a nation in crisis. And I want to ask 'What does it mean?' Well, at the very least it is clear that God views all of human social history primarily in familial terms. And says in words that actually would jar politically correct sensitivities today, that men, and particularly fathers, are critical to his designs and desires for our social welfare. There will be no peace on earth until men learn again what it really means to be a man, as God defines a man to be... This generation has been called the fatherless generation. And the loss of true fathers has had incalculable effects.[31]

Haslam bases a 'wish list for better fathers' on his experience of rarely seeing his father since his parents' divorce when he was a child.

---

[30] Holden, 'Man in the New Millennium'.

[31] Greg Haslam, 'A Day for Revival: Malachi 4', audiotape of a talk given at Stoneleigh Bible Week (Hove: New Frontiers International, 2001).

Explaining his yearning for 'a father who'd talked to me', 'a father who'd affirmed me and supported me', 'a father who'd trained me and disciplined me', 'a father who loved me,' he reveals how be believes his father's absence affected him:

> He wasn't there when I got 10 O levels and later 5 A levels. He didn't see me graduate. He didn't see me when I got my postgraduate certificate and became a teacher. He wasn't there when my first child was born, nor my second, nor my third. He didn't see me get married. And he wasn't there when I felt the call of God on my life to ministry at the age of 27. And he's never visited the church I've pastored for 21 years and he's only heard me preach one of the many thousands of sermons I've preached. And that was at the funeral of my older brother. Now fathers, I'm saying to you that you need to be there for your children. Because the thing I've missed most about my father is that he was never there to say 'well done son, I'm proud of you.' But a child needs to hear that with an ache deep in their bones.

Holden and Haslam's fatherhood discourse involves responsibility, authority, discipline and economic provision; it dovetails with separate spheres discourse. Their additional emphasis on fatherly affection and participation in the daily tasks of nurture incorporates, however, a feminist 'new' fatherhood that does not restrict childcare to women – in this it represents more than simply a reactionary backlash. Holden's commentary can also be located within the backlash, for he argues that mothers have taken an 'overbearing' parenting responsibility when men, to whom God has given primary parenting responsibility, have neglected it. This reassertion of fatherhood contains anti-feminist aspects. If, as Holden argues, 'every single one of those things' (including disciplining, loving, being affectionate, instructing children) is 'the major responsibility of us as fathers', women's importance is being minimised. A curious tension emerges: although NFI literature indicates a preference for *mothers* to stay at home as primary carers of their young children[32], here the implication is that women should take a backseat at parenting because their parenting work is less important than their husbands'. Mothers, it might be argued, are here considered less significant than fathers. Like backlash 'underclass' theorists of father absence, NFI here positions mothers as secondary compared with the indispensability of active fathers, on whose presence social health is seen to stand or fall

Holden and Haslam's discussions of father absence therefore closely echo contemporary British backlash discourse. Their conception that

[32] Wendy Virgo, *Mainly for Mothers: A Practical Discipleship Guide* (Eastbourne: Kingsway, 1997), 7-11.

they are constructing a 'biblical' fatherhood in contradistinction to the absent fatherhood favoured in contemporary Britain may not be accurate for two reasons. First, in the British social context father absence is rarely suggested as preferable, except by those concerned about individual men who are abusive to female partners or children. Second, Holden and Haslam's fatherhood ideal in fact closely resembles popular contemporary ideals.

Conclusion

This brief examination demonstrates NFI's concern with men being, as Westside's leader Chris put it, 'proper men'. I have suggested that NFI's response to questions of gender has been to adopt a primarily conservative stance that claims to be 'biblical' yet is an identifiable reflection of the 'secular' (as far as a culture with a Christian heritage can be taken to be secular) British social context. As anti-feminist elements within Britain have been concerned with the reinstatement of separate spheres masculinity, so have NFI, and central to this has been the promotion of breadwinning, responsible fatherhood. What is intriguing, though, is that adoption of cultural ideals appears not to have been an intentional formal strategy made in response to questions of social integration and mission.[33] Yet at an informal level, it is likely that individual NFI members *are* living out gendered lives in ways that they feel best synthesise biblical values and cultural beliefs for the sake of evangelism to their non-religious peers. As Chris, who expressed the desire that men be 'proper men', told me when I returned to visit Westside after my fieldwork had finished: 'we want to be normal people doing normal jobs and living normal lives, but also being Christians.'

---

[33] I make this suggestion because I have not come across any literature or recorded material by NFI leaders in the public domain to suggest otherwise. I would be grateful to receive material supporting or contradicting my hypothesis.

CHAPTER 12

New Music and the 'Evangelical Style' in the Church of England, c. 1958-1991

Peter Webster and Ian Jones

Introduction

George Carey's election as the 103rd Archbishop of Canterbury in 1990 provided many commentators with a powerful symbol of the rise and rise of the Church of England's evangelical wing over the preceding three decades. But this ascendancy was not without controversy, and most hotly debated was the change of style that an evangelical archbishop might potentially bring. Nowhere was this noted more than on the question of music: after concerns were raised over Carey's choice of music for his enthronement service, the Dean of Canterbury (the Very Revd. John Simpson) was even forced to give assurances in the press that 'evangelical songs and charismatic hand-claps will not prevent the "unique English choral tradition" from shining through'.[1] Though fundamentally this was a controversy about contrasting conceptions of music and holiness, much was assumed in passing about the nature of evangelicalism and the centrality of a popular style of worship music to it. But whilst the use of chorus and popular song by evangelicals has a long and interesting history, the place of this type of music in perceptions of evangelical identity has not always been so straightforward.

This paper is an attempt to begin to explore the notion of an 'evangelical style' in late twentieth century Britain, and the degree to which music became a defining part of that style. Much fruitful work has been done in recent years, and for different historical periods, on how historians classify religious movements and delineate the defining

[1] Paraphrased in: 'Choral Tradition at Canterbury Safe', *Church Times* 12 April 1991, 2. For more on the wider reaction to the inclusion of the All Souls' [Langham Place] Ensemble in the service, see: Robin L. D. Rees, *Weary and Ill at Ease; A Survey of Clergy and Organists* (Leominster: Gracewing Fowler Wright, 1993), 13.

features of membership or allegiance. Work on the English seventeenth century, for instance, has fruitfully posited the notions of both a Puritan and a corresponding Laudian 'style'.[2] Given the difficulty of arriving at an agreed doctrinal definition of evangelicalism in the late twentieth century, it is perhaps particularly fruitful to explore this notion of 'style'. This has particular analytical power in exploring a repertoire of activities, attitudes and taboos which may together characterise the 'evangelical'. At the same time, not all evangelicals would display evidence of each element, and the idea of a stylistic repertoire allows analysis across denominational boundaries, and over time. The notion of 'style tribes' in evangelicalism has already been explored fruitfully by Pete Ward, drawing on wider literature on 'style' from the discipline of cultural studies.[3]

This paper seeks to explore in historical perspective how new, pop-influenced worship music became a mark of the evangelical 'style' in the late 20th century Church of England. It is part of a process much wider than simply Anglicanism, but the Church of England is considered here as a manageable case study in the space available. We will argue that in many respects, evangelicals in the Church of England took up experimentation with new music comparatively late, in the 1960s and 70s, and that full identification of the new style with evangelicalism was most closely related to the growing influence of the charismatic renewal. We cannot hope to chart every aspect of that emerging relationship here, so the particular focus is on the level of *perception*, and the forging of what we will call an 'imaginative link' between evangelicals and popular music. Whilst the place of music in evangelicals' sense of their own identity is considered, we have been particularly interested to explore how that link was made in the minds of non-evangelicals. If Evangelicalism is in some senses as much a *condition* as a *confession*, it is important to recognise that identity is as much constructed externally – by non-evangelicals – as internally, by evangelicals themselves.[4]

---

[2] C. Durston and J. Eales, 'Introduction: The Puritan Ethos, 1560-1700' in C. Durston and J. Eales (eds), *The Culture of English Puritanism, 1560-1700* (Basingstoke: Macmillan, 1996), 1-31; P. Lake, 'The Laudian style: order, uniformity and the pursuit of the beauty of holiness' in K. Fincham (ed.), *The Early Stuart Church* (Basingstoke: Macmillan, 1993), 161-185.

[3] Pete Ward, 'The Tribes of Evangelicalism' in Graham Cray *et al.*, *The Post-Evangelical Debate* (SPCK/Triangle, 1997), 19-34.

[4] For a good general discussion of recent research on religious identity, see: Simon Coleman and Peter Collins, 'Introduction: Ambiguous Attachments: Religion, Identity and Nation' in Simon Coleman and Peter Collins (eds), *Religion, Identity and Change: Perspectives on Global Transformations* (Aldershot: Ashgate, 2004), 1-25.

Evangelicals and Experimentation with Popular Music for Worship

Although the realm of perception is as important as the reality, identity nevertheless has some basis in events (however subsequently interpreted), and the common association between evangelicals and popular music is no exception. Late twentieth century debates about music and 'churchmanship' must acknowledge the long history of the relationship between evangelical religion and popular music; from 18th century revivalist hymn-writers, through the Salvation Army bands and Sankey and Moody hymns of the late 19th century, and the mission and youth chorus books of the early 20th.[5] For the latter part of the 20th century, Pete Ward's invaluable book *Growing Up Evangelical* provides a sketch of post-war evangelicals' adoption of successive strands of popular musical culture for worship. Three particular phases identified by Ward are taken for granted as the backdrop to this discussion:[6]

First, Ward highlights the significance of the influential collection *Youth Praise* of 1966, compiled by the then London curate (later Bishop of Chester) Michael Baughen, with contributions from some of the brightest young evangelical minds of that new generation. Whilst not actually 'pop', a significant portion of the book employs a light swing style with the explicit intention of reflecting the cultural landscape familiar to a younger audience.

Second, Ward notes the critical importance of the charismatic movement in making extensive use of rock and folk styles – the former most obvious in the 'Jesus rock' of Larry Norman and others; the latter exemplified by the popular worship collections *Sound of Living Waters* (1974) and *Fresh Sounds* (1976). Whilst *Youth Praise* had still been hymnic and strophic in form, the material in *Sound of Living Waters* frequently tends towards a verse-chorus form, with simpler melodic material and greater repetition. Most significantly, whilst *Youth Praise* was originally designed primarily for para-church activities such as youth group meetings, *Sound of Living Waters* was intended for use in the 'normal'

---

[5] On the Wesleys, see: Erik Routley, *The Musical Wesleys* (London: Herbert Jenkins, 1968). On the Salvation Army, see Horton Davies, *Worship and Theology in England vol IV: From Newman to Martineau, 1850-1900* (Princeton NJ: Princeton University Press, 1962), 166-69. On Moody and Sankey, see Erik Routley, *Twentieth Century Church Music* (London: Herbert Jenkins, 1964), 196-99; David Bebbington, *Evangelicalism in Modern Britain. A history from the 1730s to the 1980s* (London: Routledge, 1989), 174; John Coffey, 'Democracy and Popular Religion: Moody and Sankey's Mission to Britain, 1873-75' in Eugenio F. Biagini (ed.), *Citizenship and Community: Liberals, Radicals and Collective Identities in the British Isles, 1865-1931* (Cambridge: Cambridge University Press, 1996), 93-119.

[6] Pete Ward, *Growing Up Evangelical: Youth Work and the Making of a Sub-Culture* (London: SPCK, 1996) - see particularly Chapter 5, 'Songs for Each Generation'.

course of congregational worship - be that in small week-night groups or on Sunday morning.[7] It thus presented a more direct challenge to the hegemony of traditional hymnody.

Third, Ward identifies the importance of the Restoration Movement and the new House Churches of the 1970s and 1980s for the introduction of new 'soft rock' and rock ballad styles to evangelical worship, primarily through the hugely popular *Songs of Fellowship*[8] and the musical diet of a series of major Christian conferences (notably *Spring Harvest* from 1979), both of which played a crucial part in introducing this new style to worshippers in the historic, 'mainstream' denominations.

That evangelicals have widely used these popular musical styles is indisputable (although the precise extent of this usage is part of an ongoing project of research on the part of the authors). However, the strength of the later association between evangelicals and pop has often obscured the degree to which - particularly in the 1950s and 60s - experimentation with church pop was not wholly (or even primarily) an evangelical undertaking.

Breaking the Connection: Perceptions of Pop in Church from the 1950s to the 1970s

At the beginning of our period, the perception of a strong connection between evangelicalism, or at least evangelistic endeavour, and popular worship music was commonly made within what we could loosely term 'the Anglican musical establishment'.[9] The strength of the identification is demonstrated by a frequent confusion of the terms "evangelical" and "evangelistic". Thus it was that the positive reception of the Geoffrey Beaumont Folk Mass could be interpreted as more due to 'the evangelical possibilities than by the fitness and quality of the music'.[10]

---

[7] Although it should also be said that *Youth Praise* also came to be used extensively in Sunday services in some parishes - particularly those with regular Family Services (Ward, *Growing Up Evangelical*, 149-50).

[8] Which sold 750,000 copies in its first six years (Tony Collins, 'Blockbuster Tales and Gospel Songs', *Church Times*, 1 March 1991, 8).

[9] A loose nexus of individuals and organisations regarding themselves as guardians and producers of the Anglican musical tradition, including salaried organists and choirmasters, concerned clergy, some musicologists and other professional musicians. For a discussion of this nexus and its coherence see: Peter Webster and Ian Jones, 'Anglican "Establishment" Reactions to "Pop" Church Music in England, c. 1956-1991' in Kate Cooper and Jeremy Gregory (eds), *Elite and Popular Religion: Studies in Church History*, 42, (2006), 429-41.

[10] Stephen Rhys and King Palmer, *The ABC of Church Music* (London: Hodder and Stoughton, 1967), 64.

David Lumsden, organist of New College, Oxford referred to 'the overtly evangelical intention and usually crude technique' of the recent experiments in church pop. This music was 'in effect the Sankey and Moody of our day, with the same attractions and the same limitations'.[11]

If the connection between popular styles and evangelical religion was well-established, the reality was always more complex, as can be demonstrated by the case of Charles Cleall, organist of the conservative evangelical church of St. Paul, Portman Square and a well-known church musician and columnist in *Musical Opinion*. Actively opposed to the extension of church pop into public worship, Cleall wrote in 1958 of the damage done by clergy who were 'so keen to give the people just what they wanted... utterly indifferent that it may be rubbish'. 'Thus', he concluded, 'is evangelical music detrimental to musicians, and popular songs degrade the followers of Beethoven'.[12] Indeed, though Cleall himself re-harmonised and republished *Sixty Songs from Sankey*, he limited absolutely their use to extra-liturgical mission services. For the mature believer to continue to desire the milk of these songs, when they should have progressed onto stronger food, was a 'mark of carnality; of self-gratification; of a determination, like that of Peter Pan, not to grow up'.[13] However, whilst individuals such as Cleall show that a variety of attitudes towards popular music for worship existed amongst Anglicans of evangelical backgrounds, general opinion was more likely to link evangelicals firmly with hymns and songs written in a current or recent popular idiom.

However, a new wave of experimentation with popular music for church was already beginning to leave Anglican evangelicals behind; the most celebrated and indeed notorious example being the publication of Geoffrey Beaumont's *Folk Mass* in 1956, subsequently the inspiration for further works over the following decade by the Twentieth Century Church Light Music Group (TCCLMG).[14] The appearance of the *Folk*

---

[11] David Lumsden, 'Introduction and Notes' in Gerald Knight and William Reed (General Editors), *The Treasury of English Church Music vol. V: 1900-1965* (London: Blandford 1965), xiv.

[12] In the 'Master of the Choir' column, *Musical Opinion* 969 (June 1958), 599, 601.

[13] *Sixty Songs from Sankey, newly presented for voices by Charles Cleall* (Marshall, Morgan and Scott, London, 1960), Preface [no pagination]. On Cleall, see Routley, *Twentieth Century Church Music*, 203-5. See also Cleall's *The Selection and Training of Mixed Choirs in Churches* (London: Independent Press, 1960), especially 13-22.

[14] See (all published by Weinberger of London) Appleford's *Mass of Five Melodies* and John Alldis' *Festival Te Deum; also: Thirty 20th Century Hymn Tunes by Members of the Twentieth Century Church Light Music Group* (1960); *More 20th Century Hymn Tunes* (1962) and also a collection of reflections: *Pop Goes the*

Mass and a televised performance in 1957 prompted a flood of comment from a range of 'learned' musical publications, with much of the response negative and some of it completely misunderstanding of the genre of the music (it was often - wrongly - described as 'pop' or as a 'jazz mass'[15]).

But despite the apparent ease with which its critics could mis-label it, neither Beaumont's *Folk Mass* nor the hymn tunes of the TCCLMG ever seem to have acquired an 'evangelical' tag. This was partly due to the personnel involved: Beaumont in later life became a monk at Mirfield; hymn-writer Patrick Appleford was the product of Chichester Theological College; Sydney Carter - arguably the most celebrated popular hymn-writer of the 1960s - openly professed a much more liberal brand of Christianity.[16] However, this obscuring of the historic link between evangelicalism and popular worship songs also rested upon a much wider shift in initiative towards the liberal wing of the Church of England over the 1960s, from which also came some of the loudest advocacy for experimenting with pop in church. In 1963 John Robinson's *Honest to God* appeared to open up a greater range of styles by insisting that the Church 'let the decor, the music and the architecture seal the language of the world it is meant to be transforming'.[17] The year before, Southwark Cathedral was one of several to host 'pop evensong' events featuring music provided by rhythm and beat groups.[18] Correspondingly, in the minds of church pop's most trenchant critics, the blame for its appearance was to be placed squarely at the door of what Charles Cleall called 'the Tillich-Bonhoeffer-Woolwich group'.[19] Even as late as 1995, former Director of the RSCM Lionel Dakers criticised younger clergy for jumping 'onto the popular bandwagon which dictated the preaching *in excelsis* of a predominantly social gospel with music to match it, in other words the *Honest to God* syndrome'.[20]

Of course, this was not to say that evangelical experimentation with

---

Hymn Tune; 20th Century Light Church Music in Schools and Parishes (Prism Pamphlet 14, London, 1964).

[15] Horton Davies, *Worship and Theology in England 3: The Ecumenical Century, 1900 to the Present* (Grand Rapids MI: Eerdmans , 1996 edn), 108.

[16] On Sydney Carter, see Adrian Hastings, *A History of English Christianity, 1920-1990* (London, SCM Press, 3rd edn 1991), 584.

[17] John A. T. Robinson, *Honest to God* (London: SCM Press, 1963), p. 89. For a general account of the theological climate of the period, see Hastings, *A History of English Christianity*, 536-46.

[18] *Church News*, March 1963.

[19] Charles Cleall, *Music and Holiness* (Epworth Press, London, 1964), 11.

[20] Lionel Dakers, *Places where they Sing: Memoirs of a Church Musician* (Norwich, Canterbury Press, 1995), 207.

pop was non-existent; evangelicals were amongst the pioneers of coffee-bar evangelism featuring folk and 'beat' groups, the stable of the next generation of leading evangelical musicians, such as Graham Kendrick.[21] Evangelical parishes were also amongst many in the 1960s to experiment with congregational singing led by 'beat' groups playing traditional hymns as well as newer material. Nevertheless, such experiments were sporadic, and the dominant trend amongst evangelical congregations of the time was towards the maintenance of tried and trusted forms. As Colin Buchanan has written, 'Before 1962 the trends in liturgy for Evangelicals were nil - everything was static'.[22] He might equally have been writing of church music in evangelical parishes for the same period (and in not a few cases, for most of the rest of the decade). Moreover, amidst the heightened religious turmoil of the 1960s, normal expectations of what each church party could be expected to do seem temporarily to have been suspended: a review of the church press for the period up to the early 1970s suggests that experimentation with popular music for worship was not disproportionately sponsored by any particular church tradition. As late as 1970, St. Paul's Cathedral was hosting 'Jazz Praises', with the Dean extolling the virtues of 'the pop approach to religion' to gathered journalists.[23]

Re-Forging the Link: Attitudes to Evangelicalism and 'Choruses' since the 1970s

By the mid-1970s, however, the imaginative link between evangelicals and church pop was being re-formed. That this association was becoming increasingly clear in the minds of non-evangelicals can be seen in the gradual shift in the thinking of leading church musician and writer Lionel Dakers. In his 1970 work *Church Music at the Crossroads,* Dakers had much to say about the 'New Look' of Sydney Carter and Malcolm Williamson, and what he described as the 'pop element', but implied no particular evangelical leadership in the latter. By the late 1970s this began to change. In his 1976 *Handbook of Parish Music,* Dakers asked what were the 'implications, and perhaps the threats, of the growth of the charismatic movement?' He diagnosed that much of the upsetting of the balance of formality and informality, spontaneity and order was 'reflected in a background tending more towards the

---

[21] Graham Kendrick, 'Worship in Spirit and Truth' in Stephen Darlington and Alan Kreider (eds), *Composing Music for Worship* (Norwich: Canterbury Press, 2003), 86-103.

[22] Colin Buchanan, 'Liturgy' in John C. King (ed.), *Evangelicals Today: 13 Stock-Taking Essays* (Guildford and London: Lutterworth , 1973), 61-90.

[23] 'Pop at St. Paul's', *Church Times,* 5 June 1970, 8.

Evangelical approach, where music is questioned and "traditional" music is suspect as an aid to worship.'[24] In 1983 Dakers again addressed what he dubbed the 'charismatic question', but in fact seems to elide evangelicalism with renewal, referring to his attendance at 'evangelical and charismatic' worship.[25] Over the period of the 1980s this linkage of pop and evangelicalism continued to grow in non-evangelical minds. By 1989, the visible crystallisation of different approaches to music around leading individuals of differing churchmanship was such that a conference to encourage dialogue between them was thought worthwhile. This included Lionel Dakers and Christopher Dearnley (former organist of St Paul's cathedral) as well as the Roman Catholic Stephen Dean and prominent figures in the new style such as Dave Fellingham and Phil Lawson Johnston.[26]

Nor was the progressive identification of evangelicalism and 'pop' church music confined to those outside the evangelical or charismatic spheres. Amidst a climate of optimism about the strength of Anglican evangelicalism in the 1980s, 1987 found a more pessimistic Michael Saward pondering the 'disturbing legacy' of the 1960s and 1970s. The decade, he felt, had produced a generation of evangelical clergy,

> brought up on guitars, choruses and home group discussions. Educated... not to use words with precision because the image is dominant, not the word. [...] Excellent when it comes to providing religious music, drama and art. Not so good when asked to preach and teach the Faith or to express it in writing.[27]

Furthermore, while discussing in the mid 1990s an 'evangelical identity crisis', the conservative commentator Melvin Tinker suggested that the term evangelical itself had shifted from being a noun to an adjective, 'a sociological cypher denoting those who have had a similar past – maybe converted at a Billy Graham meeting, members of the IVF [Inter Varsity Fellowship]... in their university days, folk who are keen on evangelism and having a taste for modern hymnody. This is a far cry for [sic] the theological confessional identification which marked our forbears'.[28] It is

---

[24] Lionel Dakers, *A Handbook of Parish Music* (Oxford: Mowbray, 1976), 116.

[25] Lionel Dakers, *Church Music in a Changing World* (Oxford: Mowbray, 1984), 12.

[26] The conference, held at the London Institute for Contemporary Christianity, issued in a published collection of essays; Robin Sheldon (ed.), *In Spirit and in Truth. Exploring Directions in Music and Worship Today* (London: Hodder & Stoughton, 1989).

[27] Michael Saward, *The Anglican Church Today: Evangelicals on the Move* (Oxford: Mowbray, 1987), 92.

[28] Melvin Tinker (ed.), *The Anglican Evangelical Crisis* (Fearn: Christian Focus Publications, 1995), 10.

striking that 'modern hymnody' makes it onto this list of recognizable evangelical traits.

The reasons for this growing identification are manifold and complex, and subject to ongoing research. We can, however, begin to sketch some main themes here. Perhaps the single most important factor was the growth of the charismatic movement within the Church of England. We have already noted, following Pete Ward, the charismatic and restorationist movements' championing of a soft rock style with a verse-chorus format, rather than the folk, swing and light music styles which had previously been the main focus of experimentation. The common use of the new music for mainstream church services, rather than merely for fringe events, also served to strengthen the imaginative link between evangelicals and pop church music: the 1981 report on *The Charismatic Movement in the Church of England* identified a trend towards the late 70s of the gradual 'charismaticisation' of worship in a second wave of Anglican churches, but this time primarily focused on the style of the service and often without the charismata themselves. This is perhaps the key process by which the new style of music was spread amongst evangelical Anglican parishes.

However, this spread in practice is not sufficient in itself to explain the increasing identification in theory. The process was aided more generally by the increasing visibility of evangelicals, and in particular by their use of new styles of music at major events, [29] from the Festivals of Light and *Spree* events in the early 1970s, to the success of Greenbelt and Spring Harvest over the following decades. This heightened profile was also aided by a boom in publishing activity. From the mid-1960s *Buzz* magazine serviced a growing demand amongst young evangelicals for information on popular Christian music, and certainly by the mid-1970s contributors frequently appear to assume that 'chorus-singing' would be a familiar feature of worship for many of their readers, alongside 'hand-clapping', praying 'without using a prayer book to guide you', a preacher who 'doesn't wear his dog collar' and a 'relaxing and informal' atmosphere'.[30] One 1991 survey estimated that around half of all books produced in the Christian publishing revolution of the 1980s had a strongly evangelical basis.[31] Among these were a number in

[29] Tony Jasper, *Jesus and the Christian in a Pop Culture* (London: Robert Royce, 1984), 133-156. On the moving of evangelicals 'into a broad place' see Bebbington, *Evangelicalism in Modern Britain*, 249-70.

[30] Quotations here taken from Sue Ritter's regular column in *Buzz*, February 1975, 25. Here, Ritter exhorted her readers not to become distracted by peripherals when seeking to share their faith with friends.

[31] Tony Collins, 'Beating the Bookshop Drum', *Church Times*, 22 February 1991, 8.

the mid 1980s by prominent musicians, such as Graham Kendrick, Chris Bowater and, amongst the Anglicans, Andrew Maries of St. Michael-le-Belfrey, York.[32]

The raised profile of evangelical musicians was coupled with a marked loss of impetus amongst those non-evangelical sections of the church which had taken the lead in the 1950s and 60s. The optimism and openness to experimentation and the search for a 'New Reformation' which had characterised the later part of the 1960s had given way by the early 1970s to an exhaustion, and a feeling amongst some that these experiments had not worked.[33] Those with little time for the new music for its own sake perhaps increasingly felt that the new music had failed to live up to its promise of attracting the young; it was therefore time to ensure that at least the needs of existing church members were satisfied. Moreover, after a decade of hearing that the church 'must move with the times', the early 1970s saw signs of a renewed determination to reassert the church's distinctiveness in a more unapologetic fashion.[34] By this time a level of space existed for a plurality of styles of worship, and so it became possible for those who preferred the traditional style of music to concentrate on developing and defending it in the places where it was still used, and in general to cease criticising the newer style (at least in print).[35]

Nevertheless, despite this process of liturgical fragmentation, new styles rarely remained within the sub-culture which gave them birth. If advocates of traditional church music were generally content to ignore the new music of evangelical and charismatic Anglicans so long as they kept themselves to themselves, the increased prominence of evangelicalism within the Church of England of the 1970s and 80s occasionally meant it was impossible to maintain an indifferent stance. Major events involving a spectrum of churchgoers - such as 1984's *Mission England* – were crucial in introducing the new music to different audiences. Added to this, by the late 1970s perhaps as many as half of the church's ordinands had trained in theological colleges with an evangelical tradition,[36] far outstripping the number of evangelical

---

[32] Graham Kendrick, *Worship* (Eastbourne, Kingsway, 1984); Andrew Maries, *One Heart, One Voice: The Rich and Varied Resource of Music in Worship* (London: Hodder and Stoughton, 1985); Chris Bowater, *The Believer's Guide to Worship* (Eastbourne: Kingsway, 1986).

[33] Adrian Hastings, 'All Change: The Presence of the Past in British Christianity' in Haddon Wilmer (ed.), *20/20 Visions: The Futures of Christianity in Britain* (London: SPCK, 1992), 13-29.

[34] Grave Davie, *Religion in Britain Since 1945* (Oxford: Blackwell, 1994), 36.

[35] Webster and Jones, 'Anglican "Establishment" Reactions to "Pop" Church Music'.

[36] Adrian Hastings, *A History of English Christianity, 1920-1990*, 615.

parishes available for them to serve in. Although Paul Welsby reflects that for the most part, these clergy were content to respect the existing traditions of non-evangelical parishes and make only sensitive changes,[37] the introduction of a more popular style of music and worship could occasionally create division. The featuring of the more notorious of these cases in both the church and secular press only seems to have cemented the connection between evangelicals and popular music in the minds of observers. Thus, in a letter to *The Times* in November 1990, a Revd. Peter Jones of Beckenham complained of the situation in London where 'too many clergymen are busy disbanding choirs and discarding organists, and introducing banal pop-style groups...'. 'I fear', he continued, 'that the tradition will be lucky to live beyond the turn of the century unless there is some check on the increasing intolerance towards church music being displayed by the evangelical wing of the Church of England'.[38]

Furthermore, if the wider identification of evangelicalism with pop-influenced worship music was not complete by 1991, the controversy surrounding George Carey's choice of music for his enthronement as Archbishop of Canterbury guaranteed to make it so. Against a backdrop of expectation that a 'charismatic Archbishop' would do things differently, the inclusion of the All Souls' Ensemble playing renewal-inspired songs at the exchange of the peace caused outrage in some quarters, despite the fact that most of the music for the service drew unflinchingly on the English choral tradition. Writing just before the enthronement, *The Times*' Clifford Longley reported 'the purist fear that a showcase of Anglican choral music at its best – boys' treble voices soaring to the medieval vaults - will be spoilt by the catchy holiday camp songs favoured by the "charismatic" movement of the Church, to which Dr. Carey inclines'.[39] Even the satirical TV show *Spitting Image* joined in, with a sketch of the new Archbishop proposing to change the symbol of the Church from the cross to a tambourine. Such now was the regularity of the identification between evangelicalism and the new style of worship that one Debra-Lyn Powell wrote to *The Times* after the enthronement service saying 'I feel it is necessary to rescue the term "evangelical" before it becomes completely debased by both Christians and the secular media. An evangelical', she continued, 'believes in the full inspiration and infallibility of the Scriptures and their authority and sufficiency concerning salvation, doctrine and holy living.

---

[37] Paul Welsby, *A History of the Church of England, 1945-1980* (Oxford: Oxford University Press, 1984), 212.

[38] *The Times*, 30 November 1990, 15.

[39] Clifford Longley, 'Why the Church is Wary of Carey', *The Times*, 8 April 1991, 14.

Evangelicalism has nothing to do with a "freer" form of worship, but everything to do with true, holy, joyful, reverent and sacrificial worship of God'.[40] Unfortunately for the writer, not many people seemed to be listening.

Conclusion

To conclude, the connection between evangelicalism and new 'pop' styles of worship music became a stronger one in the minds of both evangelicals and non-evangelicals over the post-Second World War period. In so doing, this displayed striking continuities with long-standing perceptions of evangelical religion through the eighteenth, nineteenth and early twentieth centuries. Even so, the connection between the new worship music and evangelical identity has not been a straightforward one. Indeed, the more inward-looking evangelicalism of the fifties and early sixties was comparatively slow to take up the new music, with little in the way of a discernible pattern to the experimentation (at least in terms of churchmanship). Even with the charismatic movement's crucial championing of more overtly 'pop' styles in the 1970s, these new songs did not become (or re-establish themselves as) a defining feature of evangelical identity until the 1980s. However, from the mid-seventies to the late eighties, the rejection of experiments with pop by the broader church, the spread of the new music into Sunday worship rather than just in mission and youth events, and the wider buoyancy of evangelicalism within the Church of England, served to ensure that by the time of George Carey's enthronement in 1991, that imaginative link was firmly established.

As a postscript, it is worth adding that ironically, at the very time of the enthronement service debate, the association between evangelicalism and the new music *in practice* was already beginning to fragment. First, evangelical worship leaders and song-writers were beginning to re-discover the richness of other, older musical traditions.[41] Second, a new generation of 'conservative evangelicals' were expressing growing reservations about the desirability and moral pedigree of the

[40] *The Times*, 19 April 1991, 15.

[41] Stuart Townend for example has drawn on Celtic rhythms in some of his more recent song-writing, whilst Graham Kendrick is one of several song-writers to have made new arrangements of popular English hymns (See the contributions of both writers to: *Songs of Fellowship* Vol. III (Eastbourne: Kingsway Music, 2003).

pop style.[42] At the other end of the spectrum some evangelical parishes and individuals were beginning to experiment with dance music and reflective 'alternative worship' services, both of which (in their different ways) stood out directly against the light pop and rock of the charismatic chorus.[43] Last, through events such as Mission England, and through a less perceptible process of gradual osmosis, so-called 'happy-clappy' choruses were beginning to find their way into services in non-evangelical parishes (albeit often without the guitar and the clapping). The final irony of this paper is that - despite these developments in reality - little had changed in the realm of perception. The commonplace imaginative link between evangelical identity and 'pop' church music appears to have remained firmly intact - at least amongst non-evangelicals.

---

[42] An account of this disquiet is given in: Michael J. Iliff, 'Worship Wars within Reformed Evangelicalism' (unpublished paper presented to the British Evangelical Identities Conference, Kings College, London, 30 July 2004).

[43] For an ethnographic study of 'alternative worship', see: Matthew Guest, '"Alternative" Worship: Challenging the Boundaries of the Christian Faith' in Elizabeth Arweck and Martin D. Stringer (eds), *Theorising Faith: The Insider/Outsider Problem in the Study of* Ritual (Birmingham: University of Birmingham Press, 2002), 35-56.

CHAPTER 13

Seen to be Remembered: Representation and Recollection in Contemporary British Evangelicalism

John Harvey

Among the recent advances in the study of Protestantism and art is the acknowledgement that, like art, Protestantism is not an undifferentiated whole. The movement comprises a shifting coalition of theological styles, subsets, churches, and individuals with diverse trajectories, at different times and in different places.[1] Protestantism also has a varied and complex visual expression, one which extends well beyond the European High Art tradition of the sixteenth and seventeenth centuries (with which the movement is commonly associated). This expression includes a visual culture of popular piety, the study of which (while still in its infancy) has shown that Protestants, in spite of their iconoclastic and iconophobic tendencies, have employed types of visual artefacts and customs of visualization as varied as their constituency is diverse. The essay contributes to this developing specificity and catholicity of approach, and involves a preliminary examination of the visual culture of the largest contemporary Protestant movement – Evangelicalism.

Up to now, chiefly American scholars have contributed to the study of Evangelical visual culture in the twentieth century. They have based their research largely upon examples produced in the United States, and aimed to describe not only the artefacts' intrinsic properties but also their significance within the broader framework of religious rites and customs, and of movements outside Evangelicalism and Protestantism.[2] In Britain, there has been comparatively little work on the material trappings of Evangelicalism used in the country during the last

---

[1] Rowland Croucher, *Recent Trends among Evangelicals* (Bromley: MARC Europe, 1986), 9, 37.

[2] See David Morgan and Sally M. Promey (eds.), *The Visual Culture of American Religions* (Berkeley, California; London: University of California Press, 2001); David Morgan, *Visual Piety: A History and Theory of Popular Religious Imagery* (Berkeley, California: University of California Press, 1998).

century.[3] Possibly this is because the artefacts have been largely either imported from the United States (like many other types of consumer goods) or are imitative of the American variety. However, one should not assume that identical artefacts transplanted into foreign soil necessarily adapt (or are adapted) in the same way. For example, the emblematic tradition of theological and homiletic discourse in British Evangelicalism may encourage a way of seeing and reading artefacts comprising pictures and verses that is more peculiar to our country than to the United States.[4]

Recent scholarship has rightly emphasized the relation between the manufacture and purchase of Evangelical artefacts and trends in consumer culture in general.[5] Nevertheless, this has often been at the expense of encouraging other perspectives. There has been little attention paid to the reciprocity and nuances of image and text; the diverse ways in which believers use artefacts as aids to devotion and as signs of affiliation; a comparison of the material and visual expressions of piety with oral and aural mediums such as hymns, prayers, and sermons; and the contrasting ways in which artefacts function in the private and individual realm of the home as distinct from the public and communal realm of the church. Moreover, there has been virtually no interaction between the scholars in this field across the Atlantic. In an attempt to address some of these deficits, this essay makes specific reference to artefacts in Britain since the late 1970s (a renascent period for some branches of Evangelicalism)[6] and the group's use of the visual as a means of propaganda and as a conduit for recalling the textual.

Like Protestantism, Evangelicalism, while bound by a general agreement on common doctrines, is a heterogeneous, ecclesio-social movement. It is found among most Protestant denominations, and describes a global enterprise committed to the spread of a historical understanding of the gospel. Historically, Evangelicalism has three

---

[3] See John Harvey, *The Art of Piety: The Visual Culture of Welsh Nonconformity* (Cardiff: University of Wales Press, 1995); *Image of the Invisible: The Visualization of Religion in the Welsh Nonconformist Tradition* (Cardiff: University of Wales Press, 2000).

[4] The emblem book was both a pictorial and a literary genre, the format comprising symbolic images as engravings to which mottoes, verses, and epigrams were attached. Of the many religious examples published in the seventeenth century, Francis Quarles's *Emblemes* (1635) was the most popular.

[5] See Colleen McDannell, *Material Christianity: Religion and Popular Culture in America* (New Haven: Yale University Press, 1995); David Morgan, *Protestants and Pictures: Religion, Visual Culture, and the Age of American Mass Production* (New York; Oxford: Oxford University Press, 1999).

[6] Oliver Barclay, *Evangelicalism in Britain 1935–1995: A Personal Sketch* (Leicester: Inter-Varsity Press, 1997), 79–113.

main phases of development, identified with: first, the Lutheran wing of the Reformation; secondly, the succession of religious revivals or awakenings in the eighteenth and nineteenth centuries; and, thirdly, since the twentieth century, the Holiness, Pentecostal, Charismatic, Fundamentalist, and neo-Reformation groups.[7] The doctrinal emphases of Evangelicalism include: conversion (through an experience of spiritual rebirth); biblicism (that is, the acceptance of the Bible as the supreme basis of authority in matters of faith and practice); activism (in preaching and sharing one's faith, principally); and crucicentrism (a focus upon the merits of Christ's redemptive sacrifice).[8] Consequently, Evangelicalism is suspicious of Roman Catholic and High Church traditions such as the saving virtues of the sacraments, ceremonies, vestments, the authority of the Established Church, the claims of episcopate, and (of particular relevance to this discussion) the use of images in the public declaration of the gospel and private devotion. Evangelicalism is, therefore, Low Church in orientation.[9]

During the seventeenth and eighteenth centuries, it was 'low' in many other respects too. The movement's mission to the masses exploited the growing means of mechanical reproduction, disseminating its message through low-cultural and ephemeral forms such as newspapers, broadsides, cheap prints and pamphlets.[10] Conversion and devotion were further encouraged by immaterial expressions of Evangelical belief, such as dramatic, emotional, and practical preaching (unadorned by elevated rhetoric and allusions to high culture, so beloved of High Churchmen);[11] the laity, for their part,

---

[7] Derek J. Tidball, *Who Are the Evangelicals?: Tracing the Roots of Today's Movements* (London: Marshall Pickering, [1994]), 219–23.

[8] D. W. Bebbington, *Evangelicalism in Modern Britain: A History from the 1730s to the 1980s*, (Unwin Hyman, 1989), 1–19; W. C. G. Proctor, *Evangelical Thought and Practice* (London: James Clarke & Co., 1946), 9–12.

[9] The term Low Church dates from the eighteenth century, and was originally applied to a group within the Church of England (or Anglican Church). Low Churchmen attributed a 'low' or unimportant position to the claims of the episcopate, priesthood, and sacraments. Today, the term Low Church also connotes concepts associated with popular piety.

[10] See Tessa Watt, *Cheap Print and Popular Piety 1550–1640* (Cambridge: Cambridge University Press, 1991).

[11] Shultze sees the same shift as having taken place in the United States, as the first stirrings of a movement towards the mass evangelism of the lower class. Quentin J. Shultze (ed.), *American Evangelicals and the Mass Media: Perspectives on the Relationship Between American Evangelicals and the Mass Media* (Grand Rapids: MI: Academie Books; Zondervan, 1990), 35; John R. Knott, *The Sword of the Spirit: Puritan Responses to the Bible*, (Chicago; London: University of Chicago Press, 1980), 4.

extemporized communal and private prayer using everyday language. In the nineteenth and early twentieth centuries, Evangelicals appealed to the lower orders of society not only by means of educational, philanthropic, and legislative endeavours to improve the worker's lot, but also by promoting modes of worship and cultural tastes consistent with the working-class milieu: sentimental songs and choruses (popularized by the American singing evangelists Dwight L. Moody (1837–99) and Ira D. Sankey (1840–1908)) whose lilt and melody that had more in common with the music hall ditty than the English anthem tradition, accompanied evangelistic and revivalist meetings;[12] Pentecostal tongues-speaking and ecstatic dance – again, imported into England from the United States – provided non-intellectual forms of religious articulation for those who were disenfranchised from the learned class and culture;[13] while banners bright, text-laden tableware, and chromolithographic prints of preachers, patriarchs, and prophets (with designs derived from artefacts commonly used to celebrate national heroes and espouse socio-political ideals) helped to cultivate an aspirant working-class religious ethos.[14]

By the end of the twentieth century, Evangelicalism in Britain (following, as it had done in the early 1900s, the lead given by United States) had requisitioned every conceivable form of mass media and merchandise: it published books and magazines, set up record companies and TV and radio stations, and produced a variety of merchandise in order to provide a now burgeoning middle class with anything from devotional aids to Christian entertainment.[15] Consequently, Evangelicalism grew to be not only a theological enterprise but also a counterculture. Today, as then, a significant aspect of this culture's visual expression is its pious 'tie-ins' – commodities which adapt secular conventions of design and imagery (as in previous centuries) and, in some cases, exhibit a relationship to the broader traditions of Christian art, the visual culture and other creative expressions of Protestantism, and (more remotely) to the cultic objects and practices of biblical times. The merchandise consists of posters, badges, brooches, tiepins, T-shirts, greetings cards, bookmarks, wall plaques, stationery, and novelty goods. Collectively, the artefacts reflect the confluence of Low-Church religion with low-cultural forms, and of mass religion with mass production. Much of it is made by small

---

[12] Ira D. Sankey, *Sacred Songs and Solos* (London: Morgan & Scott Ltd, [1874]).

[13] Walter J. Hollenweger, *The Pentecostals* (trans. by R. A. Wilson, London: SCM Press, 1976), 177–208.

[14] See Harvey, *Art of Piety*.

[15] Linda Kintz and Julia Lesage, *Media, Culture, and the Religious Right* (Minneapolis; London: University of Minneapolis Press, 1988), 3, 36, 87.

promotional businesses (of which not all are consecrated to the Evangelical cause), and retailed through Christian bookshops, church bookstalls, and by mail order.[16] More often, the artefacts express universally Christian, rather than sectarian sentiments, and so appeal across the board of Evangelical churches, Protestant denominations, and to the Roman Catholic community. Like souvenirs, these items are often cheap and affordable and, therefore, without any intrinsic prestige or preciousness beyond their associations or the sentiments they mediate. Similarly, the choice of artefact reveals who the purchaser or recipient is and with what they wish to associate themselves,[17] variously serving as a visual statement of religious identity, a seal of allegiance, an affirmation of convictions, and an externalization of the inner motions of the spirit.

In addition to serving as a tribal badge, the merchandise fosters a culture of remembering. Remembering is an obligation for Evangelicals. Throughout the Bible, God commands all men and women not to forget his word (Deuteronomy 4: 31; Psalm 119: 176), and to express their obedience by memorizing, understanding, and acting upon, as well as by presenting, it to the mind and conscience of unbelievers through evangelism (that is, preaching and personal testimony). Visual artefacts have always played a significant role in fulfilling these duties. In the seventeenth and eighteenth centuries, Scripture texts were either painted or carved on the walls of their early churches and chapels to fill the vacuum created by Calvin's ban on images. They pasted broadsheets on the walls of the domestic interior, and, in the nineteenth century hung samplers, long-stitch work, printed texts, and stencilled crockery in both their own houses and those of God – a literal interpretation of the scriptural injunction to '*shew* ... the word of God' (1 Samuel 9.27) (my emphasis).[18] Thus, the word was seen (in the sense that it was both ensured and visible) to be remembered.

---

[16] In 1974 there were some 120 independent and chains of Christian bookshop outlets in the UK. Today there are over 700, together with a further 48 art and craft suppliers (Eric A. Thorn, *Directory of Christian Organisations* (London: Pyramid Press, 1974), 19–21; Heather Wraight (ed.), *UK Christian Handbook 2002/03* (London: Christian Research, 2002), 89–95, 234–6.

[17] Michael Hitchcock and Ken Teague (eds.), *Souvenirs: The Material Culture of Tourism* (Aldershot: Ashgate Publishing Co., 2000), 8, 91; Jukka Gronow, *The Sociology of Taste* (London: Routledge, 1997), 42–3.

[18] John Calvin, *Institutes of the Christian Religion* (3 vols; Edinburgh: Calvin Translation Society, 1845, I), 120–33; John Sympson Sergrove, *The True Nature of Protestant and Christian Education: A Sermon Preached in the Parish Church of St. Luke, Chelsea* (Chelsea: G. Bryan, 1824), 12.

Identity and Evangelism

The use of artefacts to articulate identity and bring about remembrance coalesces in the context of evangelism. During the late twentieth century, Evangelicals utilized merchandise to render not only the gospel but also their own movement visible and unforgettable. Having entered the marketplace, they recognized that in a multi cultural, multi faith society Christianity was no longer the only religious option; and in an increasingly fragmented denominational and theological framework, Evangelicalism was not the only Christian option.[19] In order to secure a distinctive profile for both, Evangelicals adopted the devices, language, and gameplay of advertising. Marketing the gospel effected a significant paradigm shift: free grace became a saleable commodity, and 'the lost and lone' a large target audience. Moreover, as Evangelicals realized, sinners were not the only consumers; there were two distinct groups – unbelievers, who were being prepared to buy God (through evangelism), and believers, who were prepared to buy and use promotional merchandise in order to evangelise.

The branding of Evangelicalism required a distillation of its message into memorable and visible confessional slogans, emphasizing its doctrinal distinctives: the person, work, and the second coming of Christ, and the need for conversion. The designs for evangelistic merchandise either incorporate, or else are exclusively, biblical texts, mottoes, and catchphrases expressing a Christian viewpoint. The exception is items based upon traditional Christian symbols such as the alpha and omega, dove, cross, and fish. These are popularly realized as 22-carat hard gold-plated lapel badges and scarf pins, and plastic bumper stickers. (Originally, the fish, or *ichthus*, was a sign used among the early believers to show, clandestinely, their loyalty to Christ. Evangelicals sport the symbol to signify the same, but freely and confidently.)[20] Since the 1970s, cotton T-shirt and bag designs have had a prominent role in promoting the message *to* young people *by* young people principally. During the counterculture offensive of the 1960s, screenprinted T-shirts were the uniform of protest and disenfranchisement; a decade later, the power, action, peace, and liberation of which Evangelicals spoke was spiritual rather than political. The rationale for propagating the Word by this means (so some Evangelicals believe) is biblical, according to the following principle: The apostle Paul referred to the Christian as an 'epistle of Christ', bearing the spiritual inscription of God's word, 'known and

[19] Craig G. Bartholomew and Thorsten Moritz, *Christ and Consumerism: Critical Reflections of the Spirit of Our Age* (Carlisle: Paternoster Press, 2000), 21–5.

[20] Those outside the faith community frequently misinterpret it as an emblem for the fishmongers' guild.

read of all men' (2 Corinthians 3.3), or, as the Puritan Richard Allestree (1619–81) put it: 'the *lives* of Christians were the *transcripts* of their doctrine'.[21] Christians, thus conceived, were tangible memorials to the gospel message. The T-shirt literalizes the metaphor, transforming the wearer into a walking placard.

Wearing the Word had an Old Testament precedent too. Gems engraved with the names of the twelve tribes of Israel were incorporated into the ephod and breastplate of judgement worn by the high priest, as a permanent, visible reminder of the people whom he carried with him before God (Exodus 28.2–30). The high priest also wore, fastened at the front of his mitre, upon his forehead, the plate of the holy crown; 'a plate of pure gold, and [engraved] upon it, like the engravings of a signet 'holiness to the Lord' – a sign and authentication of the people's consecration and of their acceptance before God (Exodus 28.36–8; 39.30).[22] God also charged the Israelites to bear the brand of the Word in the form of a portion of Scripture written on a band and worn around their heads, between their eyes, and bound upon their hand. These physical appurtenances were, thus, a constant reminder to remember all his statutes and his commandments (Deuteronomy 6.2–9).[23]

Promotional companies referred to T-shirts, badges, and other forms of dress accessories as 'witness wear' – the vestment of laity, worn by a generation of Evangelicals who were ostentatious in worship and courageously 'coming out' about their faith at a time when (in the United States, especially) Evangelicalism was developing into a religious and political force to be reckoned with. These artefacts signify the God they carry with them before a lost humanity and represent not only a non-verbal and informal means of *telling* by *showing* the gospel but also a confident assertion of religious identity, and as a reminder (as much to themselves as to others) of the God whom they serve. The design imagery, some of which also reflects the ex-ecclesial affiliations and consumerist trends of young Evangelicals, tends to be imitative and parasitic. On one level, this is intentional. Evangelicalism ransacks and parodies popular logos and graphic styles unashamedly, connecting

---

[21] Richard Allestree, *The Causes of the Decay of Christian Piety; Or, An Impartial Investigation of the Ruines of Christian Religion Undermin'd by Unchristian Practice* (London: R. Norton, 1683), 24.

[22] The position of the plate on the high priest's forehead (literally, between his eyes) is also significant. In the Judaeo-Christian tradition, the forehead, being open and fully visible, was the most obvious place for a mark or seal of designation (Ezekiel 9.4; Revelation 13.16).

[23] The practice is expressed, in its present form among the Jews through the custom of wearing phylacteries – two hollow cubes containing a parchment, worn on the head and hand.

hype and hip, sacred and secular, in an attempt to dispel Christianity's air of starchy seriousness and otherworldliness, and to address the unchurched (so-called) using a graphic language that is comprehensible in terms of their culture. For example, one T-shirt design consists of a theological adaptation and amalgamation of the famous Pepsi Cola and Coca Cola slogans of the 1970s, with the words: 'Life giving, soul saving, joy filling, peace making, long suffering, load lifting, heart thrilling, rock solid Jesus Christ – he's the real thing.'

This endeavour parallels other developments in Evangelicalism during the 1970s. New translations of the Bible aimed for clarity and immediacy, by adapting the ancient texts to the everyday speech of a contemporary readership. Likewise, new hymns abandoned the theological ruminations and poetic archaisms of the previous centuries' hymnology in favour of modern idioms, prosaic statements, and musical settings influenced by contemporary popular songs. On another level, derivativeness was the fruit of Evangelicalism's own history. Unlike for example Shakerism in the United States, the movement never had a conscious and consistent visual style. The closest it achieved to a visual expression of biblical purism was in the form of the earliest Dissenting and Nonconformist places of worship. They were built using simple vernacular building techniques and were characterized by an economic, homespun, plain style and pared-down austerity which conveyed a formidable visual identity predicated on the invisibility of God, the simplicity of New Testament worship, and establishing a contradistinction to Roman Catholic and High Anglican Churches. [24]

In spite of the merchandise's street wise, contemporary (if hackneyed) graphic style, the meaning of the message very often remains resolutely unintelligible to those who are unfamiliar with the whole fabric of the Bible, of which the screenprinted quotes and catchphrases are but as loose threads. The artefacts also reveal a painful naivety regarding the reciprocity of medium and message. In some examples, image and style reflect inappropriately on the biblical text as, to quote Peter Lloyd Jones, 'visual reality clashes violently with the profundity of the religious sentiment leading to bathos'.[25] For instance, one typographic design, set in variant Old English Text type, rendered as though in polished chrome (with its connotations of motorbike culture and heavy metal music), refers to salvation as 'Heavenly Metal: It'll Rock the Hell out of You'. The often strident, triumphalist, self-

---

[24] William R. Davies, *Rocking the Boat: The Challenge of the House Church* (Basingstoke: Marshall Pickering, 1986), 140–51; Harvey, *Image of the Invisible*, 6–25.

[25] Peter Lloyd Jones, *Taste Today: The Role of Appreciation in Consumerism and Design* (Oxford: Pergamon Press, 1991), 66.

satisfied mottoes, passé allusions (devoid of Postmodern irony), such as 'Try a Close Encounter of the Real Kind', and arbitrary design styles, betray a cultural awkwardness – the absence of a developed and confident understanding of forms and their habitual significance – which is not lost on their audience.

Piety and Commodity

'Wear and share' merchandise enables Evangelicals to propagate the cause as they venture into the world. Their homes, too, are the setting for evangelistic opportunity – the place where the world comes unto them in the shape of unconverted visitors, friends, and family members. What could be called 'display and pray' merchandise, chiefly wall-mounted ornaments and utility objects meant for show, hang up the staircase and down the hall, preaching silent sermons to the weary, lost, and lone. The home is Evangelicalism's most unecclesiastical context. In the absence of traditional Christian symbols and representations (such as a crucifix, cross, and figurines of holy persons, familiar in Roman Catholic domestic interiors) plaques, posters, and ceramic mugs signify the occupants' faith. The plaques are usually 20 centimetres in height, available in a variety of shapes, and comprise veneered or laminated fibreboard, painted in wood effect or pastel colours (appropriate for almost any décor). Many examples bear inscriptions in gold- or silver-leaf stamping, together with stencilled or screen-printed pictures; and are designed to be hung on die-cast metal mouldings finished to imitate antique brass. Posters, postcards, and, latterly, photocards, are produced cheaply in a range of sizes on laminated paper and card suitable for either framing or pinning up in more informal areas of the Evangelical home, such as the bathroom, kitchen, and children's bedroom. The mugs are manufactured in white, glazed bone china; ceramic whiteware; or plastic, and decorated with transfer prints. (The more expensive range is sold gift-boxed.) They combine, somewhat jarringly, spiritual sentiment with a desperately mundane utility.

The artefacts each comprise a biblical text, inspirational maxim, creed, prayer, hymn verse, or moralizing poem, often along with a photograph, illustration, or decorative adjunct [See illustration 1]. (Increasingly, commercial prints showing Jesus and acts of Christian piety join with photographs of family, deceased relatives, and friends above the mantelpiece. As Colleen McDannell remarks of the same practice in the United States, heavenly kin and earthly kin are brought together at the family shrine.)[26] The merchandise removes Scripture from the closed covers of a book, converting it into a mobile,

---

[26] McDannell, *Material Christianity*, 34.

purposeful, and godly decoration – a perpetual memorial to the faithfulness of both God and the family.

In Victorian times, the biblical texts chosen for display were frequently alarming and confrontational. 'Prepare to Meet Thy God' was among the most popular. They warned the spectator to heed the consequences of sin, the certainty of death, and judgement to come. By contrast, contemporary examples foster a serene and reassuring ethos which aims to encourage faith in the unbeliever and pacify the believer's anxiety. Texts such as 'Peace, Be Still' and 'The Lord is my Shepherd' emphasize the consolations of God and signal the displacement of a fearless, unselfconscious, sandwich-board piety by a religious identity which is more optimistic, heartening, soft-bellied, and inoffensive, in its lack of aggression and wish to wound.[27] The appropriately anodyne, romantic naturalism of the accompanying imagery draws for the most part on God's second book – the natural world. Flowers and animals emblematize the texts' reference to God's goodness and abundant provision, and the believer's spiritual life and growth, following the imagery of the Psalms. The designs and their deployment, together with the framing devices, engender a nostalgic air of old colonialism and rustic Victorianism, while motifs and subjects recall domestic decals popular in the 1950s. These were eras more sympathetic to Evangelical values, in which, some writers argue, Evangelicals remain psychologically marooned.[28]

Evangelism is not the sole end of visualizing Scripture in these ways. The sentiments of the artefacts' texts also address the needs and experience of those belonging to 'the household of faith', just as they had in the previous two centuries. In Copley's *Memorials of Practical Piety* (1830), an example of a nineteenth-century biographical genre which portrayed the exemplary lives of contemporary Christians who had died well, the terminally ill Marianne Beuzevil reflects: 'How humbled would I be, when I consider what trifles have, this week, and do continually keep me from my retired devotions. Oh! when shall I have my heart and affections placed more entirely on heavenly

[27] Victorian text-ware incorporated consolatory verses too. Today, however, this type of verse predominates, rather than serves, as it did in the past, as sugar to the vinegar of the fire and brimstone texts.

[28] Alister McGrath, *Evangelicalism and the Future of Christianity* (London: Hodder & Stoughton, 1994), 111–22; David Wells, 'On Being Evangelical: Some Theological Differences and Similarities', in M. A. Noll, D. W. Bebbibgton and G. A. Rawlyk (eds), *Evangelicalism: Comparative Studies of Popular Protestantism in North America, the British Isles, and Beyond, 1700–1990* (Oxford: Oxford University Press, 1994), 389–410.

objects.'[29] By 'Heavenly objects' she meant spiritual realities. But they could equally have been material artefacts (like those mentioned already), elevated on the walls to remind the believer to fix their heart on goals and priorities above, when the vain and even the legitimate things of this world press too hard for attention. Today too, such heavenly objects provide a visual focus for devotion amid not only life's distractions but also the clutter of possessions that comprise the domestic environment. While sharing the same substance of such worldly trappings, the message transfigures the object, sanctifying and legitimizing its materiality by association with the divine truth, and providing an uplifting purpose and a justification for their purchase. The relative inexpensiveness of these artefacts in comparison to other household items also serves to play down their status as acquisitions.

The objectification of the Word in the home as a means to preserve piety and to express religious identity originates in the early history of the Judaism. God charged the Israelites to write his commandments on the doorposts of their houses and on their gates, once they possessed the land of promise (Deuteronomy 6.9; 11.20).[30] Previously, in the land of Egypt he had instructed them to strike the side posts and lintel of their houses with hyssop soaked in the blood of the sacrificial lamb, as a sign to the Lord to pass over (Exodus 12.7, 21–3). The blood and the Word were both visualizations of the covenantal relationship. The former was an abstract expression, made at the commencement of their wanderings, and before the composition of the Torah, as a symbol of protection, for God to see. The latter was made at the conclusion of their wanderings, as a symbol of their fidelity and obedience, for the families of Israel to see, lest they forget 'the Lord, which brought [them] forth ... from the house of bondage' (Deuteronomy 6.12). The context of the command suggests that, in all likelihood, the domestic inscriptions were also a means of teaching the children, in addition to oral instruction, and an *aide-mémoire* to instil God's commandments in their 'heart' (Deuteronomy 6.6–7).[31] The practice of setting up text-bearing artefacts on the walls of Evangelical homes retains some of the essential significance of the inscriptions on the Israelites' doorposts and gates.

---

[29] Esther Copley, *Memorials of Practical Piety: As Exemplified in the Lives of Miss Marianne Beuzeville Who Died April 10, 1828 and Mrs Bridget Byles Who Died March 17, 1829* (Holdsworth, 1830), 17.

[30] Today Jews fulfil this commandment by enclosing a parchment containing two portions of the book of Deuteronomy in a box called a *mezuzah* and fastening it to their doorposts.

[31] The Hebrews used the term the heart (*leb* or *lebab*) to denote the seat of consciousness, the governing centre of the will, personality, as well as intellectual activities, such as memory (Deuteronomy 4: 9).

The plaques, posters, plates, and prints are, in addition to being consecrated decoration, covenantal signs between God and believers – visual memorials (lest they forget) of the promises and consolations of God and of fundamental Christian duties.

The artefacts externalize Scripture (to be seen), in order for believers to internalize it (to be remembered). The practice reflects a religious culture, wherein the Word is not restricted to Sunday services but experienced daily in the home. The Evangelicals' predecessors, the Puritans, encouraged believers to read the Bible through at least once a year. They regarded the home as a school in which the children in particular and servants were to be catechized and encouraged to learn the Scripture by heart. Protestants published numerous booklets of so-called proof texts, which drew together short and pithy Bible verses to provide a shorthand corroboration of Christian doctrine, God's promises, and moral axioms.[32] Similar texts, to the same end, are found on contemporary domestic artefacts.

Evangelicals, likewise, view the inculcation of biblical knowledge in children as a priority. For this reason, they Christianize objects that children habitually use with the inscription of a Bible verse. These objects are usually accessories associated with their general education and play. The eternal and the ephemeral, the cherished and the cheap, the holy and utilitarian are conjoined, as pencils, rulers, rubbers, and sharpeners are conscripted into sacred service. They also amalgamate religious culture and consumer culture, adopting and adapting the forms of promotional merchandise by printing a biblical verse rather than the company logo on them [See illustration 2].[33] The same accessory is available bearing one of a variety of texts. Therefore, the relationship between text and support is entirely arbitrary. However, occasionally, fortuitous meaning arises from a conjunction. For example, the inevitable consonance between the inscription 'Christ Died for Us' and its support – a novelty ballpoint pen in the shape of a six-inch nail – transforms an otherwise innocuous item of stationery into a plastic imitation relic of the crucifixion [See illustration 3]. Correspondences between other artefacts and religious concepts may be forged: thus erasers speak of Christ's expunction of sin; sharpeners of the quickening and exacting nature of the spiritual life; and pencils of holy inscription. Granted, these accessories in themselves, irrespective of the accompanying text, do not convey such ideas (nor are they intended to). Nevertheless, this is neither a wilful nor (necessarily) an idiosyncratic association.

---

[32] Christopher Tolley, *Domestic Biography: The Legacy of Evangelicalism in Four Nineteenth-Century Families* (Oxford: Clarendon Press, 1987), 33.
[33] McDannell, *Material Christianity*, 239.

Evangelicals encourage a parabolic outlook on life; they are not averse to transforming everyday events and things into spiritual pictures to embody biblical truths, to serve as remembrancers and as fit objects of meditation. The Puritan writer Lewis Bayly (d. 1631) advocated that Christians contemplate every aspect of their experience, from waking to sleep, from a spiritual perspective, thereby transforming their whole world into a veritable tableau of emblems. As they prepare for bed, he suggests:

Things to be meditated upon as thou art putting off thy cloathes ... That the day is coming when thou must be barely *unstript* of *all* that thou hast in the *World* ... When thou seest thy *bed*, let it put thee in minde of thy *grave* ... Let therefore thy bed-clothes represent unto thee the mould of the earth, that shall cover thee: thy *sheets, thy winding sheet*; thy *sleep*, thy *death*, thy waking, thy *resurrection*.[34]

The object assumed religious significance only when vivified by the gloss. Once converted into a sign, it functioned as a mnemonic device. In theory, frequent exposure to the image on devotional merchandise, and to the accompanying text, helps to instil the verse in the memory. Like Bayly's object lesson, the merchandise's image is subservient to the text (text is always visually prominent), and serves to draw attention not to itself but to a higher, spiritual reality. In other words, the image is a trigger or pointer. The text defines the image's meaning and delimits its multivalence or propensity to be read in a variety of ways, not all of which might accord with sound doctrine. For this reason (and in keeping with the earliest examples of Protestant emblemature), seldom does an image appear independently of a biblical verse.

A notable exception is the drawing of hands, clasped in prayer, by the German artist Albrecht Dürer (1471–1528), who was converted under the influence of Martin Luther (1483–1546). In this example, the visual culture of popular religion meets the European high art tradition. Dürer's durable emblem of earnest piety has been, since the second half of the twentieth century, transformed and reiterated, redrawn and painted, moulded and embossed on cards, plaques, and mugs [See illustration 4]. Usually the plaques are composed of an amalgamation of techniques and components, including a plastic relief-moulding of the hands, painted in either a tarnished or a polished bronze effect, affixed to a copper-etched surface, which is in turn glued to a wood or fibreboard support. The popularity of the image derives, in part, from its appeal to the Protestants' pictorial sensibility. This is not, after all, an illegitimate icon depicting God or holy persons, intended to mediate worship; rather, it symbolizes (contemporary Evangelicals rarely pray

---

[34] Lewis Bayly, *The Practice of Piety: Directing a Christian How to Walke that He May Please God* (1611), (London: M. Allott, 1711), 174–5.

with their hands clasped together) an act of direct, biblically sanctioned worship. The artefacts based upon this drawing, when placed in the home, serve as a visual reminder for individuals and families to pray, and, when specific texts are added, as the visual adjunct to specific imprecations.

Where image and text are present together, the former functions as either an illustration, a decorative embellishment, or a backdrop. Some images are symbolic, derived directly and indirectly from the biblical signs, similes, and metaphors, while others have a looser connection, depicting picturesque scenes or the physical context of Christian worship. The lighthouse (an image popularly chosen for calendars) is an example of an indirect, biblical symbol. It is used invariably as a metaphor for either the Scripture (illustrating its propensity to enlighten) or of Christ as 'the light of the world'. The emblem, derived from nineteenth-century British hymnology, adapts the Old Testament image of the lamp or candle to the circumstances of a seafaring nation. Pictures of the sea, coastline, and harbour are the stock-in-trade of Evangelical text-pictures. They hang beside scenes of unidentified forests, fields, vales, and glens, printed with an artificiality of colour one associates with 1950s and 1960s picture postcards. The pictures represent idyllic settings of enjoyment, tranquillity, fair weather and well-being – a slice heaven on earth, as it were. The relation between picture and text is, here, casual: the picture is not an illustration but a mood setter, representing the natural world to evoke the sense of supernatural bliss and serenity and to remind the viewer of the benefits of faith in, and obedience to, the text's sentiments. Images such as these sometimes have an emblematic content too. Harbours, in the literary imagery of Protestant hymnology, are associated with the concepts of spiritual embarkation, arrival in heaven, and a safe haven from the storms of life [See illustration 5].[35] The rock in the foreground of this picture resonates in the Evangelical mindset with allusions to Christ, the rock of salvation (Psalm 28.1).[36] Likewise, fishing vessels connote those used by the disciples to fish (the metaphor for evangelism) and from which Christ preached. At first, the juxtaposition of the text 'Believe on the Lord Jesus Christ' and a picture of Alpine skiing seems wholly incongruous. However, in the Old Testament snow is a symbol of purity and cleansing from sin, which, in the New Testament, is a consequence

---

[35] Priscilla Jane Owens, 'Will your anchor hold in the storms of life', *Christian Hymns* (Bridgend: Evangelical Movement of Wales, 1977), no. 489.

[36] The rock is the Pauline metaphor for Christ and an antitype for the rock God gave to nourish the Israelites in the wilderness (1 Corinthians 10.4; Numbers 20.8–11) Toplady's hymn 'Rock of Ages, cleft for me' draws on this metaphor.

of faith in Christ (Isaiah 1.18; 1 John 1.7). In the same vein, the picture of a hovercraft on the button badge, top right, is, perhaps, an extremely oblique allusion to Christ walking on the water [See illustration 6]. Thus for those with knowledge of the Bible who see with the eye of faith otherwise neutral images are connotatively rich.

Artefacts designed to appeal particularly to young children often sacrifice the pious seriousness of the adult variety. The texts are simple, upbeat confessional statements, and gentle encouragements to praise, pray, seek, trust, do good, and be converted, and are exemplified by brightly coloured illustrations of anthropomorphic, cute and chirpy animals and insects printed on stickers, bookmarks, and badges. They serve as gifts or rewards for good behaviour. In the course of time, such artefacts (especially those given as Sunday School prizes) become mementos which evoke memories of particular places, persons, and events associated with childhood and early religious experience.

This cosy and ebullient version of Christianity also appeals to adults who are unable to heed the apostle Paul's example and relinquish 'childish things'. The advertisement for holy teddy bears (beatification by beanification) declares that: 'Holy Bears teddy bears answer to a calling. Our teddy bears honour Christian themes, the Sacraments and life-cycle occasions. Ideal as gifts for children and adults alike, each bear comes with an inspirational quote from the Bible. There is a place for Christianity in today's world'.[37] Quite how a text-bearing teddy bear provides evidence of that last assertion remains a moot point.[38] In the secular realm, promotional and fund raising teddy bears, inscribed with the names and slogans of companies and slogans, are common. The association of a teddy bear with Christianity is not an entirely arbitrary conjunction. According to medieval legend, bear cubs, which teddy bears closely resemble, were believed to be born shapeless, their form being given to them by their mother. This act became a symbol of Christianity in its capacity to reform and regenerate the heathen. Today, however, these bears project neither theology nor fable, but an

---

[37] The bears are made and distributed internationally by a company based in the United States via bookshops and by e-commerce (Horizons Distributors, 'The Original Holy Bears' [advertisement], *Christian Bookseller*, no. 8, (2000), [back cover]).

[38] Another American company called Legends of the Faith distributes 'toys that teach', including teddy bears. Sales figures for 2001 indicate that '700,000 Biblical character bears' had been sold. (They produce a range of 46 bears, covering Old and New Testament characters.) Their modest expectation is to reach 5% of the Evangelical community in the United States, representing some 4 million people. The company also offers an 'apparel line' called 'Yahwear' (Legends of the Faith, Inc., 'Legends of the Faith' [advertisement], *Christian Bookseller*, no. 14, (2000), 5).

uncomfortable amalgam of profundity and banality, and a soft-centred approach to evangelism and piety (literally so, in this case).

The use of merchandise to give form and shape to gospel and godliness has led to a convergence of the ethos of Holy Land and Disneyland, a cheapening of religious feeling, together with a gratuitous espousal of themes, motifs, devices, and, ostensibly, the ethics of advertising. As a result, the prophets' message is overlaid with a message about profit, and churches become places we now go to to shop for not only a particular brand of Christianity but also its branded goods. Evangelicals have engaged one of the central elements of contemporary culture – consumerism – while ignoring and despising every other element. Consequently, they reproduce the forms of culture uncritically (creating, to use Greenberg's expression, a 'simulacra of genuine culture'[39]), while the significance, value, and usefulness of the merchandise reflect little understanding of, or interest in, concepts of aesthetic subtlety, material and design quality, mediation, uniqueness, and ambition.

British Evangelical merchandise is kitsch in a precise and exclusive sense. It is essentially conservative – lacking the excess and eccentricity; the sense of the comic, camp, and crude; and the flamboyance or pretension more usually associated with this category of objects. What Evangelical kitsch shares with the secular variety is its espousal of the clichéd, trite, and trivial; aesthetic mediocrity; and a devaluation of true feeling by association with processes of commodification, plasticity, imitativeness, and affectation.

Most Evangelicals would not consider the hardware of their religion as a species of kitsch. The heterogeneity of the movement (as of any other community) prevents the evolution of a consensual criteria of judgement; class, gender, race, age, and social and intellectual identity all condition opinions as to what is kitsch.[40] More importantly, as Sternberg observes, the 'recognition of kitsch comes from the way things are looked at, from the way they affect you'.[41] Evangelicals, for the most part, stand in need of a more highly developed visual literacy and familiarity with high-art forms (the acquired self-consciousness and cultivated standards regarding taste and tastelessness) with, and against, which to perceive what is trashy and tacky. Aesthetic principles

---

[39] Clement Greenberg, 'Avant-Garde and Kitsch' in *Perceptions and Judgements, 1939-1944*, John O'Brian (ed.), *Clement Greenberg: The Collected Essays and Criticism*, vol. 1, Chicago: University of Chicago Press, 1986), (5-22), 12.

[40] Frank Burch Brown, *Good Taste, Bad Taste, and Christian Taste: Aesthetics in Religious Life* (New York: Oxford University Press, 2000), 3–4.

[41] Jacques Sternberg, *Kitsch* (1971) Marina Henderson (ed.), (London: Academy Editions; St. Martin's Press, 1972), 1–2.

and issues are rarely considered relevant in the cult(ure) of Evangelicalism. Consequently, they regard religious artefacts (as things in themselves) to be neither beautiful nor ugly, nor intended to illicit visual gratification, nor to embody aesthetic virtue for its own sake. Rather, these products are intended to serve God's glory and 'man's' good. (This is deeply utilitarian merchandise.) The Evangelicals' esteem of religious artefacts (thus conceived) is based upon the object's objective and the message's meaning. (The pleasure of the text is, again, paramount.)

The paraphernalia of Evangelicalism has turned the abstract and didactic word into a concrete sign. Whatever benefits there are in terms of establishing religious identity and stimulating piety, such artefacts as those hung on domestic walls sacramentalize the Word. It is as though the mere presence of the word (elevated like the host) imparts grace. Alternatively, they risk turning the Word into a talisman, with which to ward off evil and doubt. Paradoxically, the ubiquitous presence of the Word, on almost every conceivable object undermines the very process of remembrance that it has intended to encourage. After all, what motivation is there to memorise that which is everywhere and constantly visible?

Long before the commodification of Christianity, believers were consumers of the Word in a very different sense. They ingested Scripture by committing verses to heart through diligent study, reciting it repeatedly, and by applying the texts not to objects but to their lives: the Christian, wrote the Puritan Thomas Watson (1620–86), 'copies out the Word in his daily walk'.[42] Thus, one could conjecture that, just as the nature of Evangelical piety shapes the character of the visual artefacts, so too the nature of the artefacts shapes the character of Evangelical piety (and of evangelism, for that matter). In other words, the quality of the visual culture may serve as an index to the quality of the faith. Only now are speculations like these being aired, and cautiously. In this respect, contemporary scholarship lags behind much earlier attempts to theorize. Indeed, it was the first Protestants who identified the reciprocity of faith and its fabric: how inappropriate doctrine gives rise to false representations of God and holy persons, which in turn corrupt a proper view of religion. Some of them, and their successors, addressed this observation with whitewash and hammers. Today a subtler and more intelligent response is required.

---

[42] Thomas Watson, *The Godly Mans Picture, Drawn with a Scripture-Pensil; Or, Some Characteristical Notes of a Man that Shall Go to Heaven* (London: Thomas Parkhurst, 1666), 82.

1. Advertisement for 'Colonial Charm Plaques' (1980s), 26 x 20 cm

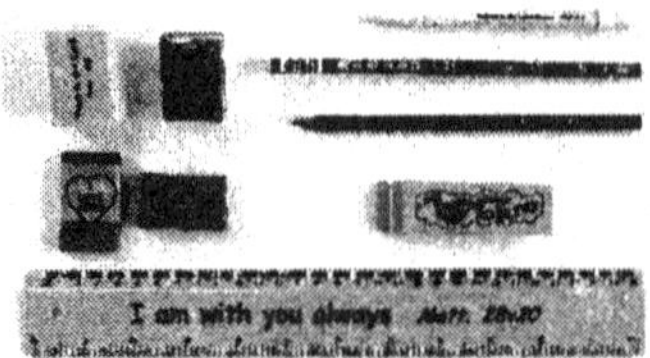

2. Text-bearing stationary: ruler, erasers, pencil sharpeners, pencils, and ballpoint pen (1981–2002)

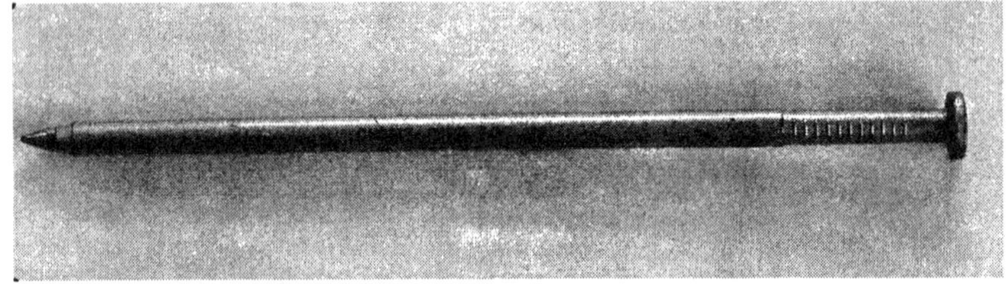

3. Text-bearing ballpoint pen in the shape of a nail (1980s) 17 cm

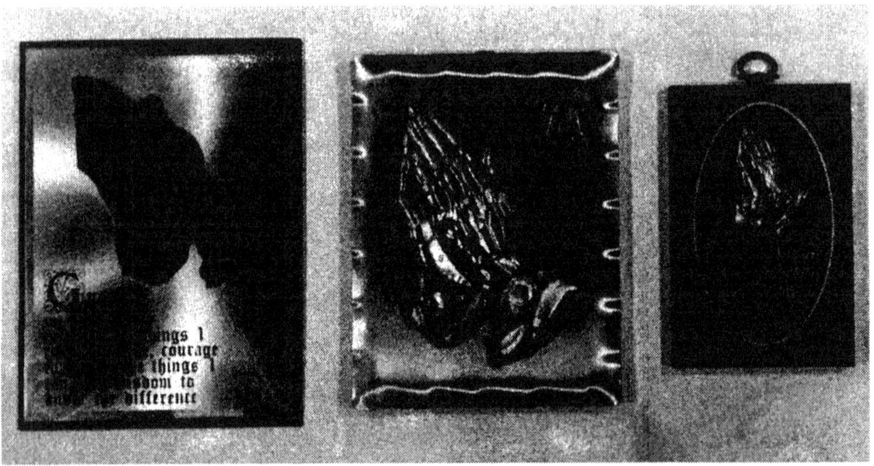

4. Plaques: praying hands (1980s) 19 x 15 cm (left); praying hands with 'Grant me the serenity' (1980s) 21 x 16 cm (centre); A&F Canada; praying hands with 'Bless This House' (2002) 15 x 10 cm (right)

5. Calendar picture: 'He who believes in Me has everlasting life' (2001)
12 x 14 cm

6. Badges (1981) 3.8 cm diameter

CHAPTER 14

'The Prince of Pastoral Preachers': The Oxford Sermons of Francis Chavasse

Andrew Atherstone

Francis Chavasse was one of the leading evangelicals within the Church of England between the 1880s and the 1920s.[1] He was the second Principal of Wycliffe Hall in Oxford, influencing a generation of young evangelical clergymen, and under his leadership the Hall went through one of the most vibrant periods of its history.[2] In 1900 he succeeded J. C. Ryle as Bishop of Liverpool, where he ministered for almost a quarter of a century, consolidating the evangelical cause within that new urban diocese. Yet Oxford was Chavasse's first love and amongst his lasting legacies to the city are the Oxford Pastorate (founded in 1893 as an evangelical chaplaincy for the University)[3] and St Peter's College (founded in 1928 as a hall for evangelical undergraduates).[4] Through his widespread influence Chavasse helped to mould Anglican evangelical identity.

Chavasse first sprang to prominence not as a theological college

---

[1] The standard biography is J. B. Lancelot, *Francis James Chavasse, Bishop of Liverpool* (Oxford: Blackwell, 1929). See also 'The Undergraduate Diary of Francis Chavasse 1865-1868' edited by Andrew Atherstone, in Mark Smith & Stephen Taylor (eds.), *Evangelicalism in the Church of England c.1790-c.1900*, Church of England Record Society vol. 12 (Woodbridge: Boydell, 2004), 109-282.

[2] Andrew Atherstone, 'The Founding of Wycliffe Hall, Oxford', *Anglican and Episcopal History* 73 (March 2004), 78-102.

[3] G. Ian F. Thomson, *The Oxford Pastorate: the First Half Century* (London: Canterbury Press, 1946); Mark A. Smith, 'A Foundation of Influence: The Oxford Pastorate and Elite Recruitment in Early Twentieth-century Anglican Evangelicalism' in Deryck W. Lovegrove (ed.), *The Rise of the Laity in Evangelical Protestantism* (London: Routledge, 2002), 202-13.

[4] Eric H. F. Smith, *St Peter's: the Founding of an Oxford College* (Gerrards Cross: Colin Smythe, 1978); William A. Evershed, 'Party and Patronage in the Church of England 1800-1945: a Study of Patronage Trusts and Patronage Reform' (D.Phil, Oxford University, 1985), 230-82; Selwyn Gummer, *The Chavasse Twins* (London: Hodder & Stoughton, 1963), 112-28.

principal or as a senior bishop, but as a pastor and preacher. In 1877, aged just thirty, he was appointed rector of St Peter-le-Bailey, Oxford, one of the 'quadrilateral' of large evangelical churches in the centre of the city. There for twelve years he developed an influential ministry amongst both townsfolk and undergraduates. His personal popularity and preaching ministry drew crowds. St Peter's was filled every Sunday evening with 600 eager listeners and so great was Chavasse's following that his friend, Canon Christopher at St Aldate's, often quipped, 'Brother, mind you don't enlarge your church, for if you do I shall have no congregation left.'[5] Chavasse's Oxford sermons are the focus of this chapter. Amongst his surviving papers in the Bodleian Library are 26 volumes containing detailed and closely-written notes on over 700 sermons, the vast majority of which are from his regular preaching ministry, Sunday by Sunday, at St Peter's.[6] He was convinced that the kingdom of God would be built 'not by the force of legions, nor by the power of intellect, but by teaching and preaching.'[7] These addresses provide a unique insight into Chavasse's theological and pastoral priorities, which lay at the heart of his evangelical identity.

There was 'quiet amusement' amongst Chavasse's congregation when, at the start of each sermon, he announced the number of his 'heads' – usually three, sometime two or four.[8] In imitation of his method, this chapter will examine some broad themes which emerge from his preaching ministry, under four 'heads'. Chavasse's sermons are earnest not erudite; devotional not doctrinal; compassionate not combative; and assured not alarmist.

Earnest not Erudite

Chavasse was not a polished orator. He spoke extempore, but without great eloquence and sometimes with 'an occasional slight stutter', brought on by tiredness and overwork.[9] After one stammering sermon he wrote in his diary, 'painful for the flesh: good for the Spirit'.[10] Nor was Chavasse a scholar. Although he read widely, he made no show of erudition, even when called to preach in the University pulpit. There

---

[5] *Oxford Journal Illustrated*, 11 February 1914, 6.

[6] Bodleian Library, MSS Chavasse dep. 45-73. I am grateful to the Master, Fellows and Scholars of St Peter's College, Oxford for permission to use these papers. In the following quotations, Chavasse's notes have been expanded into full prose, to aid readability.

[7] 'His Charge to Evangelize the World' (1893), MS Chavasse dep. 68, fo. 113.

[8] H. D. S. Sweetapple (ed.), *Parochial Sermons of Bishop Chavasse: Advent to Whit-Sunday* (London: SPCK, 1938), xi-xii.

[9] *Parochial Sermons*, xi; Lancelot, *Chavasse*, 42.

[10] Chavasse Diary, 10 August 1873, MS Chavasse dep. 22.

was no attempt to quote from ancient authors or obscure theologians. Chavasse insisted that the preacher should not speak 'with eloquence or rhetoric, but in a way suited to arrest, teach, and help his hearers.'[11] As a rule, he told his trainee preachers at Wycliffe Hall, sermons should use small words and short sentences, conveying the message in the simplest terms.[12] He observed:

> Much of our preaching, our testimony for Christ, is beyond our hearers. Eloquence, scholarship, subtlety of thought, profound learning are great gifts of God, but should simply not obscure God's message. He is a bad shepherd that holds the hay too high for the sheep. ... Ah, let us remember our great duty to be simple.[13]

That applied equally well for dons as for dustmen. For example, from Balliol College, Oxford it was admitted that Chavasse had 'succeeded where many abstruse theologians had failed' because instead of offering 'something original and elaborate' he gave them 'milk for babes'.[14] In this Chavasse followed the style of his mentor and predecessor at St Peter's, Henry Linton, who once described himself as 'a plain man, preaching to plain people'.[15] The method proved effective. One of Chavasse's Wycliffe Hall ordinands, L. H. E. Ffrench, reflected that he was not a great 'pulpit orator', like some who could be heard in the University, 'but as a preacher to an ordinary mixed congregation in a parish church he appeared to many to be without a rival.' Likewise William Fletcher, curate at Holy Trinity, Oxford from 1878 to 1882, recalled: 'He was not a great preacher like Magee or Liddon, but excellent for an ordinary parish congregation, and his sermons went home to men's hearts.'[16] Henry Sweetapple, an undergraduate at Queen's College in the 1880s, declared: 'we hung spellbound upon the words of that prince of pastoral preachers'.[17]

Chavasse's earnestness breathes through every sermon. It is seen, for example, in his calls for Christians to be courageous in the face of opposition, to resist conformity to the world, to battle with sin and seek 'total consecration', to love the Bible and be dedicated in prayer, to persevere amidst hardship, rejoice in suffering and be reverent in

---

[11] 'Apostolic Preaching' (1886), MS Chavasse dep. 65, fo. 12.

[12] 'The Making of a Sermon', Pastoral Lectures, MS Chavasse dep. 77, fo. 17.

[13] 'The Home Missionary' (1883), MS Chavasse dep. 59, fos 88-9.

[14] Mary F. Smith, *Arthur Lionel Smith, Master of Balliol: A Biography and Some Reminiscences* (London: Murray, 1928), 256.

[15] Henry Linton, *Sermons Preached in the Parish Church of St Peter-le-Bailey, Oxford* (Oxford: Parker, 1878), vi.

[16] Lancelot, *Chavasse*, 125-6.

[17] *Parochial Sermons*, v.

worship. It is evident in his appeals for the church to resist that 'awful trinity' which were corrupting British society (the three Is: impurity, infidelity and intemperance),[18] and his declarations about divine judgment upon individuals and nations through tragedy and disaster.[19] These are some of the recurrent themes in Chavasse's preaching. What they have in common is a plain-speaking urgency. He warned that when someone wants 'flowery, oratorical, sensational preaching' it is a sure sign that spiritual decline has set in.[20] On another occasion he chastised lukewarm churches with their lukewarm clergy: 'Their doctrine is pure, style unimpeachable, sermons models of persuasive rhetoric, but they are unreal and miss the mark.'[21] Observing the lack of earnestness displayed by many preachers and congregations, he lamented:

> There is a large church in a suburb of a great city far away from Oxford crowded by a fashionable congregation, who flock thither not merely because of exquisite music, but because it seems to be the great aim of the preacher to preach smooth things, to avoid saying anything that could stir up a saint or awaken a sinner, to take the cross out of Christianity, and to make religion, as one of the people said, "easy Sunday after Sunday". ... If this day that preacher were to change his tone and preach no more vapid and colourless sermonettes, but Christ in all his fulness, and warn his complacent hearers of sinfulness and worldliness and indifference, that scandalized congregation would forsake him in disgust.[22]

Chavasse was certainly not a preacher of 'smooth things'. He considered it his 'duty to reprove and call to repentance', constantly exhorting his parishioners to turn to Christ.[23] They were left in no doubt about 'the exceeding sinfulness of sin' and the catastrophic results of human rebellion against God.[24] For example, in a sermon on 'The Doom of the Wicked', he warned his hearers that they may be popular preachers, Sunday School teachers, district visitors, church workers, even temperance reformers and still end up in the 'everlasting fire' of

---

[18] 'The National Recognition of God' (1887), MS Chavasse dep. 66, fo. 16.

[19] John Wolffe has recently argued that evangelical sermons linking national sin and national calamity began to wane after Prince Albert's death in 1861, but Chavasse preached frequently on this theme during the 1870s and 1880s. See John Wolffe, 'Judging the Nation: Early Nineteenth-Century British Evangelicals and Divine Retribution' in Kate Cooper and Jeremy Gregory (eds.), *Retribution, Repentance, and Reconciliation* (Woodbridge: Boydell, 2004), 291-300.

[20] 'Spiritual Decline' (1881), MS Chavasse dep. 55, fo. 28.

[21] 'Lukewarmness' (1879), MS Chavasse dep. 49, fo. 9.

[22] 'Ahab's Righteousness' (1880), MS Chavasse dep. 52, fos 103-4.

[23] 'Apostolic Preaching' (1886), MS Chavasse dep. 65, fo. 11.

[24] 'The Conviction of Sin' (1880), MS Chavasse dep. 51, fo. 102.

hell. They may subscribe to missionary societies, help to build churches and schools, or give away money to the poor, and still be eternally condemned.[25] The preacher proclaimed: 'Oh that I had a voice of thunder and a tongue of brass that I might warn you of your danger'.[26]

One corollary of these stark truths was the urgency of evangelism, in which Chavasse led by example. He reiterated the biblical imperative to be involved in evangelism before philanthropy – of the necessity not to build hospitals and orphanages but to feed 'the starving souls of Oxford' with the good news of Christ and to take that message to the heathen tribes around the globe.[27] A second corollary was the urgent need to turn to Christ without delay, and Chavasse took every opportunity to hammer this point home. For example, on 31 August 1878 there was a railway accident at Sittingbourne Station in Kent in which five people were killed, including a former member of St Peter's. Then, on 3 September, the *Princess Alice,* a passenger steamer, collided with a collier on the River Thames and sank in under five minutes with the loss of over 600 lives. The following Sunday Chavasse suspended his planned sermon series and preached instead on the imminence of death. He proclaimed:

> From that wrecked train at Sittingbourne and from that sinking steamer on the Thames, from the new made graves and desolate homes and vanished forms, comes a voice from God to England: "Be ye also ready."[28]

These exhortations were delivered not with a dusty academic tone (nor indeed with a stern or fierce countenance), but with a heart-felt longing to see lives changed and God glorified. One close friend, Bishop Knox of Manchester, described Chavasse as 'a little man, rather deformed, a stammerer, but alive with the fire of divine love'.[29]

Devotional not Doctrinal

Chavasse's primary aim in all his preaching was to promote personal response to Jesus Christ. Week after week he exhorted his congregation to adore Christ, imitate Christ, cling to Christ, turn to Christ, hear Christ, trust in Christ, speak for Christ, work for Christ, love Christ, rest on Christ. As he freely acknowledged, 'My own danger is always to be

---

[25] 'The Doom of the Wicked' (1880), MS Chavasse dep. 54, fo. 27.
[26] 'The Delay of the Bridegroom' (1878), MS Chavasse dep. 48, fo. 41.
[27] 'The Compassionate Teacher' (1886), MS Chavasse dep. 64, fo. 146.
[28] 'The Ascension of Elijah' (1878), MS Chavasse dep. 47, fo. 113.
[29] Edmund A. Knox, *Reminiscences of an Octogenarian, 1847-1934* (London: Hutchinson, 1934), 73.

preaching evangelistic sermons'.[30] No matter what the Bible passage, the call to respond to Christ was always just as passionate. Chavasse explained: 'As every hamlet and village has a road which leads to London, so every text leads us to Christ.'[31] Elsewhere he declared:

> Every Book speaks of or leads up to Him. He is the great centre and subject of Holy Scripture. To Him History and Parable and Poem and Prophecy all lead up and in Him they find their highest fulfilment.[32]

This desire to exalt the Saviour should have two consequences for sermons, Chavasse insisted. First, every preacher must point to Christ and not to himself. He told his ordinands at Wycliffe Hall:

> The minstrel who sings before you to show his skill will be praised for his wit and rhyme and voice, but the courier who hurries in breathless to bring you a message will be forgotten in the message that he brings.[33]

Likewise he warned his congregation at St Peter's:

> The preacher may hide Christ. Hearers may go away and say what an able man, what a fine sermon, what wealth of language, poetry of thought, naturalness of delivery – *and Christ may be forgotten*. ... Oh that in every Sermon preached in this Church the messenger may be forgotten in his message, the Servant lost in the Master. One of the best tests of a Sermon is whether it fixes our thoughts on Christ.[34]

Second, every preacher must exalt Christ, not doctrine – not Christian theology, still less evangelical dogma. The Christian faith, Chavasse proclaimed, 'all centres round not a doctrine or a dogma but a Person'.[35] Although he preached surprisingly little from Paul's epistles (more often from 1 Kings than from Romans, and almost as often from the Psalms as from all of Paul's epistles put together), yet still he sought to follow the apostle's example in this regard:

> The centre, the heart of St Paul's preaching was a Person. He spoke not so much of atonement as of Christ atoning, not so much of salvation as of the Saviour, not so much of Christianity as of Christ. We need a Person. It is good to have a clear and well-defined Creed; but alone this satisfies the intellect not the heart. We need someone we can love and who can love us,

---

30 'The Making of a Sermon', Pastoral Lectures, MS Chavasse dep. 77, fo. 4.
31 'A Joyful Conversion' (1877), MS Chavasse dep. 45, fo. 8.
32 'The Creed of St Paul' (1881), MS Chavasse dep. 55, fo. 122.
33 'The Making of a Sermon', Pastoral Lectures, MS Chavasse dep. 77, fo. 2.
34 'Bartimaeus: His Healer' (1878), MS Chavasse dep. 47, fo. 52.
35 'The Creed of St Paul' (1881), MS Chavasse dep. 55, fo. 119.

> who can feel with us and help us. We want a living and divine Friend accessible at all times.[36]

Therefore Chavasse advised a group of senior clergy to avoid 'philosophical sermons' and to preach 'not of Christianity but of a personal Christ, not a mere string of cold hard formulae ... Nothing but a living Christ will satisfy craving hearts touched by God's Spirit.'[37] Likewise he reminded a group of ordination candidates: 'Our message is not philanthropy, not poetry, not politics, but Christ. Not a thing, a system, an Institution, but a Person – Christ.'[38] This principle is particularly evident in Chavasse's preaching on the atonement. In sermon after sermon he proclaims that Christ is a Saviour from sin. Seldom, however, does he attempt to explain *how* Christ saves from sin. Although he believed firmly in the doctrine of substitutionary atonement, its mechanics are rarely explored. Christ, rather than the cross of Christ, was the primary focus of his preaching.

Speaking to his predominantly evangelical congregation at St Peter's, Chavasse frequently warned them about the dangers of focussing upon doctrine rather than devotion. It is 'not enough to hold the pure faith, to be members of a pure Church', he insists.[39] Nothing can be a substitute for a 'personal and experimental intimate acquaintance' with God.[40] He described barren 'head knowledge' in these terms:

> We hold most correct and orthodox views. ... We can give good definitions and talk most ably about doctrines. We have a keen eye for error and can scent out with wonderful precision the slightest approach to heresy.[41]

Yet this barren orthodoxy, says Chavasse, can become 'a garment of self-righteousness' which must be renounced when we approach Christ. In a similar vein, he repeatedly warned his listeners:

> We may be zealous for truth, simply in the interests of a party – we may be an earnest Churchman, a staunch Protestant, a decided Evangelical, a conscientious Nonconformist without one reference to God's glory.[42]

---

[36] 'Apostolic Preaching' (1886), MS Chavasse dep. 65, fo. 9.
[37] 'The Minister a Witness' (*c.*1885), MS Chavasse dep. 74, fo. 127.
[38] 'Ministers, the Prophets of God' (*c.*1883), MS Chavasse dep. 74, fo. 65.
[39] 'Spiritual Building' (1880), MS Chavasse dep. 52, fo. 51.
[40] 'Strength from Knowing God' (1921), MS Chavasse dep. 70, fos 127-8.
[41] 'Bartimaeus: His Coming to Christ' (1878), MS Chavasse dep. 47, fos 69-70.
[42] 'The Training of the Forgiven' (1880), MS Chavasse dep. 51, fo. 122.

> Brothers, why do you expect pardon? ... Because you are a Churchman, a Protestant, an Evangelical? Good! But the holding of certain views, unless they influence our life, will not open the gate of Heaven.[43]

> Look to it, brothers. You say you have faith – where is the fruit? ... It is vain to say, "I am a Churchman, orthodox, a champion of truth, a successful controversialist". We will be judged according to our works.[44]

> Brothers, many of us in this Church have been reared from children in the great Evangelical truths which have done so much for mankind. We hold fast to the Word of God as the sole rule of faith, we maintain the great truths won back at the Reformation, of Justification by faith only and the Priesthood of the laity. ... And there is a danger of stopping there, of living on the traditions of the past, of uttering certain shibboleths, of repeating as if charms certain set phrases, of glorying in the mere possession of a glorious name, of glibly reciting belief in certain great doctrines, and of condemning, pitying, despising others who speak not as we speak and think not as we think. My brothers, one of the most hideous and repulsive sights is that of dead Evangelicalism, of men and women who profess to hold, and who can repeat with unfaltering accuracy, the doctrines of their creed, but who lack love, reality, devotion, zeal, unction – whom their friends may count as living, but Christ calls dead.[45]

Orthodox Christians, Chavasse maintained, must continually cry for the power of the Holy Spirit, so that 'old creeds and catechisms and articles of faith cease to be dead and dry things and become living realities'.[46] Elsewhere he praised the example of the Church Pastoral Aid Society for being 'a witness to Evangelical Truth, not narrowed and dead and fossilized, but living and beautiful and strong and as wide as Christ Himself.'[47]

Compassionate not Combative

Although Chavasse warned against a barren orthodoxy which was devoid of Christ, he still desired his congregation at St Peter's to be doctrinally orthodox. Indeed he told them that it was their duty to be 'intolerant of error'.[48] They should

---

[43] 'The Creed of St Paul' (1881), MS Chavasse dep. 55, fo. 120.
[44] 'The Rule of the Judgment' (1881), MS Chavasse dep. 56, fo. 38.
[45] 'The Giver of the Spirit' (1885), MS Chavasse dep. 62, fos 93-4.
[46] 'Access to God' (1879), MS Chavasse dep. 49, fo. 107.
[47] CPAS Sermon (nd), fo. 23, MS Chavasse dep. 73 (loose papers).
[48] 'Christian Intolerance' (1881), MS Chavasse dep. 55, fo. 17.

> contend with holy jealousy for the preservation of the faith. Scepticism, immorality, lawlessness, the great foes that assailed the Church in Jude's day, have lost none of their power. ... we must meet and drive them back.[49]

He applauded 'the stern denunciation of these treacherous foes of Jesus Christ', though warning that ceaseless conflict tends to 'mar and stunt our spiritual life'.[50] He encouraged his hearers not to use 'violent measures' or 'carnal weapons' but, nevertheless,

> to be true protestants and protest by every right means against the leaven that they might expose its real character, destroy confidence in its promotion and check its growth. Christ comes with His eyes of Flame and searches our hearts. What does He find? Are any of us tolerant of error and of sin in our Church? Do we close our eyes to it, pretend not to see it, or weakly bewail what we do not try to denounce? ... if error, distinct and deadly, be preached or inculcated and we hold our peace, none liking to speak, we are verily guilty. ... The cause may be timidity, indolence or a false liberalism which excuses error and evil – but the end will be, must be, misery and shame and the anger of God.[51]

Some of Chavasse's sternest rebukes were reserved for Christians who lacked the 'moral courage' or 'holy boldness' to stand for the truth. However, it is Chavasse's compassion, rather than a desire for combat, which shines through his sermons. He was famed for his indefatigable pastoral care and 'personal work'. In Liverpool it won him the epithet 'The People's Bishop'. In Oxford it was rumoured that he knew personally 10,000 individuals. As he reminded a clerical conference, a clergyman must not just be a good preacher but a compassionate pastor:

> "One visit", said a layman to me only yesterday, "is worth three Sermons". Men will listen to, support, and love a Clergyman who has knelt with them in their cottage or drawing room, has bent over their sick beds and caressed their little children, has been at their side in every time of joy and sorrow, a ready sympathizer and an unobtrusive friend. "He is a good man and a fine preacher", it is often said, "but we never see him except in the pulpit."[52]

He advised his students at Wycliffe Hall to keep their mornings for sermon preparation and their afternoons for home visiting. Every clergyman should visit for at least twelve hours a week, in which time,

---

[49] 'Spiritual Building' (1880), MS Chavasse dep. 52, fo. 49.
[50] Ibid., fo. 50.
[51] 'The Searcher of Hearts' (1885), MS Chavasse dep. 62, fos 70-1.
[52] 'The Work of a Congregation' (*c.*1880), MS Chavasse dep. 74, fos 51-2.

he calculated, they should manage at least 25 visits in the countryside or 40 visits in the town.[53]

Chavasse's deep pastoral concern is evident in the way he approached controversial issues from the pulpit. He avoids an aggressive and polemical position. His Wycliffe ordinands were repeatedly advised not to preach 'controversial discourses'.[54] For example, he told them:

> Never run down Rome in the pulpit. Only preach controversial sermons when circumstances compel – then let them be fair, truthful, temperate, logical and clear. Preach positive truth and teach the whole truth – at the same time, fortify the minds of your people against Roman error by inculcating the distinctive doctrines of the English Church.[55]

Chavasse did speak periodically against modern liberal theories and certain Roman doctrines, even describing them as satanic deceptions. Yet such criticisms are both brief and scarce. Never do they dominate a sermon. He did not rail against error, in the style of some Victorian contemporaries. Likewise, Chavasse never denounced individuals or churches. Only once in 700 sermons does he tackle a false teacher by name.[56] Instead he aimed to oppose wrong thinking 'not by denunciation, but by pressing home the truth. Man cannot exist on negations'.[57]

Chavasse pleaded with his congregation at St Peter's to adopt a similar approach when dealing with error. Those in the wrong deserved compassion not contempt:

> You will never convince a man that he is wrong by clever scoring, by smart sayings, by crushing argument, by sharp declaiming. You will only embitter him and make him hold fast to error; but if he sees that you are not seeking to gain an intellectual victory over him, that you care for him and desire to set him right, not in the interest of a party or clique but because you wish to benefit him, he will listen, weigh and yield.[58]

---

[53] 'Visiting the Whole', Pastoral Lectures, MS Chavasse dep. 77, fo. 52.

[54] 'The Clergyman and his Treatment of Unbelief / Doubt', Pastoral Lectures, MS Chavasse dep. 77, fo. 36.

[55] 'The Clergyman and his Treatment of Romanism', Pastoral Lectures, MS Chavasse dep. 77, fo. 30.

[56] The lone exception is Chavasse's contradiction of a preacher at the City Temple in London, who on Good Friday 1889 declared that Jesus Christ had no more died to purchase the forgiveness of mankind than had Thomas Cranmer; 'The Ways of the Lord' (1889), MS Chavasse dep. 67, fo. 48.

[57] 'On Toleration of Evil' (1889), MS Chavasse dep. 67, fo. 78.

[58] Ibid., fos 78-9.

This was particularly the case when ministering to someone in danger of becoming a Roman Catholic

> Roman fever must never be treated with harshness, ridicule, dogmatism, or good-natured advice not to think about such things, but with discrimination, patience, sympathy, and candour.'[59]

The same rule applied when speaking to sceptics or honest doubters. The minister should never show signs of anger, contempt or surprise, but sympathy, sorrow and patient encouragement.[60] Chavasse exhorted his hearers:

> Brothers, see how Christ deals with real honest doubt – not sternly, not scornfully, but very pityingly, as something to excite compassion not anger. ... Brothers, if we have to deal with doubters let us imitate Christ. Be tender, sympathetic ... do not scold, frown, turn aside in horror. Doubt disappears fastest before love.[61]

Assured not Alarmist

In the final decades of the nineteenth century, many Christians in Oxford (townsfolk as much as undergraduates) were troubled by the rise of new scientific and historical theories which challenged the Bible's veracity and undermined traditional orthodoxy. Chavasse summed up the unsettled atmosphere as follows:

> At this very moment not a few Christians have dragged their anchor. A storm fierce and unexpected has burst upon them. The authority of the Old Testament Scriptures is being questioned. New and difficult theories are being put forth. ... And the majority of us are busy men and women who have little time for searching out hard questions. ... We are in danger of leaving our moorings and of making shipwreck of our faith. What can we do?[62]

Chavasse's response to these difficulties was not one of alarm but of confident assurance. Indeed he used it as part of his evangelistic appeal

---

[59] 'The Clergyman and his Treatment of Romanism', Pastoral Lectures, MS Chavasse dep. 77, fos 24-5.

[60] 'The Clergyman and his Treatment of Unbelief / Doubt', Pastoral Lectures, MS Chavasse dep. 77, fo. 36.

[61] 'Appearances of the Risen and Ascended Saviour: To the Doubter' (1882), MS Chavasse dep. 56, fos 126-7.

[62] 'The Risen Christ and the Old Testament Scriptures' (1892), MS Chavasse dep. 68, fo. 14.

– that Christ would not only provide pardon for sin, strength for the weary, and peace for the guilty conscience, but also 'give truth to your Intellect'.[63] He was convinced that 'Reason is the foe and exposer of Credulity, but the servant and helpmeet of Faith.'[64]

Yet Chavasse never offered his congregation reasoned arguments in defence of traditional Christianity. He did not attempt to justify his own position, but boldly declared it to be the truth. Martin Wellings has recently observed that Anglican evangelicals in the late nineteenth century often responded to evolutionary theory by simply ignoring it,[65] and Chavasse is a case in point. He followed his own warning to his Wycliffe ordinands not to deal with scientific questions in the pulpit unless they were competent students of science.[66] For example, when preaching on the Fall he never once mentioned or even alluded to Charles Darwin, Thomas Huxley or evolutionary theory. He was happy to sit on the fence over whether some of the details in Genesis 3 (such as the tree, the fruit and the serpent) are literal fact or allegory, but he did not raise the possibility that the Fall was not an historical event.[67] Likewise he naturally assumed that the other narratives of Scripture are historical facts – that Noah took two of every animal into an ark, that Lot's wife was turned into a pillar of salt and that the walls of Jericho miraculously fell. Only occasionally did he acknowledge that these events had been questioned by modern scientists and historians. For instance, beginning a Lent series on Jonah and the big fish, Chavasse admits that 'to scoffers it has proved an unfailing fund for scorn', but still insists that it is 'neither a fable, nor a legend, nor an allegory, but a history'.[68] When asked to justify this conviction, the preacher replies only that 'it is recorded in the Word of God' and that it was viewed as a historical fact by Jesus Christ, 'the Faithful and True witness' who 'cannot lie or deceive or be mistaken'.[69]

Rather than expressing alarm at attacks upon traditional Christian teaching, Chavasse reassured his congregation that God is in control and therefore all will be well. Although the Bible was assaulted on all sides, one day it would be proved true and Christianity would be

---

[63] Sermon on John 6.68 (nd), fo. 11, MS Chavasse dep. 73 (loose papers).

[64] 'Faith the Condition of Performance' (1881), MS Chavasse dep. 55, fo. 135.

[65] Martin Wellings, *Evangelicals Embattled: Responses of Evangelicals in the Church of England to Ritualism, Darwinism and Theological Liberalism 1890-1930* (Carlisle: Paternoster, 2003), 196-8.

[66] 'The Clergyman and His Treatment of Unbelief / Doubt', Pastoral Lectures, MS Chavasse dep. 77, fo. 36.

[67] 'The First Sin' (1883), MS Chavasse dep. 58, fo. 43; 'The First Temptation' (1893), MS Chavasse dep. 68, fo. 86.

[68] 'The Flight from God' (1885), MS Chavasse dep. 62, fo. 1.

[69] 'In the Deep' (1885), MS Chavasse dep. 62, fo. 17.

vindicated. In the meantime they need not be unsettled in their faith, but should renew their trust in God. This optimism in the future is a frequent theme in Chavasse's preaching. For example, he compared the nineteenth century to the fifteenth century, when new developments such as the revival of Greek learning, the invention of printing and the discovery of America troubled the church:

> Steam and electricity and the wonderful discoveries of science have again ushered men into fresh fields of knowledge and capability and have again landed us in a similar state of criticism, speculation and unrest. And fearful and fainthearted men are beginning to cry out for the "Ark of God" and to deal blind blows against Science which they deem the foe of Christianity. Brethren, we need not fear. Scientific research is still in its childhood. Some of its followers flushed with success and with new knowledge may from time to time broach strange opinions and utter bitter and unchristian words. We have but to wait. Science and Revelation are not foes but sisters.[70]

Forty years later, in the 1920s, Chavasse still held the same confidence:

> We live at the beginning of a new age in which Scientific Discovery and Historical Research have brought a flood of new knowledge. This new light is not a foe to be feared but a friend to be welcomed.[71]

Speaking of the creation narratives, he expressed his optimism that science would eventually be found 'to be a real elucidator of God's words. ... The faith of the Church in God as the Creator will in the long run be stronger and more real because the "noise of battle" has rung louder and louder round the first chapter of Genesis.'[72]

A similar bold assurance is seen when dealing with other aspects of biblical criticism. For example, beginning a sermon series on blind Bartimeus, Chavasse frankly acknowledged the contradictions between the different synoptic accounts, but continued:

> There are not a few apparent discrepancies in the Gospels; they try our faith, they exercise our ingenuity, but were we but in possession of *all* the facts, their reconciliation would be easy.[73]

In similar vein, he declared elsewhere:

---

[70] 'Faith in the Creator' (1880), MS Chavasse dep. 53, fos 10-1.
[71] 'The Spirit of Truth' (1922), MS Chavasse dep. 70, fo. 135.
[72] 'Faith in the Creator' (1880), MS Chavasse dep. 53, fo. 11.
[73] 'Bartimaeus: His Blindness' (1878), MS Chavasse dep. 47, fo. 41.

> We need not fear the "Higher Criticism", as it is called. Many of its upholders in our own Land are men of devout and reverent minds, who love the Bible as much as we do and desire only to discover the truth. At present they have not said the last word. Thirty years ago the Gospels were passing through a like trial. To some timid minds it seemed as if they must perish in the fire. Today their truthfulness, their authority, their divine origin are more strongly established than ever. They have lost nothing but a few human notions which had gathered round them. And in 30 years our children shall find that the Old Testament has come through its trial as victoriously. A few human ideas respecting it shall have gone – like the seaweed or the shellfish which the storm sweeps from the rock – but the impregnable rock of Scripture shall stand unhurt while "at its feet the baffled billows die". We have Christ's word for its Divine origin. On that word let us rest.[74]

As can be seen, Chavasse did not pretend that there were no difficulties with the classic Christian doctrines. He freely admitted that he did not have many answers in the face of modern sceptical scholarship. Yet he continued to proclaim the Bible's teaching with undaunted confidence and exhorted his congregation to do the same. This was particularly the case with the doctrine of the atonement. He was happy to accept the connection between the death of Christ and the forgiveness of sins as 'a great, and at present unexplained mystery, just because it comes from God'.[75]

Conclusion

In conclusion, the heart of Francis Chavasse's evangelical identity is revealed in his Oxford sermons. They show his theological and pastoral priorities – earnestness and devotion in response to the call of Christ; compassion for the troubled and confused; assurance in the face of hostile critics. These were the dominant motifs in Chavasse's ministry at St Peter's and beyond, as he rose to be a leader of the Anglican evangelical movement. They were attractive emphases and he quickly won his way into the hearts of his hearers. It was for good reason that they called him 'the prince of pastoral preachers'.

---

[74] 'The Risen Christ and the Old Testament Scriptures' (1892), MS Chavasse dep. 68, fo. 18.

[75] 'Salvation through Faith' (1880), MS Chavasse dep. 53, fo. 109.

CHAPTER 15

'Take My Life': Evangelical Spirituality And Evangelical Identity

Ian M. Randall

In his significant study, *Trust and Obey: Explorations in Evangelical Spirituality,* David Gillett covers major features of evangelical spirituality – conversion, assurance, the cross, the Bible, holiness, active service and prayer. He also raises four questions about evangelical spirituality which have to do with an understanding of evangelical identity. First, he sees evangelicals as having valued spontaneity, for example in prayer, while having little appreciation of liturgical prayer or of silence. Secondly, he suggests that evangelicals have concentrated on inward spirituality, while placing less emphasis on the sacraments. In the third place, he notes that evangelicals have proclaimed personal salvation, but have shown a degree of impatience with the idea of the Church as an institution. Finally, he describes evangelicals as being aware of themselves as a people of light in the midst of darkness, which can lead to isolation and a ghetto mentality.[1] Throughout his study Gillett draws from evangelical history. I want to pick up on these four specific points and illustrate that historically there has been a considerable degree of diversity and complexity in these areas of spirituality. This in turn has meant that evangelical identity, although shaped by core values, has been expressed in a rich variety of ways. In my own study of evangelical spirituality between the First and Second World Wars, I found four main strands – Keswick holiness, the Wesleyan tradition, Reformed approaches and Pentecostal/charismatic spirituality. Each of these had significant internal variations.[2] In his

---

[1] D. K. Gillett, *Trust and Obey: Explorations in Evangelical Spirituality* (London: DLT, 1993), 34-9.

[2] I. M. Randall, *Evangelical Experiences: A Study in the Spirituality of English Evangelicalism, 1918-1939* (Carlisle: Paternoster Press, 1999); cf. my wider survey, *What a Friend we have in Jesus* (London: DLT, 2005).

book *Holiness in Nineteenth-Century England*,[3] David Bebbington considers three evangelical traditions (Calvinist, Wesleyan and Keswick) and also the High Church Tradition, and he has a further analysis of holiness in the recent book edited by Stephen Barton, *Holiness Past and Present* (2003).[4]

This study seeks to contribute to the on-going exploration of evangelical spirituality by examining aspects of evangelical thinking in England in the period from the 1880s to the First World War. By the 1880s the spirituality of the Keswick Convention and associated conventions, with their teaching about the deeper spiritual life, had entered the evangelical bloodstream, and thinking about spiritual experience was to the fore among many evangelicals. After the First World War the unity of evangelicalism in Britain was broken, with deep divisions opening up between liberal and conservative evangelicals. The spirituality of the liberal evangelicals – found in the Anglican Evangelical Group Movement, the Methodist Fellowship of the Kingdom, the Genevan movement and the Oxford Group – was open and forward-looking. The outlook they espoused created a rift between them and the conservative evangelicals found at Keswick, in traditional Wesleyan holiness movements, within the Brethren or among the Pentecostals. But before this break the evangelical world embraced and held together wide variations in theology and practice. Thus in the 1880s the breadth of thinking about expressions of spirituality among evangelicals was such that what might have been thought to be High Church fifty years before was now regarded and described as 'decidedly Evangelical'.[5]

Spontaneity and Liturgy in Prayer

The method of spontaneous prayer was widely employed among evangelicals in the period being studied. Often those who prayed had an expectation that God would answer in specific ways. Thus Charles Haddon Spurgeon, minister of the Metropolitan Tabernacle, London, said to his congregation on one occasion: 'Dear friends, we are a huge church, and should be doing more for the Lord in this great city. I want us, tonight, to ask him to send us *some new work*; and if we need money to carry it on, let us pray that *the means may also be sent*.' Spurgeon asked

[3] D. W. Bebbington, *Holiness in Nineteenth-Century England* (Carlisle: Paternoster Press, 2000).
[4] D. W. Bebbington, 'Holiness in the Evangelical Tradition', in S. C. Barton (ed.), *Holiness Past & Present* (London: T & T Clark, 2003), 298-315.
[5] D. W. Bebbington, *Evangelicalism in Modern Britain: A History from the 1730s to the 1980s* (London: Routledge, 1995), 146-9.

a number of people to come up on the platform to pray about this, and during the prayer it seemed that Spurgeon 'knew that the answer had come'. A few days later Mrs Anne Hillyard, a widow, wrote to Spurgeon offering him the enormous sum of £20,000 to found an orphanage. One of those who had prayed on the platform that evening, who was then a student at Spurgeon's College, commented later (in the 1890s) about this event: 'Surely the Orphanage was born of prayer.'[6] When Spurgeon himself was suffering from one of his periodic bouts of illness, he wrote: 'Perhaps if the church met for prayer, I should be speedily restored.' The prayer took place, and Spurgeon reported: 'As soon as the church had resolved to meet for special prayer for me, I began rapidly to recover.'[7] The thinking behind such prayer was that precise petitions were made and answers – often dramatic answers – were received in line with these petitions.

Given this perspective, it is not surprising that Spurgeon and others did not wish to use set or written prayers. Such prayers did not allow a person to bring to God in his or her own words the actual needs that existed. Even an Anglican leader like J.C. Ryle, who became the first Bishop of Liverpool in 1880, asserted: 'As to praying out of a book, it is habit I cannot praise. If we can tell doctors the state of our bodies without a book, we ought to be able to tell the state of our souls to God. I have no objection to a man using crutches, when he is first recovering from a broken limb....But if I saw him all his life on crutches, I should not think it a matter for congratulation.'[8] Ryle did, of course, use set prayers in public worship. Spurgeon was happy to produce a volume of morning and evening Bible readings, with brief comments and suitable hymns, which was published first as *The Interpreter,* and was widely used by Nonconformists and also by well-known Anglicans such as the Earl of Shaftesbury. But Spurgeon always refused to include set prayers with his readings. Explaining this, he wrote: 'I have been earnestly urged to add prayers, but my conscience will not allow me to do so, although it would greatly increase the sale of the work...To some persons the use of forms of prayer appears to be lawful; but as I cannot coincide with that opinion, it would be the height of hypocrisy for me to compose prayers for the use of others.'[9] David Gillett's case, that evangelicals do not value liturgy, seems well founded.

However, other evangelicals were happy to have books of prayers to

---

[6] C. H. Spurgeon, *Autobiography: Compiled from his diary, letters, and records by his wife and his private secretary* (4 vols: I; London: Passmore and Alabaster, 1899), 168.

[7] Spurgeon, *Autobiography*, III, 246.

[8] J. C. Ryle, *Practical Religion* (Cambridge: James Clarke & Co., 1959 [1878]), 64.

[9] Spurgeon, *Autobiography*, III, 319.

be used along with the reading of the Bible as an aid to devotion. According to G.W.E. Russell, a journalist and politician who in 1915 wrote a history of the evangelical movement, the use of *Family Prayers*, a book compiled by Henry Thornton, a banker, an MP, and a member of the campaigning group of evangelicals in Clapham (the Clapham Sect), was a distinctive sign of nineteenth-century evangelicalism.[10] Russell recalled that in his own family there were daily family prayers and that his father read prayers from books by William Wilberforce, the best known member of the Clapham group, by Thornton, or by Ashton Oxenden, bishop of Montreal.[11] Another widely-used book, also entitled *Family Prayers*, was by Edward Bickersteth, a prime mover in the formation of the Evangelical Alliance in 1846. His book of prayers, published in 1842, contained a complete course for eight weeks, and also forms of prayers for special occasions like moving house or choosing a school, and for saints' days.[12] In 1862 Joseph Wigram, the evangelical Bishop of Rochester, wrote *The Cottager's Family Prayers*, based on biblical themes. He spoke about households kneeling together, and suggested that 'one of them should read a proper form of prayer, and all the others follow him'. They should, he advised, repeat the Lord's Prayer and close with the blessing.[13] Manuals of prayer assisted devotion in many Anglican evangelical homes in the later nineteenth century.

Some Nonconformists were also willing to use aids to prayer. Samuel Chadwick, a powerful figure within the Methodist holiness constituency from the 1890s, who became Principal of Cliff College, Derbyshire, used Catholic devotional manuals and the Anglican Prayer Book, especially during Lent. He had a particular interest in the spirituality of the mystics and considered, when commenting on this, that 'such praying may need to be learned at the feet of instructors'.[14] For many evangelicals who attended the Keswick Convention, both Anglican and Free Church, Handley Moule was a highly respected guide in the area of spirituality. He became Principal of the newly formed Ridley Hall, Cambridge, in 1880, having been Dean of Trinity College. In 1885, through hearing Evan Hopkins expounding Keswick

---

[10] I. Bradley, *The Call to Seriousness* (London: Jonathan Cape, 1976), 180.

[11] G. W. E. Russell, *A Short History of the Evangelical Movement* (London: Mowbray and Co., 1915), 142.

[12] M. Hennell, *Sons of Prophets: Evangelical leaders of the Victorian Church* (London: SPCK, 1979), 39.

[13] See N. A. D. Scotland, *Evangelical Anglicans in a Revolutionary Age, 1789-1901* (Carlisle: Paternoster Press, 2004), 349-50.

[14] N. G. Dunning, *Samuel Chadwick* (London: Hodder & Stoughton, 1933), 20; D. Howarth, *How Great a Flame* (Cliff College, 1982), 34-5.

teaching on holiness at a Convention at Polmont, Scotland, Moule had a deeper experience of surrender to God. As James Gordon puts it in his fine book, *Evangelical Spirituality*, Moule 'had found the answer to inner deficiency and Keswick had found an eloquent spokesman of impeccable standing among Evangelicals'.[15] In his book *The Call of Lent*, Moule advocated taking the Lord's Prayer as a framework and also spoke of the 'great work' of meditation. In the process of turning thoughts into prayers, Moule suggested, a person's soul 'shapes its thoughts into words addressed to its eternal Friend, and so the thought is both defined and hallowed'.[16] The use of silence was also commended by Moule. Noting that this discipline had been used in all ages, and especially by the Quakers, Moule commented that it had 'come into recognition and use in a new degree latterly among ourselves, and from many sides testimony is given to its spiritual value'. He continued: 'To let the articulate activities of the mind, as much as may be, lie still, while the consciousness in a profound quiet simply recollects the Lord and hearkens before Him, not least when this is done in company together, is a method of devotion assuredly fitted to foster in the inner world both light and peace.'[17]

The benefit deriving from the use of liturgy in corporate worship has been an area of dispute among evangelicals. Horton Davies, in *Worship and Theology in England*, delineates what he calls the 'School of Spontaneity' in the Free Churches in the early twentieth century, a school which took the view that 'to retain a liturgy is to remain in the adolescent stage of the spiritual life'.[18] A Baptist, F. B. Meyer, who was the leading international Keswick speaker, is seen by Davies as one of the 'rebels' against the 'school of spontaneity'; Meyer incorporated in public worship both liturgical forms and free expressions of praise.[19] A similar approach was taken by Peter Taylor Forsyth, an outstanding Congregational theologian who had studied at Aberdeen University and who, after ministering at Emmanuel Church, Cambridge, became Principal of Hackney College, London, in 1901. Forsyth has been called a 'Barthian before Barth', but this evaluation does not reflect fully Forsyth's deep personal experience: as he famously put it regarding his

---

[15] J. Gordon, *Evangelical Spirituality: From the Wesleys to John Stott* (London: SPCK, 1991), 206.

[16] H. C. G. Moule, *The Call of Lent* (London: SPCK, 1917), 78-9.

[17] Moule, *Call of Lent*, 80.

[18] Horton Davies, *Worship and Theology in England, Vol. 5: The Ecumenical Century* (London: OUP, 1962), 350.

[19] Horton Davies, *Worship and Theology*, V, 380.

own journey, the 'lover of love' became 'an object of grace'.[20] Forsyth was deeply concerned to connect evangelical theology with ministry. In his *Soul of Prayer*, published in 1916, he wrote: 'Public prayer, therefore, should be in the main liturgical, with room for free prayer.' He argued for the use of 'those great forms which arose out of the deep soul of the Church before it spread into sectional boughs or individual twigs'.[21] Handley Moule, as an Anglican, was an upholder of the Church of England's liturgy. 'Dream not', he said, 'that the life of faith can be its true self in neglect of the holy adorations and praises and confessions of the Lord's congregation. Expect rather to find in every public prayer of our blessed Liturgy light, truth and help tenfold.'[22] David Gillett is right to highlight the way some evangelicals, even those whose church tradition is liturgical, have been wary of what has been seen as formal prayer. Others, however, have viewed liturgy as helpful.

Virtually all evangelicals, whatever their views about liturgical prayer, have used set forms of worship in the form of hymns. Edward Bickersteth produced *Christian Psalmody* in 1833, and his son, Edward Henry Bickersteth, edited a replacement entitled *Hymn Companion to the Book of Common Prayer*. In the later nineteenth century this was the most used book in evangelical Anglican parishes in England. *Hymns Ancient and Modern* appealed to High Church parishes.[23] As Ian Bradley traces in his examination of the world of Victorian hymns, *Abide with Me*,[24] new hymns such as 'Blessed Assurance' and 'To God be the glory', by the amazingly prolific American hymnwriter, Fanny Crosby, became hugely popular with evangelicals on both sides of the Atlantic. At the Keswick Convention, a British hymnwriter, Frances Ridley Havergal, the daughter of a Church of England clergyman, was of crucial significance. In 1880 *The Life of Faith*, Keswick's semi-official mouthpiece, carried an article on 'Miss Havergal's experience of the Deeper Life', suggesting that one of her hymns, 'Take my life, and let it be consecrated Lord to Thee', 'may be said to have lifted Christians of all denominations to a higher standard of devotedness, and has preached the doctrine of the Deeper Life in a most engaging and persuasive manner'.[25] Havergal's hymn 'Like a river glorious' was seen

---

[20] P. T. Forsyth, *Positive Preaching and the Modern Mind* (London: Hodder and Stoughton, 1906), 281. For more on Forsyth, see T. Hart (ed.), *Justice the True and Only Mercy* (Edinburgh: T & T Clark, 1995).

[21] P. T. Forsyth, *The Soul of Prayer* (London: C. H. Kelly, 1916), 54.

[22] H. C. G. Moule, *Thoughts on Christian Sanctity* (London: Seeley & Co., 1885), 103.

[23] Scotland, *Evangelical Anglicans*, 357.

[24] I. Bradley, *Abide with me: The world of Victorian hymns* (London: SCM, 1997).

[25] *The Life of Faith*, 1 July 1880, 127.

as summing up the Convention's message about entering into 'God's perfect peace'. F. S. Webster, Rector of All Souls, Langham Place, London, writing in 1907 about Keswick hymns, considered the sentiment in the following lines from this hymn to be crucial:[26]

Stayed upon Jehovah,
Hearts are fully blest,
Finding as He promised,
Perfect peace and rest.

The use of such hymns, which were central to the corporate spirituality of many evangelicals, was an example of the way in which liturgy functioned as a shaper of evangelical identity.

The Place of Holy Communion

'Evangelical spirituality', says Gillett, 'has most often existed with reasonably infrequent celebrations of Holy Communion – monthly or even quarterly'. The exception he notes is the Brethren, with their weekly observance of 'the Breaking of Bread'.[27] It is often thought that the trend towards frequent communion in the Church of England in the later nineteenth century was attributable to the Anglo-Catholic Movement. Horton Davies, however, argued that it was the evangelicals of the nineteenth century who could rightly be claimed as pioneers in restoring Holy Communion to a central place in Anglican worship.[28] Handley Moule was one who promoted this emphasis. For the benefit of Keswick readers, and others, Moule published booklets in the 1880s on aspects of the devotional life, including Holy Communion. Moule's *Outlines of Christian Doctrine* described communion as 'an hour with God, with the Son of God'. He continued: 'It is a blessed hour of remembrance, of meditation; but far more. It is an hour in which He speaks to us, and as it were sensibly touches us, in the ordinance of, not our invention, but His command. The holy Bread, the holy Cup, are received as from His hand, as truly (to faith) as they were received at the first Administration.'[29] In 1895 Moule was awarded a DD for his scholarly edition of Bishop Ridley's volume, *On the Lord's Supper*. Moule later wrote that Holy Communion was a 'personal interview with the

[26] F. S. Webster, 'Keswick Hymns', in C. F. Harford (ed.), *The Keswick Convention: Its Message, Its Method and Its Men* (London: Marshall Bros., 1907), 214.
[27] Gillett, *Trust and Obey*, 37-8.
[28] Horton Davies, *Worship and Theology in England, Vol. 1: From Cranmer to Hooker 1534-1603* (London: OUP, 1961), 223.
[29] H. C. G. Moule, *Outlines of Christian Doctrine* (London: Hodder & Stoughton, Rev. ed. [1890]), 242.

Lord'.[30] By the First World War, in *The Call of Lent*, Moule could comment: 'Far more now than in days which I can well recall it is the usage of earnest English Christians to communicate often. The holy Sacrament...certainly suggests no reason in itself against such frequency; and to many souls the frequency brings a benefit untold.'[31]

As a representative of Keswick, Moule was part of a movement that had been deeply affected by Romantic sensibilities. The same was true of F. B. Meyer, who introducing weekly Communion in the 1880s at Melbourne Hall, Leicester, a Baptist congregation of 1,500 people, and subsequently when he was minister of the unusually upper-class Baptist congregation meeting at Regent's Park Chapel, London.[32] Love of the natural elements, a typical feature of Romanticism, led Meyer to value the tangible substances of bread and wine. He argued that to eat the bread of the 'Sacrament' (the term he used) and to meditate on what Christ did was to 'incorporate Him into our texture', just as to eat everyday bread was to absorb the influence of heaven and earth, rain, cloud and soil.[33] He described the 'Holy Supper' as 'always a great means of grace and nourishment'.[34] Other evangelicals who also argued for more frequent Communion were driven by different forces. A number of Anglican evangelical leaders who were committed to reaching the working classes advocated at least a monthly celebration of Holy Communion and also introduced evening communions since they were concerned that the working classes should have access to the Sacrament. Many people in domestic service worked during the day on Sundays.[35] The Earl of Shaftesbury, the leading Anglican evangelical champion of the poor, was highly critical of the conservatism of some clergy. He wrote:

> Now if it were given out by a large body of the ministers of the Church that they would administer the Communion in the evening, many of the poor with whom we have to deal would be likely to attend; but if it is to be given out that the ministers of the Church of England will never consider their convenience and necessities, they will certainly stay away

---

[30] H. C. G. Moule, *At the Holy Communion: Helps for Preparation and Reception* (London: Seeley Service & Co., 1914), 113.

[31] Moule, *Call of Lent*, 82.

[32] For Meyer see I. M. Randall, *Spirituality and Social Change: The Contribution of F. B. Meyer (1847-1929)* (Carlisle: Paternoster Press, 2003).

[33] *Baptist Times*, 12 November 1909, 811.

[34] F. B. Meyer, *The Future Tenses of the Blessed Life* (London: Morgan & Scott, [1894]), 66.

[35] Scotland, *Evangelical Anglicans*, 352-4.

> from the churches altogether. And how, I ask you, in such a refusal, can the Church of England call herself the 'Church of the people'.[36]

Those who valued the Reformed tradition of Word and Sacraments were also drawn to a high view of the Lord's Supper, reflecting something of the continuing influence of John Calvin's thinking. Thus J. C. Ryle spoke of 'a spiritual presence of Christ in the Lord's Supper to every faithful communicant', while also making it clear that there was 'no local corporal presence in the bread and wine to any communicant'.[37] Horatius Bonar, who had a ministry of over fifty years in Scotland and who died in 1889 when minister of Chalmer's Memorial Free Church in Edinburgh, made considerable use of the traditional Scottish Presbyterian extended seasons of Holy Communion to foster spiritual encounter. The same was true of Bonar's friend, Robert Murray McCheyne, a minister in Dundee. In this tradition Holy Communion was a 'sweet silent sermon'. Christians came face to face with the mystery and wonder of the grace of God, and were nourished. This is expressed magnificently in one of Bonar's communion hymns. Here are two verses:

> Here O my Lord, I see thee face to face;
> Here would I touch and handle things unseen,
> Here grasp with firmer hands the eternal grace,
> And all my weariness upon thee lean.
>
> Here would I feast upon the bread of God,
> Here drink with Thee the royal wine of heaven.
>
> Here would I lay aside each earthly load,
> Here taste afresh the calm of sin forgiven.[38]

C. H. Spurgeon, who also identified with the Calvinist tradition, spoke of the Lord's Supper as conveying the 'real presence of Christ'.[39] In line with what Spurgeon considered to be 'apostolic precedents', at the Metropolitan Tabernacle a communion service was held each Sunday evening and Spurgeon encouraged regular participation.[40] He told the

---

[36] E. Hodder, *The Life and Work of the Seventh Earl of Shaftesbury, KG* (London: Cassell & Co., 1888), 743.

[37] J. C. Ryle, *Knots Untied* (London: C.J. Thyme, 1898), 173-4.

[38] Gordon, *Evangelical Spirituality*, 144-5, citing H. Bonar, *Hymns by Horatius Bonar* (London, 1904), 235.

[39] 'Mysterious Visits', in *"Till He Come": Communion Meditations and Addresses by C. H. Spurgeon* (London: Passmore & Alabaster, 1894), 17.

[40] Spurgeon, *Autobiography*, IV, 72.

Tabernacle congregation in 1883: 'I have been in the habit of coming to the Lord's table every first day of the week now for many years...Has it lost it's freshness? Oh, dear, no!'[41] Six years later he made a similar, deeply personal statement: 'I love to come every Lord's day to the Communion table; I should be very sorry to come only once a month, or, as some do, only once a year. I could not afford to come as seldom as that. I need to be reminded, forcibly reminded, of my dear Lord and Master very often. We do so soon forget, and our unloving hearts so soon grow cold'.[42] Spurgeon also encouraged more informal celebrations of communion. A volume of Spurgeon's communion addresses, *Till He Come*, explains that a number of the addresses were delivered to 'the little companies of Christians,- of different denominations, and of various nationalities,- who gathered around the communion table in Mr. Spurgeon's sitting room at Mentone'.[43] When Spurgeon's health was poor he spent time recuperating in Mentone, in the south of France. Referring to his travels abroad, Spurgeon said in 1888: 'It is most delightful, when travelling, to remember Christ in your own room, where two or three brethren meet together.'[44] The Lord's Supper was central to Spurgeon's spiritual life.

Despite the emphasis found in C. H. Spurgeon and in F. B. Meyer on the place of Holy Communion, the tendency in much evangelical Free Church Sunday worship was to focus attention on preaching, prayer and singing. In Congregational and Baptist churches the communion was often a separate service, attended by only a section of the worshipping community. In his *Lectures on the Church and the Sacraments* (1917), P. T. Forsyth stated: 'Our idolatry of the popular preacher needs to be balanced by more stress on the Sacraments.'[45] For Forsyth, ministers themselves were 'sacramental elements, broken often, in the Lord's hands, as He dispenses His grace through us'.[46] In his theological writing Forsyth particularly pressed home the power of the Cross of Christ, and this flowed over into his thinking about the sacraments. He resolutely opposed any suggestion that there was automatic spiritual

---

[41] 'What the Lord's Supper sees and says', *Metropolitan Tabernacle Pulpit* [*MTP*] Vol. 39, No. 2595, on 1 Cor. 11.26, delivered 1 July 1883, 537.

[42] 'The Greatest Exhibition of the Age', *MTP*, Vol. 39, No. 2307, 1 Cor. 11.26, delivered 5 May 1889, 220.

[43] *"Till He Come"*, preface.

[44] 'The Lord's Supper: A Remembrance of Jesus', *MTP*, Vol. 34, No. 2038, Lk 22:19, delivered 19 August 1888, 451-2.

[45] P. T. Forsyth, *The Church and the Sacraments* (London: Independent Press, 1917, 2nd ed., 1947), 232. A. J. MacDonald, in *The Evangelical Doctrine of Holy Communion* (Cambridge: W. Heffer & Sons Ltd., 1930), 299-300, does not do justice to Forsyth's thinking.

[46] Forsyth, *Soul of Prayer*, 108.

power in the sacraments, commenting on one occasion that he had been 'more moved and blessed by the word and prayer of a Scottish peasant or an East Coast fisherman with the sacramental experience', than by a High Mass he had attended in Cologne.[47] Yet Forsyth insisted that the bread and wine were more than memorials. 'In some mysterious way', he averred, 'the life of God is conveyed into the life of the worshipper through the medium of the material elements which are consumed in the course of the meal.'[48] For Forsyth, as a preacher in the Reformed tradition, the Sacraments were 'the acted Word – variants of the preached Word. They are signs, but they are more than signs. They are the Word, the Gospel itself, visible, as in preaching the Word is audible...[This] is Christ in a real presence giving anew His redemption'.[49] Through Holy Communion evangelicals were brought again to the cross of Christ.

The One, Holy, Catholic, Apostolic Church

As indicated by the title of P.T. Forsyth's book, there was a close link in his thinking between the church and the sacraments. Is it true, as David Gillett, suggests, that evangelicals display a degree of impatience with the institutional church? It seems so. In an essay in the volume *Evangelical Ecclesiology: Reality or Illusion?* (2003), Bruce Hindmarsh asks: 'Is Evangelical Ecclesiology an Oxymoron?' He sees evangelicals as bearing witness to the underlying unity of the people of God, but from an examination of early evangelicalism he concludes that there was no distinctively evangelical doctrine of church order and that while celebrating the spiritual union of all the regenerate people of God the movement itself was marked by separatism. As examples of these schisms, John Wesley and George Whitefield divided over the doctrines of Calvinism, Wesley and the Moravians spit over quietism in spiritual experience, and the Countess of Huntingdon went through evangelical chaplains like serial lovers.[50] It is difficult to see in such experiences much of a vision of the One Holy, Catholic, Apostolic Church. Worse still, as Derek Tidball points out, an evangelical classic like R. A. Torrey's *What the Bible Teaches*, makes no reference whatsoever to the church.[51]

---

[47] Forsyth, *The Church and the Sacraments*, 150.
[48] Forsyth, *The Church and the Sacraments*, 162.
[49] Forsyth, *The Church and the Sacraments*, 176.
[50] B. Hindmarsh, 'Is Evangelical Ecclesiology an Oxymoron?', in J. G. Stackhouse, Jnr, (ed.), *Evangelical Ecclesiology: Reality or Illusion*, (Grand Rapids, Mich.: Baker, 2003), 31-4.
[51] D. J. Tidball, *Who are the Evangelicals?* (London: MarshallPickering, 1994), 160.

Yet not all evangelicals have been indifferent to church tradition. J.C. Ryle was utterly committed to the historic Reformed doctrinal foundation (as he saw it) of the Church of England. Nonetheless, for him the most important test of the teaching heard in any church was not whether it was said by 'Father or Reformer, – Bishop or Archbishop, – Priest or Deacon'. For Ryle the only question to ask was: 'Is the thing said Scriptural?' 'If it is, he continued, 'it ought to be received and believed. If it is not, it ought to be refused and cast aside'. Ryle feared what he called the 'servile acceptance' of all that was said by 'the parson'. The call, 'Hear the Church', was, in Ryle's view, a mark of a misguided approach to ministry. The true minister said: 'Hear the Word of God'.[52] Other Anglican evangelicals of that period echoed Ryle's thinking. H. W. Webb-Peploe, a Prebendary of St Paul's Cathedral and a leading London evangelical Anglican (one who advocated Keswick teaching on receiving sanctification by faith – teaching which Ryle criticised), upheld the necessity for thoroughly biblical preaching and measured churches by this standard. At the same time, Webb-Peploe spoke of himself as a strict Churchman, and wanted the Keswick platform to remain largely Anglican. He believed, however, that the Keswick message, 'All One in Christ Jesus', called for a unity that drew together denominationally disparate evangelicals, and believed that this could be achieved when evangelicals were committed to listening to God's Word together.[53]

Indeed it was precisely through such expressions of Christian co-operation as Keswick or the Evangelical Alliance that later nineteenth-century evangelicals saw the unity, holiness, catholicity and apostolicity of the Church being exhibited. From the 1880s to the period immediately before the outbreak of the First World War, there were great hopes among many evangelicals for increased international co-operation. Conferences at Northfield, Massachusetts, USA, organised by D. L. Moody, America's leading evangelist, inspired a new generation of evangelicals to seek 'the evangelisation of the world in this generation'. The international Evangelical Alliance movement was growing rapidly at this juncture, and its emphasis on catholicity was consistent with this theme of the universality of mission. The Alliance also pioneered pan-denominational celebrations of Holy Communion. At an Evangelical Alliance conference in 1881 J. C. Ryle spoke of the Alliance's testimony to the unity of 'the whole Catholic Church', and in 1884 there was a call for 'genuine catholicity' from a Swiss-American, Philip Schaff, who was a professor at Union Theological Seminary, New York. Shaff, who from the 1860s until his death in 1893 was a central

---

[52] Ryle, *Practical Religion*, 85.

[53] J. C. Pollock, *The Keswick Story* (London: Hodder & Stoughton, 1964), 111.

personality in the international Evangelical Alliance movement, was a respected speaker in America, Britain and across Europe.[54] The roots of Schaff's spirituality were in German pietism. Schaff envisaged the possibility of the ultimate coming together of the Roman Catholic, Protestant and Orthodox Churches in one body.[55] Samuel Chadwick, the Methodist leader, had similarly expansive views. Norman Dunning, Chadwick's colleague and biographer, heard Chadwick say that in another life he would have chosen to be a Catholic abbot, and Chadwick, who believed in the 'Real Presence' at the eucharist, has been described as a 'high church' Methodist.[56] There have been influential evangelicals who have held to a high view of the Church.

A few evangelicals in the Church of England in the 1870s and 1880s, influenced by High Church thinking and practice, were promoting what they called 'Evangelical Catholic' principles. The most prominent, who deserves greater attention than he is usually given, was George Howard Wilkinson, who was appointed Bishop of Truro in 1883, having been Vicar of St Peter's, Eaton Square, London – a church which, under his ministry, became known as perhaps the leading parish church in England.[57] In 1877, E. W. Benson, then Bishop of Truro and later Archbishop of Canterbury, encouraged Wilkinson to pass on 'what you understand and express by "Evangelical-Catholic" teaching'.[58] Wilkinson had an interest in promoting eucharistic and monastic life, and was the prime mover behind the founding of the Community of the Epiphany, in Truro, in 1883. Another evangelical who espoused catholic thinking was Arthur James Mason, Wilkinson's biographer, who was the Church of England's first Canon Missioner and in 1895 was appointed Lady Margaret Professor of Divinity in Cambridge. These figures did not fit neatly into ecclesiastical categories. When Wilkinson's appointment as Bishop of Truro was announced, the conservative

---

[54] *Evangelical Christendom*, 1 December 1881, 367; 1 October 1884, 316; cf. I. Randall and D. Hilborn, *One Body in Christ: The History and Significance of the Evangelical Alliance* (Carlisle: Paternoster Press, 2001), chapter 6. The Evangelical Alliance's basis of faith (1846) included the 'obligation...of the Lord's Supper'.

[55] P. D. Jordan, *The Evangelical Alliance for the United States of America, 1847-1900* (New York and Toronot: Edwin Mullen, 1982), 75. See also N. M. Railton, *No North Sea* (Leiden: Brill, 2000), 183-4.

[56] Dunning, *Chadwick*, 20; W. Strawson, 'Methodist Theology 1850-1950', in R. Davies, A. R. George, and G. Rupp, eds., *A History of the Methodist Church in Great Britain* (3 vols: I; London: Epworth, 1983), 221; Randall, *Evangelical Experiences*, 101.

[57] V. Smith, D. Hilary and M. Melrose, *St. Peter's Eaton Square (1827-1998)* (London: St. Peter's, 1998), 10.

[58] A. J. Mason, *Memoir of George Howard Wilkinson*, II, (London: Longmans, Green and Co., 1909), 10.

evangelical Anglican weekly, *The Record*, captured the ambiguity felt about Canon Wilkinson's evangelicalism. It wrote: 'Thankful as we feel for the [Canon's] evangelistic zeal...we cannot but express an earnest hope that in his new position of increased power and responsibility he may be led to a more complete view of Scriptural truth. The mixture of high sacramentarian doctrine with the most earnest and faithful preaching of the Gospel has hitherto produced a painful confusion in his teaching as a whole.' The High Church camp, for its part, considered that 'serious High Churchmen' would not follow Wilkinson. [59]

Dietrich Voll, in a study of this phenomenon of 'Catholic evangelicalism', suggested that the way in which it was associated with Anglican parish missions showed its essential evangelicalism.[60] John Kent vigorously opposed this view, arguing that the missions the Catholic evangelicals undertook drew their inspiration from Roman Catholic tradition rather than evangelical revivalism. It is true that Wilkinson did not identify with the 'Evangelical party' in the Church of England, and Kent has suggested that Wilkinson had abandoned his evangelical distinctives by the 1870s.[61] The debate about the Catholic evangelicals has surfaced again recently in Martin Wellings' discussion of evangelical responses to ritualism.[62] Were they in fact evangelicals? Certainly they placed stress on personal conversion. Arthur James Mason wrote 'The Ministry of Conversion', in which he recommended John Wesley, George Whitefield and Charles Finney. In one passage, in which unusually for the times he used feminine rather than masculine language, he spoke about 'a truly contrite soul which has found her way to the Living Saviour, and has felt the touch of His hand...and is walking in His way within the unity of the Church, has the right to believe herself absolved and justified from her past sins and set right with God forthwith.'[63] This description of conversion uses classic evangelical terms, but includes the more 'catholic' emphasis on following Christ 'within the unity of the Church'. Wilkinson and others such as William Cadman at Holy Trinity, Marylebone, an evangelical who introduced higher and more aesthetic forms of worship in the 1880s, were, Bebbington argues, influenced both by high churchmanship and public taste. Cadman was ready to move 'with the

---

[59] Mason, *Memoir of George Howard Wilkinson*, II, 18-19; cf. D. Voll, *Catholic Evangelicalism* (London: The Faith Press, 1963), 71.

[60] Voll, *Catholic Evangelicalism*, chapter 2.

[61] J. Kent, *Holding the Fort* (London: Epworth Press, 1978), 242-3; cf., 236-94.

[62] M. Wellings, *Evangelicals Embattled* (Carlisle: Paternoster Press, 2003), 29-30.

[63] A. J. Mason, 'The Ministry of Conversion', in A. W. Robinson, (ed.), *Handbooks for the Clergy* (London: Longmans & Co., 1902), 115, cited by Voll, *Catholic Evangelicalism*, 81-2.

taste of the times'.[64] Here were evangelicals whose spirituality was being remoulded.

In the case of Wilkinson, Kent's argument that he abandoned his evangelicalism by the 1870s seems doubtful. On 19 February 1874 Wilkinson had a breakfast appointment, arranged by a leading evangelical layman, Sir Thomas Beauchamp, with an American, Robert Pearsall Smith. At this point Robert and his wife Hannah were gaining prominence in Britain as advocates of the teaching that spiritual victory was by trust in Christ, by 'the rest of faith'. This teaching was soon to be spread in modified form by Keswick. Wilkinson noted in his dairy the effect of his meeting: 'A day to be remembered – P. Smith told me of Peace and Rest in Christ.' He and Smith met on several subsequent occasions. Wilkinson was clearly drawn to this movement of spiritual renewal within evangelicalism. Later in 1874, Wilkinson and his wife were among the hundred or so people, including Evan Hopkins and F. B. Meyer, two future Keswick leaders, who attended a significant conference at Broadlands in Hampshire. Wilkinson, who addressed the conference, spoke of enthusiastically (as did others) of Hannah Pearsall Smith as the 'life and heart of the whole gathering' and described her charming way of disarming the 'dear theologians', as she often called them.[65] Eight years later, on 12 November 1882, preaching at St Peter's, Eaton Square, Wilkinson asked:

> Is there any one here who has never yet known the happiness of realising that the past is entirely done away with?....It came to me very quietly....Long after I had taught other people and brought them into happiness, I myself had no inward rest. I sat quietly in my room, at every spare moment, with my Bible, and I asked God by the Holy Spirit to show me what I have tried to show you this morning... And, in His great Son, as calmly and as quietly as a little child when the mother stoops to kiss it, quietly Rest came into my soul.[66]

This language was typical of evangelicals in the Keswick network, suggesting that Wilkinson's own experience resulted from his conversations with Pearsall Smith.

During Wilkinson's later ministries, as Archbishop of St Andrews and then Primus of the Scottish Episcopal Church, the description 'Catholic evangelical' was used less often, although he was described as combining High Church doctrine with the 'devotion of the Dissenting prayer-meeting'. But it was particularly in the 1880s that Wilkinson was seen as a creative exemplar of a high evangelicalism. St Peter's, Eaton

---

[64] Bebbington, *Evangelicalism*, 148.
[65] Mason, *Memoir of George Howard Wilkinson*, I, 321-2.
[66] Mason, *Memoir of George Howard Wilkinson*, I, 41.

Square, where he introduced a daily eucharist and also prayer meetings on mid-week evenings and where he attracted very large congregations, was talked of in 1883 as 'the centre of a novel kind of Church life'.[67] Wilkinson appreciated hymnody and used a great variety of hymns, from Horatius Bonar to John Keble, to focus on the cross at eucharist services. In commenting on his practice 'he pointed out how still more beautiful some well-known Evangelical hymns became when used sacramentally'.[68] Later, in his Episcopal oversight of the clergy of the Truro Diocese, particularly of those clergy commencing ministry, Wilkinson sought to achieve high standards of consecration. He had a dread, said his friend Henry Scott Holland (who became Regius Professor of Divinity at Oxford) of an 'unconverted ministry'.[69] As an example of his biblicism, Wilkinson gave a Sunday afternoon Bible Reading at St Peter's at which he expounded Peter's First Epistle and brought out the practical application. 1,800 people attended. At a certain point in his address Wilkinson gave an opportunity to those who found the exposition too long to leave; only about 100 did so.[70] James Paige, the Baptist minister in Truro from 1877 to 1894, who had been brought up in Anglicanism before becoming a Baptist, and who had trained at Spurgeon's College, said of Wilkinson that 'those who had the privilege of knowing him, even though differing from him in creed, could not help being attracted by his great spirituality of mind'.[71] Paige felt an affinity with the conversionist spirituality of a Catholic evangelical.

The Local Community

'Conversion', says Gillett, 'can lead to the ghetto; it can reject more than is necessary of the wider culture...It can produce its own super-spiritualized culture, replete with taboos and idiosyncrasies.'[72] The description is an apt one. Early nineteenth-century opposition to the theatre, for example, can be illustrated by the response of Francis Close, the dominant Anglican evangelical leader in Cheltenham, to the burning down in 1839 of Cheltenham's Theatre Royal. Close saw this as 'an act of God'. Because of the influence of Close in the town the theatre

---

[67] Voll, *Catholic Evangelicalism*, 72-3, citing *The Standard*, 19 January 1883.

[68] Mason, *Memoir of George Howard Wilkinson*, II, 79.

[69] Mason, *Memoir of George Howard Wilkinson*, II, 67; cf. Voll, *Catholic Evangelicalism*, 73, 115.

[70] Mason, *Memoir of George Howard Wilkinson*, II, 94-5.

[71] Mason, *Memoir of George Howard Wilkinson*, II, 64; 'Memoirs of Ministers', *Baptist Handbook* (London: Baptist Union, 1925), 315-16.

[72] Gillett, *Trust and Obey*, 39.

was not rebuilt until 1891.[73] Doreen Rosman, in *Evangelicals and Culture,* showed that there were significant numbers of nineteenth-century evangelicals who enjoyed a wide variety of cultural activities.[74] But there were also many who were wary of the seduction of culture. In 1876 Spurgeon attacked the way in which 'modern culture', 'intellectual preaching' and 'aesthetic taste' were being embraced within Nonconformist life. He called for a spiritual protest.[75] Changes in attitude were apparent, however, by the end of the nineteenth century. By that time, as Nigel Scotland notes, the early evangelical opposition to reading novels, for instance, had virtually disappeared.[76] In the early twentieth century Samuel Chadwick could note (with regret) that Methodists 'of social standing' went to the theatre, danced and played cards. He could not, however, get them to prayer meetings.[77]

The relationship of evangelicals to sport illustrates changing attitudes. In the 1870s the idea that there might be a connection between Nonconformist chapel life and sport would have seemed incongruous, but the next two decades saw sport being widely embraced by evangelicals. In 1889 a sports column appeared in the *Northamptonshire Nonconformist,* signed by 'Biceps'. The writer stated that he believed with all his heart in the 'trite but true' maxim, *Mens sana in corpore sano.* Without a sound body, he argued, a sound mind was often impossible. He continued:

> Give me good sound sport, free from cruelty and torture of dumb animals – that is barbarity not sport – and I am happy. Were the Studds any worse missionaries because they were the foremost cricketers of the day? Is a man a poorer Christian because he can pull stroke in an eight, do a spin across the country, play a sound game of football, or distinguish himself on the cricket field? Nay, I trow not.[78]

The reference to leading Christian cricketers is significant. In 1882 C. T. Studd, who three years later was one of the 'Cambridge Seven' missionaries to China with Hudson Taylor's China Inland Mission, was seen by the *Cricketing Annual* as the leading all-round cricketer in England. He and his two brothers each captained the Cambridge

---

[73] Scotland, *Evangelical Anglicans,* 217-18.

[74] See D. Rosman, *Evangelicals and Culture* (London: Croom Helm, 1984), 152.

[75] *The Sword and the Trowel,* July 1876, 306; cf. Bebbington, *Holiness in Nineteenth-Century England,* 48-9.

[76] Scotland, *Evangelical Anglicans,* 216.

[77] Randall, *Evangelical Experiences,* 94.

[78] *Northamptonshire Nonconformist,* February 1889, cited by H. McLeod, '"Thews and Sinews": Nonconformity and Sport', in D. Bebbington and T. Larsen (eds.), *Modern Christianity and Cultural Aspirations* (Sheffield Academic Press, 2003), 42.

University cricket team. C. T. Studd's spiritual outlook was deeply affected by Hannah Pearsall Smith's book, *The Christian's Secret of a Happy Life*, and by the response to God expressed in Frances Ridley Havergal's words:

> Take my life, and let it be consecrated, Lord, to thee.
> Take my moments and my days; let them flow in ceaseless praise.

Although Studd was to leave the world of cricket, he never regretted his early sporting involvement.[79] One of Studd's later missionary associates in central Africa, Alfred Buxton, describing missionary advance there which was being led by Studd, believed that opposition to the Christian message was waning and that 'the Devil's bowling is going to pieces'.[80] J. C. Ryle enjoyed watching cricket and took the unusual view that two subjects were essential in education – English history and games.[81] Cricket was one sport which enjoyed widespread evangelical support.

'Biceps' was keen to show that women as well as men could be involved in sport and that a variety of sports could be commended. He drew attention to the achievements of Northampton's College Street Baptist hockey team and to the benefit gained by young ladies in Doddridge Congregational Chapel through their weekly aerobics class. Their exercises, directed by Miss Jeannie Mayger, were, he suggested, 'to the manifest improvement of their physique'.[82] Football clubs were launched by churches. John Ripsher, the leading influence behind the formation of Tottenham Hotspur in 1882, for example, was a prominent member of All Hallows Church, Tottenham, and of the evangelical Young Men's Christian Association. The YMCA was used as the team's first headquarters and club members attended scripture lessons.[83] Another popular sport was tennis. At Ferme Park Baptist Church, Hornsey, the church's Tennis Club had to reply to allegations in 1901 that single men and women at the club were indulging in 'improper behaviour'. Tennis clubs were widely regarded as 'marriage markets'.[84] Sometimes evangelical ministers were hailed as sportsmen. Joseph Roxburgh, who became pastor of Princes Street Baptist Church,

---

[79] N. P. Grubb, *C.T. Studd: Cricketer and Pioneer* (London: Lutterworth Press, 1933), 30-1, 38-9.

[80] I. M. Randall, *Entire Devotion to God* (Ilkeston, Derbys: The Wesley Fellowship), 10.

[81] I. D. Farley, *J.C. Ryle: First Bishop of Liverpool* (Carlisle: Paternoster Press, 2000), 137.

[82] McLeod, '"Thews and Sinews": Nonconformity and Sport', 29.

[83] Scotland, *Evangelical Anglicans*, 227, citing P. Soar, *Tottenham Hotspur: The Official Illustrated History* (Hastings: Hilton Publishers, 1997), 11-13.

[84] McLeod, '"Thews and Sinews": Nonconformity and Sport', 42.

Northampton, in 1906, was lauded in a local newspaper as one who 'has pleaded all along for the entire development of manhood and womanhood – body, mind and spirit. He is athletic...an all-round cricketer, having captained several clubs, a swimmer and a seasoned cyclist.' His piety was 'of the robust order' and it was reckoned that this would appeal to young men, 'in whose interests a large part of his active life has been spent'.[85]

This last phrase is crucial in understanding the piety of people like Joseph Roxburgh. Recreation was not simply for the sake of personal gratification. There was a desire to reach out and help others. Gillett comments that at its best corporate evangelical spirituality produces a strong missionary commitment.[86] In Lambeth, where F. B. Meyer was minister from 1892 (at the Congregational church, Christ Church, Westminster Bridge Road), he rented a tumble-down factory for gymnastics and for carpentry. He decided, because of the level of stealing and rowdiness, that he had 'got hold of the right sort' of young people.[87] Meyer's weekly Sunday afternoon Brotherhood meeting, which he started in 1893, grew to 800 men. He picked up ideas from a Brotherhood meeting at George Street Chapel in Liverpool. Pleasant Sunday Afternoon (PSA) meetings for men were, in the 1890s, as large as 1,000 in several Nonconformist churches. With Meyer's Brotherhood, evangelism and social action went hand in hand. An influx of some of the 'roughest class of working men' in Lambeth was bound to highlight social needs.[88] Through the Brotherhood Meyer opened an evening school for adults, and the Education Inspector assessed this as having the best results in London. As well as being 'an institution for soul-winning', the Brotherhood was also an expression of Meyer's belief in community.[89]

Anglican evangelical leaders were also involved in social ministry. Active social concern was not as evident in the Anglican-dominated Keswick constituency, and in 1893 *The Life of Faith* gave evidence of this lack of awareness when it suggested that compared to reaching the rich, work among the poor was 'comparatively easy'.[90] But many individual Anglican evangelicals committed themselves to the alleviation of suffering. The best known was the Earl of Shaftesbury, whose biographer, Edwin Hodder, writing in 1884, recalled how Shaftesbury spoke of himself as an 'Evangelical of the Evangelicals' and considered

---

[85] McLeod, '"Thews and Sinews": Nonconformity and Sport', 38-9.
[86] Gillett, *Trust and Obey*, 39.
[87] M. J. Street, *F.B. Meyer: His Life and Work* (London: S.W. Partridge, 1902), 98.
[88] Randall, *Spirituality and Social Change*, 109.
[89] *British Weekly*, 19 October 1905, 37.
[90] *The Life of Faith*, 8 February 1893, 108.

it was from evangelicals that most of the great philanthropic movements of the nineteenth century had sprung.[91] Shaftesbury's most notable achievement as an MP was legislation that greatly improved the working conditions of adults and children. Among his many other concerns were the conditions in which the mentally ill were housed. Through his activities Acts were passed ensuring better provision of asylums. In his analysis of Shaftesbury's inner, spiritual life, Hodder noted that belief in Christ's Second Coming stimulated Shaftesbury in all his work.[92] J. C. Ryle, in Liverpool, was one of the main promoters of the city's Commission of Inquiry into Unemployment, set up in 1894. In a passage in *Practical Religion*, Ryle dealt with the concern for the poor from the parable of the rich man and Lazarus. He spoke about the danger of the sin of selfishness and the danger of riches. 'I am sure there never was a time', Ryle averred, 'when all classes in England had so many comforts and so many temporal good things.' But he saw an utter disproportion between what better-off people spent on themselves and what they gave to the poor. The problem, as he saw it, was love of self. For Ryle it was not fear of hell, nor hope of heaven, nor any sense of duty, that would lead to concern for the poor. He was emphatic: 'Oh no! The disease of selfishness is far too deeply rooted to yield to such secondary motives as these. Nothing will ever cure it but an experimental knowledge of Christ's redeeming love.'[93] Spirituality was foundational.

The bias of many evangelicals of this period was towards the disadvantaged and the vulnerable. Josephine Butler was a prominent Victorian who took up the cause of women and girls who were exploited. Although reluctant to be identified with the evangelical wing of the Church of England, Butler affirmed core evangelical convictions.[94] She campaigned successfully for the repeal of the Contagious Diseases Acts, under which prostitutes were given health inspections while no action was taken regarding their clients. She argued that if employment opportunities for women were improved, prostitution would decrease. Butler pressed for the age of consent for lawful sexual intercourse to be raised from twelve to sixteen, and this goal was achieved in 1885. She spoke in that period of her campaigns as having advanced since they were 'openly baptised, so to speak, in the name of Christ', and she thought she had observed in the 'sceptical and worldly atmosphere of Parliament' something she had never observed before – 'signs of a

[91] Hodder, *Life and Work of the Seventh Earl of Shaftesbury*, 519.
[92] Hodder, *Life and Work of the Seventh Earl of Shaftesbury*, 523.
[93] Ryle, *Practical Religion*, 213-18.
[94] L. S. Nolland, *A Victorian Feminist Christian* (Carlisle: Paternoster Press, 2004), 43-8.

consciousness of a spiritual strife going on'.[95] Thomas Barnardo, too, was an evangelical who had a huge social impact. When he died in 1905, at the age of sixty, his homes had brought up 60,000 destitute children. It was largely through his influence that the 1891 Custody of Children Act came into being, protecting the rights of vulnerable, neglected children.[96] F. B. Meyer became well known for his contribution to the rehabilitation of offenders. During his ministry in Leicester in the 1880s he discovered that men coming out of prison were quickly drawn back into crime. With the co-operation of the governor, he visited the prison each morning, taking discharged prisoners to a coffee house for a plate of ham. He estimated that he had provided over 4,500 breakfasts by the time he left Leicester in 1888. Meyer also found ex-prisoners employment, and when manufacturers were reluctant to assist he launched a business himself. A minority of those he sought to help, Meyer admitted, 'turned out very badly', but he claimed that many were converted and the prison population was reduced.[97] Social improvement was undergirded by spiritual change.

Did this imply a social gospel? This term began to be used increasingly in the late 1880s and 1890s by Baptist leaders such as John Clifford, the best known advocate of what was called the 'Nonconformist Conscience'.[98] For evangelicals like Clifford and Meyer, the social gospel was the application of the gospel to society. Nonconformists as a whole looked to the Liberal Party as a vehicle for achieving their hopes of a better society. Prior to the 1880 general election Spurgeon wrote and distributed leaflets in the boroughs of Lambeth and Southwark urging voters not to elect a Conservative, as had happened at the last election, but to support the Liberal candidates. He wrote:

> Are we to have another six years of Tory rule? This is just now the question. Are we to go on invading and slaughtering, in order to obtain a scientific frontier and feeble neighbours? How many wars may we reckon upon between now and 1886? What quantity of killing will be done in that time, and how many of our weaker neighbours will have their houses

[95] M. G. Fawcett and E. M. Turner, *Josephine Butler* (London: Association for Moral & Social Hygiene, 1927), 99-100.

[96] J. W. Bready, *Doctor Barnardo: Physician, Pioneer, Prophet* (London: George Allen & Unwin, 1930), 208-9, 259.

[97] See F. B. Meyer, *The Bells of Is: Or Voices of Human Need and Sorrow* (London: Morgan & Scott [1894]).

[98] See D. M. Thompson, 'The Emergence of the Nonconformist Social Gospel in England', in K. Robbins, (ed.), *Protestant Evangelicalism: Britain, Ireland, Germany and America c1750 – c1950: Essays in Honour of W.R. Ward* (Oxford: Blackwell, 1990), 255-80.

> burned and their fields ravaged by this Christian (?) nation? Let those who rejoice in War vote for the Tories; but we hope they will not find a majority in Southwark.[99]

Spurgeon was adamantly opposed to the Conservative administration's aggressive foreign policy in the Balkans, South Africa and Afghanistan. The two Liberal candidates Spurgeon endorsed were elected. Voting patterns among Free Church evangelicals were to become more varied in the twentieth century, with the rise of socialism and the Labour Party and also because some Free Church evangelicals, like many Anglican evangelicals, began to vote Conservative. F.B. Meyer, in an address to the Baptist Union assembly at Huddersfield in 1906, asserted that Baptists shared with socialists a desire for peace, for old age pensions and for better housing, and that these would come as the gospel created 'a kingdom of social justice'.[100] Such a community-orientated spiritual vision was to become less evident in the decades that followed, but it is a significant part of evangelical identity.

Conclusion

To what extent has evangelical spirituality been wary of liturgy, cautious about the sacraments, weak in its ecclesiology and uninvolved in the wider community? All these features have been present in evangelical thinking. However, this is not the whole story. Evangelicals, who value the Bible, have also valued forms of prayer that have expressed great biblical themes. Spontaneous prayer, which can lack such themes, has not always been their preference. There has always been a mixture of the liturgical and the free in evangelical devotion. James Paige, the Truro Baptist minister, could speak warmly of an occasion when Bishop G. H. Wilkinson, the high church evangelical, led a united prayer meeting.[101] In their thinking about the Lord's Supper, evangelicals have adopted various theological positions. The Lord's Supper helped C. H. Spurgeon to focus on the cross and to connect with the tradition of the church. He spoke about 'the simple breaking of bread and the pouring out of wine' being observed by the church through the ages.[102] For evangelicals the church is the setting where the Word and the Sacraments nourish believing people, but it is also a place

[99] Reproduced in M. K. Nicholls, *C.H. Spurgeon – The Pastor Evangelist* (Didcot: Baptist Historical Society, 1992), 65.

[100] *British Weekly*, 4 October 1906, 611, 630. See D. Thompson, 'John Clifford's Social Gospel', *Baptist Quarterly*, Vol. 31, No. 5 (1986), 204.

[101] Mason, *Memoir of George Howard Wilkinson*, II, 64.

[102] 'The Object of the Lord's Supper', *MTP*, Vol. 51, No. 2942, 1 Cor. 11. 26, del. On 2 September 1877, 320.

of conversion. Evangelical ecclesiology is mission-shaped. P. T. Forsyth typically pronounced: 'The Apostolic succession has no meaning except as the Evangelical succession. It does not mean...a historic line of valid ordinations unbroken from the Apostles to the last curate...But it is the succession of those who experience and preach the Apostolic Gospel of a regenerating redemption.'[103] Finally, have evangelicals neglected the wider community? This has been the case at times, but evangelical activism has always been a powerful force pushing outwards. Commitment to the spread of the gospel has led evangelicals to search for ways, as F. B. Meyer expressed it in 1902, in which the gospel can be 'incarnated again' in the wider community.[104] There have been significant evangelicals whose contribution to evangelical spirituality and identity has been liturgical, sacramental, ecclesial and communal.

[103] Forsyth, *Church and Sacraments*, 110.

[104] *Free Church Year Book* (London: National Council of the Evangelical Free Churches, 1902), 94. From an address by Meyer on 'Twentieth Century Evangelism'.

CHAPTER 16

The Missionary Statesman and the Missionary Saint: Henry Venn's Life of Francis Xavier

Mark A. Smith

In 1862, there emerged, after a gestation of almost one and a half decades a historical work penned by Henry Venn one of the nineteenth century's most influential Evangelical missionary statesmen. His topic was not the history of the CMS – an institution he had already steered for more than twenty years.[1] Nor one of the heroes of the Protestant Missionary pantheon like John Eliot or Henry Martyn but, rather surprisingly, a great champion of Roman Catholic Missions, Francis Xavier. In writing *The Missionary Life and Labours of Francis Xavier,*[2] Venn was choosing, as his own biographer subsequently noted, 'to express opinions which could not fail to be misinterpreted' and so, rather less surprisingly, the book was soon enveloped in controversy. The early 1860s have been identified as a period of relative calm in English Protestant/Catholic relations situated between the high point of papal aggression in the early 1850s and the squalls caused by the Murphy riots of the 1866-7.[3] Nevertheless, relationships remained uncomfortable and a work on Xavier (perhaps especially one which omitted the usual honorific 'saint' from its title) by so prominent an Evangelical was bound to invite suspicion.

The first substantial review appeared within a few months of publication in the December number of what was still virtually the house journal of the Clapham strand of English Evangelicalism – the

---

[1] W. Knight, *Memoir of Henry Venn B.D. Prebendary of St Paul's, and Honorary Secretary of the Church Missionary Society* (London: Longman, 1882), iii-iv. For biographical information on Venn, see also T. E. Yates, *Venn and Victorian Bishops abroad* (London: SPCK, 1978).

[2] Henry Venn, *The Missionary Life and Labours of Francis Xavier taken from his own correspondence with a sketch of the General Results of Roman Catholic Missions among the heathen* (London: Longman, 1862).

[3] See, for example, J. Wolffe, *The Protestant Crusade in Great Britain 1829-1860* (Oxford: Oxford University Press, 1991), 247.

Christian Observer. As one would expect from a journal with this pedigree the review was relatively favourable. The *Life*, the anonymous reviewer concluded,

> is not meant to charm the idler, but to instruct the Christian student on some of the most important questions connected with God's work on earth. It is a wise book, and we say much in saying that it is in every way worthy of its author, and of those glorious principles which, in his connection with the Church Missionary Society, he has so long and ably represented.[4]

From the point of view of the *Christian Observer*, Venn's work was useful on a number of levels. It exposed the true nature of Xavier's missionary methods, especially his reliance on the secular power of the Portuguese state and his mass baptisms of infants whose parents remained heathen. It also demonstrated their ultimate failure. With respect to Xavier himself Venn had illustrated his autocratic and restless character, and exploded his subsequent reputation as a worker of miracles. In short

> he shows that he was no model for a Christian missionary, and that in his hands the work of converting the heathen was an utter failure. More than this, he proves that Romish missions are a heartless, hollow enterprise; that wherever her emissaries go, and on whatever field they enter, they scatter only the seeds of superstition, which hasten to a barren harvest or a premature decay.[5]

Nevertheless, the *Observer* assured its readers, Venn's work was not blindly critical of Xavier, 'Mr Venn writes of him without prejudice, and even with some partiality. He sees in him much to admire. He is "to his virtues very kind".' This was, needless to say, not the verdict of Roman Catholic reviewers. Stirred by the notice in the *Christian Observer*, the first of these appeared in the following year in the *Home and Foreign Review*[6] Here the reviewer took a relatively moderate line, 'Mr Venn', he noted, 'has certainly demonstrated that Father Bouhours's biography of the saint (well known in this country through Dryden's translation) is deformed by many gross and extravagant fictions.'[7] In this respect, suggested the reviewer, 'If Mr Venn has served the truth, he has also served the cause of Catholicism,' for, 'to feed the religious life on

---

[4] *Christian Observer*, (Dec 1862), 913.

[5] Ibid.

[6] *Home and Foreign Review*, II (1863), 172-89.

[7] Ibid., 172.

falsehood is indeed to build on a foundation of sand.'[8] Nevertheless, he had not succeeded in his main objects which seemed to have been,

> 1. To prove that St. Francis worked *no* miracles.
>
> 2. To prove that his character had many defects, *e.g.* insincerity, restlessness, fickleness; in short that he was not really a saint.
>
> 3. To prove that he would have effected little or nothing in the field of conversion without the aid of the civil power; in Mr Venn's technical language that he was always prone to "lean on the arm of the flesh."
>
> 4. To prove that Catholic missions in general during the last three centuries have been a failure; that all conversions on a large scale have been either "military" or purchased by unlawful compliances; and that, in either case, they have been only "nominal."[9]

Moreover, in Venn's writing, the reviewer detected more than a hint of jealousy,

> Protestants are tempted to disparage a Christianity which the "arm of flesh" has any share in bringing about, because they have become so accustomed to the dilettante, ineffectual way in which their own missions are carried on that they think a more vigorous system must have something wrong about it...their missions as a whole remain without fruit; the nations whom they are intended to convert are *not* converted.[10]

In the following year, H. J. Coleridge, writing in the *Dublin Review* took a much less conciliatory line, Venn's work, he asserted roundly was to be classified as a piece of 'controversial literature',[11] which sought to deny the miracles of the saint because their existence was fatal to the protestant position. Neither was it a particularly compelling piece of polemic,

> Were it not for certain qualities which provoke no light sentence of moral condemnation, Mr Venn's book would be highly amusing to any reader possessed already of a moderate knowledge of the subjects of which it treats. There is an artless and unconscious simplicity about its blunders and absurdities that reminds us of some of those delightful descriptions of

---

[8] Ibid., 173.
[9] Ibid., 174.
[10] Ibid., 186.
[11] *Dublin Review*, NS, 3, (July 1864), 28.

> the manners and customs of a strange country, which visitors for a few weeks occasionally publish for the edification of their friends.[12]

Eschewing the caution of the *Home and Foreign Review*, Coleridge proceeded to assert the genuineness of all of Xavier's reported miracles, including several which his colleague had accepted as legendary.[13]

Were the Catholic reviewers correct in identifying Venn's *Life of Xavier* with the genre of anti-Catholic controversial literature? There is certainly material in the work that could be used to substantiate such a view. However the verdict of most recent historians would appear to be decisively against it. For the existing modern literature on Venn, insofar as it mentions the *Life* at all, places it in the context not of missionary tensions with Rome but of a domestic dispute within the Church of England. It is regarded pure and simple as a commentary on the idea of 'a missionary bishop' and placed in an entirely different genre – that of missionary primer.[14]

This view clearly has much to commend it. The notion that missions should be concerned not just to take the Christian message to the heathen but to take the church in all its fullness – with a bishop at its head – had been canvassed with growing enthusiasm since the 1830s. It had been given a powerful boost by the Tractarian movement and its most vocal supporters by mid-century were Tractarian-influenced High Churchmen like Samuel Wilberforce.[15] Venn, who regarded episcopacy as the crown rather than the foundation of the church, objected to the notion of missionary bishops on several inter-connected grounds many of which found their way into his interpretation of Xavier. Of these, the most important seems to have been a concern about the damaging effects of the introduction of a potentially despotic Episcopal authority into a mission situation to which it was unsuited.[16] Venn noted at the outset of his work,

> Many prevailing sentiments of the present day, even in Protestant countries, respecting Missions, find their counterpart in some of the most striking features in the history of St Francis Xavier, such as... the notion

[12] Ibid., 27.

[13] Ibid., 49-64.

[14] This is the virtual consensus of modern scholarship. See, for example, Yates, *Venn*, 108-9; W. R. Shenk, *Henry Venn – Missionary Statesman* (New York: Orbis Books, 1983), 24-37; P. Williams, ' "Not Transplanting": Henry Venn's Strategic Vision', in K. Ward and B. Stanley (eds), *The Church Mission Society and World Christianity* (Cambridge: Eerdmans, 2000), 155.

[15] Yates, *Venn*, 100-105.

[16] See, for example, Williams, ' "Not Transplanting"', 154-5; Yates, *Venn*, 109.

that an autocratic power is wanted in a Mission, such as a Missionary Bishop might exercise.[17]

The deleterious effects of such a policy are illustrated by references to the authoritarian tendencies implicit in Xavier's model of mission and then summed up thus:

Even if Xavier had better understood the work of Missions, there was one great fault in his system which would have proved fatal to success. He attempted to carry everything by authority. He constantly inculcated the supreme merit and advantage of implicit obedience to himself. The sequel of his history will show how completely this system failed to form an efficient body of coadjutors. Xavier's history will, therefore, afford a useful caution against a notion, too much countenanced at the present day, that an ecclesiastical head of a Mission is needed to secure efficiency by uniformity of action, and to counteract the evils which may arise within a Mission from the contrariety of individual opinions. Such absolute power may consist with the government of a settled Christian Church, where the relation between ecclesiastical authority and the pastoral function has been defined by canons, and by experience. But no canons or regulations have been yet laid down for Missions to the heathen.[18]

Venn, was not just opposed to prelacy in principle but also because he connected it with two further dangers – the temptation of over-reliance on the temporal advantages of links with the state and the inhibition of local initiative. Xavier's close links with, and reliance on political power are a constant theme of Venn's writing. Initially, the concentration is on Xavier's support of and by the power of the Portuguese imperium. As a consequence, Venn noted,

it is difficult to conceive more splendid worldly attractions to any enterprise, and greater temporal advantages for its prosecution, than those which accompanied the call of Xavier to become "the Apostle of India."[19]

However, even in his mission to Japan, which lay substantially outside the influence of the Portuguese, the policy of reliance on political power continued to be dominant. Xavier's, success in winning by diplomacy the patronage of a local ruler for his mission is described and then, Venn concludes,

Xavier erected a Mission upon the treacherous foundations of secular support. With the honest intention of promoting Christianity, he

---

[17] Venn, *Life*, iii.
[18] Ibid., 146.
[19] Ibid., 18.

> introduced into the work the elements of political intrigue and complications, which soon sprang up and choked whatever "good seed" such' as that which his native assistants, 'Paul, Cosmo, and Fernandez were labouring to disseminate.[20]

This enterprise was effectively destroyed by persecution in the seventeenth century and

> Thus the Mission planted by Xavier was extinguished in blood, after existing for nearly ninety years; and this *through the same political power on which Xavier had leaned in all his Missionary enterprises.*[21]

The reliance on political power was, in Xavier, a specific example of a general tendency to rely on an "arm of flesh" rather than the power of the gospel. This was manifest at its most extreme in Xavier's resort not just to political influence but also to military power in order to establish his missions. This Venn illustrated by reference to Xavier's advocacy of a military expedition against Jaffnapatam in Ceylon and by citing a maxim attributed to Xavier that, 'Missionaries without muskets do never make converts to any purpose.'[22]

Perhaps of even greater concern to Venn, however, was the second danger of Episcopal authoritarianism – that it might suppress the local and indigenous initiatives that were crucial to the future health of the Church. Such dangers were the subject of an extensive commentary in the *Life* as illustrated by the following passage on the task of the missionary,

> That work is so varied, and its emergencies so sudden, that the evangelist must be left to act mainly on his own responsibility and judgment. It pre-eminently requires independence of mind, fertility of resource, a quick observance of the footsteps of Divine Providence, a readiness to push forward in that direction, an abiding sense in the mind of the Missionary of personal responsibility to extend the kingdom of Christ, and a lively conviction that the Lord is at his "right hand." These qualifications are, like all the finer sentiments of Christianity, of delicate texture; they are often united with a natural sensitiveness; they are to be cherished and counselled rather than ruled; they are easily checked and discouraged if "headed" by authority. Yet these are the qualities which have ever distinguished the Missionaries who win the richest trophies, and advance the borders of the Redeemer's kingdom. Among such a body of workmen no formidable difficulties will arise from the contrariety of individual opinions; and such as do arise will be easily composed by affectionate,

---

[20] Ibid., 209. See below for Paul, Cosmo and Fernandez.

[21] Ibid., 209-10.

[22] Ibid., 258-9.

> Christian, and wise counsels, whether offered on the spot, or transmitted from Europe.[23]

Perhaps even more compelling than this overt defence of the CMS model, however, was the tone adopted by Venn in describing the work of Xavier's native assistant in Japan. His attitude to this native catechist is clear from the outset, 'It is impossible,' noted Venn, 'to contemplate the story of Paul Anger, without recognising in it a signal instance of the providence of God, which has often thus facilitated the entrance of His gospel into a dark region.'[24] Later Venn, quotes Xavier directly in asserting that 'Paul diligently preaches the gospel day and night'. [25] We also hear that,

> The zeal of Paul for the religion he had embraced proved itself to be eminently sincere. He devoted whole days and nights to the instruction in Christian doctrine of his parents, relatives, and friends of every age and rank, and he exhorted them with such success, that within three months he brought over to Christianity his mother, his wife, his male and female relatives, and no small number of his other friends and former intimates.[26]

Thus, we are perhaps intended to conclude, the Japanese church would have prospered had it not been for, 'the defective foundation laid by Xavier'[27] – defects, we are meant to understand, in both theology and practice.[28] Here we are close to the heart of Venn's famous concern for the development of strong self-supporting indigenous churches and his sensitivity to the danger of any model of mission that inhibited the development of a native pastorate or fostered a relationship of dependency.

It is one of the ironies of the Roman Catholic commentaries on the *Life of Xavier* that the reviewers appeared to believe they had scored a hit when they found Venn criticising the saint in respect of activities for which the missionaries of the High Church Universities Mission to Central Africa might also be held accountable. 'Has he never heard,' asked the *Home and Foreign Review*,

> of the armed incursions made by the Oxford and Cambridge missionaries, headed by Bishop Mackenzie, upon the Ajawas in South Africa, - incursions which, according to the candid confessions of Mr Rowley, it

[23] Ibid., 146-7.
[24] Ibid., 174.
[25] Ibid., 181.
[26] Ibid., 179. Venn is also complimentary about Xavier's 'simple' European assistants Cosmo and Fernandez. Ibid., 176-7.
[27] Ibid., 300.
[28] Ibid., 182, 209.

> was afterwards found were wholly unjustifiable? One would think it would be time enough for him to attack St. Francis after he had duly bewailed and expressed his abhorrence of such monstrous acts as these.[29]

With this part of the review at least Venn might have been delighted and had his primary purpose been to criticise the High Church model of mission under the cover of a biography of Xavier, it would have presented the unusual spectacle of a Roman Catholic being criticised for being too much like an Anglican High Churchman rather than *vice versa.* It would also, like the campaign for a Martyrs Memorial in Oxford,[30] have been a difficult tactic to counter. A High Church response would have risked a public identification of their understanding of the appropriate form of mission with that of the papacy –strengthening the impression that they represented a Romanising tendency within the Established Church. It is understandable, therefore that the main Anglican High Church periodical, *The Christian Remembrancer* seems to have chosen not to review Venn's work.

To the extent that the *Life of Xavier* is to be regarded as a defence of the CMS model of mission and a critique of the alternatives it should not be assumed, however, that the Roman Catholics and Anglican High Churchmen were its only targets. Venn is critical throughout the work of the temptation to be swayed by the 'romance of missions' or to indulge in undue asceticism.[31] Both these characteristics might be linked with Catholic and High Church missions but they were associated too with a radical protestant approach to missions which stressed faith rather then the use of means as the proper keynote of missionary activity. It is perhaps no coincidence that the review in the *Christian Observer* detected a striking resemblance between the character of Xavier as depicted by Venn and that of the apostle of radical Protestantism, Edward Irving. Indeed, on the question of miracles

---

[29] *Home and Foreign Review,* II, (1863), 184. See also, *Dublin Review,* NS, 3, (July 1864), 39. Both reviewers did, however, also refer to Bishop Macdougall of Labuan with whom Venn may have had rather more sympathy. For an account of the tragic UCMS mission led by MacKenzie, see Owen Chadwick, *Mackenzie's Grave* (London: Hodder and Stoughton, 1959).

[30] The Martyrs Memorial effectively challenged Tractarian Churchmen to declare their allegiance to the English reformation or publicly be seen not to do so. For the most recent account of the campaign see, A. Atherstone, 'The Martyrs Memorial at Oxford', *Journal of Ecclesiastical History,* 54 no 2, (April 2003), 278-301.

[31] Venn, *Life,* iii, 13. For Venn's opposition to asceticism see also Shenk, Henry Venn, 51.

Xavier was revealed to have been, 'less a fanatic than Irving was.'[32] It is here that the character of Venn's Evangelicalism emerges with the greatest clarity. If he was heir to the liberal and generous spirit of the Evangelicalism of Wilberforce and his circle so he also inherited its enlightenment caution about supernatural interventions in general and the miraculous in particular. Such assumptions lay at the root of his concept of missions. Indeed, for Venn, modern missionary work differed from that described in the New Testament precisely in respect of the fact that 'ours is not a miraculous dispensation.'[33] It should come as no surprise therefore, that it was to William Paley that Venn directed his readers on the reputed miracles of Xavier, 'as presenting an illustration of the contrast between false pretensions to miraculous powers and the truth of the Gospel History of our Lord and his Apostles.'[34] The continuing vitality of Claphamite perspectives within a key evangelical institution in the age of Shaftesbury and the *Record* is an important indicator of the persistent diversity of evangelical styles and of the complexity of the process of cultural change within the movement as a whole. Moreover, the existence of an audience for such views is clearly a necessary feature of any attempt to understand the character of British evangelicalism in the Victorian period and therefore requires further investigation.

Such considerations emerge even further into the foreground if we consider the *Life of Xavier* in the light of a third genre of evangelical writing. A clue here is given by Yates' helpful summary of Venn's daily routine. The day began, we are told at 8am with family prayers, followed by breakfast and a brisk walk to the office in Salisbury Square. Venn stayed at his desk until 5pm often taking only a cup of coffee and a bun for lunch. Dinner was at 6.30pm and frequently spent in conversation with a missionary visitor whom Venn had brought home to quiz on the progress of his station. From 8pm until 10pm Venn roped his family into his work, persuading his children to read him missionary reports while he took notes. At 10pm family prayers would signal the end of the day for the bulk of the household but Venn himself would continue to work on CMS papers until 1 in the morning or even longer during busy periods.[35] Yates later notes, apparently without conscious irony, that, 'As a man of letters he showed his breadth of mind by devoting his spare hours to a life of the great Roman Catholic

[32] *Christian Observer*, (Dec 1862), 911. Mrs Oliphant's biography of Irving had appeared earlier in the same year.

[33] Venn to Barton, 27 January 1862, cited in Williams, ' "Not Transplanting"', 152.

[34] Venn, *Life*, 89.

[35] Yates, *Venn*, 13-14. The account is based on that of Venn's son Henry.

missionary of the sixteenth century Francis Xavier.'[36]

It seems unlikely that a man whose time was quite so fully occupied as Henry Venn's should have laboured for 14 years simply to produce a work of polemic against Roman Catholic or Anglo-Catholic models of mission. He was certainly interested in what might be learnt either positively or negatively from the life and missionary labours of Xavier in furthering the protestant missionary enterprise. However, as Venn indicated clearly in the introduction to the work, he was also interested in the details of Xavier and his missions for their own sake – because,

> The history of modern Roman catholic Missions to heathen countries forms an important subject of inquiry with all who take an interest in the progress of Christianity. One of the most remarkable periods in this history is that which extends from the middle of the sixteenth to the middle of the seventeenth centuries. It was then that the Jesuit Missionaries and some of the ablest men appeared in the field.[37]

Venn was convinced that the true nature of these missions, like those of the CMS could be gleaned only from authentic materials that revealed the motives and methods of the missionary – materials like the missionary journals and letters that formed his own daily reading. He was thus drawn to Xavier because of the survival of such materials, because, as he claimed, 'the life of Xavier is, the only authentic source from which an *internal* view of the life and labours of a Romish Missionary can be obtained.'[38] The *Life* then, should be considered first and foremost not as a polemic though it has some polemical characteristics nor even as a missionary primer though it is certainly that too, but as a work of Ecclesiastical History.

The market in evangelical church history writing had been cornered by the first decade of the nineteenth century by that close associate of Claphamite Evangelicalism Joseph Milner. His *History of the Church of Christ,* which had reached a third edition by 1812, was a foundational text for many an evangelical home education and was famously credited by Newman with first instilling in him a love of the Fathers.[39] Milner had tackled the issue of writing about the pre-reformation centuries by seeking to uncover within the Catholic Church a tradition of 'real Christianity'. In so doing, as John Walsh has noted, 'Milner showed considerable ingenuity in discovering Evangelicals in unlikely

---

[36] Ibid., 14.

[37] Venn, *Life*, i

[38] Ibid. The emphasis is mine.

[39] Much the best analysis of the importance and content on Milner's work remains, J. D. Walsh, 'Joseph Milner's Evangelical Church History', *Journal of Ecclesiastical History*, X (1959), 174-87.

corners of Church History.'[40] His heroes included Cyprian and Ambrose as well as Augustine, Gregory the Great and St Bernard. However, from the twelfth century onwards, with the arrival on the scene of serious proto-protestant candidates like the Waldensians, such heroes become thinner on the ground. Bernard who he described as 'the last of the fathers'[41] is also the last to receive really substantial treatment. Other likely candidates tend to receive short shrift, Francis of Assisi, for example, was dismissed as a fanatic. 'His practices of devotion,' noted Milner, were,

> monstrous, and he seems ever to have been the prey of a whimsical imagination. Pride and deceit are not uncommonly connected with a temper like his... Francis sought for glory among men by his follies and absurdities and he found the genius of the age so adapted to his own, that he gained immense admiration and applause.[42]

In the thirteenth century Grosseteste did impress by his defiance of papal claims, as did Bradwardine in the fourteenth by his stand against Pelagianism but these were isolated figures in a narrative increasingly dominated by Lollards and Hussites.[43] By the eve of the Reformation catholic heroes are no longer to be found and Erasmus, for example, while praised as a restorer of learning was condemned for his lack of religious seriousness.[44]

Joseph Milner's history, even as continued by his brother Isaac, only reached 1530. Henry Venn in seeking to add what might be regarded as a further chapter to this evangelical historiographical enterprise had set himself a difficult task. Xavier after all was not just a post-reformation Catholic – a man who, given every opportunity to embrace evangelical truth, had failed to do so. He was also a counter-reformation saint and a Jesuit to boot. How might such a figure be approached?

In line with his project of uncovering a tradition of real Christianity Milner had tended to allow the spiritual fervour of his pre-reformation subjects to compensate for their evident theological shortcomings – giving a priority to devotion over doctrine as a sign of real Christianity. St Bernard, for example,

---

[40] Walsh, 'Joseph Milner', 179.

[41] J. Milner, *The History of the Church of Christ*, 3rd edn, (London: Cadell and Davies, 1812), III, 416.

[42] Milner, *History*, IV, 22. Milner's suspicion of Francis seems to have been a response to his association with the miraculous and especially the 'stigmata'.

[43] Milner, *History*, IV, passim.

[44] Milner, *History*, V, 258, 349-50.

> was deeply tinged with a predeliction for the Roman hierarchy; he had imbibed most of those errors of his time, which were not directly subversive of the Gospel; and the monastic character, which, according to the spirit of the age, appeared to be the greatest glory, seems to have much eclipsed his real virtues, and prevented his progress in true evangelical wisdom.[45]

But

> His genius was truly sublime, his temper sanguine, his mind active and vigorous. The love of God appears to have taken deep root in his soul, and seems to have been always steady, though always ardent. His charity was equal to his zeal; and his tenderness and compassion to Christian brethren went hand in hand with his severity against the heretical, the profane, and the vicious. In humility he was truly admirable...His heartfelt dependence on Christ, and his heavenly affections were incontestably strong.[46]

Moreover, having described Bernard's godly death, Milner felt able to conclude with remarkable confidence, 'thus, through faith and patience, did he, at length, inherit the promises'![47] Similarly, in the case of Grossteste, Milner, noted,

> To have so much enlarged on the character and transactions of a man, so little distinguished, in regard to evangelical knowledge, as bishop Grosseteste was, from the common herd of papists in his time, might seem to need an apology, were I not sensible, that the eminence of his PRACTICAL godliness demonstrates that he must have been in possession of the fundamentals of Divine Truth.[48]

This was essentially the approach that Venn adopted in his discussion of Xavier. His doctrine, his missionary methods and some aspects of his character are consistently condemned.[49] Venn also called into question some aspects of Xavier's spirituality and there was a tendency to attribute 'the more healthy tone of religion', which he sometimes detected, to the lingering effects of Xavier's early acquaintance with Protestantism.[50] However, Venn also retained a keen sense of the virtues

---

[45] Milner, *History*, III, 414.
[46] Ibid., 415.
[47] Ibid., 416.
[48] Milner, *History*, IV, 57.
[49] Venn, *Life*, 17, 39, 78.
[50] In particular Venn questioned Xavier's preparedness to endure suffering, linking it to his doctrine of purgatory rather than 'the exercise of a lively faith in the divine presence, or of anticipations of future glory, such as we meet with in the writings of St Paul'. Ibid., 116. On the influence of Protestantism, see, for example, Ibid., 7, 39.

of his subject. Some of these are presented as traits of character with no necessary connection to his religion. Thus Venn notes that Xavier, 'was of a generous noble and loving disposition'[51] and that his authority,

> was never pressed in a way to offend the feelings of his brethren. Its exercise is blended with so much tenderness of affection, and with such expressions of personal humility and Christian courtesy, as cannot but excite our admiration at the *natural* magnanimity of the man.[52]

Other virtues, however, are clearly more spiritual in character. Xavier's letters, for example, 'breathe throughout a fervent devotion to God, and an ardent zeal for bringing the heathen into the fold of the visible Church of Christ.'[53] As a missionary, 'Xavier was perfectly sincere in his determination to follow the call of God'[54] and 'his standard of spiritual religion was far higher than that of his associates.'[55] For Venn, Xavier's mission was fatally undermined by his failure to 'arm himself with that Gospel which is "the power of God unto salvation"' – meaning evangelical doctrine in general and a vernacular translation of the scriptures in particular.[56] Nevertheless in a number of respects, Xavier was presented as being worthy of imitation by Protestant missionaries. These included his 'energy in his calling', his 'maintaining a bold position as a Christian Missionary,' his 'sympathy for his fellow labourers', his 'zeal as a peace-maker', and particularly one suspects from the point of view of he secretary of the CMS, 'the fullness and frequency of his communications with the Church at home.'[57] Venn also characteristically identified Xavier as, 'exercising an important influence in favour of Missions' in genuine Claphamite mode,

> More especially in respect of the native races he acted the part of a true Missionary, maintaining their rights against the oppression and injustice of his own countrymen, and treating them as possessing the same feelings and capacities as their more civilised fellow men.

Venn's commendation of the Jesuit saint, limited and fenced with caveats though it was, did cause some disquiet among his more protestant reviewers. Both the *Christian Advocate* and the *Record* felt obliged to point up the contrast between Xavier and modern evangelical

---

[51] Ibid., 145.
[52] Ibid., 125. The emphasis is mine. See ibid., 250 for a further example.
[53] Ibid., 3.
[54] Ibid., 175.
[55] Ibid., 8.
[56] Ibid., 259.
[57] Ibid., 251-54.

missionaries rather more starkly than they understood Venn to have done. For the *Christian Advocate,*

> he that is least among our faithful and devoted modern missionaries, may safely be pronounced to be greater than he. He had much in him, no doubt, which was eminent and admirable, and worthy of all imitation; but the Gospel which he preached was, in many respects, not the Gospel of St. Paul.[58]

The *Record* chose to embroider Venn's contrast between the death of Xavier off the coast of China with that of the missionary Rosine Krapf in Ethiopia with the comment

> The difference is this: that the heroism of Rosine Krapf was in the cause of God's truth, that of Xavier in that of the world's perversion of it. And therefore the one is forgotten, while the other is remembered; the one despised while the other is applauded. Is it any wonder that the world should love its own?[59]

Nevertheless, in this quarter at least Venn's reputation did carry the day. Although The *Record* began its piece by noting, 'the curious contrast between the subject of the biography and the author of it" it concluded by noting 'No recommendation from us is needed to a book of Mr Venn's on such a subject. He has the right to speak, and we rejoice that he has spoken.'

In High Church circles, the evangelical notion of the invisible church, which underlay the historiographical strategy of both Milner and Venn, was often suspected as a devious route by which the true nature of the Church could be diluted in favour of dissenters. The *Life of Xavier* demonstrates the capacity of the evangelical doctrine of the invisible church, generously interpreted, to act as a bridge not only between Anglican and Nonconformist evangelicals but also between evangelicals and Catholics whether of the Roman or Anglican variety, thus helping to mitigate the tendencies to conflict inherent in their theological and ecclesiological systems. It also underlines the willingness of some evangelicals to trace the boundaries of real Christianity in devotional as well as doctrinal terms. That such views did not always triumph and that they were not always reciprocated should not blind us to their importance as a contribution to evangelical identity even at inauspicious moments in the nineteenth century. Nor should their twentieth-century re-emergence in some sectors of charismatic

---

[58] *The Christian Advocate and Review edited by Clergymen of the Church of England,* III, (May 1863), 229.

[59] *Record,* (Dec 15, 1862), 4.

evangelicalism, for example, be regarded as a novelty.

AFTERWORD

What's Right with Evangelicalism?

Derek Tidball

Evangelicalism has a remarkable capacity to provoke opposition, criticism, and even ridicule. Recently Robert Beckford has presented a series of tendentious television programmes, entitled God is Black, in which he sought to connect the vibrancy of evangelical life in the UK with the growing power of conservative African religion. I could understand a little better how he could reach his jaundiced conclusions when I discovered how he defined evangelicals. Evangelicals, he told the *Church of England Newspaper,* are people with a very literal approach to the Bible and conservative ethics arising from a narrow reading of the Bible, other-worldly, that is, spiritualising everything and with a stress on evangelism and witness.[1] Such a starting point is bound to produce a distorted picture and will inevitably produce unreliable conclusions. Having been born and brought up in an evangelical subculture and having now been at the heart of national evangelicalism for over thirty years I do not recognise Beckford's definition as doing anything like justice to the evangelicalism I have known. The most charitable comment that could be made is that it is like seeing oneself in a fairground hall of mirrors. The image you see is undeniably you, but the image is so distorted as to be almost beyond recognition.

The critics of evangelicalism are numerous, both within and without. We shall briefly document a few of them.[2] They certainly leave us in no doubt about what's wrong with evangelicalism. But the danger of allowing the critics to take the floor too much is that we too easily forget the good features and wholesome aspects that lie at the heart of evangelicalism. We fall into the trap of the Children of Israel, who when they encountered difficulties in the desert, longed to return to oppression in Egypt rather than rejoicing in the benefits of freedom. In

---

[1] *Church of England Newspaper*, 10th June, 2004, 13.

[2] Elsewhere I have categorised them as cultural despisers, intellectual detractors, charismatic critics and evangelical dissenters. See *Who are the Evangelicals?* (London: Marshall Pickering, 1994), 24-30

the light of this I seek to answer the question, "What's right with evangelicalism?" I do not do so defensively, or because I want to shut my ears to the critics. I am aware of the flaws in the movement and have been critical of it in print myself before.[3] I recognise that not everyone's experience is as positive as mine and the voices which cry of distress and perplexity need to be heard as well as those voices which spur evangelicals on to greater authenticity as a gospel driven and bible-centred movement.

Critical Voices

Major academic critiques are found in Barr and Harris who seek - not altogether convincingly - to tie evangelicals into a fundamentalist mindset.[4] In Harris' case her selection of supporting evidence is extraordinary if she was seeking to present a picture of mainstream evangelicalism. Copious attention is paid to the Dutch neo-Calvinism with comparatively little being paid to John Stott, Martyn Lloyd-Jones, the Evangelical Alliance or popular movements which are the natural habitat of evangelicals. Many criticisms, however, are less academic in their approach.

Criticisms from the Margins

Several critical voices are heard among those on the margins of the movement. Alistair Ross, a Baptist minister, wrote of the pain he experienced during his training in an evangelical theological college and the disillusion and experience of the dark night of the soul which resulted from, in his view, an abuse of power, damaging judgmentalism and narrow-mindedness.[5] It propelled him on a spiritual journey to discover a faith which is psychodynamically aware, spacious, rather than suffocating, and enables his true self to be expressed.

Best known among the critics of recent days is Dave Tomlinson, a former leader among the newer charismatic house churches. He writes not only of the struggles of those who find evangelicalism intellectually stifling and narrowly conformist, but also of the need for evangelicalism to sever its marriage to modernity and undergo a paradigm shift and produce a post-evangelicalism that resonates with contemporary post-

---

[3] See Tidball, *Evangelicals*, e.g., 237-40.

[4] J. Barr, *Fundamentalism* (London: SCM, 1977), and H. Harris, *Fundamentalism and Evangelicals* (Oxford: Clarendon Press, 1998).

[5] A. Ross, *Evangelicals in Exile: Wrestling with Theology and the Unconscious* (London: Darton, Longman and Todd, 1997).

modern culture.[6] The book gave rise to a flurry of debate and Nick Mercer, among others, contributed a piece recounting the spiritual evolution which led him to feel distinctly uncomfortable with some of the more protestant aspects of faith, the negatively reactive ones, and to re-evaluate liturgical worship which his evangelical friends found suspect.[7] But as Michael Saward wrote in the same volume, such "hemmed-in experience" as Mercer and Tomlinson speak of is not characteristic of all evangelicals by any means and many Anglican evangelicals, including himself, broke out of that beleaguered mentality long ago without jettisoning their evangelicalism.

The most recent voice from exile is Gordon Lynch, who endorses the view that evangelicalism can be judgemental and that in its handling of those who doubt or explore alternative life-styles it can be "abusive". He argues that many, including himself, begin to question evangelicalism because their experience – experiences of pain, friendship and love – raises questions which do not fit neatly into evangelical discourse. The core of the problem, as he sees it, is that although evangelicalism preaches that God loves us, 'the way in which this love is understood in Evangelical discourse tends to support hierarchical and patriarchal structures, a dependence on "approved" Evangelical sources for finding out the truth about life, and a pressure to conform to certain standards of behaviour whether or not these are really essential to a morally and spiritually healthy life'.[8]

Criticisms from Within

Firmly committed Evangelicals also have a robust ability to engage in self-criticism. A constant stream of publications fall within the genre of what in higher education would currently be called an 'SED', a Self-evaluation Document. Richard Mouw whose book *The Smell of Sawdust*[9] was the inspiration for this lecture, confesses to three common defects in evangelicalism: namely, anti-intellectualism; otherworldliness and a separatistic spirit. I am less persuaded that 'otherworldliness' is characteristic of contemporary British evangelicalism, at least by comparison with evangelicalism immediately after the Second World War. In my childhood we may have sung 'This world is not my home,

---

[6] D. Tomlinson, *The post evangelical* (London: Triangle, 1995).

[7] N. Mercer, 'Living intimately with strangers – a post-evangelical pilgrimage' in, *The Post- evangelical Debate* (London: Triangle, 1997), 57-75.

[8] G. Lynch, *Losing my Religion: Moving on from Evangelical Faith* (London: Darton, Longman & Todd, 2003), 13.

[9] R. Mouw, *The Smell of Sawdust: What Evangelicals Can Learn from their Fundamentalist Heritage* (Grand Rapids, MI: Zondervan, 2000), 24.

I'm just a passing through' with gusto but the song is unknown now, unsung now and would not be true if it was. There is lively debate among sociologists in the USA as to how 'this-wordly' evangelicals are becoming and whether the changes of lifestyle, focus and attitudes amount to an accommodation with the contemporary world that will prove fatal.[10] Of course, some sections are more otherworldly than others, but in the UK the general loss of a credible eschatology, after the demise of premillennial adventism, the rediscovery of the evangelical social conscience following Lausanne in 1974, and the general growth of wealth and comfort in suburban churches, which is one of the streams through which evangelical currents flow strongly, means that evangelicals are very much at home in this world. The anti-intellectualism has been explored thoroughly, forcefully and, to my mind, persuasively by Mark Noll in *The Scandal of the Evangelical Mind*.[11] The separatism to which Mouw alludes works itself out in Britain somewhat differently since our tradition of established church and the place of evangelicals within both it and the university sector means we have a more nuanced separatist mindset. What is characteristic of British evangelicalism is a tendency to fragmentation. The combination of evangelicalism's emphasis on personal religion, on fulfilling our personal calling, together with the premium put on being right before God and accountable to him alone, leads to a fatal chemical reaction that causes evangelicals to split from one another for the most trivial of reasons.[12] We believe in an unrestrained free enterprise religious economy, often, I think, to our detriment.

What surprises me is that Mouw does not list the restrictive nature of the evangelical subculture to which others refer. Kenneth Myers, in a critique of the evangelical church which makes many pertinent criticisms about its selling out to a quest for power and success, argues that it is extraordinary how modern evangelicalism is more concerned 'with doing than with knowing' and that, while we happily disagree on the nature of the atonement, sacraments, eschatology, once-saved always saved and church order, we are all agreed, according to him,

---

[10] See, *inter alia*, J. D. Hunter, *American Evangelicalism* (New Brunswick: Rutgers University Press, 1983), idem. *Evangelicalism: The Coming Generation* (Chicago: Chicago University Press, 1987), C. Smith, *American Evangelicalism: Embattled and Thriving* (Chicago: Chicago University Press, 1998), J. M. Penning & C. E. Smidt, *Evangelicalism: The Next Generation* (Grand Rapids: Bakers, 2002).

[11] M. A. Noll, *The Scandal of the Evangelical Mind* (Grand Rapids: Eerdmans, and Leicester: IVP, 1994).

[12] Evidence can be found in the new so-called ministry organisations and agencies which are constantly opening up, as illustrated by the various *UK Christian Directories*, as well as in the numerous church splits and newly founded churches that spring up.

about behaviour patterns that are not even discussed in Scripture and these become the ties that bind rather than 'belief systems that are the entire substance of scripture'.[13]

But enough of the criticisms. Evangelicals are aware of them, capable of making them themselves and of reflecting on them with a view to correcting where they believe they should. Given the criticisms, however, what is it that makes evangelicalism the most vibrant wing of the church in the UK and continues to make it attractive? Success does not, of course, guarantee rightness, anymore than the number of people eating at McDonalds guarantees their food is nutritious. But it should make us want to explore the question with an open mind. We know that it is not perfect, contains flaws, and could improve, but lest in the welter of criticism we forget the factors that are commendable, let us consider what it is that is right about evangelicalism.

Identifying what's Right about Evangelicalism

One critic, Gordon Lynch, generously acknowledges that evangelicalism is not all bad. He lists the strengths in a series of factors I would not have considered, but nonetheless recognise. He speaks of evangelicalism's:

- strong commitment to helping others and making a difference in the world;
- ability to welcome people who might otherwise be socially isolated;
- willingness to think and act in counter-cultural ways;
- underlying ethos that can empower in democratic ways (e.g., a deaf church).[14]

My own list would be somewhat different: Assuming that evangelicalism is a coalition of groups, churches, institutions and individuals who share a common core set of commitments, as, for

[13] Kenneth A. Myers, 'A Better Way: Proclamation instead of Protest', in M. Horton (ed.), *Power Religion* (Chicago: Moody Bible Institute, 1992), 48. Noll refers to a related tendency for evangelicals to act first and only apply their minds to problems later, *Scandal*, 243. A different perspective expressing concern about the dominance of subcultural issues over classic beliefs is found in D. H. Williams, *Retrieving the Tradition and Renewing Evangelicalism* (Grand Rapids, MI: Eerdmans, 1999), 212-216

[14] Lynch, *Losing*, xx.

example, outlined by Bebbington[15] and a common set of doctrine, as outlined by Packer and Oden,[16] I identify, under six broad headings, features where evangelicalism has, I believe, got it right, three of which are theological and three of which are sociological:

Theological Strengths

A Belief in a Living God[17]

When John Stott recently published his book *Evangelical Truth*[18] he chose to use a trinitarian framework to expound the defining essence of evangelical truth. Longer back it was sufficient to say, as he did, that evangelicals were gospel people and Bible people.[19] But today, I believe, we must start with God, for the understanding of God seems to me to be what often distinguishes evangelicals from others in the church. For many even within the church God seems to have no voice of his own, to be a remote object of study, to be either totally other or, at the other extreme, just like the boy next door. Characteristic is the masterclass in Religion and Philosophy my son has just undertaken at school, aged 12, where he was asked by his practising Christian teacher as two initial exercises to write on 'I blame God for' and 'What God should apologise to people for'. It is in the unique combination of features of the evangelical view of God that their distinctiveness lies.

He is an awesome God. The evangelical God is a powerful creator, who brought the world into existence (though we may differ on the mechanism he used to do so) and who will bring about the recreation of all things in his time. Creation does not merely exist - it exists by him, through him and for him. He still actively upholds creation and still performs miracles, shapes history, determines destinies and works out his sovereign plans. He is holy in essence, morally pure and altogether righteous. He is a sovereign to be approached with reverent fear, not looked down upon by his creation.

He is a gracious God. He is love from start to finish. He bestowed love on Israel and pledged himself in faithful covenant to them. In the

---

[15] David Bebbington, *Evangelicalism in Modern Britain: A history from the 1730s to the 1980s* (London: Unwin Hyman, 1989), 2-17. Bebbington highlights conversionism, activism, biblicism and crucicentrism.

[16] J. I Packer and Thomas Oden, *One Faith: The Evangelical Consensus* (Downers Grove, IL, IVP, 2004)

[17] I am aware that at each point below evangelicals would differ over the exact formulations and finer details among themselves, but the substantive points nonetheless remain. I have resisted documenting the debates, for example, about creationism, atonement or open theism.

[18] J. Stott, *Evangelical Truth* (Leicester: IVP, 1999).

[19] J. Stott, *What is an Evangelical?* (London: CPAS, 1977).

Old Testament as well as the New he is 'full of compassion and abounding in love'. There is a continuity in revelation between the two Testaments. Love was not wrestled out of a reluctant God at Calvary; rather the cross was the result of an ultimate expression of his love. Holiness and mercy, power and love, law and grace, majesty and meekness are blended in one God.

He is a living God. He is still active in his world. We are theists not deists. He is neither remote nor impotent. He is active in rescuing people from the rule of darkness and bringing them into his kingdom of light. He is engaged in transforming his world and reconciling it to himself. He is also working out his judgement in the world as Romans 1 suggests.

He is a communicating God. Though mysterious and beyond our comprehension, he does not leave us to fumble around in the dark making what we can of the scattered and opaque clues he has left for our benefit. He reveals himself and makes himself known, to the extent that we can bare and that we need to know about him. He mostly reveals himself through human means, human persons, human documents, human experiences, human history, and above all through the perfect human, Jesus, the second Adam, situated in one historic human culture. Yet, these revelations are stamped with his hallmark, and so are trustworthy and reliable revelations of his person. Too often, the church is so preoccupied with the human dimension of revelation, e.g. in using the tools of literary criticism to understand the scriptures, that it fails to encounter the God who makes himself known through them. Yet, he is knowable and longs to enter into and engage in a relationship with people.

He is a trinitarian God. This we share with many others. Truth to tell we have sometimes believed more in a binitarian God and some evangelicals have been in danger of adopting a 'Jesus only' approach to the faith that has excluded the Father and the Spirit. But Charismatic renewal revived a living experience of the Spirit for many and equally revived the robust theological understanding of the Spirit inherited through the Puritans leading us now to be more solidly trinitarian. Recent evangelical theology, too, has been for different reasons very explicitly Trinitarian.

A Belief in a Transforming Gospel

At the heart of the evangelical message is the preaching of grace – 'grace unspeakable' as P. T. Forsyth described it.[20] This speaks of the undeserved love of God who takes the initiative in removing every

[20] Cited in J. Gordon, Evangelical Spirituality: From the Wesleys to John Stott (London: SPCK, 1991), 1 *ff.*

obstacle to our relationship with him, forgives all our sin and provides us with assurance by adopting us into his family. Consequently, and only as a consequence of God's initiative, we can experience the transforming power of grace in our lives. From that so many things follow:

Evangelicals place a premium on the cross and resurrection in their theological framework and make that their focus where others might place creation (as in some forms of Catholicism), incarnation (as in Orthodoxy), or the Spirit (as in some forms of Pentecostalism). I readily confess that evangelicals have neglected these others emphasises with the result that their neglect has led to some distortions, as for example, in a devaluing of this world's creation and culture. But the emergence of a greater balance in contemporary evangelicalism, where neglected truths have been rediscovered, should not be at the expense of the atonement. There the evangelical emphasis seems to me to mirror the priorities of scripture from Genesis to Revelation.

Evangelicals may differ to some degree on their interpretation of the cross but historically the interpretation of penal substitution has been their central but not exclusive understanding of Christ's death.[21] Some would want to argue that it is the defining evangelical interpretation of the cross. In spite of voices to the contrary, this interpretation still has much to commend it and is not nearly as lacking in resonance with contemporary culture as some intellectuals make out.[22]

Evangelicals place a premium on conversion as an initiation into a life in which grace is experienced. The evangelical conversion experience of the First Evangelical Awakening was precisely an experience in which grace was tasted, felt, and known experimentally. It was not some empty ritualistic rite of passage in which a person responded to the appeal of the evangelist but felt nothing.[23] The consequence of this is that there are some who have experienced grace and others who have not. The evangelical is keen for all to experience grace and that cannot be wrong. The emphasis on experience that lies at the root of the evangelical tradition makes it ironic that evangelicalism is criticised today for being too rational, too cerebral, and too word-

---

[21] Since originally writing these words a vigorous debate has erupted among evangelicals about penal substitution. The literature on the issue is copious and the current debate can be charted both in recently published books, the web site of the Evangelical Alliance, and in *Christianity* magazine.

[22] See, for example, G. Jenkins, *In My Place – The Spirituality of Substitution* (Cambridge: Grove, 1999).

[23] See G. Rawlyck, *Is Jesus your Personal Saviour? In search of Canadian Evangelicalism in the 1990s* (Montreal & Kingston: McGill University Press, 1996), 9-30

oriented. Until very recently it was anything but. 'Join the CU: annual subscription your mind' used to be the common jibe against evangelicals. Now evangelicals are easily dismissed as 'happy clappy'. But it was not always so. Our desire to reason the faith since the Second World War and to encourage evangelical scholarship that was able to give credible answers to faith-debilitating biblical scholarship, has perhaps led to an unhealthy over correction, creating an experiential vacuum which Charismatic renewal came to fill.

Evangelical spirituality places a premium on that grace being daily experienced. We believe in grace upon grace. The practice of the daily Quiet Time as a key devotional tool in evangelical spirituality found its purpose precisely in the renewing of one's relationship with God on a daily basis, and finding fresh supplies of grace for the day ahead. It is not true that evangelical spirituality was always excessively personal and lacking in any corporate dimension. Apart from family prayers, evangelicals have always encouraged participation in small groups activities, from Wesley's class meetings onwards, and in wider, even sacramental, worship. But the heart of it all lay in one's need for grace, for discovering more about grace and being transformed by grace. Evangelicals have recently broadened their appreciation of other forms of spirituality but have often done so, I regret to say, at the expense of understanding and renewing their own tradition.[24]

Evangelicals place a premium on grace as a transforming power in our lives. The accusation that conversion is viewed as a superficial commercial transaction that leaves the sinner unreformed but possessing a ticket to heaven, or that justification by faith is merely a legal fiction, undoubtedly applies to a small stream of shallow evangelical teaching. But it is misdirected as far as most evangelical preaching is concerned. Regeneration goes hand in hand with sanctification, conversion goes hand in hand with transformation of character, orientation, world view, purpose in life, social relations and even political obligations. Grace, once experienced, goes on flowing in free forgiveness and is used by the Spirit to transform people towards maturity in Christ. Not for nothing have some tried to capture the essence of evangelicalism as 'convertive piety' or 'conversion piety'.[25] Holiness has always been a central concern of evangelicals.

Evangelicals place a premium on grace being experienced by others, and so are concerned to share the good news. From this the drive for

---

[24] The most recent publication on this topic is I. Randall, *What a Friend We Have In Jesus* (London: Darton, Longman and Todd, 2005). It offers a number of helpful corrections to distorted claims about evangelical spirituality.

[25] See S. Grenz, *Renewing the Centre* (Grand Rapids, MI: Baker, 2000), 46-7, citing both Donald Dayton and Roger Olson.

evangelism that some would see as the key evangelical distinctive arises.

Evangelicals make grace a priority and resist division on the basis of 'lesser' matters, such as church government or eschatological schema, while distancing themselves from those who frame the gospel in other terms. This leads to an 'alternative' ecumenism which is every bit as real and often a good deal more effective than the 'official' ecumenical movement. The ethical battles of recent days have somewhat called the centrality of grace into question as other tests are being posited as evidence of genuine Christianity. But I believe grace is still the foundation of evangelicalism and will never be supplanted by other priorities, however keen evangelicals might be to live ethically before God.

A Belief in a Useful Bible

Perhaps the importance given to the Bible is the best-known characteristic of evangelicalism and deservedly so, especially in comparison with the way other sections of the church use (or often do not use) it. Evangelicals write Bible commentaries, sponsor Bible Conferences and weeks, publish and distribute Bibles, set up Bible Colleges and are encouraged to read the Bible daily. They hold true to the reformation heritage of *sola scriptura* and view the Bible as both the normative rule and final authority for Christian belief and practice (2 Tim. 3:16-17). The original claim of *sola scriptura* was made over against the authority and tradition of the church which could prove all too fallible. In reality the Bible has never been the only resource for Evangelicals and there is an awareness that making it so can lead to any private judgement or individual interpretation of it being supreme in reality rather than the Bible itself being so.[26] The assertion of *sola scriptura* needs to be reaffirmed in new ways today, especially over and against the dictates of cultural fashion.

Having said this, a number of myths cloud the picture. First, the way in which the Bible's authority has been formulated by evangelicals has differed down the centuries. There is, for example, a difference between Wesley and Simeon's formal view of scripture and that of the later Princetonians. Second, evangelicals are not literalists. They take the Bible seriously and seek to abide by its teaching but, even the most literal have, at least, an implicit hermeneutic and can judge between, for example, the continuing validity of some Old Testament laws and the temporary nature of others. Third, few, if any, believe that inspiration

---

[26] On these matters see, A. N. S. Lane, 'Sola Scriptura? Making Sense of a Post-Reformation Slogan', in Philip Satterthwaite and David Wright (eds.), *A Pathway into the Holy Scripture* (Grand Rapids, MI: Eerdmans, 1994), 297-327.

took the form of dictation, bypassing the human authorship of scripture. Fourth, their love of the Bible was not an end in itself but a means of leading them to Christ and of Christlike living. It is not a dead text but a living word through which God communicates. Fifth, all the tools of mind and heart should be deployed in unlocking the Bible and leading one to know the God of the Bible.

There is also a wide gulf between the evangelical view of scripture as understood, on the one hand, by contemporary evangelical theologians like Professors Anthony Thiselton and Kevin Vanhoozer, to name but two, the conservative view of how to interpret scripture, as traditionally taught say by John Stott or other evangelical statesmen who have championed expository preaching, and, on the other hand, the popular use of scripture by others. Listening to much evangelical preaching suggests to me that the Bible is in fact not an authority but a tool, even a weapon. Many popular preachers I hear use the Bible as drunks use a lamppost, more for support than illumination. It leaves much to be desired. Much work needs to be done by scholars on how the Bible is actually used by evangelicals and what informal hermeneutics really are in operation, especially if we wish to help each other to handle the Bible with greater wisdom.

But what's right about evangelicalism is both the formal and practical exposure it gives to the Bible. It takes seriously that this is the book of the people of God, and beyond that God's message to the world. It views the Bible as more than a manual of private devotion. It is also a book of public truth. However inadequate, evangelicalism seeks to unlock its message and not ignore or neglect its teaching. It still seeks to bow to the authority of the Bible and relate ever-changing contemporary scholarship and understanding of scientific and moral issues to it. Scripture, rather than culture, is the final word. For all their imperfections, in letting God be God, in their understanding and living of grace and in their submission to the Bible, evangelicals are surely right.

Sociological Strengths

Evangelicalism is a Popular Movement

Many scholarly portraits of evangelicalism do not pick up the popular ethos of the movement.[27] Socially it is essentially a movement of ordinary people, not composed of academics, the powerful, or of

[27] An excellent exception to this is J. A. Carpenter, *Revive Us Again: The Reawakening of American Fundamentalism* (New York & Oxford: Oxford University Press, 1997), 13-32.

establishment figures (though it has a share of these and evangelical history has been blessed by them).[28] Many scholarly debates I read miss this feature altogether and speak as if evangelicalism only inhabits scholarly publishing houses and academia. But its natural habitat is more that of the mission halls, tin tabernacles, youth clubs, and of Bible conventions and conferences like Keswick, Filey and Spring Harvest. Its prime publications have been *The Christian*, *Crusade Magazine*, *The Life of Faith*, and *The Christian Herald*, rather than the *Church Times*. Its written media finds expression in publishers like Kingsway, and the old Marshall, Morgan and Scott. True, there were (or are) the Bash camps, Crusaders in Public Schools, Christian Unions in our Universities and Apollos which can hold its head high as an academic publisher. And they have contributed greatly to the movement but that is not where the majority have encountered evangelicalism. In camps and house parties, missions and conferences, in prayer meetings and sacred concerts, evangelicalism has had an extraordinary ability to create powerful, even if temporary, communities. It bonds people through the gospel, across denominational, generational and cultural barriers and binds them into a community of mutual help and sacrificial service. Soul in the City, an event that mobilised thousands of evangelicals to engage in projects to better inner city life in the summer of 2004, is an impressive, but not untypical, example.

In this way, an immense mission and philanthropic network has emerged that functions as an effective, yet informal, ecumenism. This type of ecumenism sets aside many of the questions beloved by theologians and religious bureaucrats for the sake of the gospel. Torry Johnson, the founder of Youth for Christ, was once asked whether he was a separatist or not and typically replied, 'I was neither a come-outer nor a go-inner. I am just a worker'.[29] Of course the work can suffer from wasteful duplication, lack of strategic thinking, short-termism and the over-stretching of scarce resources. But at least while others are talking, evangelicals are working. Mission, both evangelistic and social, is in the DNA of evangelicals.

The core beliefs and principles of evangelicalism, as well as its ethos, are transmitted through popular communicators and entertaining, storytelling preachers; and through hymns and songs: from Wesley's powerful hymn 'And can it be' and Sankey's sacred songs, 'There were ninety and nine' and 'There is power in the blood', through 'Blessed Assurance', 'Amazing Grace', 'Trust and Obey' and 'Great is Thy faithfulness' to the songs of Kendrick and Redman. The style is

---

[28] The relative absence of such figures means they tend to be feted and given prominence when they exist.

[29] Quoted by Carpenter, *Revive Us Again*, 56.

consistently in tune with the popular culture of the day the style of Music Hall, of the Light Programme (as it was) and of clubs and the pop scene rather than of organ and oratorios. Not for nothing did Bishop Richard Holloway, having accused Evangelicalism of 'adolescent arrogance and intemperateness', of being incapable of thinking beyond simple explanations and theories, of downplaying creation and incarnation, and above all of moralism, once write that evangelical innovative worship 'makes worship accessible to people in a way that the more developed liturgies do not. More people go to discos than to high opera, and one of the courageous things about evangelicals is their ability to embrace bad taste for the sake of the gospel'.[30]

Consistent with this has been a willingness to look to lay leaders, those without theological training or official sanction as much as to bishops, clergy or theologians. This feature goes back at least to Selina, Countess of Huntingdon, and William Wilberforce. It was exemplified most in Lord Shaftesbury but it was equally seen in the twentieth century in the place variously occupied by Sir William Joynson-Hicks, John Laing, Montague Goodman, Tom Rees, Lindsay Clegg and Douglas Johnston, and continues today.

Some years ago John Kent reviewed a book I had written on Evangelicalism in the Expository Times and commented that it was 'a further contribution to the drive to establish the respectability of Evangelicalism...' (which) he wrote, 'is no simple aim because Evangelicalism is essentially "popular religion" in a protestant form'.[31] On reflection I think Kent is right – and in that lies not something of which to be ashamed but something of which to boast, for Christ spent his time ministering among ordinary people. Evangelicalism may not be unique in this, since Roman Catholicism can display some of the same tendencies. Nonetheless here is something precious to value.

It strikes me that we really still await a popular cultural history of evangelicalism, at least of the twentieth century; one that picks up the feel of the crusades, missions and conventions from the viewpoint of committed participants rather than disinterested observers and writes not just using the evidence of the minute books of its primary agencies and the published addresses of public spokespersons, but one that captures the oral history of the ordinary participant in the movement. Anything less must be inadequate and a distortion of evangelicalism's true character.

---

[30] 'Evangelicalism: An Outsider's Perspective', in R. T. France and A. E. McGrath (eds.), *Evangelical Anglicans: Their Role and Influence in the Church Today* (London: SPCK, 1993), 182.

[31] *Expository Times*, 106 (94-5), 125.

Evangelicalism is a Flexible Movement

Dave Tomlinson called for a paradigm shift and for a leaving behind of the old evangelical paradigm with its reference points, things taken for granted and certainties and for the adoption of a new paradigm for a postmodern age.[32] There seem a number of problems with his analysis which make me cautious about responding to his call too eagerly. First, I am unsure that postmodernity is the culture that in any significant way is going to replace modernity rather than a transition stage en route to a more enduring cultural format. More importantly, I think his analysis misunderstands evangelicalism. Evangelicalism is not and never has been a fixed paradigm that refuses to change. It is a living tradition which constantly reinvents itself, expressing itself in new and relevant ways, going, though not uncritically, with the ebb and flow of cultural transition.

Most histories of evangelicalism support the point. In America, for example, Joel Carpenter's history of the Reawakening of American Fundamentalism between 1920-50 shows 'the movement has never been stagnant or purely reactionary. It is based on an evolving ideology subject to debate, and dissension: a theology that adapts to changing times'.[33] In Canada, George Rawlyck, as mentioned previously, began his study of evangelicalism by highlighting the difference in world view, thought form and expression between the evangelical testimonies of converts in the 1790s, 1850s, 1920s and 1990s, before identifying the common core that contemporary evangelicals sign up to like the Bible, witnessing, prayer, conversion, and the centrality of the cross. But even here, he notes, 'to be born again is no longer a badge of evangelical honour, apparently, or even something to be carefully glossed over; or even hidden from public view'.[34] He, unlike David Wells,[35] does not regard the formulations of Jonathan Edwards as the inflexible benchmark for all time and welcomes the 'experiential and relational' emphasis of contemporary evangelicalism, though he fears it might be capitulating to consumerism. David Bebbington, similarly, has brilliantly documented the changing forms of evangelicalism in Britain since the 1740s.[36]

Recent evangelicalism, rightly or wrongly, has undergone change in its understanding of doctrines (e.g. women in ministry, and the doctrine

---

[32] Tomlinson, *The Post Evangelical*, 86-7.

[33] Carpenter, *Revive Us Again*, cover comment.

[34] G. Rawlyck, *Is Jesus your Personal Saviour? In search of Canadian Evangelicalism in the 1990s* (Montreal and Kingston: McGill University Press, 1996), 9-30 and 214.

[35] David Wells, *No Place for Truth* (Leicester: IVP, 1992).

[36] Bebbington, *Evangelicalism in Modern Britain*.

of hell); in lifestyle (e.g. attitudes to alcohol, films and dancing) and in style and technique. Truth to tell, far from being reactionary, evangelicalism has often been in the vanguard of change in the church because it is always driven by a passionate concern to share the gospel and to do so by any means. It would be interesting to cross reference the number of churches that have adopted the latest communication tool, namely, 'powerpoint' with the doctrinal stance of the church. My guess is that of the churches who have adopted it, the overwhelming majority are evangelical. Billy Graham was certainly in the vanguard of the communications revolution last century and sought to capture every means of communication – colour magazines, landline relay, radio, TV, film, satellite transmission – and press them into service in the cause of the gospel. He was often ahead of even the professionals in doing so. A recent sociological textbook has estimated, typically, that 80% of Christian presence on the World Wide Web is evangelical.[37]

J. D. Hunter tends to see all change as decay and all accommodation as fatal. Indeed the matter is complex and no change is neutral. The adoption of new methods of communication have an impact not only on the way we convey the message but the message itself and the nature of the community that bears the message. As McLuhan taught us, 'the medium is the message'. None of these changes can or should be embraced uncritically (as they might be in the secular world) nor resisted uncritically (as they might be in some other sections of the church). Evangelical history provides plenty of evidence of evangelical segments who have sought to make the gospel so relevant that they have eventually left the fold altogether and most frequently petered out into nothingness.[38] That leads naturally to my final point.

Evangelicalism is a Conviction Movement

What many perceive to be a weakness in evangelicalism is, in reality, a strength. Many criticise it for its dogmatism, strong boundaries and unconventional convictions and argue that faith in the contemporary world should be more open to debate and negotiation, and less demanding in the expectations it has of those who identify with it. These criticisms were reflected in many of the works mentioned at the start of this essay.

---

[37] K. J. Christiano, et.al., *Sociology of Religion: Contemporary Developments* (Walnut Creek, CA: Alta Mira, 2002), 245-6.

[38] See *inter alia*, S. Bruce, *Firm in the Faith* (Aldershot: Gower, 1984), M. Hopkins, *Nonconformity's Romantic Generation: Evangelical and Liberal Theology in Victorian England* (Carlisle: Paternoster, 2004), and I. Randall, *Evangelical Experiences: A Study of Spirituality of English Evangelicalism 1918-1939* (Carlisle: Paternoster, 1999).

But sociological wisdom suggests otherwise. Here I refer to two debates that cross the Atlantic from the United States. First, there is debate that was initiated by Dean Kelley,s book *Why Conservative Churches are Growing*, first published in 1972.[39] At the time, churches, denominations and sects that were not only holding their own against advancing secularism but growing, were those who confounded popular ideas about needing to be reasonable, tentative and undemanding and adopted dogmatic beliefs and imposed strong expectations on their members.

Ample research evidence, such as that by Steve Bruce who studied the growing vitality of CUs in contrast to the demise of SCM groups in British Universities,[40] supports this theory. Bruce concludes that you cannot build strong organisations around non-dogmatic beliefs. Distinct organisations need to have 'beliefs that are sufficiently different to those shared by the rest of the world'[41] to attract people, maintain their commitment and inspire their active participation in worship, giving or mission. This explains why evangelical, charismatic and catholic churches are surviving in the current climate better than others. Evangelical churches have a much better track record than other wings of the church at getting members out, getting them to give and getting them to engage in various mission activities than others. I can remember the envy of some of my colleagues in ministry when I was last in local church ministry at our ability to do just that.

None of this, of course, means that any dogmatism will do or that all dogmatism is, in and of itself, right. The beliefs have to be justified on other grounds and evangelicalism has certainly had a capacity to be dogmatic about a number of issues on which scripture speaks with a more ambiguous voice than we have admitted. Even so, I am glad to belong to a wing of the church that makes new members, retains those members and mobilises its members more than others – a faith, in other words, which is alive, vibrant and active, because it is not adopting 'an uncertain sound' as it conveys its message.

Secondly, there is the debate between James Hunter and Christian Smith. Hunter takes a pessimistic stance in arguing that virtually any accommodation to culture on the part of evangelicalism spells its demise.[42] Christian Smith, however, adopts an optimistic stance and

---

[39] D. Kelley, *Why Conservative Churches are Growing* (New York: Harper & Row, 1972). The book sparked a fierce debate and has generated a great deal of literature and alternative theories but at the end of the day their remains a core of truth in Kelley's thesis, even if it has to be applied with care.

[40] Bruce, *Firm in the Faith*.

[41] Bruce, *Firm in the Faith*, 89

[42] Hunter, *American Evangelicalism*; idem. *Evangelicalism: The Coming Generation*.

argues that evangelicalism is best placed to remain a thriving religious stream. Fundamentalism, he comments, can never enduringly thrive because it is too distant from mainline culture; liberalism cannot do because it is too assimilated in mainline culture. In contrast to both these movements, evangelicalism maintains the right balance of distance and belonging; of distinctiveness yet involvement. There are other weakness, he warns, which will frustrate its achievement of its goals. Even so, from a sociological viewpoint religion is best placed to advance when it sits where evangelicalism does and is simultaneously embattled and thriving.[43]

Conclusion

Last year I asked a missionary to China if he could give me a run down of what was happening in the church there. His reply was, 'What have you heard, because anything you have heard is bound to be true?' That strikes me as apt for evangelicalism too. It is a very diverse movement, as it has always been. It is constantly changing and adapting to the new philosophical and cultural context which it inhabits. It is flawed, yes, although perhaps, as Christian Smith has argued in a second work in relation to the USA, in need of demythologising and not quite so scary as its media image suggests. The popular image is of a well-bonded, homogeneous subculture that contains some unsavoury features of the Christian Right, who are all bigoted and fanatical. This is certainly true of some segments of evangelicalism though they are not large in Britain. On some issues evangelicals are more conservative than the general populace but in many respects, whatever the rhetoric of their well-known spokespersons, they are quite able to live as constructive citizens within modern, multicultural, pluralistic, even secular, democracies without exclusivism, imperialism or intolerance.[44]

The criticisms are sometimes misplaced and obscure the benefits of evangelicalism which we have outlined. What's right about it, above all, in my view, is as John Stott once put it, aware of the potential pitfalls of arrogance, that evangelicals contend they 'are plain Bible Christians, and that, in order to be a biblical Christian it is necessary to be an evangelical Christian.'[45]

---

[43] Smith, *American Evangelicalism.*

[44] C. Smith, *Christian America? What Evangelicals Really Want* (Berkeley: University of California Press, 2000), 224-7.

[45] J. Stott, *Christ the Controversialist* (London: Tyndale Press, 1970), 32.

Index

www.ingramcontent.com/pod-product-compliance
Lightning Source LLC
LaVergne TN
LVHW020538100826
845148LV00010B/1518

* 9 7 8 1 6 0 6 0 8 6 0 3 2 *